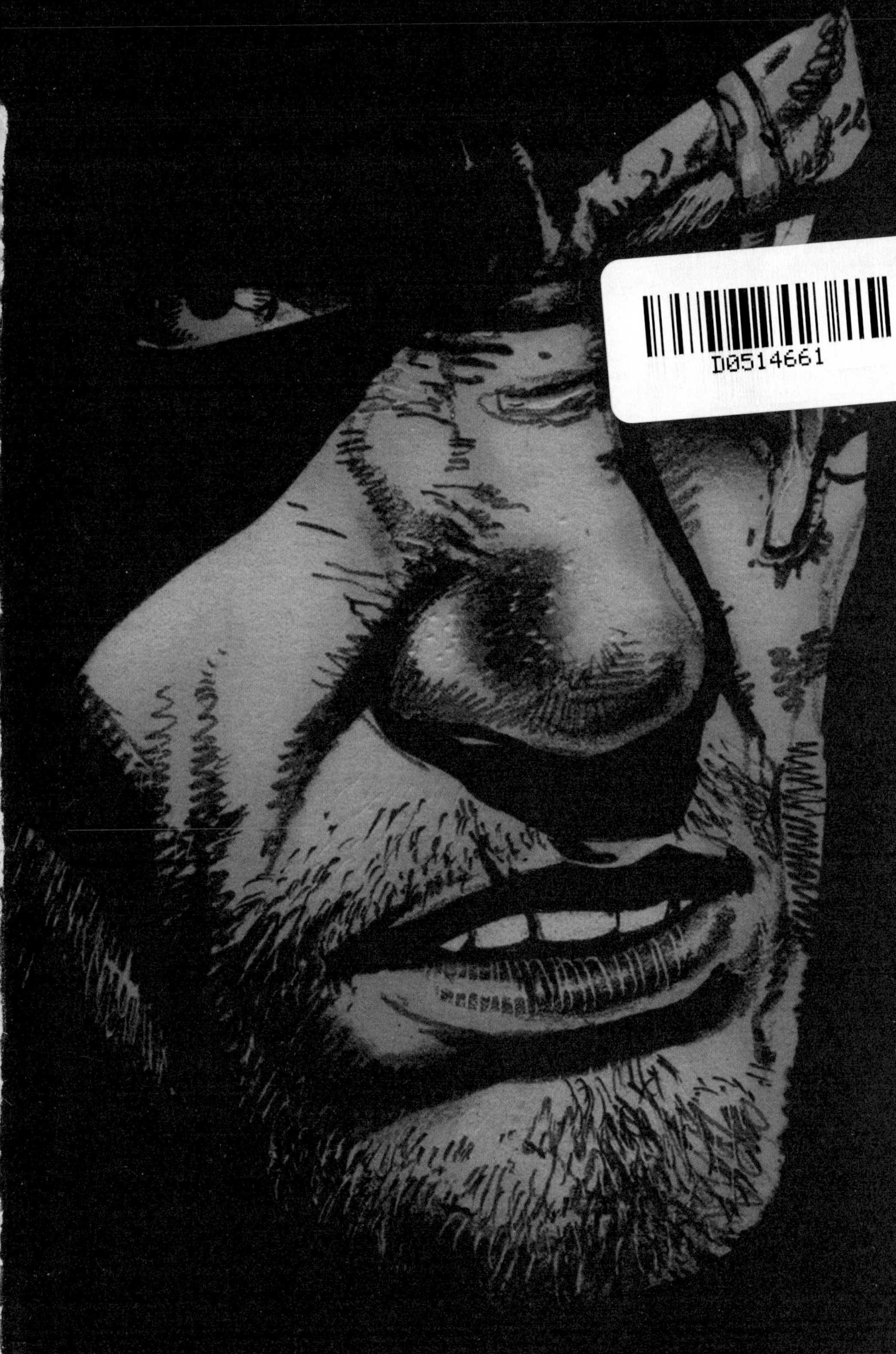

JOHN CONSTANTINE

HELLBLAZER

PHANTOM PAINS

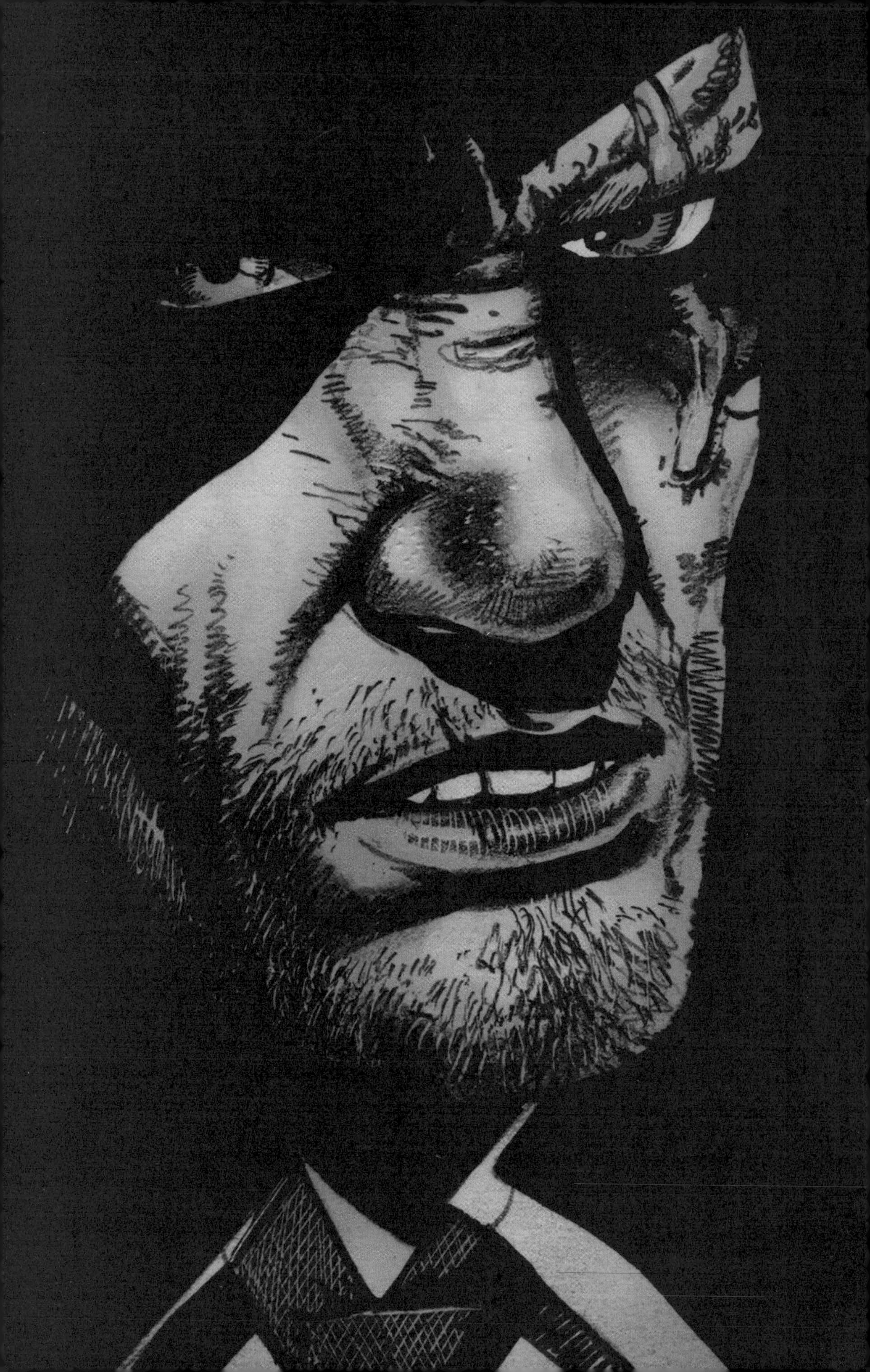

JOHN CONSTANTINE
HELLBLAZER
PHANTOM PAINS

Peter Milligan writer

PHANTOM PAINS
Giuseppe Camuncoli layouts
Stefano Landini finishes
Gael Bertrand Guest Artist – "Gemma's Story"

HIGH-FREQUENCY MAN, INSIDE
Simon Bisley artist

Trish Mulvihill Brian Buccellato colorists

Sal Cipriano letterer

Simon Bisley cover artist

THE
JOHN CONSTANTINE
HELLBLAZER

READER'S GUIDE

Look for these other important **HELLBLAZER** collections:
LADY CONSTANTINE
PAPA MIDNITE
CHAS — THE KNOWLEDGE
ALL HIS ENGINES
PANDEMONIUM

SHELLY BOND Editor – Original Series GREGORY LOCKARD Assistant Editor – Original Series
IAN SATTLER Director – Editorial, Special Projects and Archival Editions ROBIN WILDMAN Editor ROBBIN BROSTERMAN Design Director – Books

KAREN BERGER Senior VP – Executive Editor, Vertigo BOB HARRAS VP – Editor-in-Chief

DIANE NELSON President DAN DIDIO and JIM LEE Co-Publishers GEOFF JOHNS Chief Creative Officer
JOHN ROOD Executive VP – Sales, Marketing and Business Development AMY GENKINS Senior VP – Business and Legal Affairs NAIRI GARDINER Senior VP – F
JEFF BOISON VP – Publishing Operations MARK CHIARELLO VP – Art Direction and Design JOHN CUNNINGHAM VP – Marketing
TERRI CUNNINGHAM VP – Talent Relations and Services ALISON GILL Senior VP – Manufacturing and Operations DAVID HYDE VP – Publicity
HANK KANALZ Senior VP – Digital JAY KOGAN VP – Business and Legal Affairs, Publishing JACK MAHAN VP – Business Affairs, Talent
NICK NAPOLITANO VP – Manufacturing Administration SUE POHJA VP – Book Sales COURTNEY SIMMONS Senior VP – Publicity BOB WAYNE Senior VP – S

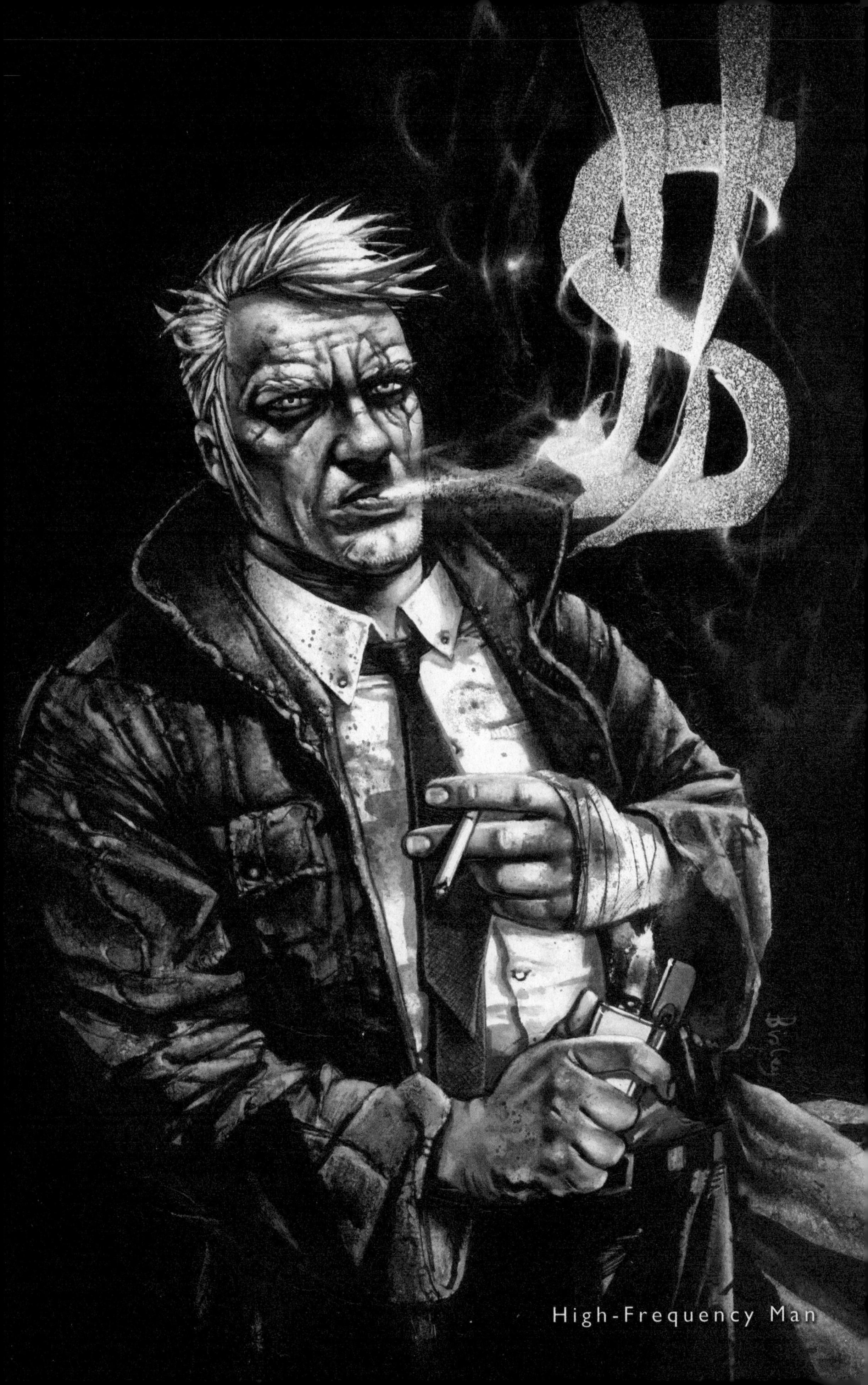

High-Frequency Man

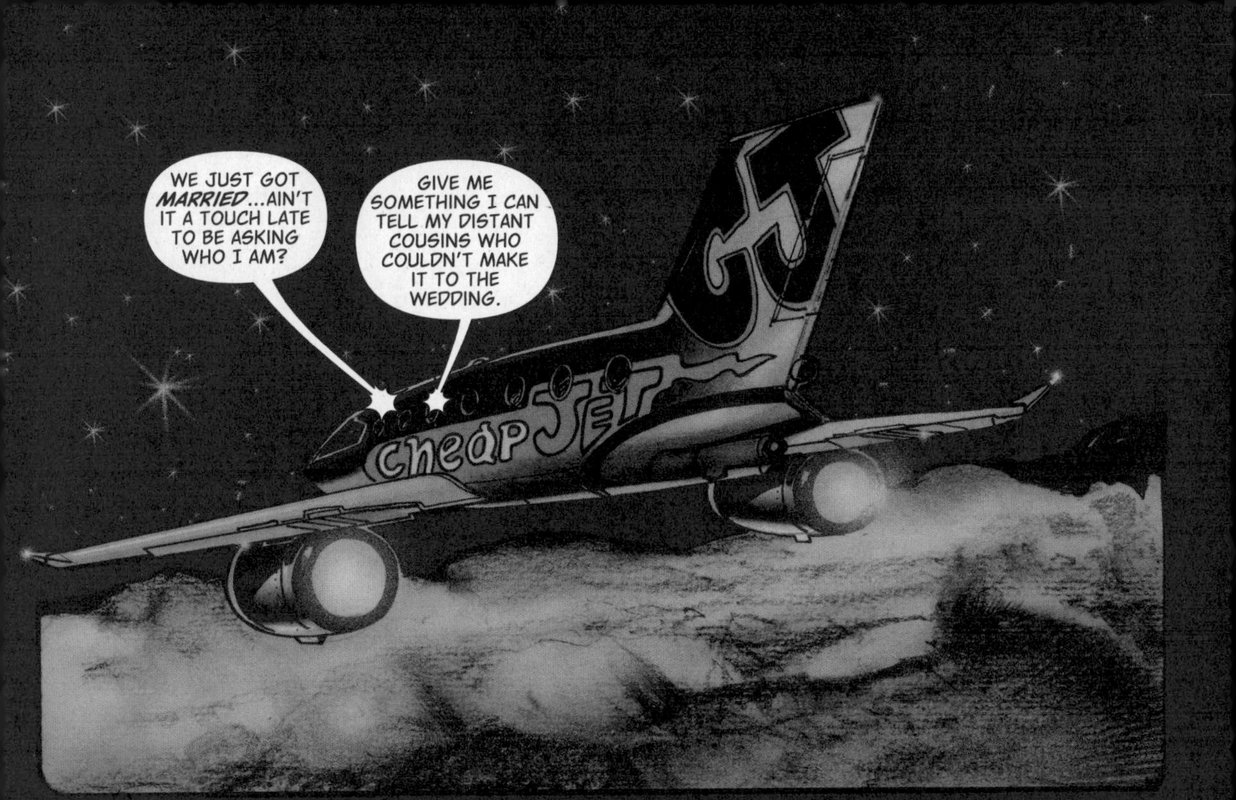
WE JUST GOT *MARRIED*...AIN'T IT A TOUCH LATE TO BE ASKING WHO I AM?
GIVE ME SOMETHING I CAN TELL MY DISTANT COUSINS WHO COULDN'T MAKE IT TO THE WEDDING.
CheapJet

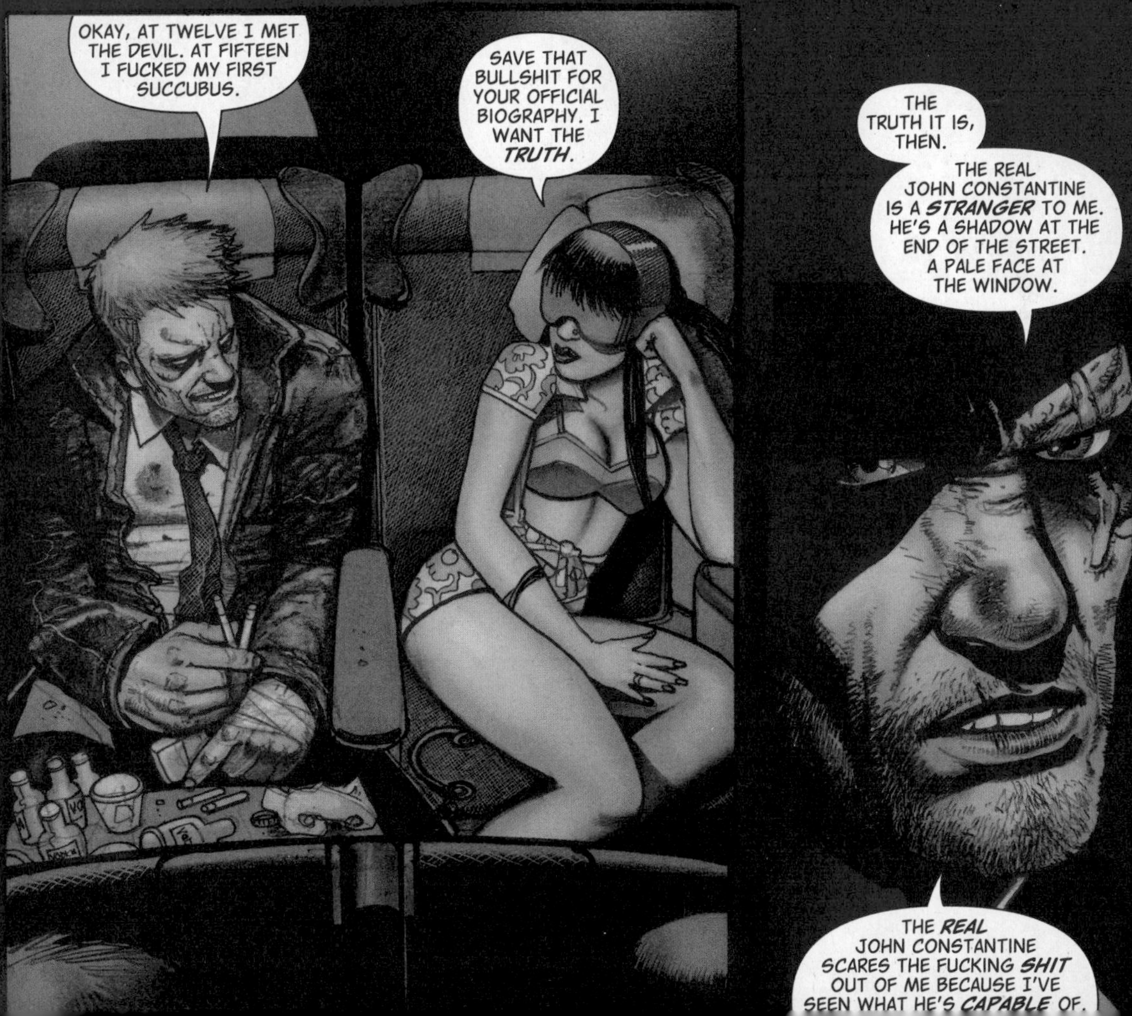
OKAY, AT TWELVE I MET THE DEVIL. AT FIFTEEN I FUCKED MY FIRST SUCCUBUS.
SAVE THAT BULLSHIT FOR YOUR OFFICIAL BIOGRAPHY. I WANT THE *TRUTH*.
THE TRUTH IT IS, THEN.
THE REAL JOHN CONSTANTINE IS A *STRANGER* TO ME. HE'S A SHADOW AT THE END OF THE STREET. A PALE FACE AT THE WINDOW.
THE *REAL* JOHN CONSTANTINE SCARES THE FUCKING *SHIT* OUT OF ME BECAUSE I'VE SEEN WHAT HE'S *CAPABLE* OF.

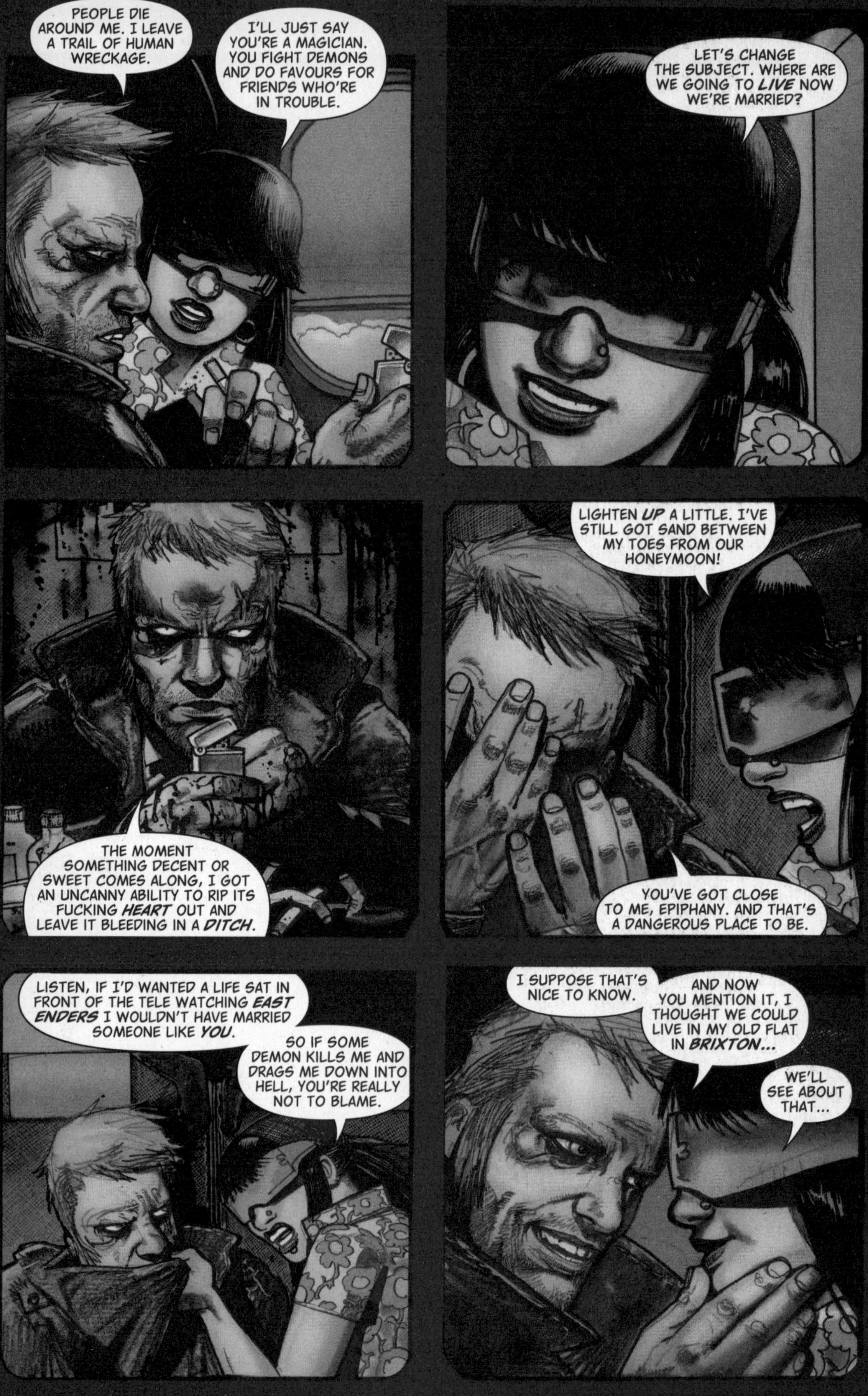
PEOPLE DIE AROUND ME. I LEAVE A TRAIL OF HUMAN WRECKAGE.
I'LL JUST SAY YOU'RE A MAGICIAN. YOU FIGHT DEMONS AND DO FAVOURS FOR FRIENDS WHO'RE IN TROUBLE.
LET'S CHANGE THE SUBJECT. WHERE ARE WE GOING TO *LIVE* NOW WE'RE MARRIED?
THE MOMENT SOMETHING DECENT OR SWEET COMES ALONG, I GOT AN UNCANNY ABILITY TO RIP ITS FUCKING ***HEART*** OUT AND LEAVE IT BLEEDING IN A ***DITCH***.
LIGHTEN *UP* A LITTLE. I'VE STILL GOT SAND BETWEEN MY TOES FROM OUR HONEYMOON!
YOU'VE GOT CLOSE TO ME, EPIPHANY. AND THAT'S A DANGEROUS PLACE TO BE.
LISTEN, IF I'D WANTED A LIFE SAT IN FRONT OF THE TELE WATCHING ***EAST ENDERS*** I WOULDN'T HAVE MARRIED SOMEONE LIKE ***YOU***.
SO IF SOME DEMON KILLS ME AND DRAGS ME DOWN INTO HELL, YOU'RE REALLY NOT TO BLAME.
I SUPPOSE THAT'S NICE TO KNOW.
AND NOW YOU MENTION IT, I THOUGHT WE COULD LIVE IN MY OLD FLAT IN ***BRIXTON...***
WE'LL SEE ABOUT THAT...

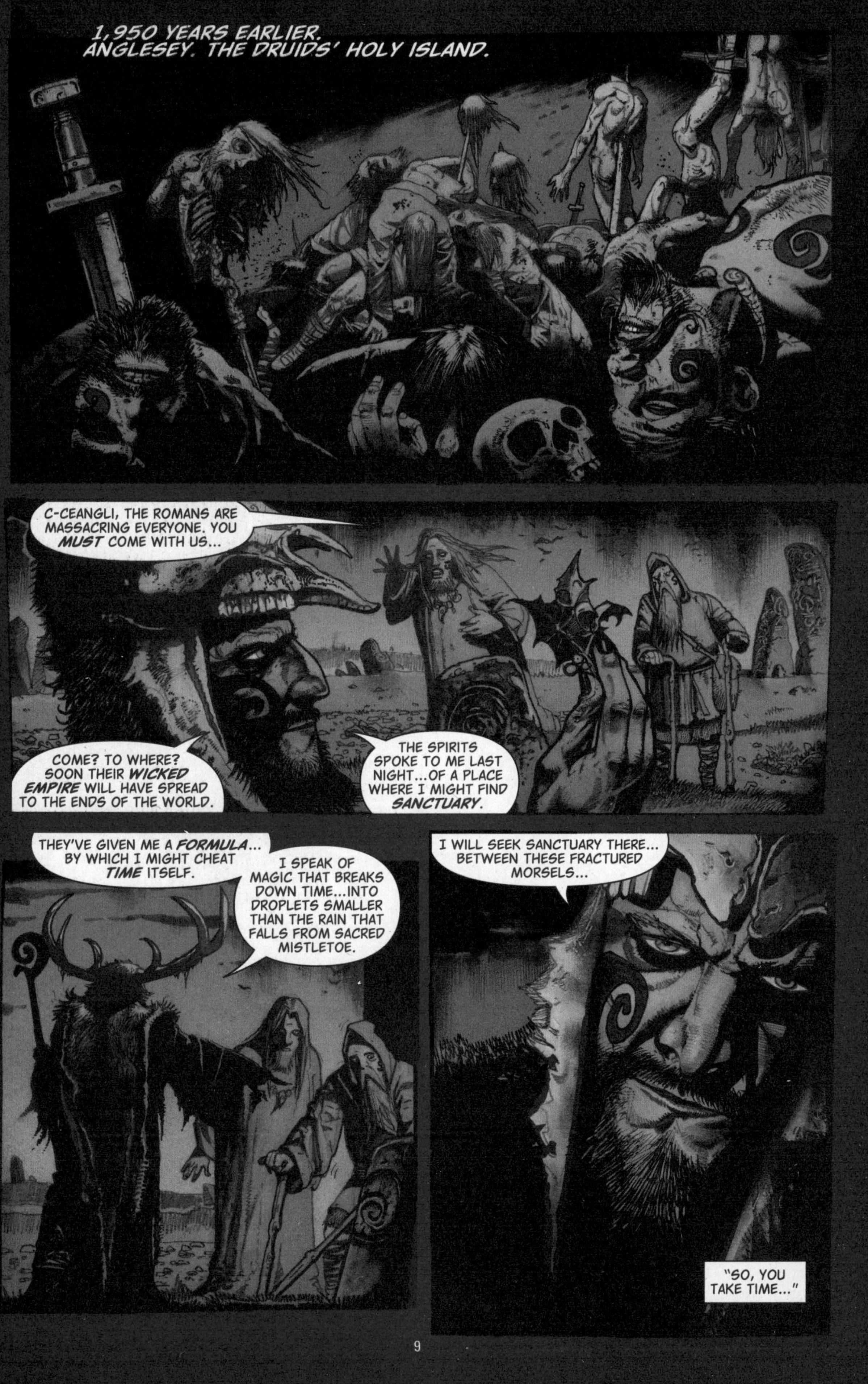
1,950 YEARS EARLIER.
ANGLESEY. THE DRUIDS' HOLY ISLAND.
C-CEANGLI, THE ROMANS ARE MASSACRING EVERYONE. YOU *MUST* COME WITH US...
COME? TO WHERE? SOON THEIR *WICKED EMPIRE* WILL HAVE SPREAD TO THE ENDS OF THE WORLD.
THE SPIRITS SPOKE TO ME LAST NIGHT...OF A PLACE WHERE I MIGHT FIND *SANCTUARY*.
THEY'VE GIVEN ME A *FORMULA*... BY WHICH I MIGHT CHEAT *TIME* ITSELF.
I SPEAK OF MAGIC THAT BREAKS DOWN TIME...INTO DROPLETS SMALLER THAN THE RAIN THAT FALLS FROM SACRED MISTLETOE.
I WILL SEEK SANCTUARY THERE... BETWEEN THESE FRACTURED MORSELS...
"SO, YOU TAKE TIME..."

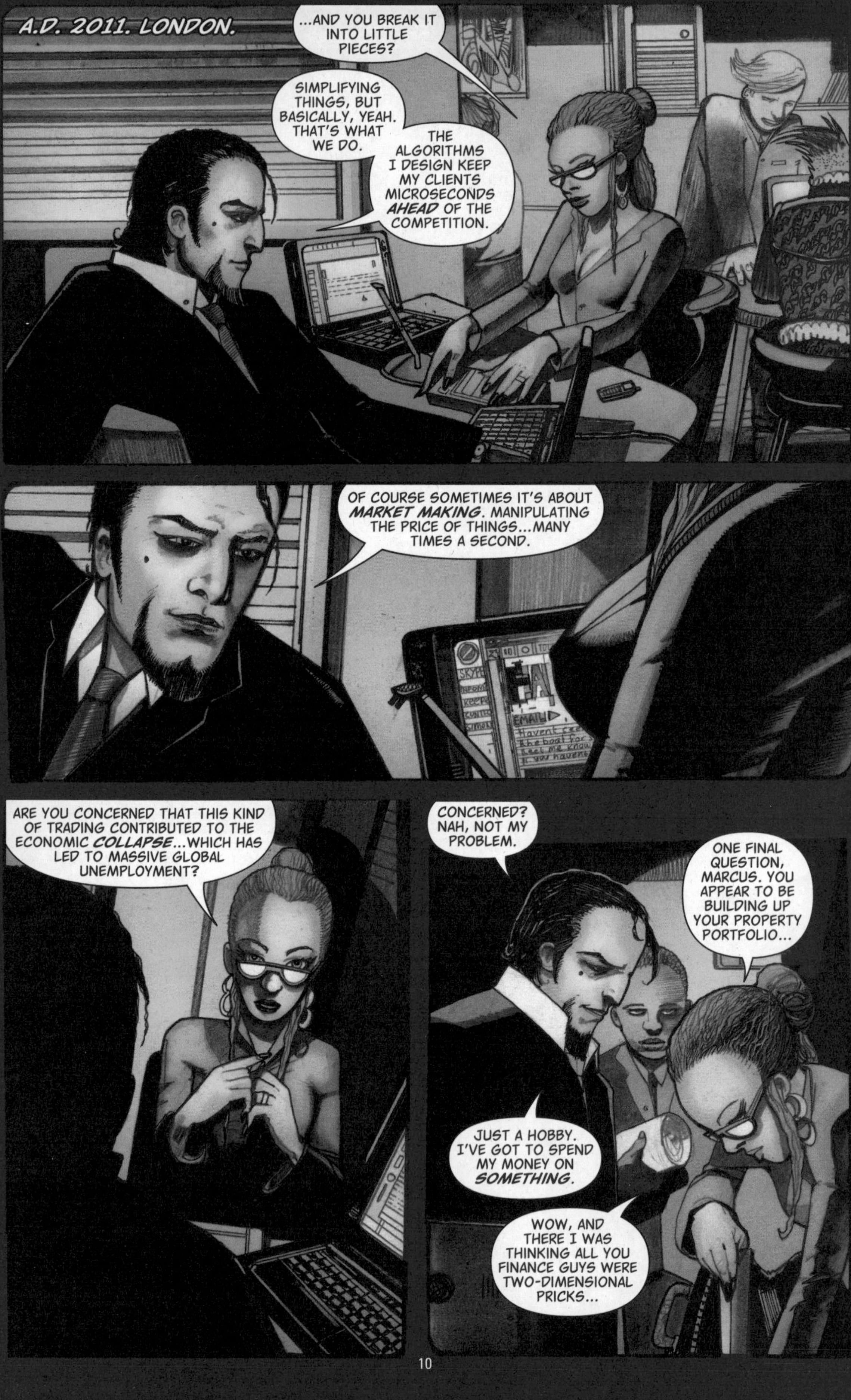
A.D. 2011. LONDON.
...AND YOU BREAK IT INTO LITTLE PIECES?
SIMPLIFYING THINGS, BUT BASICALLY, YEAH. THAT'S WHAT WE DO.
THE ALGORITHMS I DESIGN KEEP MY CLIENTS MICROSECONDS AHEAD OF THE COMPETITION.
OF COURSE SOMETIMES IT'S ABOUT MARKET MAKING. MANIPULATING THE PRICE OF THINGS...MANY TIMES A SECOND.
ARE YOU CONCERNED THAT THIS KIND OF TRADING CONTRIBUTED TO THE ECONOMIC COLLAPSE...WHICH HAS LED TO MASSIVE GLOBAL UNEMPLOYMENT?
CONCERNED? NAH, NOT MY PROBLEM.
ONE FINAL QUESTION, MARCUS. YOU APPEAR TO BE BUILDING UP YOUR PROPERTY PORTFOLIO...
JUST A HOBBY. I'VE GOT TO SPEND MY MONEY ON SOMETHING.
WOW, AND THERE I WAS THINKING ALL YOU FINANCE GUYS WERE TWO-DIMENSIONAL PRICKS...

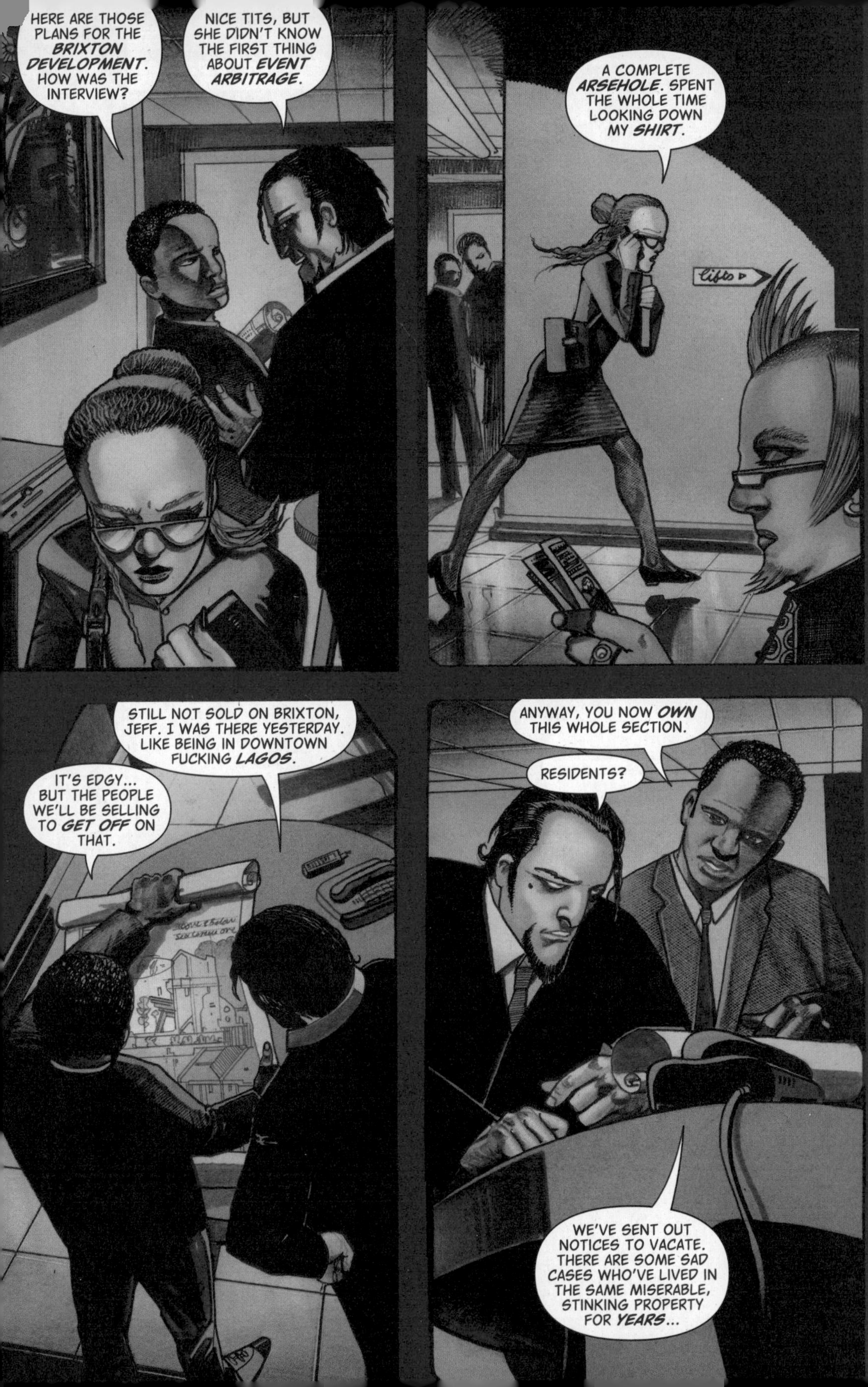
HERE ARE THOSE PLANS FOR THE BRIXTON DEVELOPMENT. HOW WAS THE INTERVIEW?
NICE TITS, BUT SHE DIDN'T KNOW THE FIRST THING ABOUT EVENT ARBITRAGE.
A COMPLETE ARSEHOLE. SPENT THE WHOLE TIME LOOKING DOWN MY SHIRT.
lifts
STILL NOT SOLD ON BRIXTON, JEFF. I WAS THERE YESTERDAY. LIKE BEING IN DOWNTOWN FUCKING LAGOS.
IT'S EDGY... BUT THE PEOPLE WE'LL BE SELLING TO GET OFF ON THAT.
ANYWAY, YOU NOW OWN THIS WHOLE SECTION.
RESIDENTS?
WE'VE SENT OUT NOTICES TO VACATE. THERE ARE SOME SAD CASES WHO'VE LIVED IN THE SAME MISERABLE, STINKING PROPERTY FOR YEARS...

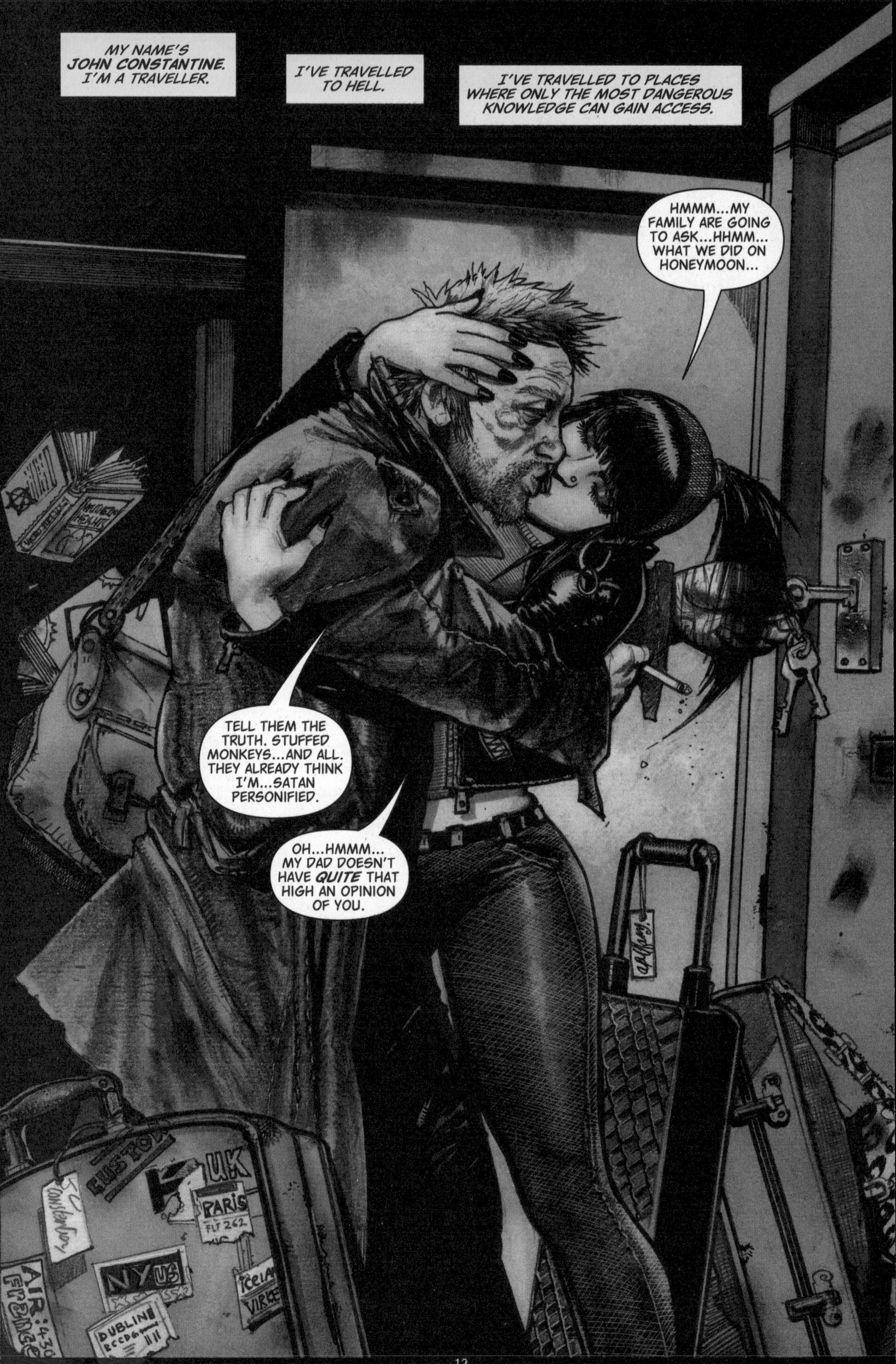
MY NAME'S JOHN CONSTANTINE. I'M A TRAVELLER.
I'VE TRAVELLED TO HELL.
I'VE TRAVELLED TO PLACES WHERE ONLY THE MOST DANGEROUS KNOWLEDGE CAN GAIN ACCESS.
HMMM...MY FAMILY ARE GOING TO ASK...HHMM... WHAT WE DID ON HONEYMOON...
TELL THEM THE TRUTH. STUFFED MONKEYS...AND ALL. THEY ALREADY THINK I'M...SATAN PERSONIFIED.
OH...HMMM... MY DAD DOESN'T HAVE QUITE THAT HIGH AN OPINION OF YOU.
UK
PARIS
FLT 262
NY US
DUBLIN

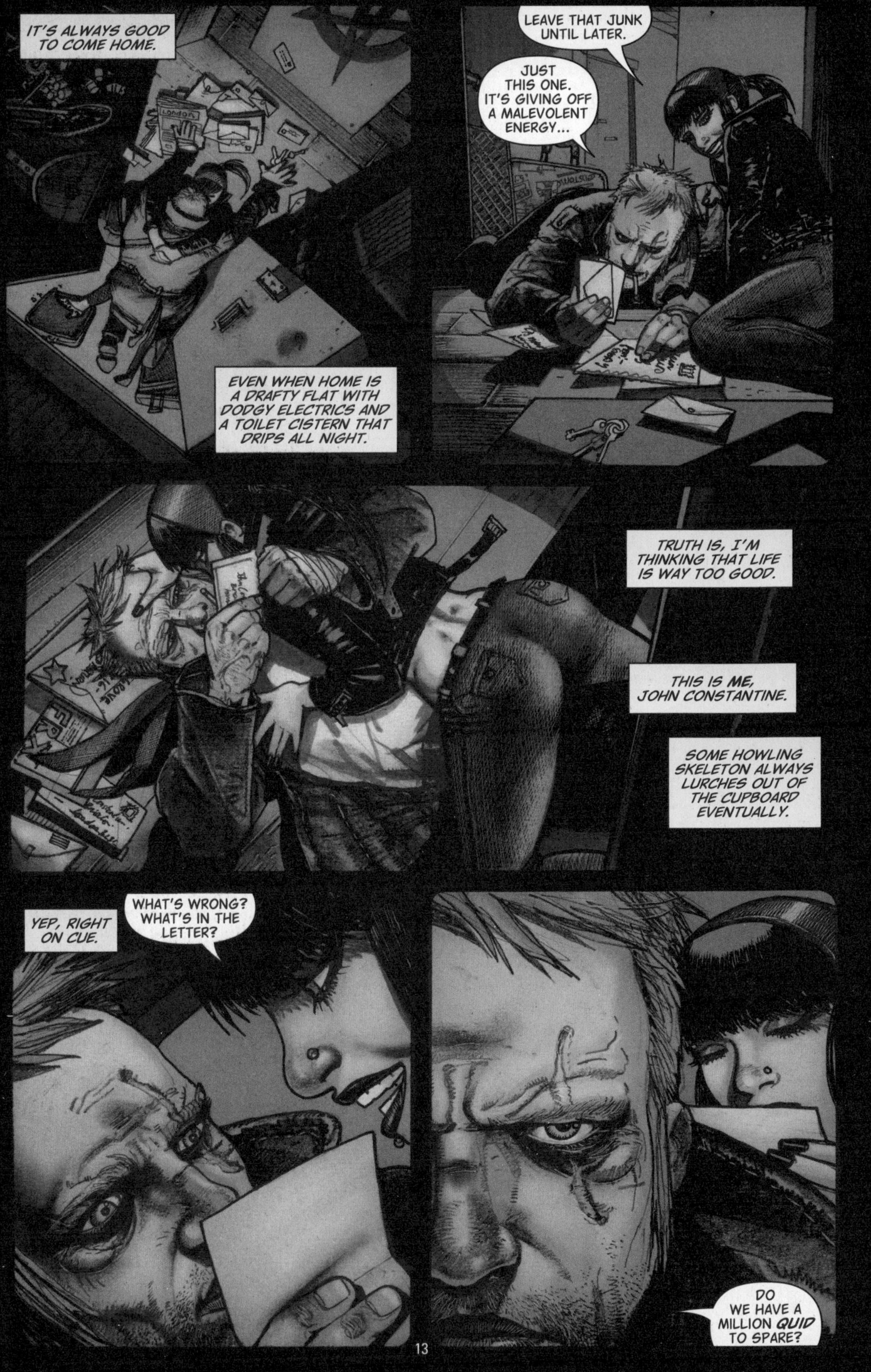
IT'S ALWAYS GOOD TO COME HOME.
EVEN WHEN HOME IS A DRAFTY FLAT WITH DODGY ELECTRICS AND A TOILET CISTERN THAT DRIPS ALL NIGHT.
LEAVE THAT JUNK UNTIL LATER.
JUST THIS ONE. IT'S GIVING OFF A MALEVOLENT ENERGY...
TRUTH IS, I'M THINKING THAT LIFE IS WAY TOO GOOD.
THIS IS ME, JOHN CONSTANTINE.
SOME HOWLING SKELETON ALWAYS LURCHES OUT OF THE CUPBOARD EVENTUALLY.
YEP, RIGHT ON CUE.
WHAT'S WRONG? WHAT'S IN THE LETTER?
DO WE HAVE A MILLION QUID TO SPARE?

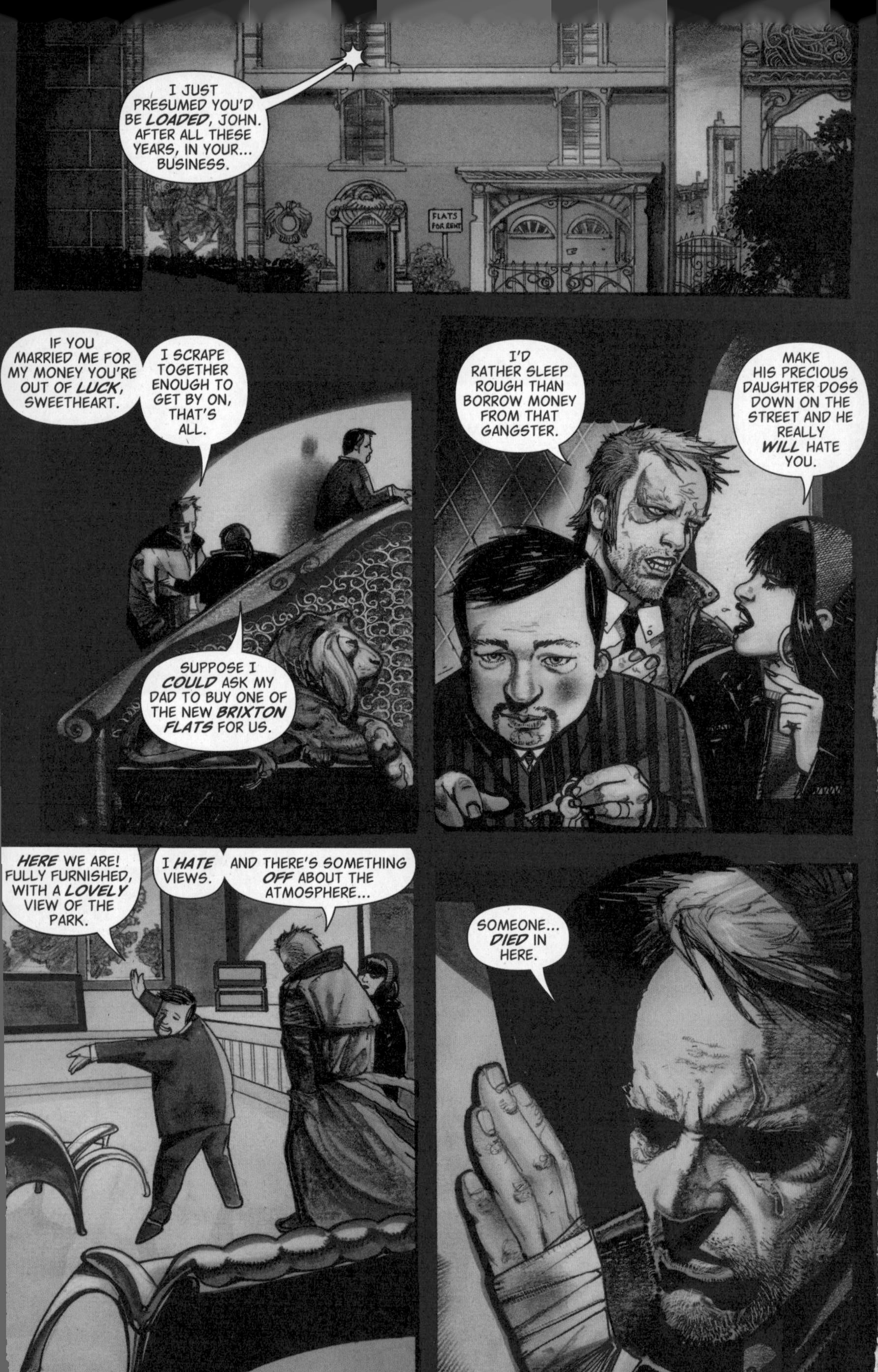
I JUST PRESUMED YOU'D BE *LOADED*, JOHN. AFTER ALL THESE YEARS, IN YOUR... BUSINESS.
IF YOU MARRIED ME FOR MY MONEY YOU'RE OUT OF *LUCK*, SWEETHEART.
I SCRAPE TOGETHER ENOUGH TO GET BY ON, THAT'S ALL.
SUPPOSE I *COULD* ASK MY DAD TO BUY ONE OF THE NEW *BRIXTON FLATS* FOR US.
I'D RATHER SLEEP ROUGH THAN BORROW MONEY FROM THAT GANGSTER.
MAKE HIS PRECIOUS DAUGHTER DOSS DOWN ON THE STREET AND HE REALLY *WILL* HATE YOU.
HERE WE ARE! FULLY FURNISHED, WITH A *LOVELY* VIEW OF THE PARK.
I *HATE* VIEWS.
AND THERE'S SOMETHING *OFF* ABOUT THE ATMOSPHERE...
SOMEONE... *DIED* IN HERE.
FLATS FOR RENT

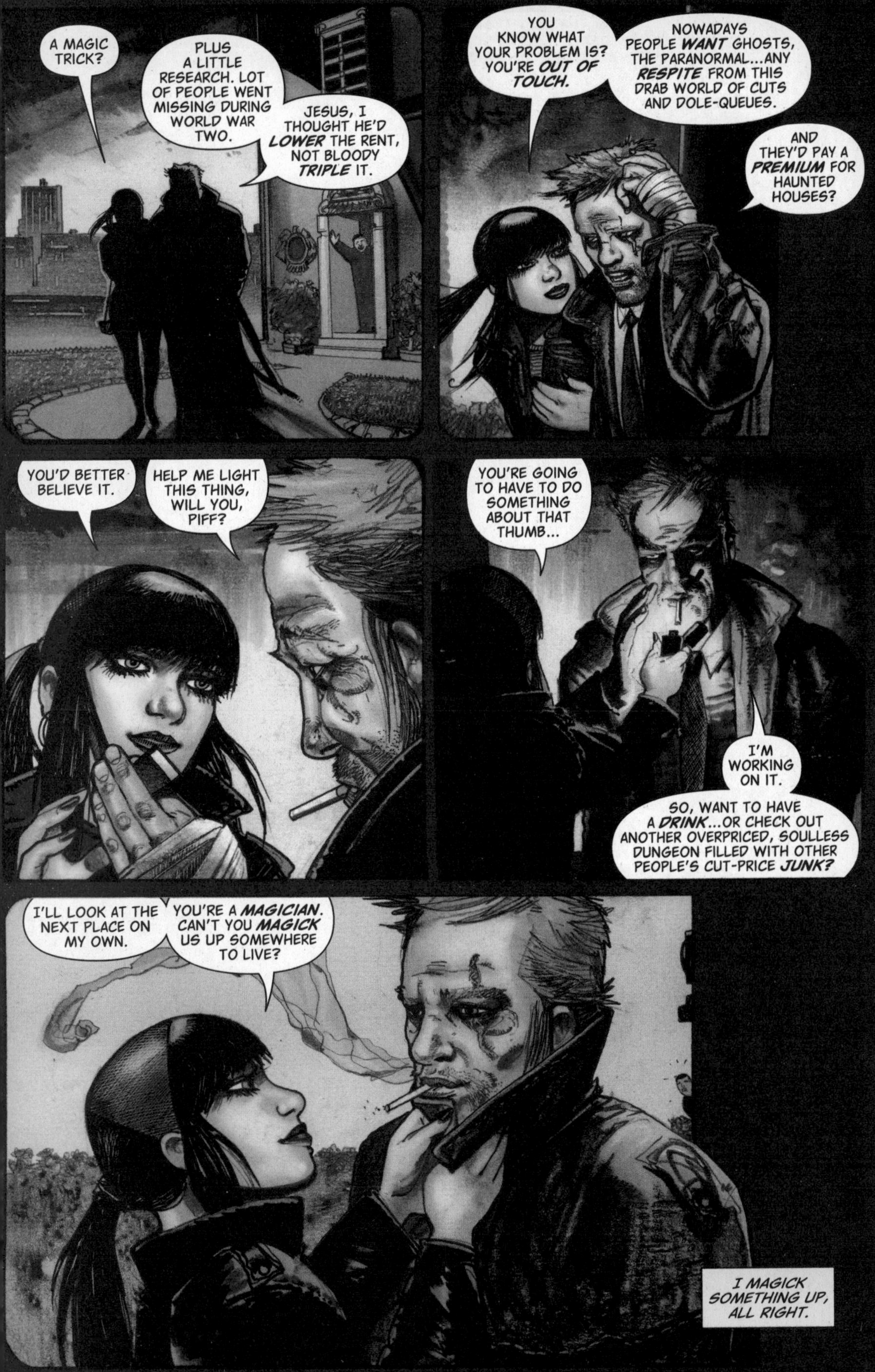
A MAGIC TRICK?
PLUS A LITTLE RESEARCH. LOT OF PEOPLE WENT MISSING DURING WORLD WAR TWO.
JESUS, I THOUGHT HE'D LOWER THE RENT, NOT BLOODY TRIPLE IT.
YOU KNOW WHAT YOUR PROBLEM IS? YOU'RE OUT OF TOUCH.
NOWADAYS PEOPLE WANT GHOSTS, THE PARANORMAL...ANY RESPITE FROM THIS DRAB WORLD OF CUTS AND DOLE-QUEUES.
AND THEY'D PAY A PREMIUM FOR HAUNTED HOUSES?
YOU'D BETTER BELIEVE IT.
HELP ME LIGHT THIS THING, WILL YOU, PIFF?
YOU'RE GOING TO HAVE TO DO SOMETHING ABOUT THAT THUMB...
I'M WORKING ON IT.
SO, WANT TO HAVE A DRINK...OR CHECK OUT ANOTHER OVERPRICED, SOULLESS DUNGEON FILLED WITH OTHER PEOPLE'S CUT-PRICE JUNK?
I'LL LOOK AT THE NEXT PLACE ON MY OWN.
YOU'RE A MAGICIAN. CAN'T YOU MAGICK US UP SOMEWHERE TO LIVE?
I MAGICK SOMETHING UP, ALL RIGHT.

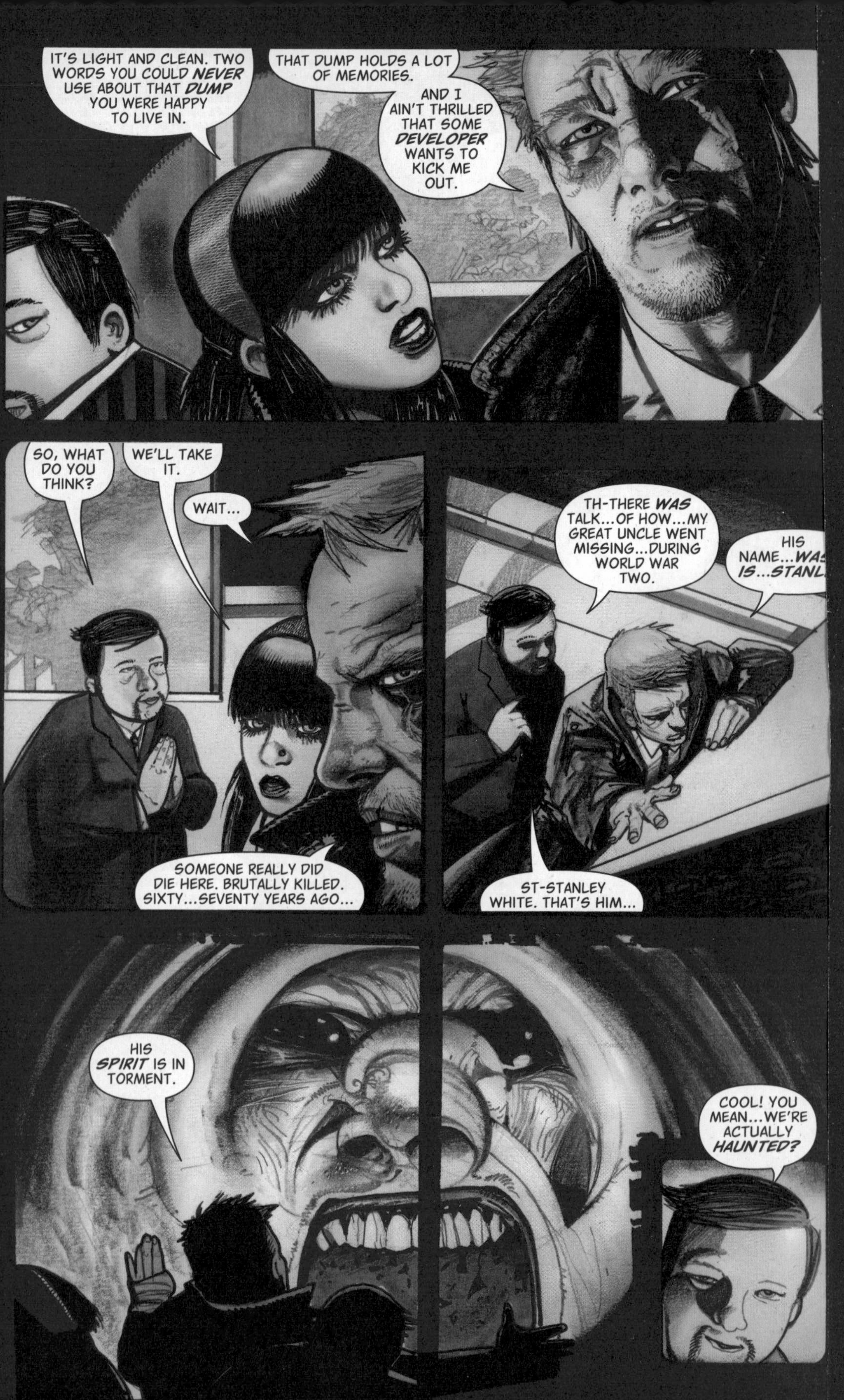
IT'S LIGHT AND CLEAN. TWO WORDS YOU COULD NEVER USE ABOUT THAT DUMP YOU WERE HAPPY TO LIVE IN.
THAT DUMP HOLDS A LOT OF MEMORIES.
AND I AIN'T THRILLED THAT SOME DEVELOPER WANTS TO KICK ME OUT.
SO, WHAT DO YOU THINK?
WE'LL TAKE IT.
WAIT...
SOMEONE REALLY DID DIE HERE. BRUTALLY KILLED. SIXTY...SEVENTY YEARS AGO...
TH-THERE WAS TALK...OF HOW...MY GREAT UNCLE WENT MISSING...DURING WORLD WAR TWO.
HIS NAME...WAS IS...STANL
ST-STANLEY WHITE. THAT'S HIM...
HIS SPIRIT IS IN TORMENT.
COOL! YOU MEAN...WE'RE ACTUALLY HAUNTED?

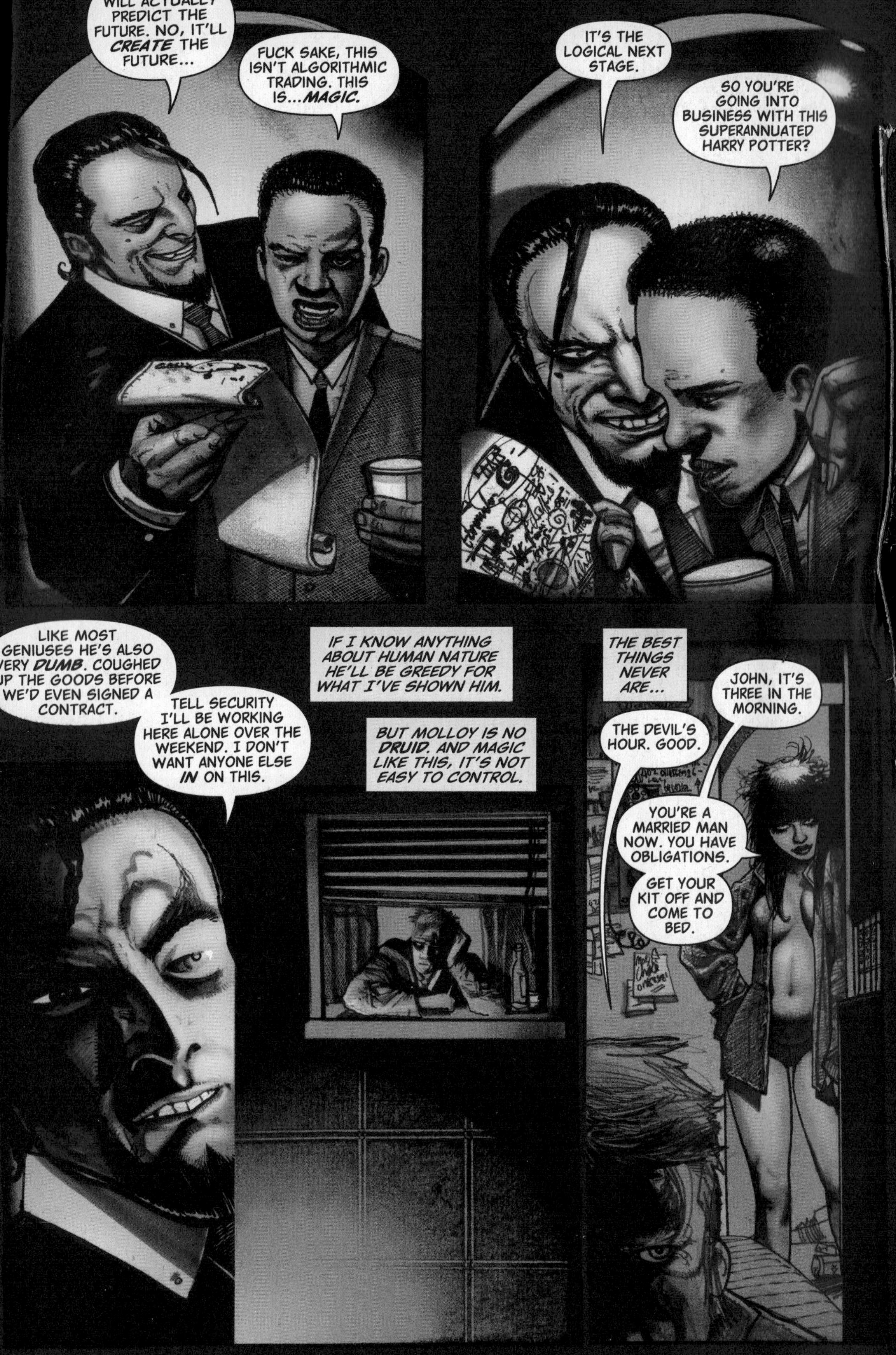
THIS... WILL ACTUALLY PREDICT THE FUTURE. NO, IT'LL CREATE THE FUTURE...
FUCK SAKE, THIS ISN'T ALGORITHMIC TRADING. THIS IS...MAGIC.
IT'S THE LOGICAL NEXT STAGE.
SO YOU'RE GOING INTO BUSINESS WITH THIS SUPERANNUATED HARRY POTTER?
LIKE MOST GENIUSES HE'S ALSO VERY DUMB. COUGHED UP THE GOODS BEFORE WE'D EVEN SIGNED A CONTRACT.
TELL SECURITY I'LL BE WORKING HERE ALONE OVER THE WEEKEND. I DON'T WANT ANYONE ELSE IN ON THIS.
IF I KNOW ANYTHING ABOUT HUMAN NATURE HE'LL BE GREEDY FOR WHAT I'VE SHOWN HIM.
BUT MOLLOY IS NO DRUID. AND MAGIC LIKE THIS, IT'S NOT EASY TO CONTROL.
THE BEST THINGS NEVER ARE...
JOHN, IT'S THREE IN THE MORNING.
THE DEVIL'S HOUR. GOOD.
YOU'RE A MARRIED MAN NOW. YOU HAVE OBLIGATIONS.
GET YOUR KIT OFF AND COME TO BED.

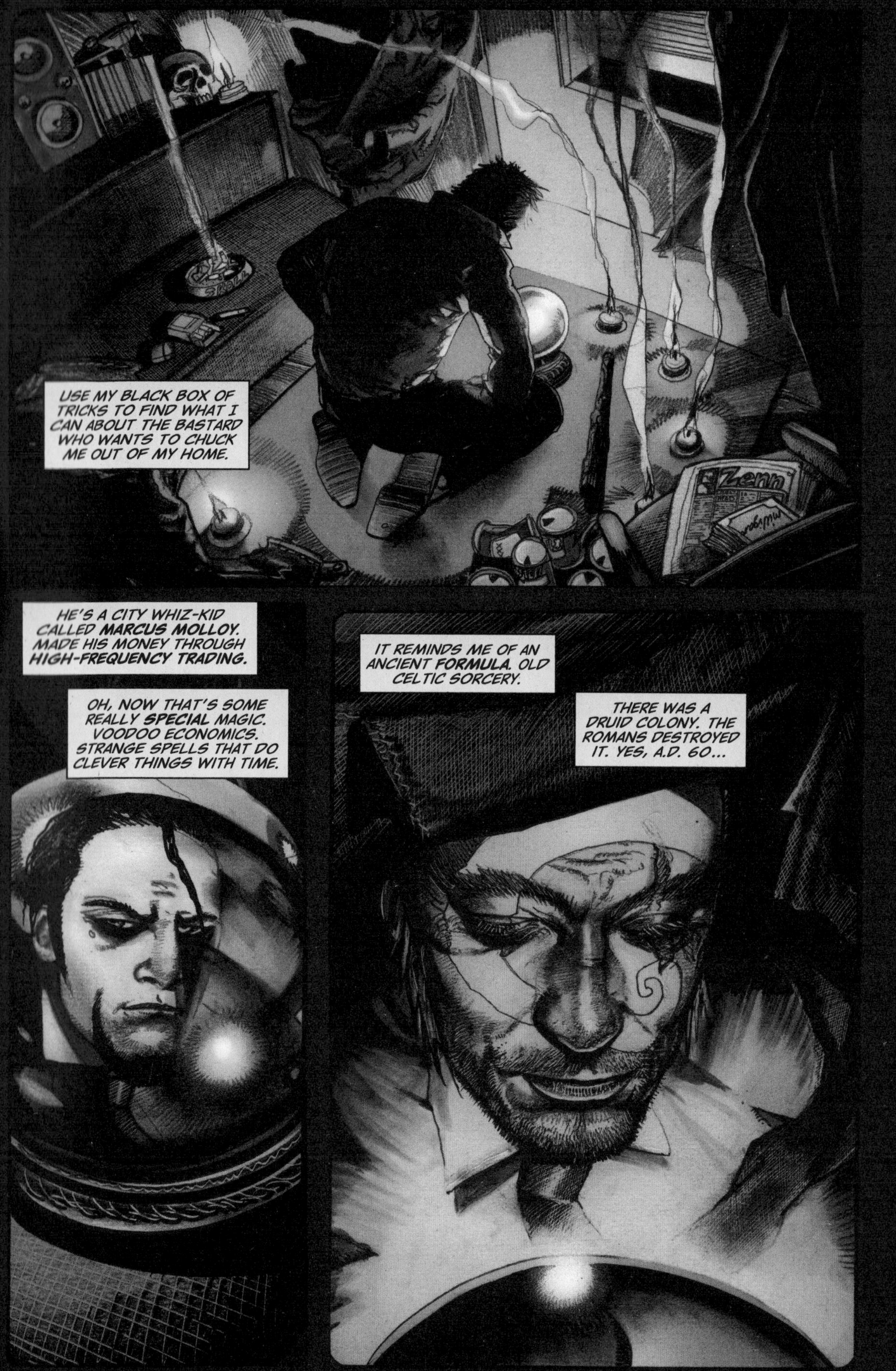
USE MY BLACK BOX OF TRICKS TO FIND WHAT I CAN ABOUT THE BASTARD WHO WANTS TO CHUCK ME OUT OF MY HOME.
HE'S A CITY WHIZ-KID CALLED MARCUS MOLLOY. MADE HIS MONEY THROUGH HIGH-FREQUENCY TRADING.
OH, NOW THAT'S SOME REALLY SPECIAL MAGIC. VOODOO ECONOMICS. STRANGE SPELLS THAT DO CLEVER THINGS WITH TIME.
IT REMINDS ME OF AN ANCIENT FORMULA. OLD CELTIC SORCERY.
THERE WAS A DRUID COLONY. THE ROMANS DESTROYED IT. YES, A.D. 60...

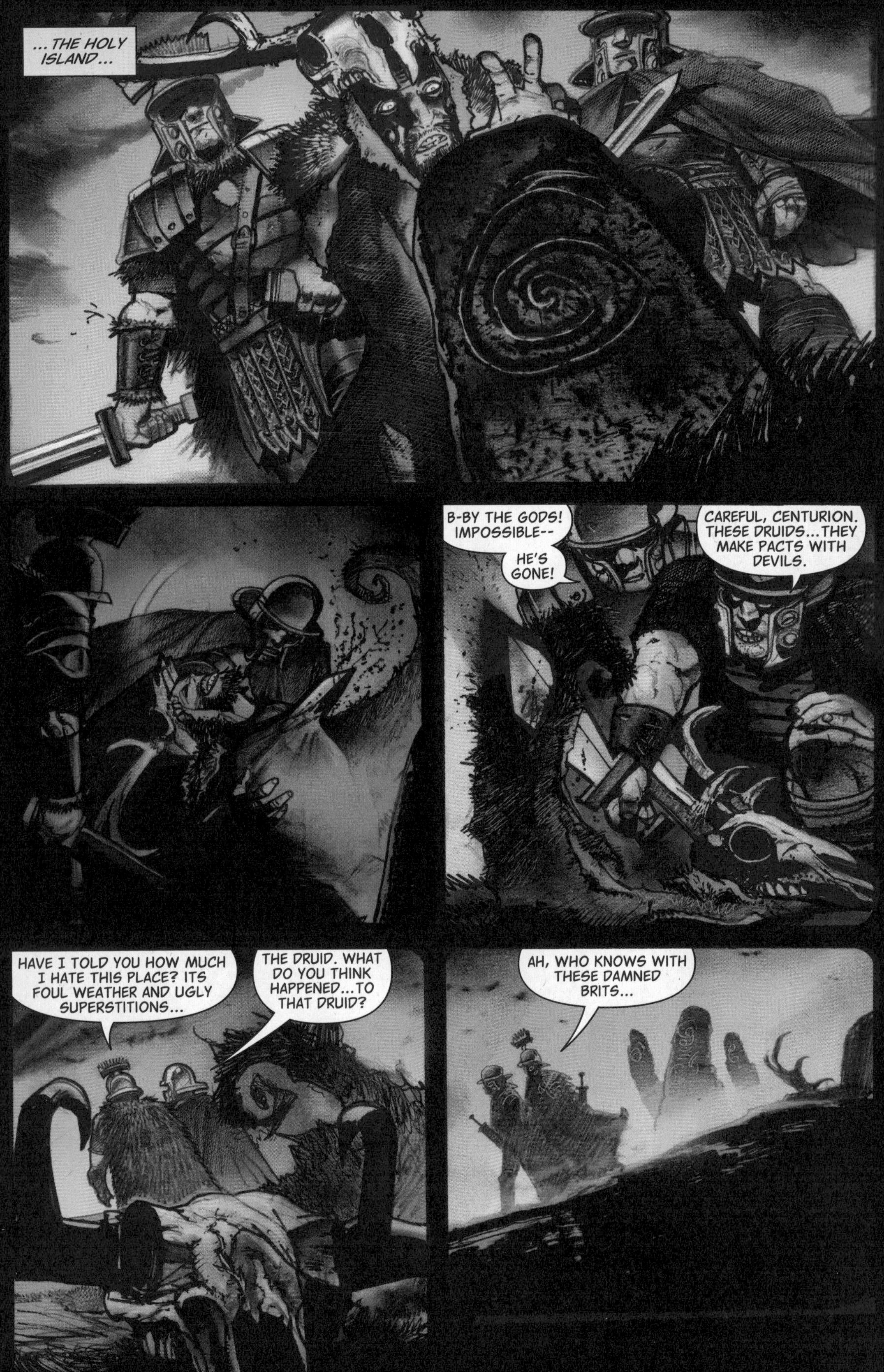
...THE HOLY ISLAND...
B-BY THE GODS! IMPOSSIBLE--
HE'S GONE!
CAREFUL, CENTURION. THESE DRUIDS...THEY MAKE PACTS WITH DEVILS.
HAVE I TOLD YOU HOW MUCH I HATE THIS PLACE? ITS FOUL WEATHER AND UGLY SUPERSTITIONS...
THE DRUID. WHAT DO YOU THINK HAPPENED...TO THAT DRUID?
AH, WHO KNOWS WITH THESE DAMNED BRITS...

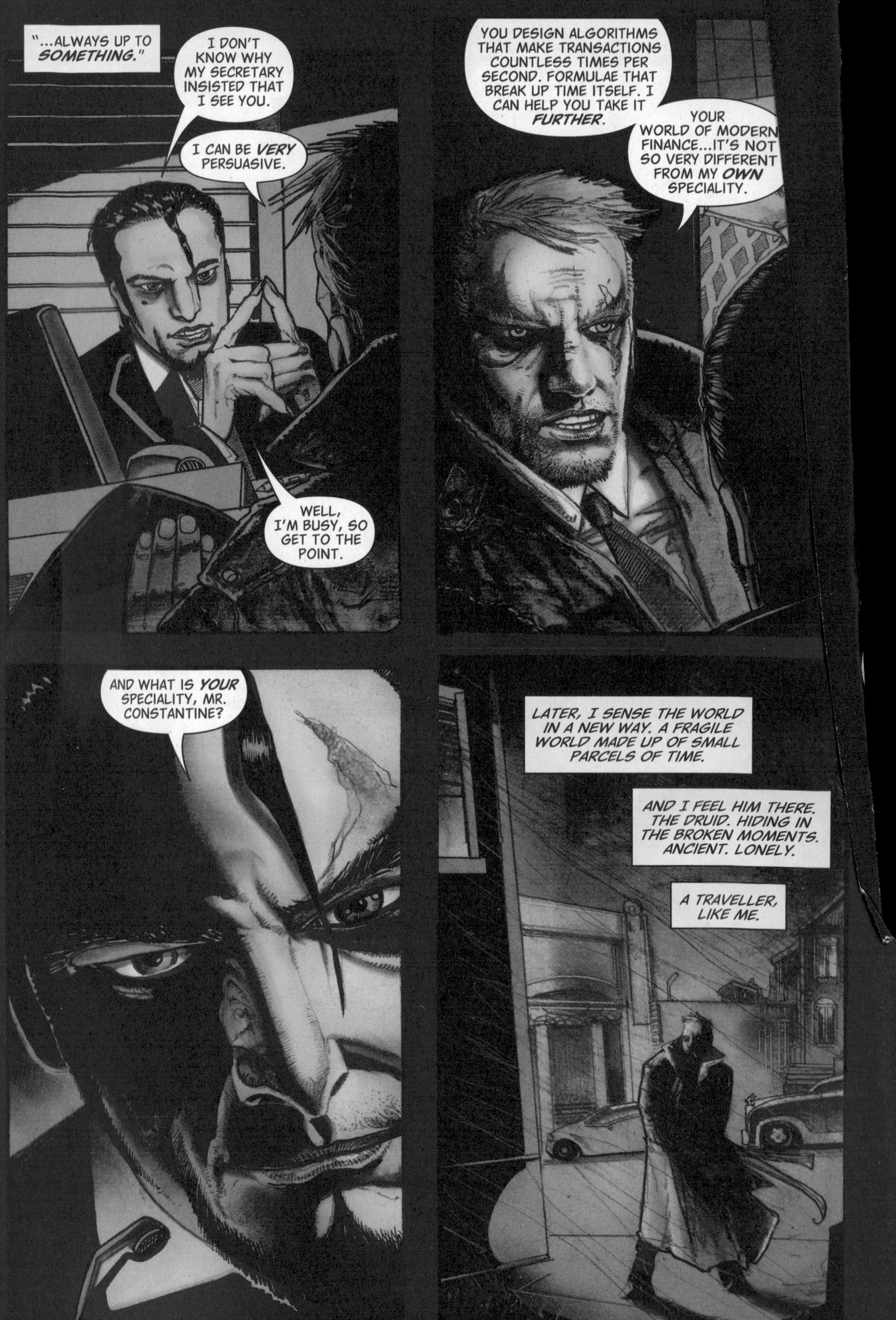
"...ALWAYS UP TO *SOMETHING*."
I DON'T KNOW WHY MY SECRETARY INSISTED THAT I SEE YOU.
I CAN BE *VERY* PERSUASIVE.
WELL, I'M BUSY, SO GET TO THE POINT.
YOU DESIGN ALGORITHMS THAT MAKE TRANSACTIONS COUNTLESS TIMES PER SECOND. FORMULAE THAT BREAK UP TIME ITSELF. I CAN HELP YOU TAKE IT *FURTHER*.
YOUR WORLD OF MODERN FINANCE...IT'S NOT SO VERY DIFFERENT FROM MY *OWN* SPECIALITY.
AND WHAT IS *YOUR* SPECIALITY, MR. CONSTANTINE?
LATER, I SENSE THE WORLD IN A NEW WAY. A FRAGILE WORLD MADE UP OF SMALL PARCELS OF TIME.
AND I FEEL HIM THERE. THE DRUID. HIDING IN THE BROKEN MOMENTS. ANCIENT. LONELY.
A TRAVELLER, LIKE ME.

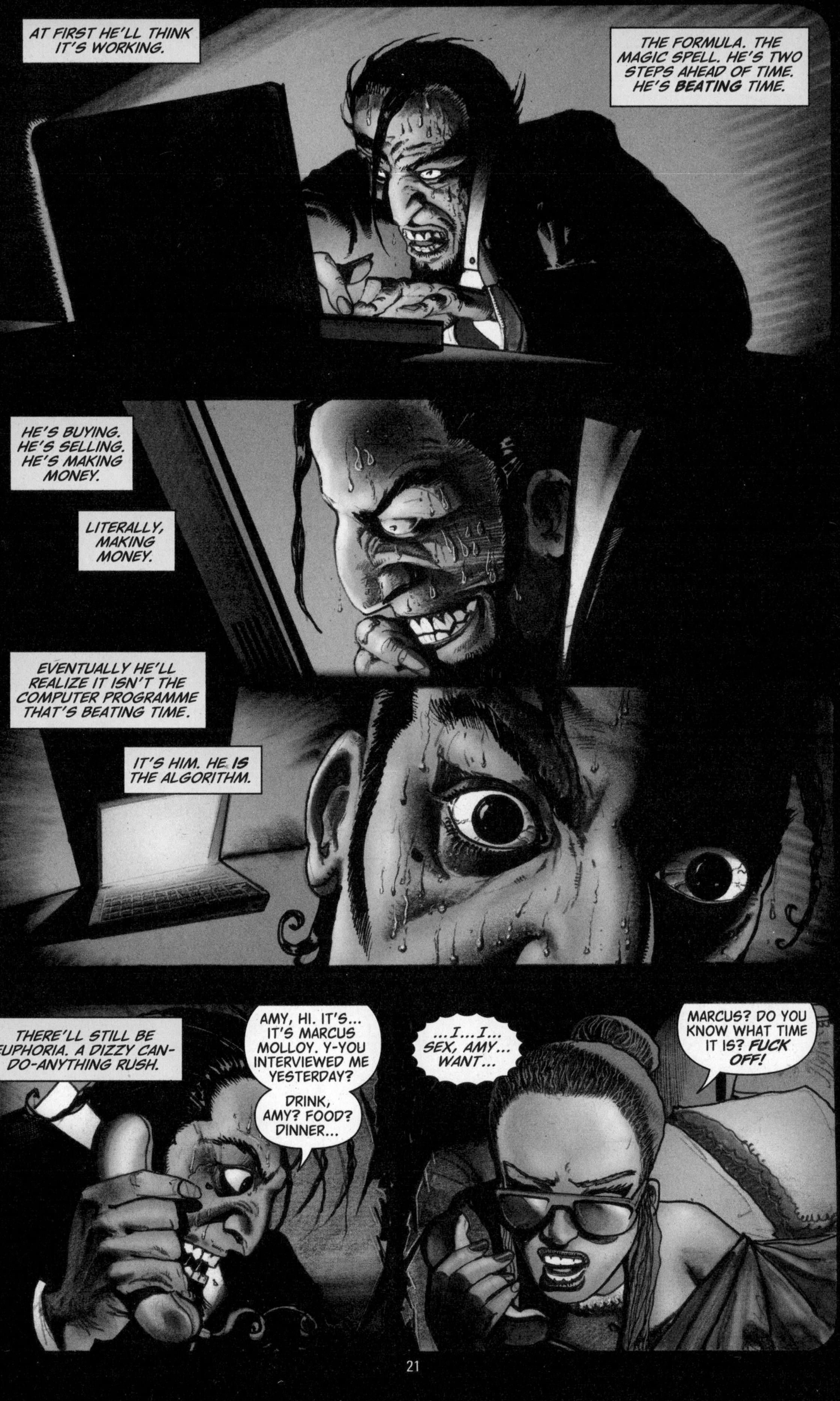
AT FIRST HE'LL THINK IT'S WORKING.
THE FORMULA. THE MAGIC SPELL. HE'S TWO STEPS AHEAD OF TIME. HE'S BEATING TIME.
HE'S BUYING. HE'S SELLING. HE'S MAKING MONEY.
LITERALLY, MAKING MONEY.
EVENTUALLY HE'LL REALIZE IT ISN'T THE COMPUTER PROGRAMME THAT'S BEATING TIME.
IT'S HIM. HE IS THE ALGORITHM.
THERE'LL STILL BE EUPHORIA. A DIZZY CAN-DO-ANYTHING RUSH.
AMY, HI. IT'S... IT'S MARCUS MOLLOY. Y-YOU INTERVIEWED ME YESTERDAY?
DRINK, AMY? FOOD? DINNER...
...I...I... SEX, AMY... WANT...
MARCUS? DO YOU KNOW WHAT TIME IT IS? FUCK OFF!

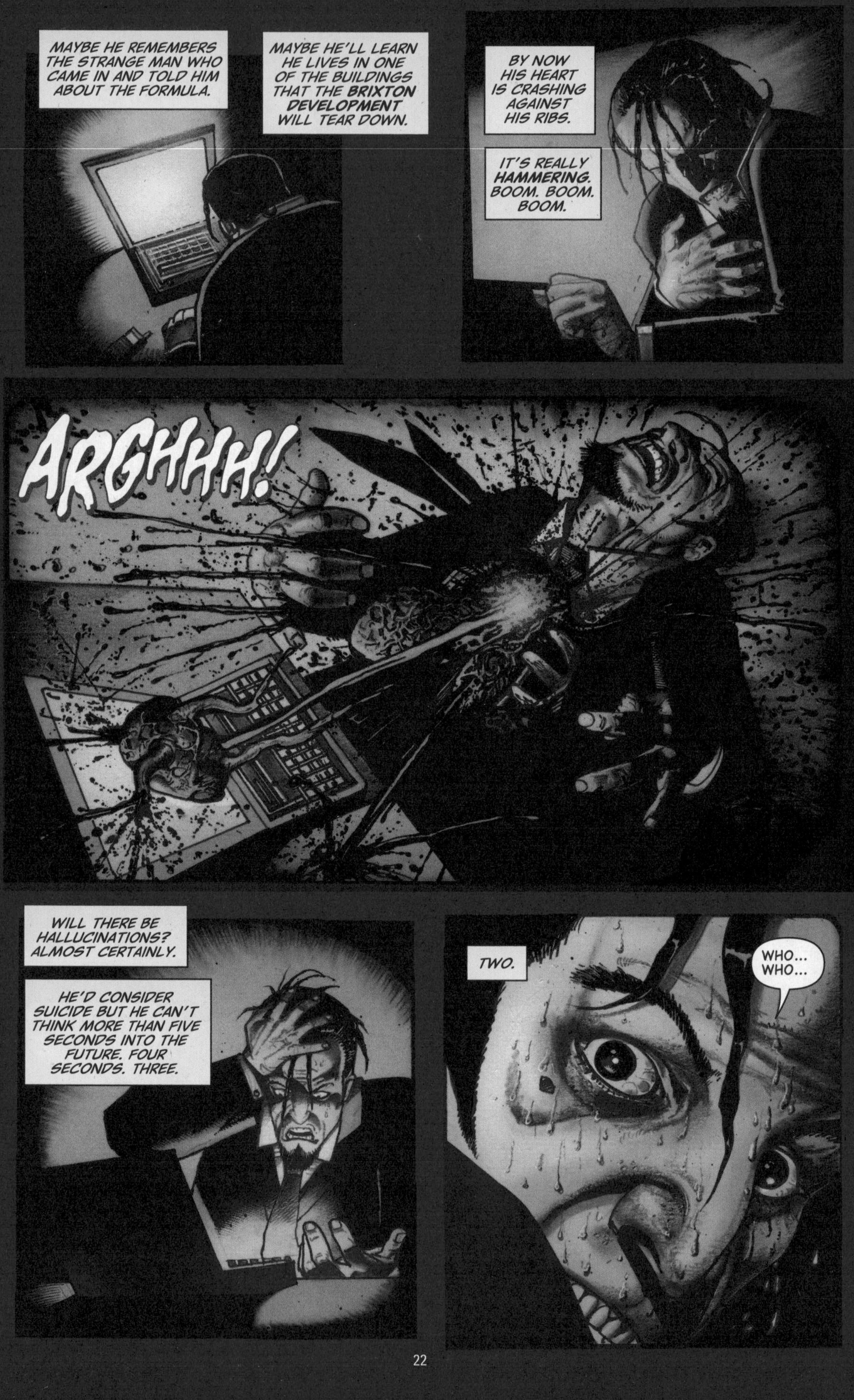
MAYBE HE REMEMBERS THE STRANGE MAN WHO CAME IN AND TOLD HIM ABOUT THE FORMULA.
MAYBE HE'LL LEARN HE LIVES IN ONE OF THE BUILDINGS THAT THE BRIXTON DEVELOPMENT WILL TEAR DOWN.
BY NOW HIS HEART IS CRASHING AGAINST HIS RIBS.
IT'S REALLY HAMMERING. BOOM. BOOM. BOOM.
ARGHHH!
WILL THERE BE HALLUCINATIONS? ALMOST CERTAINLY.
HE'D CONSIDER SUICIDE BUT HE CAN'T THINK MORE THAN FIVE SECONDS INTO THE FUTURE. FOUR SECONDS. THREE.
TWO.
WHO... WHO...

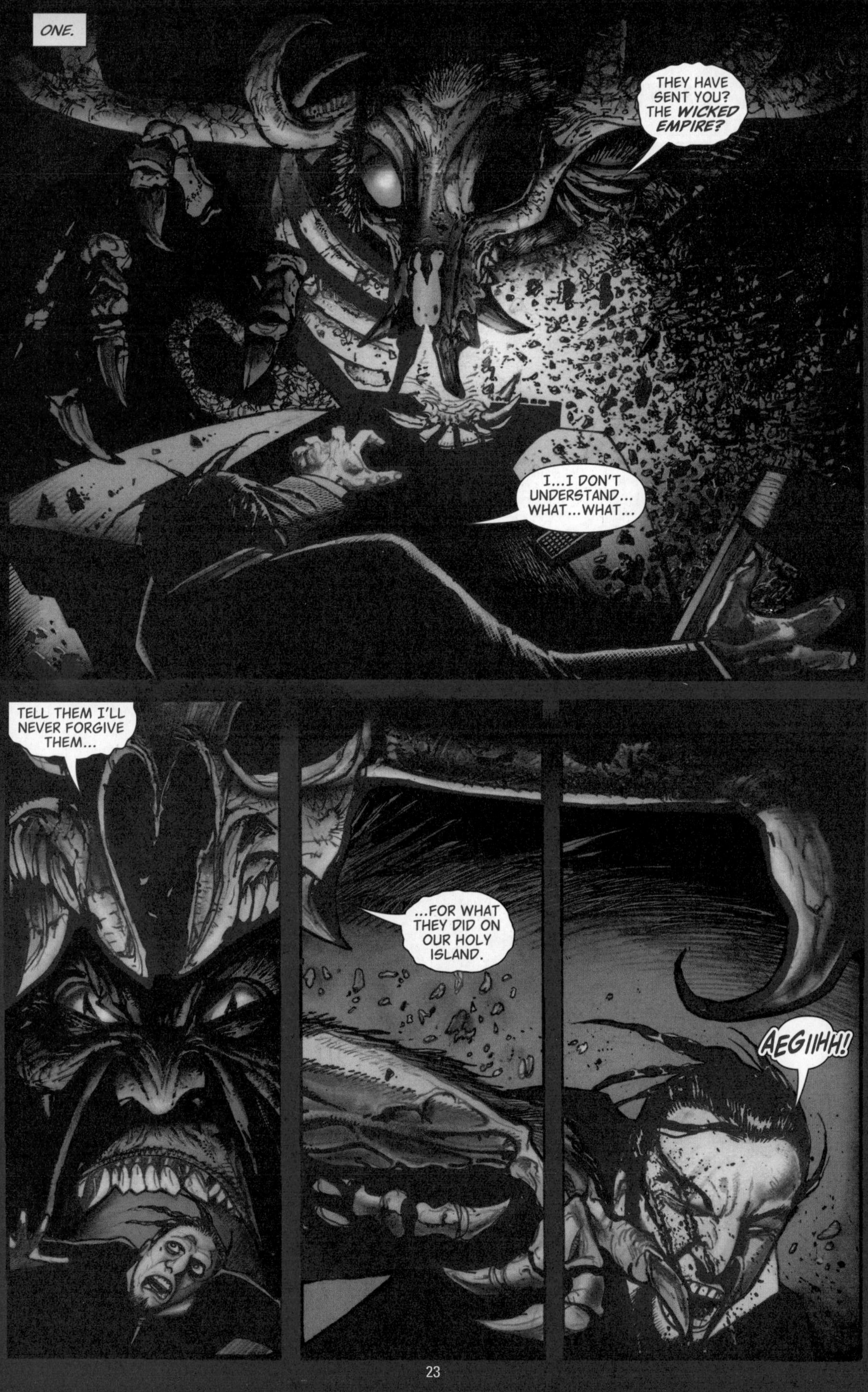
ONE.
THEY HAVE SENT YOU? THE WICKED EMPIRE?
I...I DON'T UNDERSTAND... WHAT...WHAT...
TELL THEM I'LL NEVER FORGIVE THEM...
...FOR WHAT THEY DID ON OUR HOLY ISLAND.
AEGIIHH!

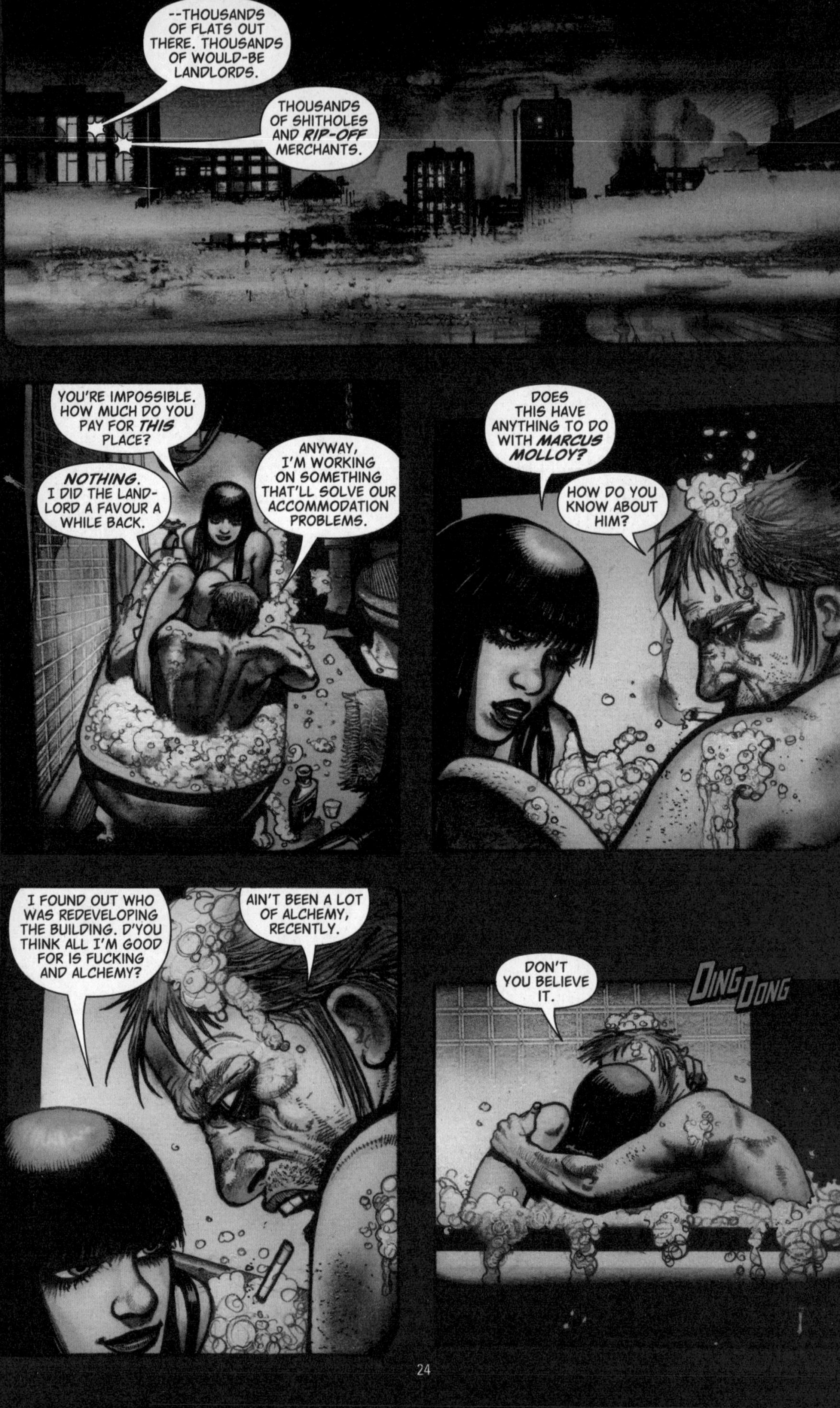
--THOUSANDS OF FLATS OUT THERE. THOUSANDS OF WOULD-BE LANDLORDS.
THOUSANDS OF SHITHOLES AND RIP-OFF MERCHANTS.
YOU'RE IMPOSSIBLE. HOW MUCH DO YOU PAY FOR THIS PLACE?
NOTHING. I DID THE LAND-LORD A FAVOUR A WHILE BACK.
ANYWAY, I'M WORKING ON SOMETHING THAT'LL SOLVE OUR ACCOMMODATION PROBLEMS.
DOES THIS HAVE ANYTHING TO DO WITH MARCUS MOLLOY?
HOW DO YOU KNOW ABOUT HIM?
I FOUND OUT WHO WAS REDEVELOPING THE BUILDING. D'YOU THINK ALL I'M GOOD FOR IS FUCKING AND ALCHEMY?
AIN'T BEEN A LOT OF ALCHEMY, RECENTLY.
DON'T YOU BELIEVE IT.
DING DONG

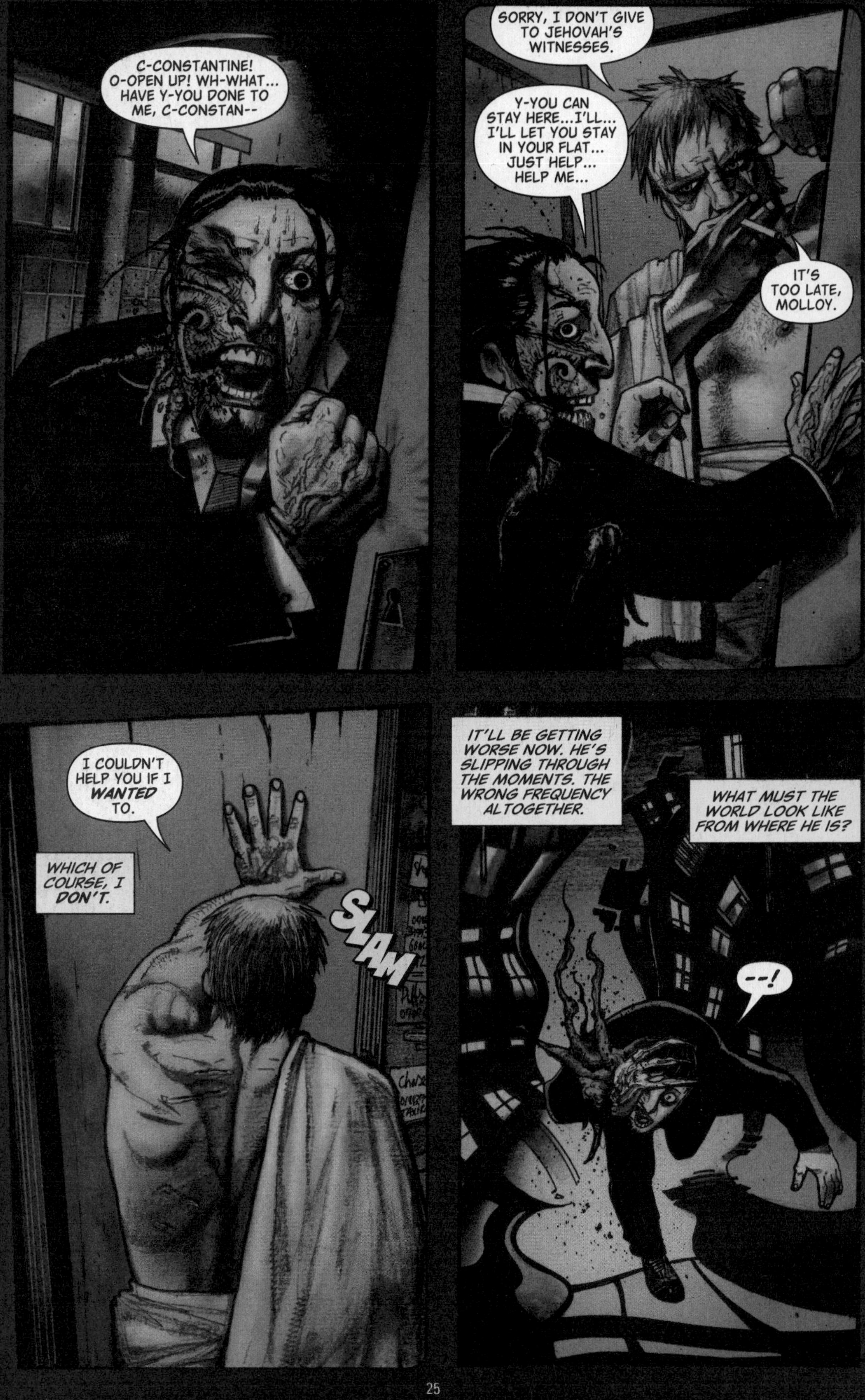

C-CONSTANTINE! O-OPEN UP! WH-WHAT... HAVE Y-YOU DONE TO ME, C-CONSTAN--
SORRY, I DON'T GIVE TO JEHOVAH'S WITNESSES.
Y-YOU CAN STAY HERE...I'LL... I'LL LET YOU STAY IN YOUR FLAT... JUST HELP... HELP ME...
IT'S TOO LATE, MOLLOY.
I COULDN'T HELP YOU IF I *WANTED* TO.
WHICH OF COURSE, I DON'T.
SLAM
IT'LL BE GETTING WORSE NOW. HE'S SLIPPING THROUGH THE MOMENTS. THE WRONG FREQUENCY ALTOGETHER.
WHAT MUST THE WORLD LOOK LIKE FROM WHERE HE IS?
--!

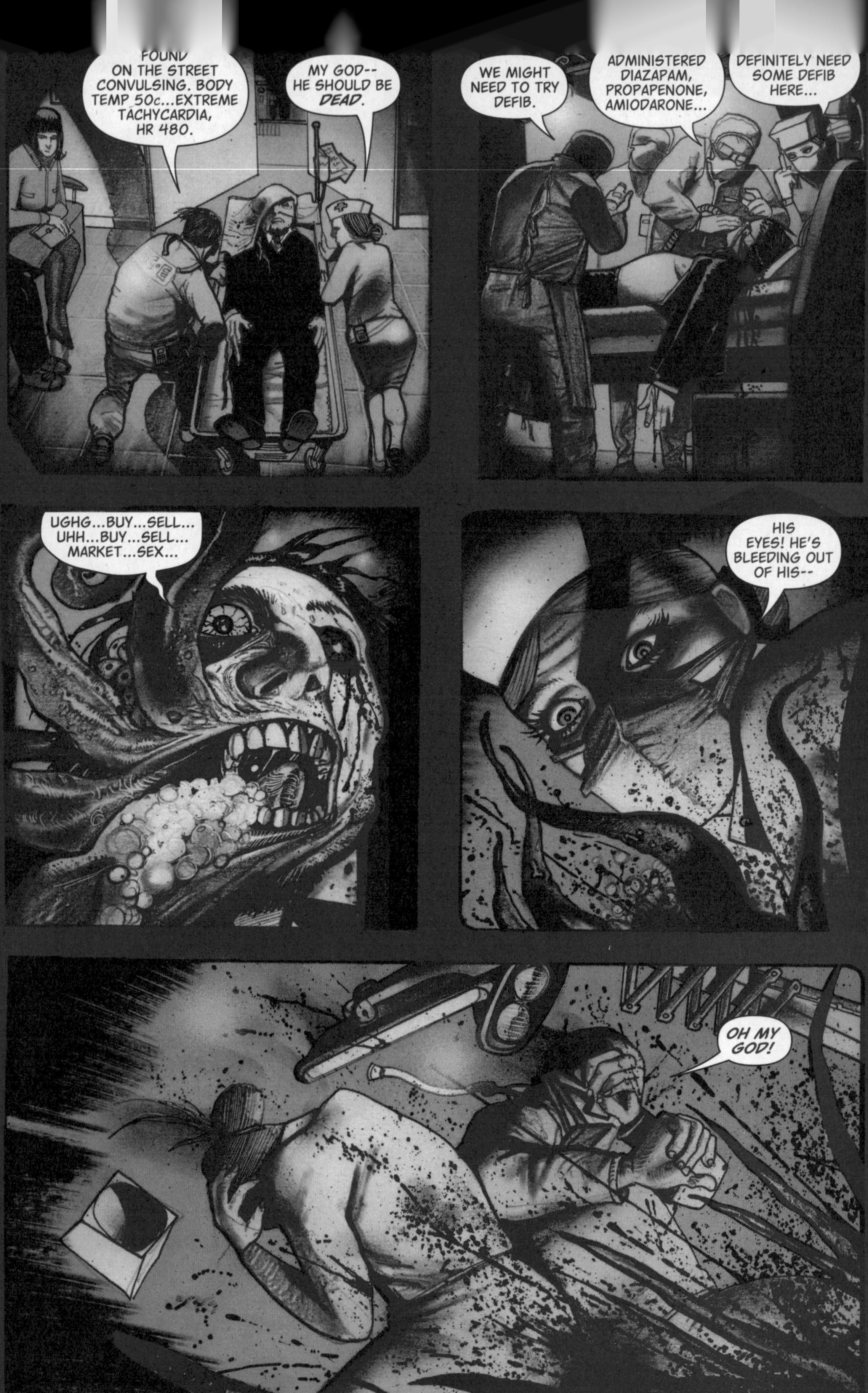
FOUND ON THE STREET CONVULSING. BODY TEMP 50c...EXTREME TACHYCARDIA, HR 480.
MY GOD-- HE SHOULD BE DEAD.
WE MIGHT NEED TO TRY DEFIB.
ADMINISTERED DIAZAPAM, PROPAPENONE, AMIODARONE...
DEFINITELY NEED SOME DEFIB HERE...
UGHG...BUY...SELL... UHH...BUY...SELL... MARKET...SEX...
HIS EYES! HE'S BLEEDING OUT OF HIS--
OH MY GOD!

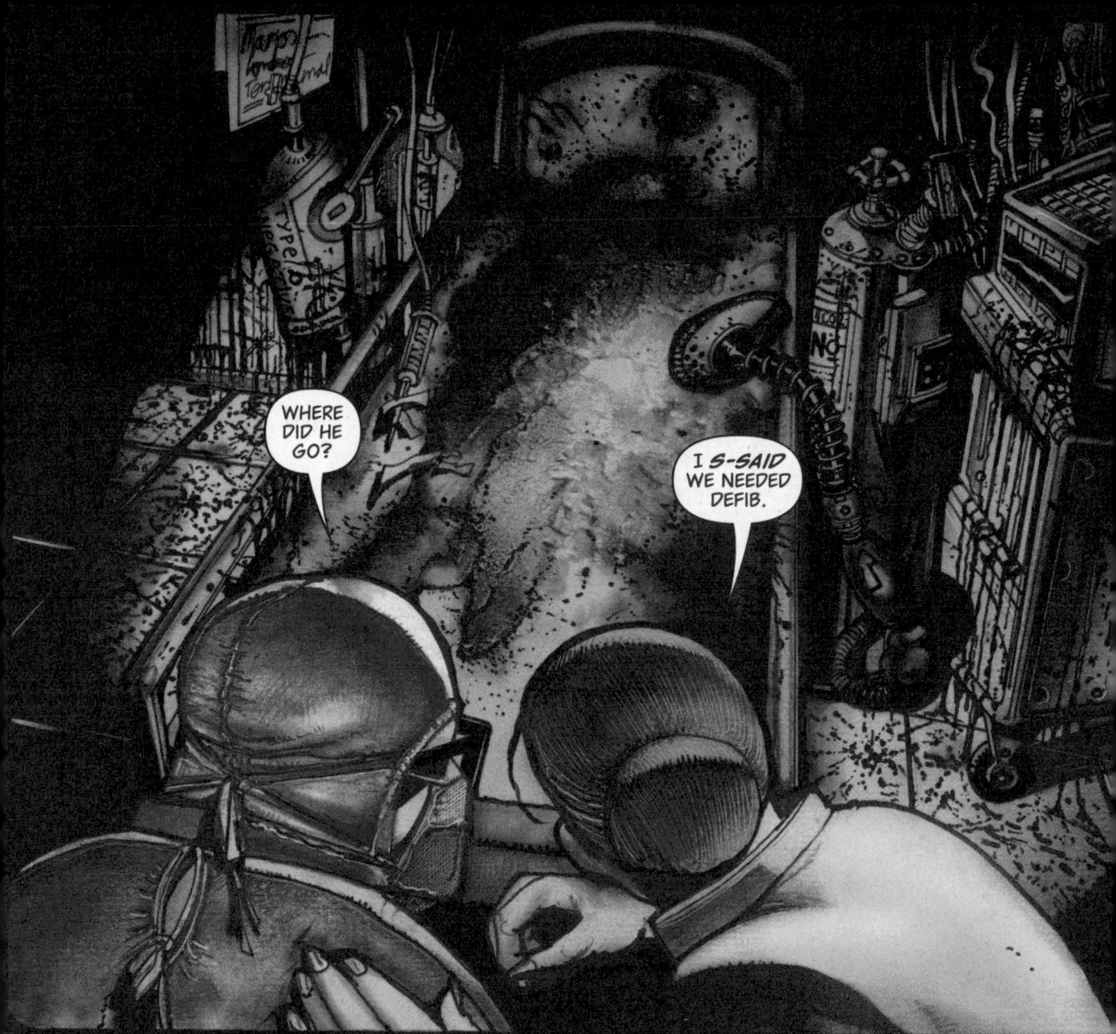
WHERE DID HE GO?
I S-SAID WE NEEDED DEFIB.
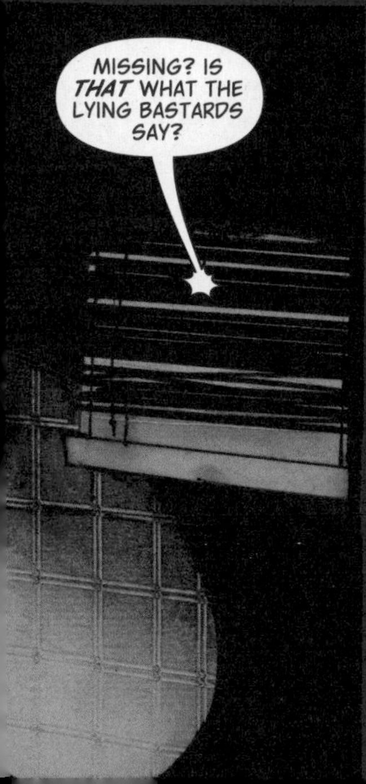
MISSING? IS THAT WHAT THE LYING BASTARDS SAY?
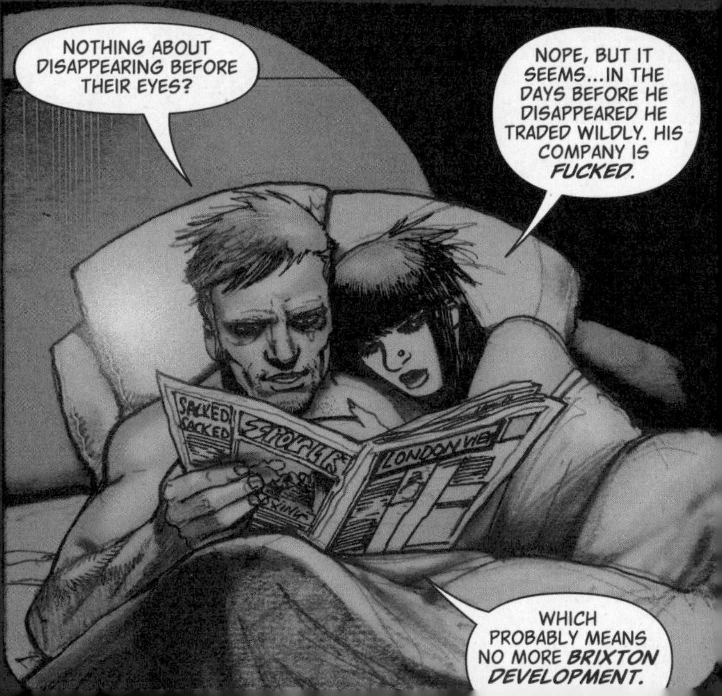
NOTHING ABOUT DISAPPEARING BEFORE THEIR EYES?
NOPE, BUT IT SEEMS...IN THE DAYS BEFORE HE DISAPPEARED HE TRADED WILDLY. HIS COMPANY IS FUCKED.
WHICH PROBABLY MEANS NO MORE BRIXTON DEVELOPMENT.

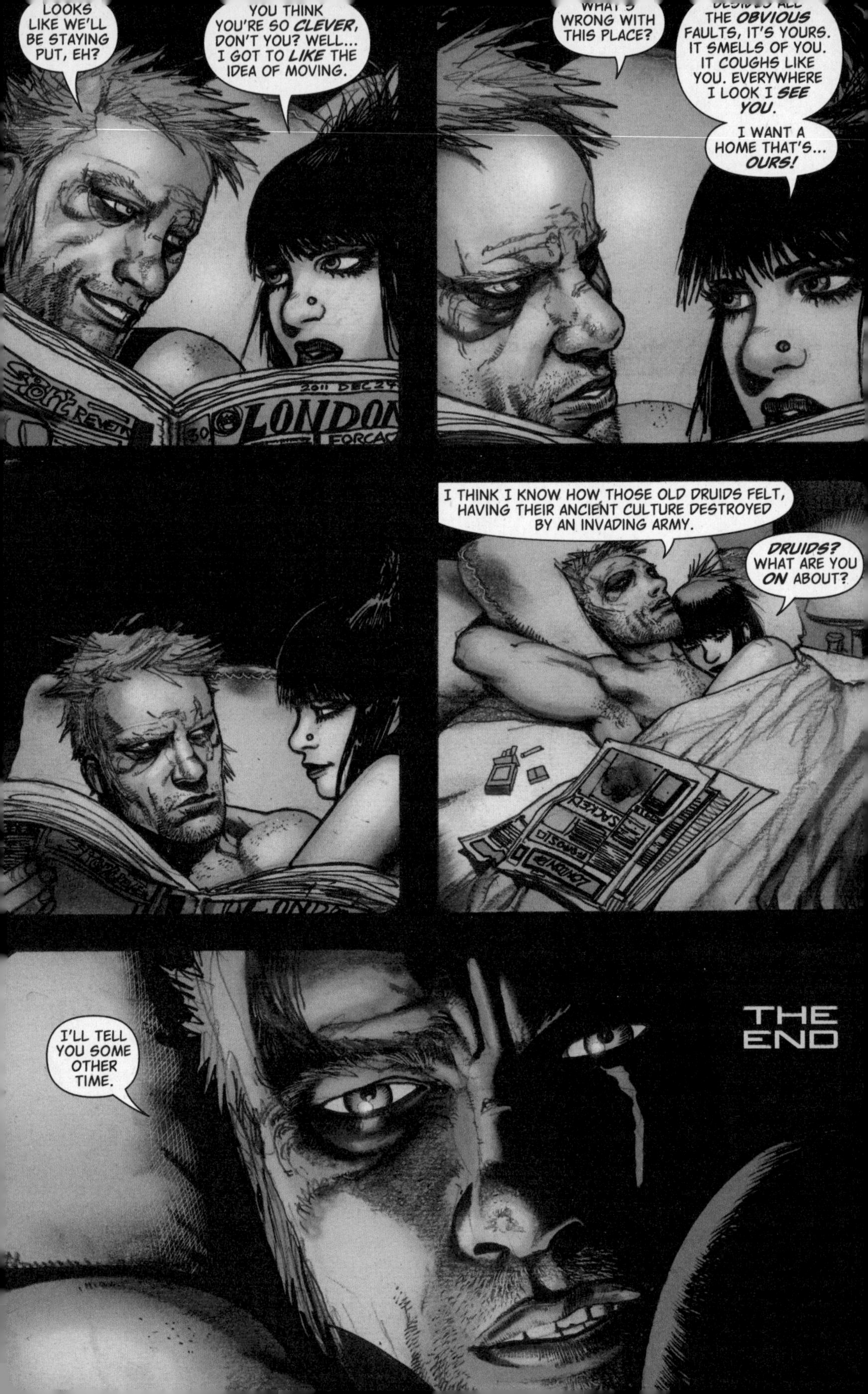
LOOKS LIKE WE'LL BE STAYING PUT, EH?
YOU THINK YOU'RE SO *CLEVER*, DON'T YOU? WELL... I GOT TO *LIKE* THE IDEA OF MOVING.
WRONG WITH THIS PLACE?
THE *OBVIOUS* FAULTS, IT'S YOURS. IT SMELLS OF YOU. IT COUGHS LIKE YOU. EVERYWHERE I LOOK I *SEE YOU*.
I WANT A HOME THAT'S... *OURS!*
I THINK I KNOW HOW THOSE OLD DRUIDS FELT, HAVING THEIR ANCIENT CULTURE DESTROYED BY AN INVADING ARMY.
DRUIDS? WHAT ARE YOU *ON* ABOUT?
I'LL TELL YOU SOME OTHER TIME.
THE END

Phantom Pains, Part One

John Thumb

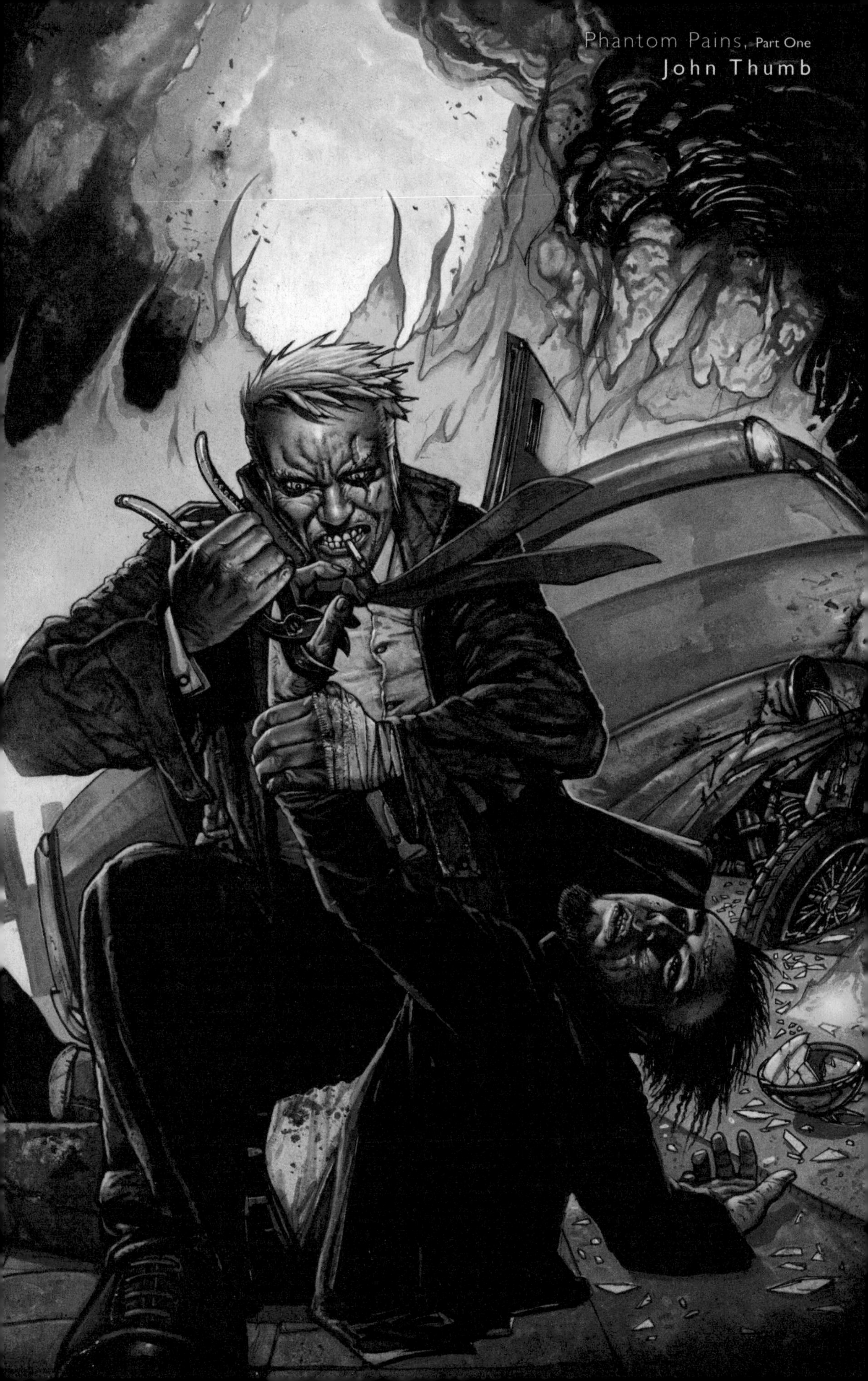

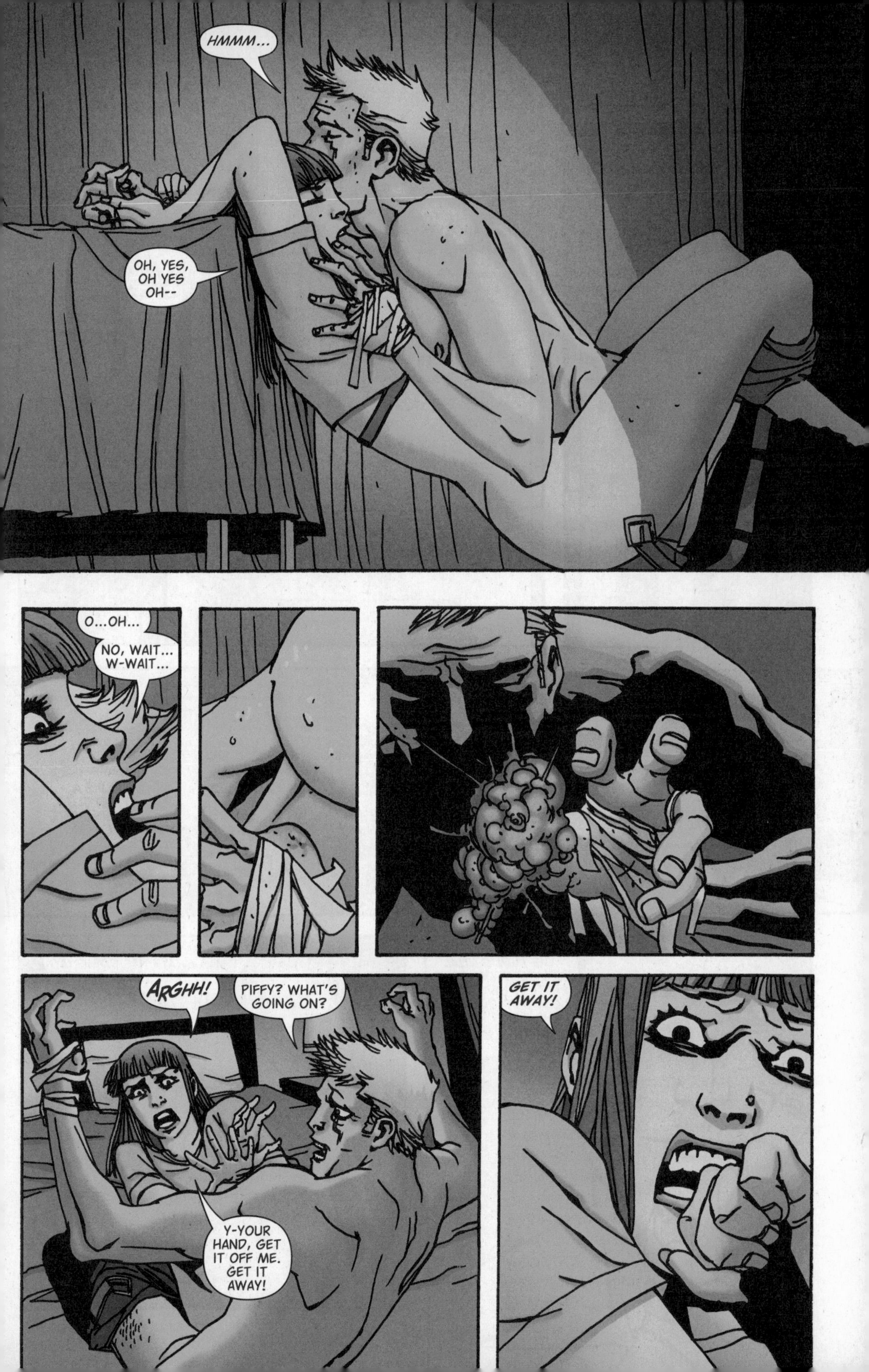
HMMM...
OH, YES, OH YES OH--
O...OH...
NO, WAIT... W-WAIT...
ARGHH!
PIFFY? WHAT'S GOING ON?
Y-YOUR HAND, GET IT OFF ME. GET IT AWAY!
GET IT AWAY!

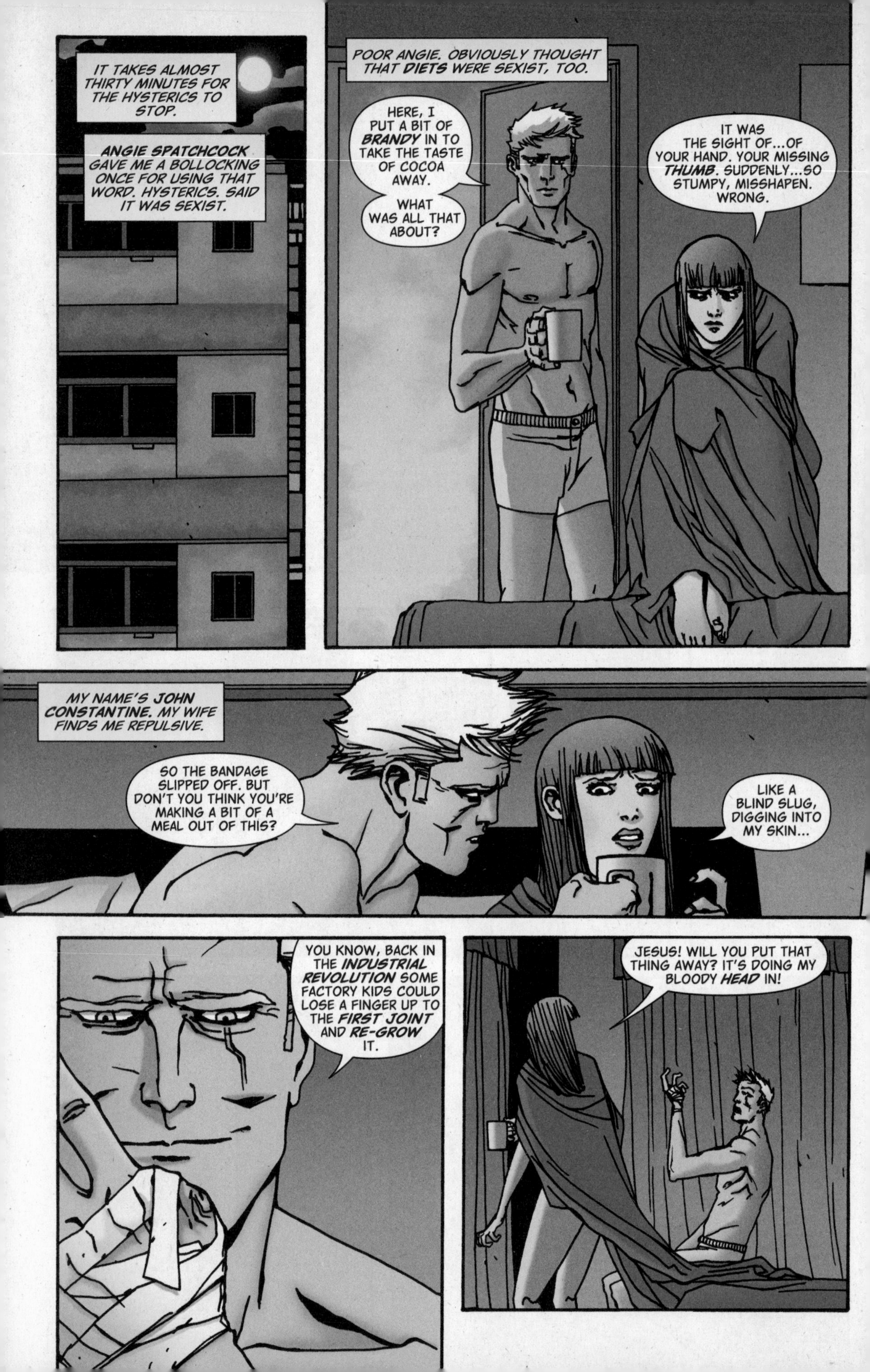
IT TAKES ALMOST THIRTY MINUTES FOR THE HYSTERICS TO STOP.
ANGIE SPATCHCOCK GAVE ME A BOLLOCKING ONCE FOR USING THAT WORD. HYSTERICS. SAID IT WAS SEXIST.
POOR ANGIE. OBVIOUSLY THOUGHT THAT DIETS WERE SEXIST, TOO.
HERE, I PUT A BIT OF BRANDY IN TO TAKE THE TASTE OF COCOA AWAY.
WHAT WAS ALL THAT ABOUT?
IT WAS THE SIGHT OF...OF YOUR HAND. YOUR MISSING THUMB. SUDDENLY...SO STUMPY, MISSHAPEN. WRONG.
MY NAME'S JOHN CONSTANTINE. MY WIFE FINDS ME REPULSIVE.
SO THE BANDAGE SLIPPED OFF. BUT DON'T YOU THINK YOU'RE MAKING A BIT OF A MEAL OUT OF THIS?
LIKE A BLIND SLUG, DIGGING INTO MY SKIN...
YOU KNOW, BACK IN THE INDUSTRIAL REVOLUTION SOME FACTORY KIDS COULD LOSE A FINGER UP TO THE FIRST JOINT AND RE-GROW IT.
JESUS! WILL YOU PUT THAT THING AWAY? IT'S DOING MY BLOODY HEAD IN!

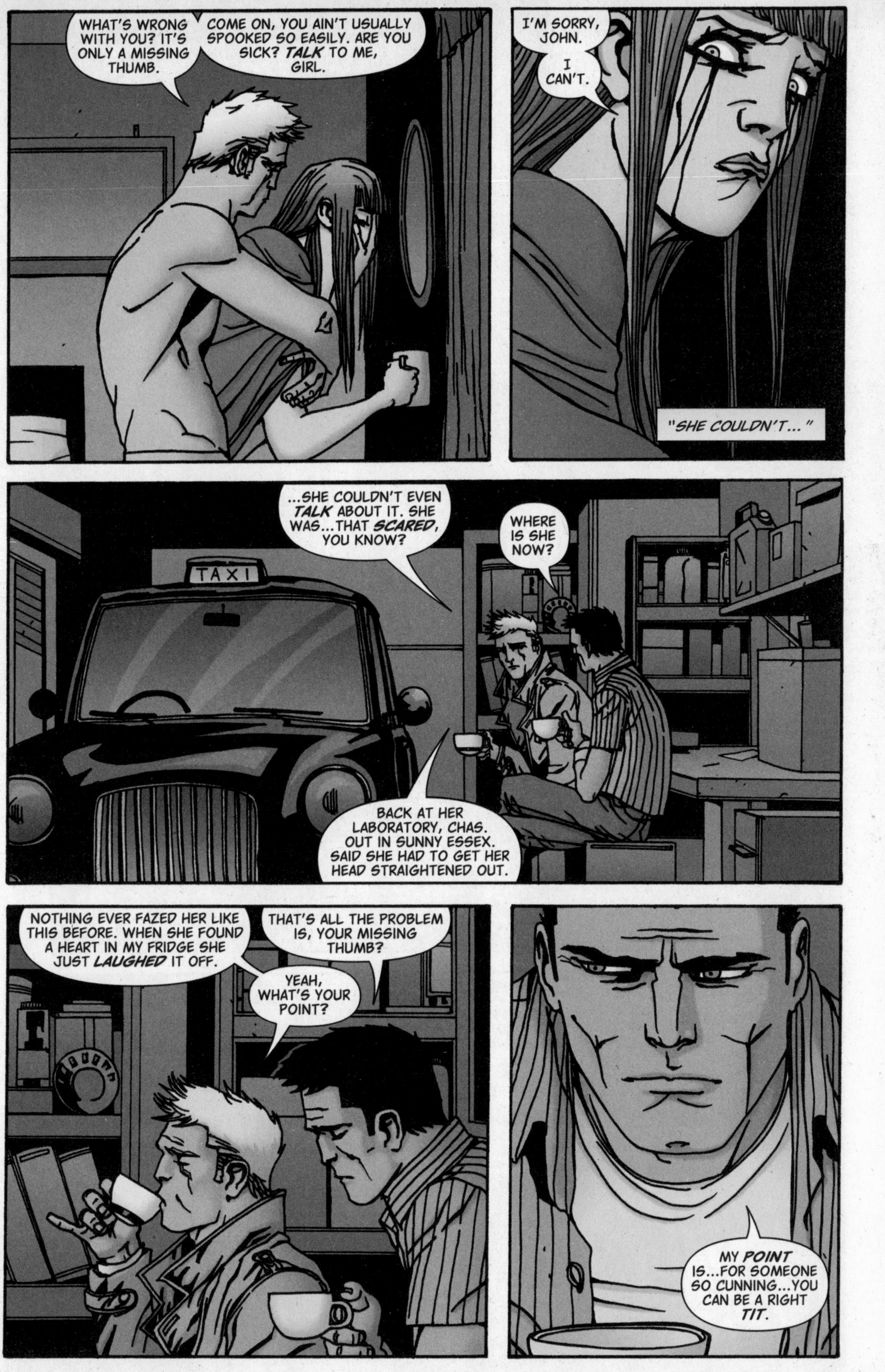
WHAT'S WRONG WITH YOU? IT'S ONLY A MISSING THUMB.
COME ON, YOU AIN'T USUALLY SPOOKED SO EASILY. ARE YOU SICK? TALK TO ME, GIRL.
I'M SORRY, JOHN.
I CAN'T.
"SHE COULDN'T..."
...SHE COULDN'T EVEN TALK ABOUT IT. SHE WAS...THAT SCARED, YOU KNOW?
WHERE IS SHE NOW?
TAXI
BACK AT HER LABORATORY, CHAS. OUT IN SUNNY ESSEX. SAID SHE HAD TO GET HER HEAD STRAIGHTENED OUT.
NOTHING EVER FAZED HER LIKE THIS BEFORE. WHEN SHE FOUND A HEART IN MY FRIDGE SHE JUST LAUGHED IT OFF.
THAT'S ALL THE PROBLEM IS, YOUR MISSING THUMB?
YEAH, WHAT'S YOUR POINT?
MY POINT IS...FOR SOMEONE SO CUNNING...YOU CAN BE A RIGHT TIT.

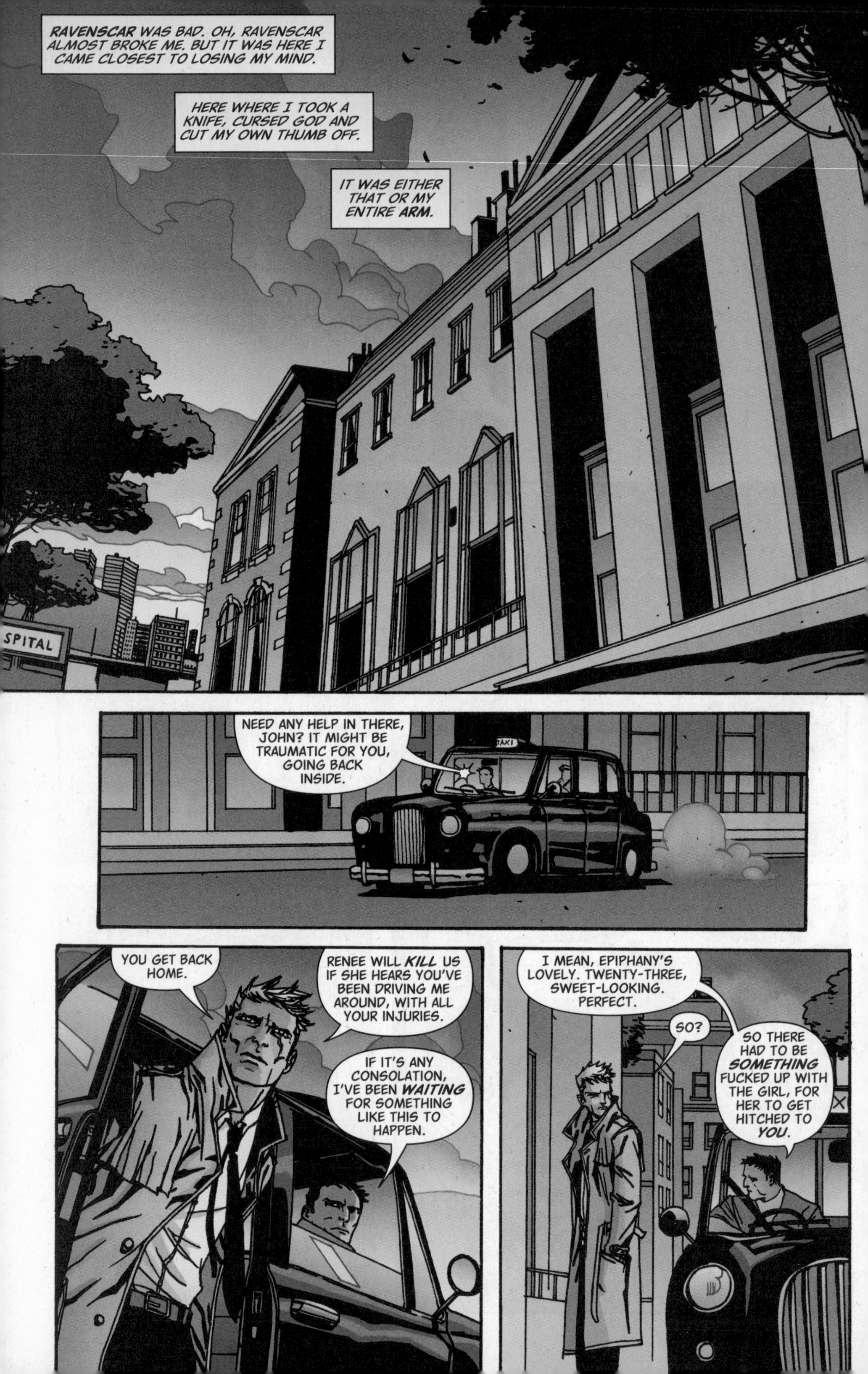
RAVENSCAR WAS BAD. OH, RAVENSCAR ALMOST BROKE ME. BUT IT WAS HERE I CAME CLOSEST TO LOSING MY MIND.
HERE WHERE I TOOK A KNIFE, CURSED GOD AND CUT MY OWN THUMB OFF.
IT WAS EITHER THAT OR MY ENTIRE ARM.
SPITAL
NEED ANY HELP IN THERE, JOHN? IT MIGHT BE TRAUMATIC FOR YOU, GOING BACK INSIDE.
TAXI
YOU GET BACK HOME.
RENEE WILL KILL US IF SHE HEARS YOU'VE BEEN DRIVING ME AROUND, WITH ALL YOUR INJURIES.
IF IT'S ANY CONSOLATION, I'VE BEEN WAITING FOR SOMETHING LIKE THIS TO HAPPEN.
I MEAN, EPIPHANY'S LOVELY. TWENTY-THREE, SWEET-LOOKING. PERFECT.
SO?
SO THERE HAD TO BE SOMETHING FUCKED UP WITH THE GIRL, FOR HER TO GET HITCHED TO YOU.

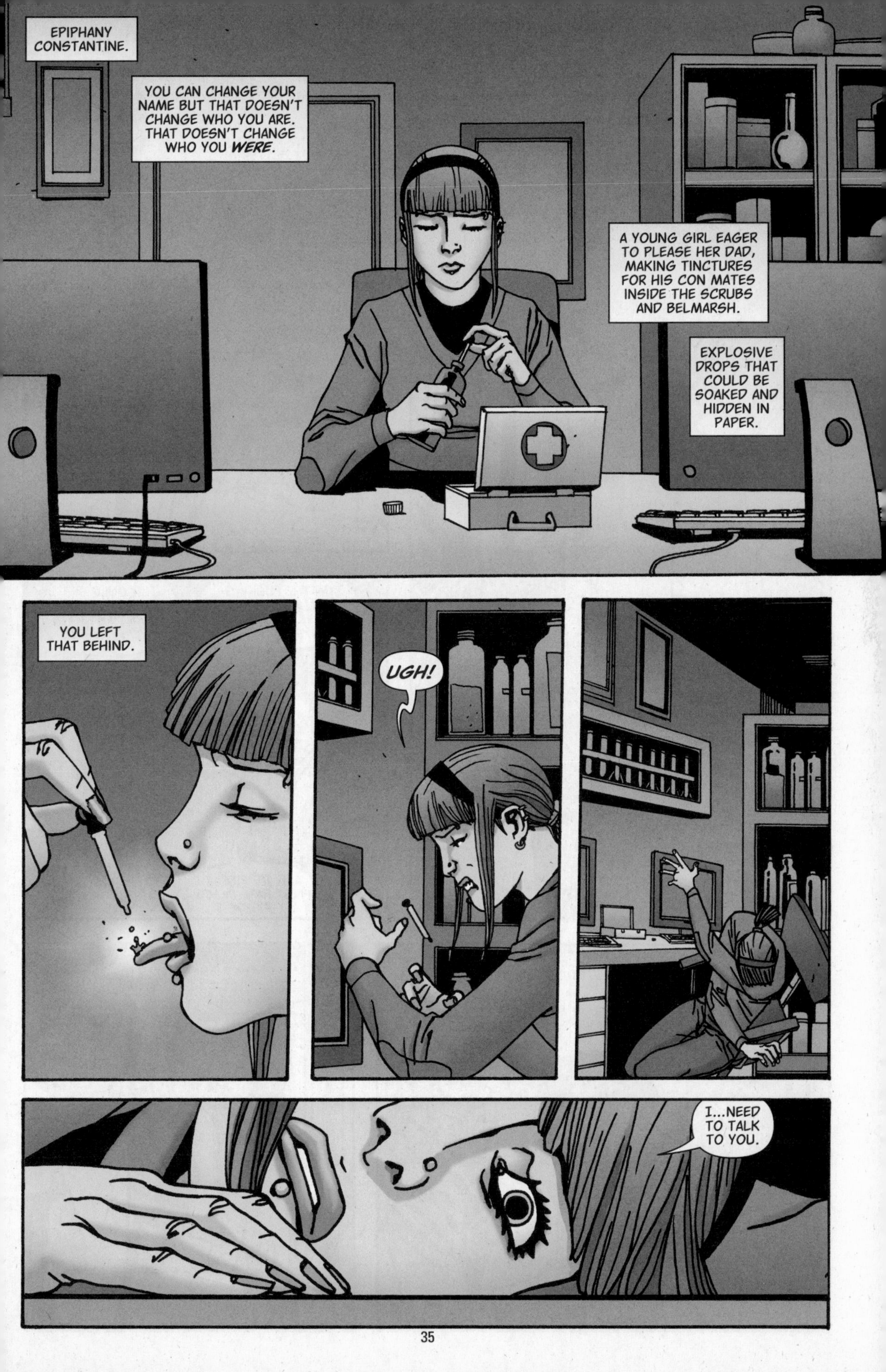
EPIPHANY CONSTANTINE.
YOU CAN CHANGE YOUR NAME BUT THAT DOESN'T CHANGE WHO YOU ARE. THAT DOESN'T CHANGE WHO YOU *WERE*.
A YOUNG GIRL EAGER TO PLEASE HER DAD, MAKING TINCTURES FOR HIS CON MATES INSIDE THE SCRUBS AND BELMARSH.
EXPLOSIVE DROPS THAT COULD BE SOAKED AND HIDDEN IN PAPER.
YOU LEFT THAT BEHIND.
UGH!
I...NEED TO TALK TO YOU.

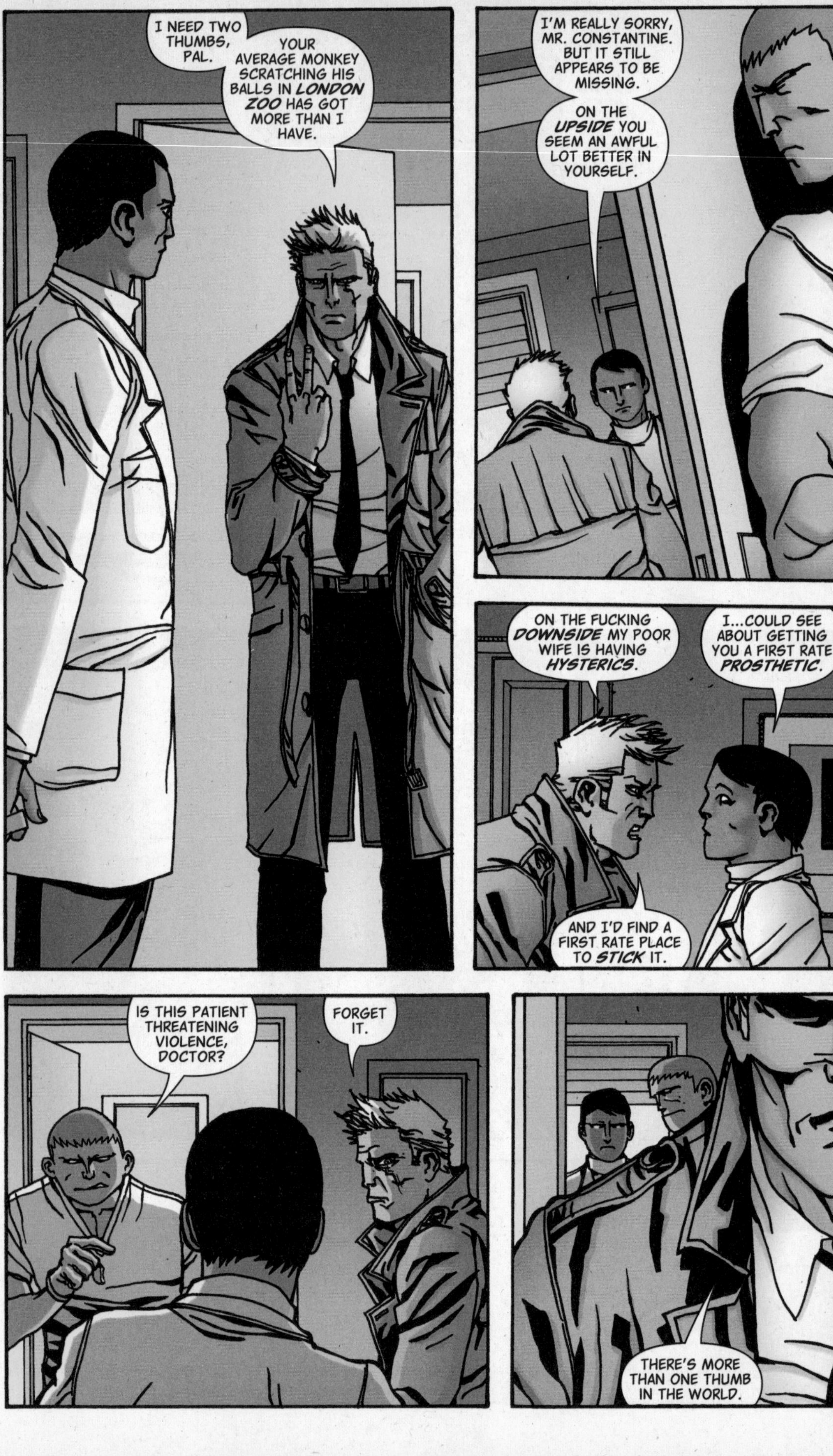
I NEED TWO THUMBS, PAL.
YOUR AVERAGE MONKEY SCRATCHING HIS BALLS IN LONDON ZOO HAS GOT MORE THAN I HAVE.
I'M REALLY SORRY, MR. CONSTANTINE. BUT IT STILL APPEARS TO BE MISSING.
ON THE UPSIDE YOU SEEM AN AWFUL LOT BETTER IN YOURSELF.
ON THE FUCKING DOWNSIDE MY POOR WIFE IS HAVING HYSTERICS.
I...COULD SEE ABOUT GETTING YOU A FIRST RATE PROSTHETIC.
AND I'D FIND A FIRST RATE PLACE TO STICK IT.
IS THIS PATIENT THREATENING VIOLENCE, DOCTOR?
FORGET IT.
THERE'S MORE THAN ONE THUMB IN THE WORLD.

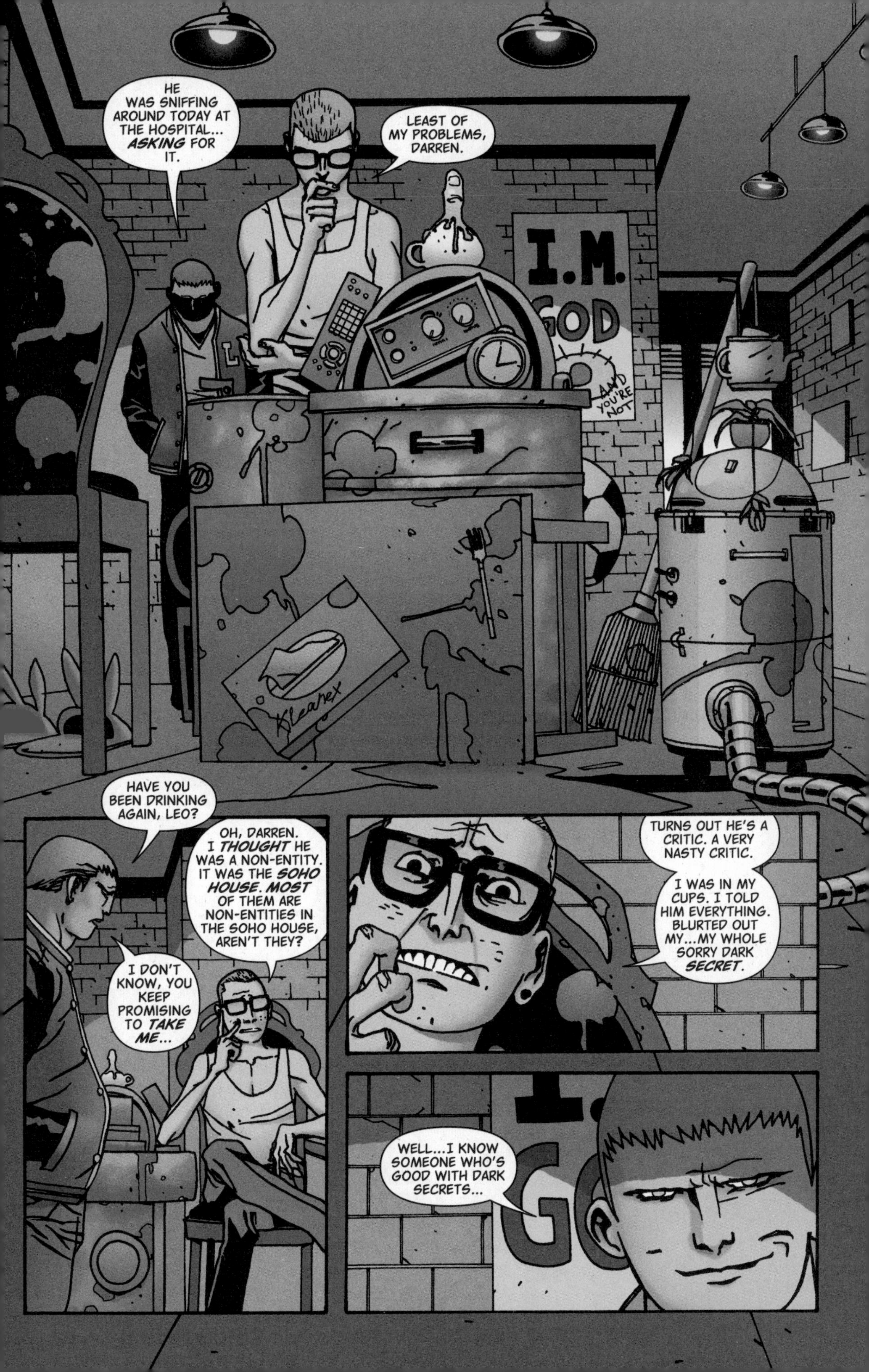
HE WAS SNIFFING AROUND TODAY AT THE HOSPITAL... ASKING FOR IT.
LEAST OF MY PROBLEMS, DARREN.
I.M. GOD
AND YOU'RE NOT
Kleanex
HAVE YOU BEEN DRINKING AGAIN, LEO?
OH, DARREN. I THOUGHT HE WAS A NON-ENTITY. IT WAS THE SOHO HOUSE. MOST OF THEM ARE NON-ENTITIES IN THE SOHO HOUSE, AREN'T THEY?
I DON'T KNOW, YOU KEEP PROMISING TO TAKE ME...
TURNS OUT HE'S A CRITIC. A VERY NASTY CRITIC.
I WAS IN MY CUPS. I TOLD HIM EVERYTHING. BLURTED OUT MY...MY WHOLE SORRY DARK SECRET.
WELL...I KNOW SOMEONE WHO'S GOOD WITH DARK SECRETS...

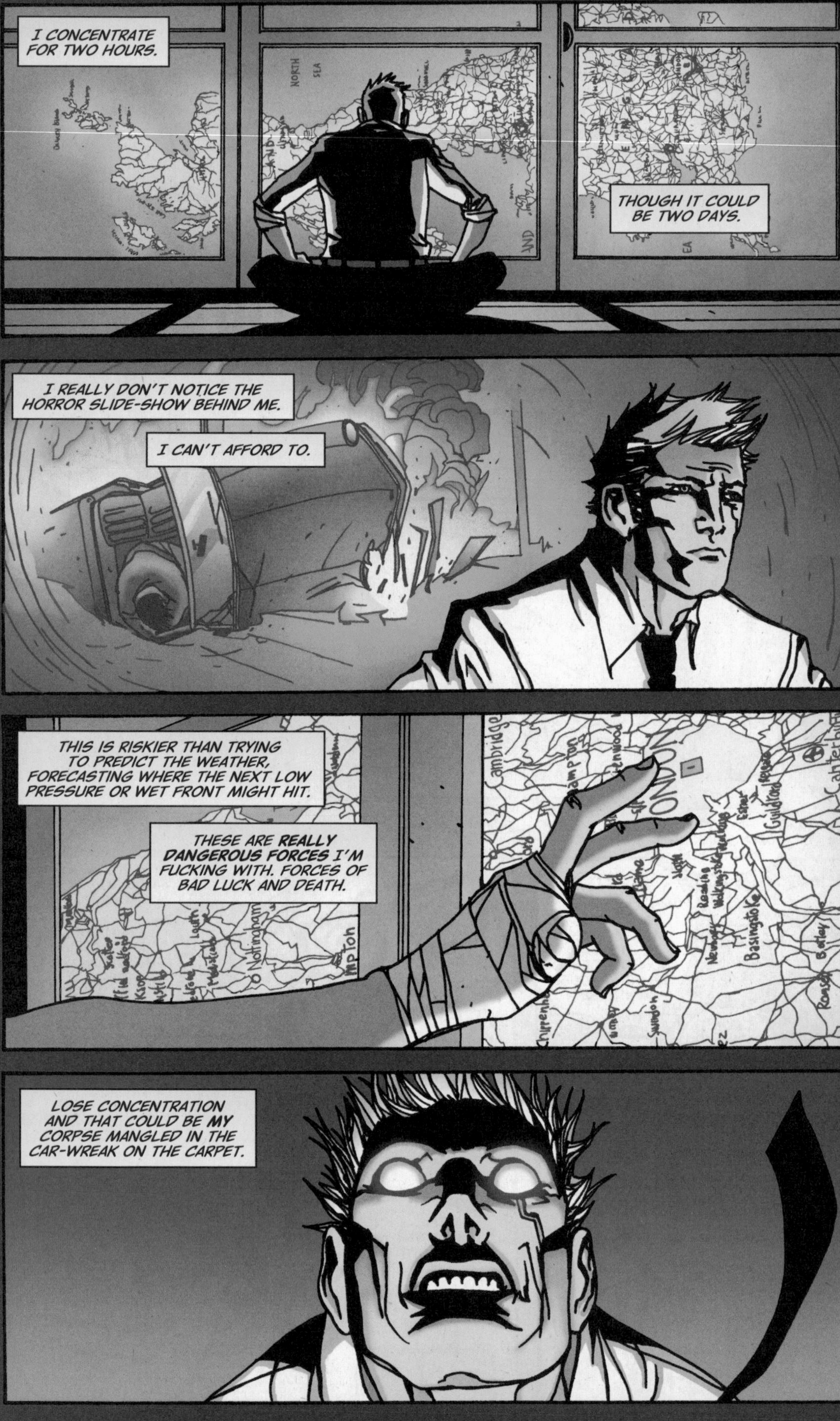
I CONCENTRATE FOR TWO HOURS.
THOUGH IT COULD BE TWO DAYS.
I REALLY DON'T NOTICE THE HORROR SLIDE-SHOW BEHIND ME.
I CAN'T AFFORD TO.
THIS IS RISKIER THAN TRYING TO PREDICT THE WEATHER, FORECASTING WHERE THE NEXT LOW PRESSURE OR WET FRONT MIGHT HIT.
THESE ARE REALLY DANGEROUS FORCES I'M FUCKING WITH. FORCES OF BAD LUCK AND DEATH.
LOSE CONCENTRATION AND THAT COULD BE MY CORPSE MANGLED IN THE CAR-WREAK ON THE CARPET.

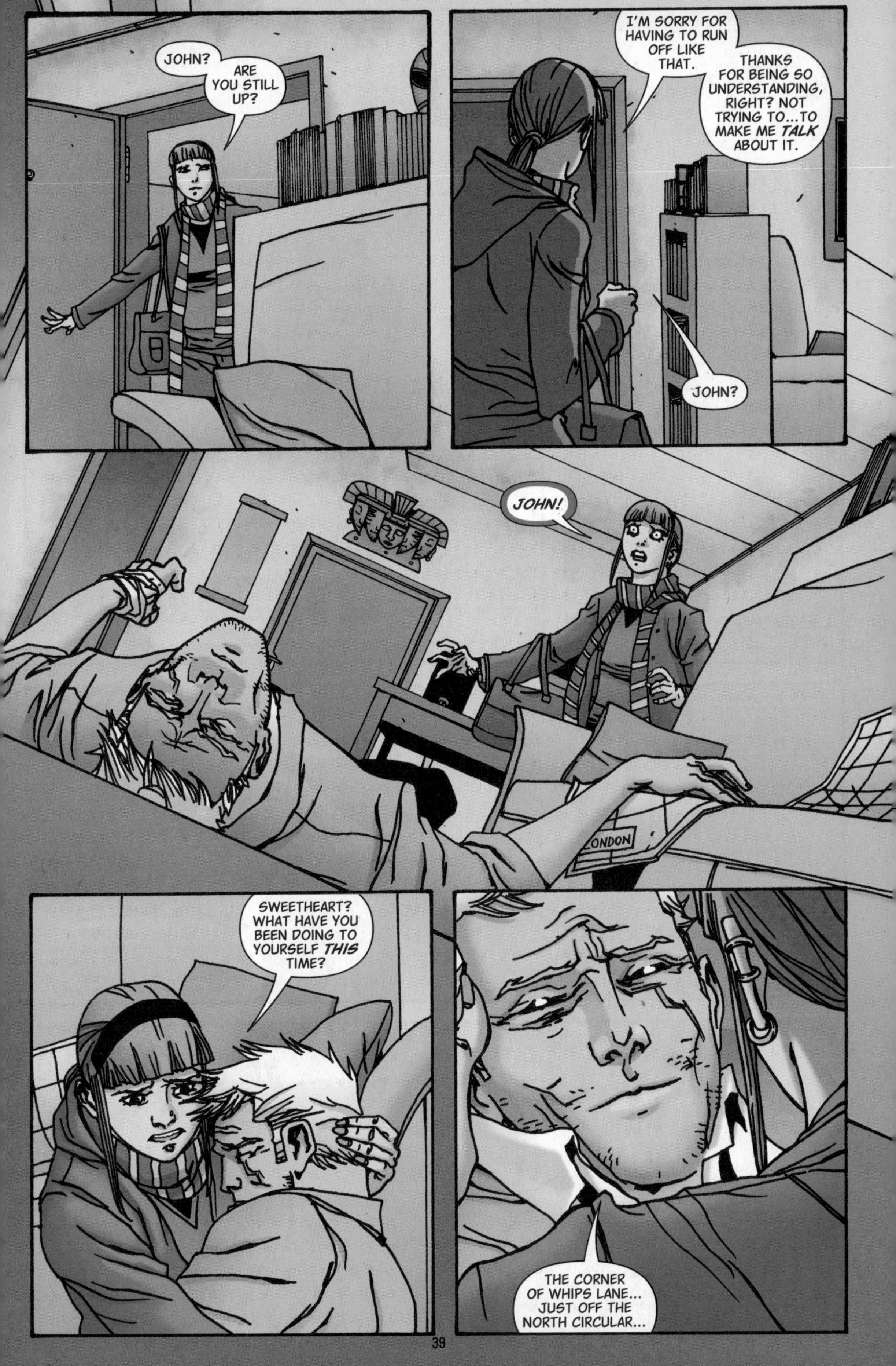
JOHN?
ARE YOU STILL UP?
I'M SORRY FOR HAVING TO RUN OFF LIKE THAT.
THANKS FOR BEING SO UNDERSTANDING, RIGHT? NOT TRYING TO...TO MAKE ME *TALK* ABOUT IT.
JOHN?
JOHN!
LONDON
SWEETHEART? WHAT HAVE YOU BEEN DOING TO YOURSELF *THIS* TIME?
THE CORNER OF WHIPS LANE... JUST OFF THE NORTH CIRCULAR...

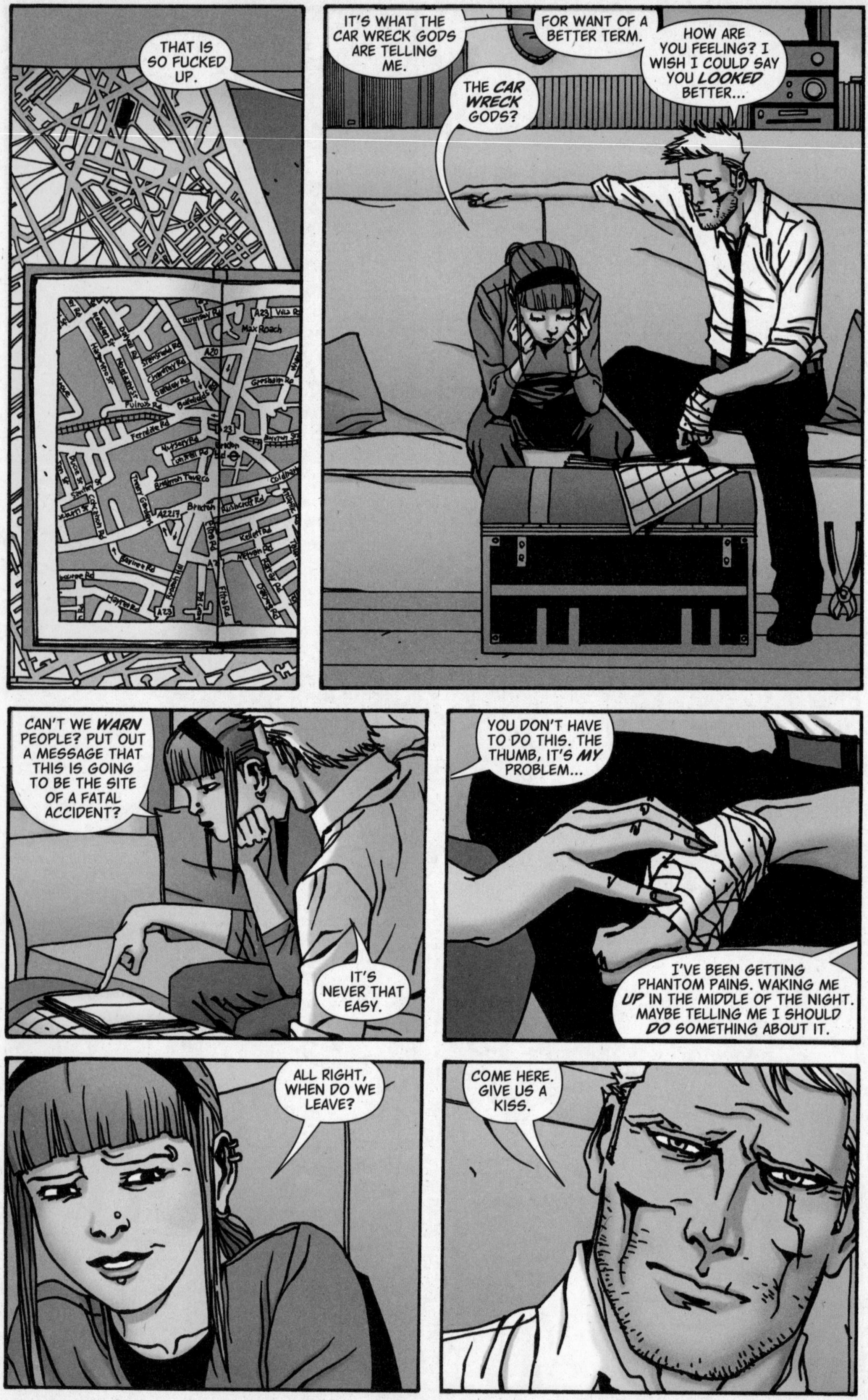
THAT IS SO FUCKED UP.
IT'S WHAT THE CAR WRECK GODS ARE TELLING ME.
FOR WANT OF A BETTER TERM.
THE CAR WRECK GODS?
HOW ARE YOU FEELING? I WISH I COULD SAY YOU LOOKED BETTER...
CAN'T WE WARN PEOPLE? PUT OUT A MESSAGE THAT THIS IS GOING TO BE THE SITE OF A FATAL ACCIDENT?
IT'S NEVER THAT EASY.
YOU DON'T HAVE TO DO THIS. THE THUMB, IT'S MY PROBLEM...
I'VE BEEN GETTING PHANTOM PAINS. WAKING ME UP IN THE MIDDLE OF THE NIGHT. MAYBE TELLING ME I SHOULD DO SOMETHING ABOUT IT.
ALL RIGHT, WHEN DO WE LEAVE?
COME HERE. GIVE US A KISS.

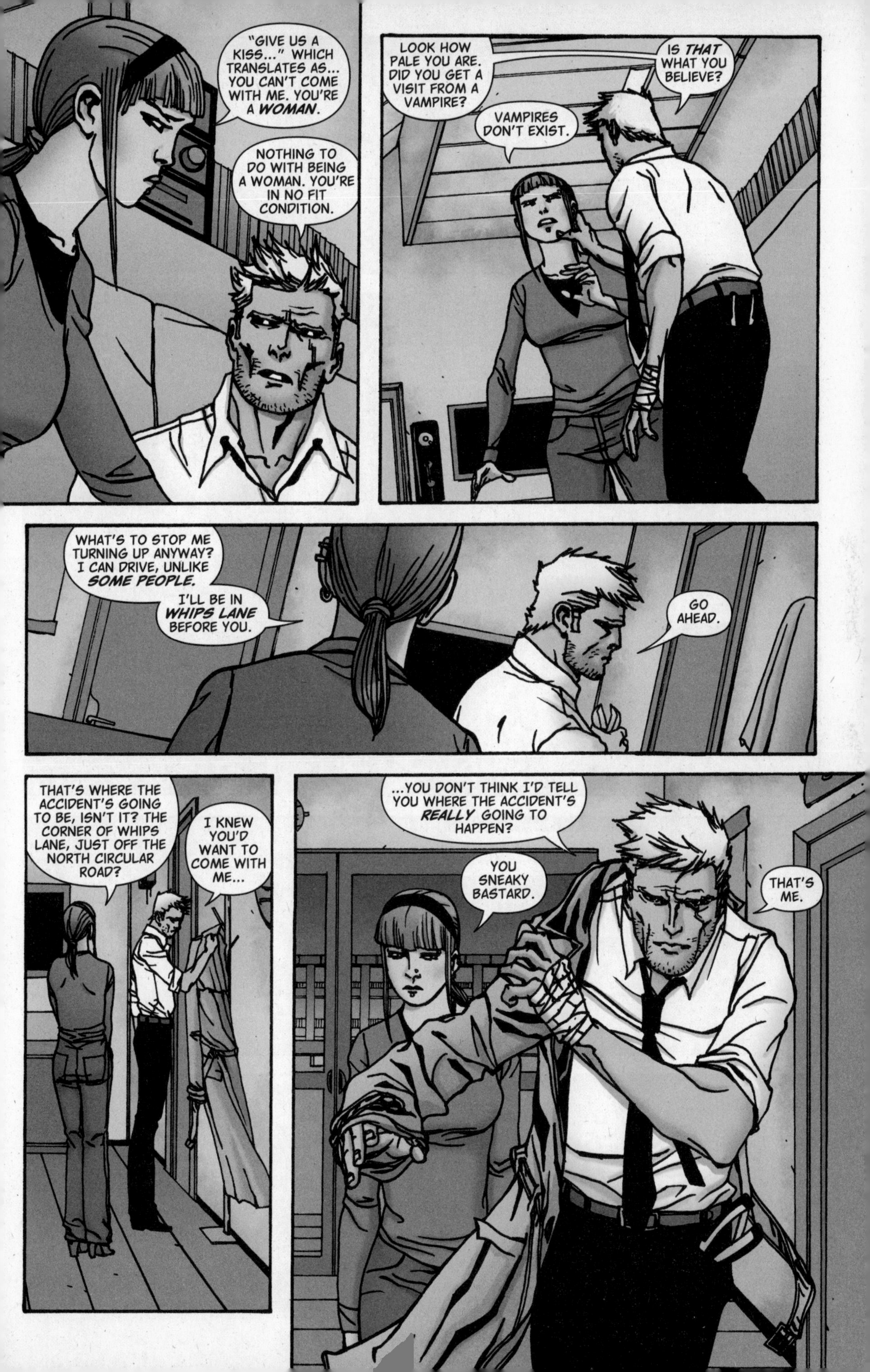
"GIVE US A KISS..." WHICH TRANSLATES AS... YOU CAN'T COME WITH ME. YOU'RE A *WOMAN*.
NOTHING TO DO WITH BEING A WOMAN. YOU'RE IN NO FIT CONDITION.
LOOK HOW PALE YOU ARE. DID YOU GET A VISIT FROM A VAMPIRE?
VAMPIRES DON'T EXIST.
IS *THAT* WHAT YOU BELIEVE?
WHAT'S TO STOP ME TURNING UP ANYWAY? I CAN DRIVE, UNLIKE *SOME PEOPLE.*
I'LL BE IN *WHIPS LANE* BEFORE YOU.
GO AHEAD.
THAT'S WHERE THE ACCIDENT'S GOING TO BE, ISN'T IT? THE CORNER OF WHIPS LANE, JUST OFF THE NORTH CIRCULAR ROAD?
I KNEW YOU'D WANT TO COME WITH ME...
...YOU DON'T THINK I'D TELL YOU WHERE THE ACCIDENT'S *REALLY* GOING TO HAPPEN?
YOU SNEAKY BASTARD.
THAT'S ME.

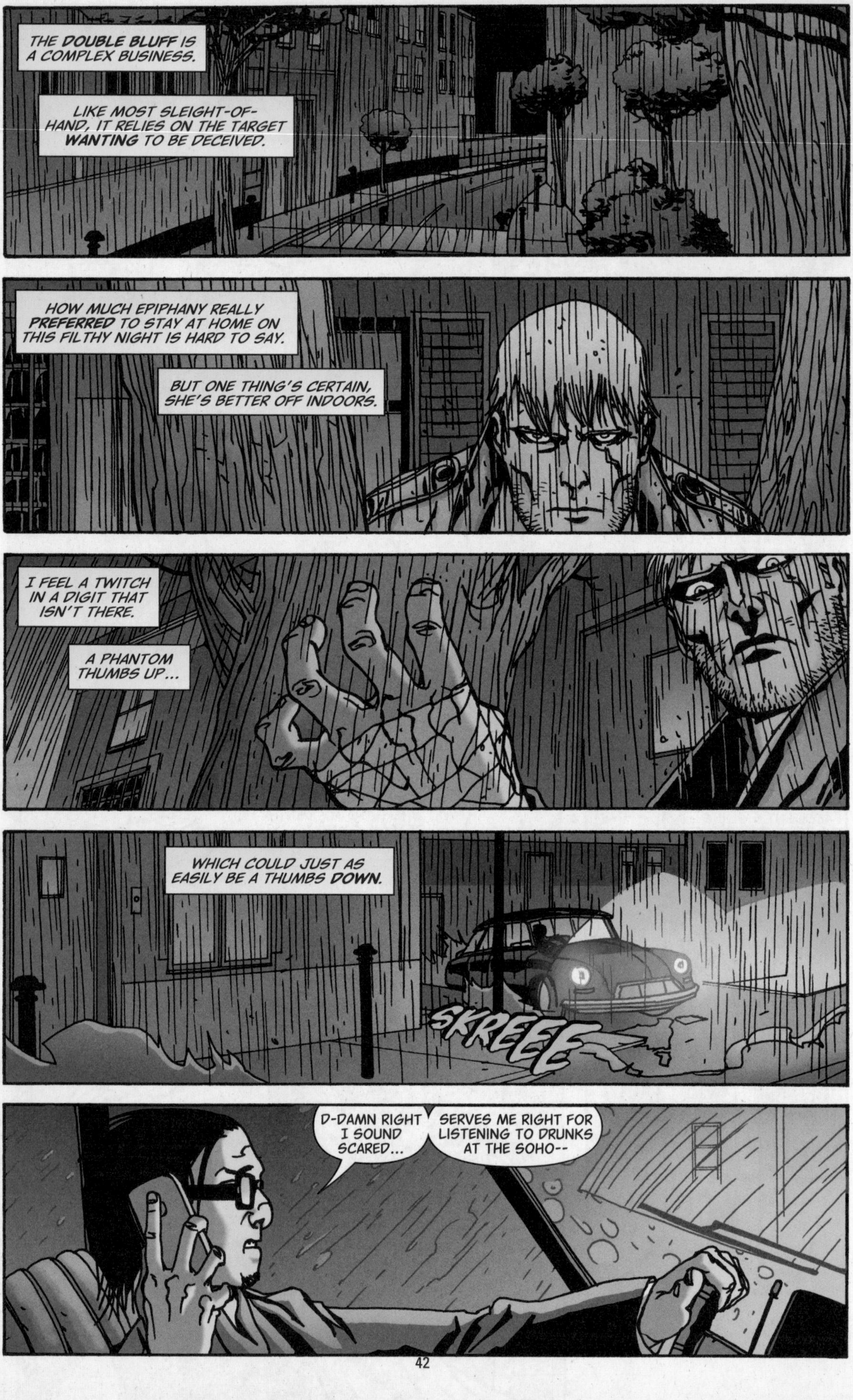

THE DOUBLE BLUFF IS A COMPLEX BUSINESS.
LIKE MOST SLEIGHT-OF-HAND, IT RELIES ON THE TARGET WANTING TO BE DECEIVED.
HOW MUCH EPIPHANY REALLY PREFERRED TO STAY AT HOME ON THIS FILTHY NIGHT IS HARD TO SAY.
BUT ONE THING'S CERTAIN, SHE'S BETTER OFF INDOORS.
I FEEL A TWITCH IN A DIGIT THAT ISN'T THERE.
A PHANTOM THUMBS UP...
WHICH COULD JUST AS EASILY BE A THUMBS DOWN.
SKREEE
D-DAMN RIGHT I SOUND SCARED...
SERVES ME RIGHT FOR LISTENING TO DRUNKS AT THE SOHO--

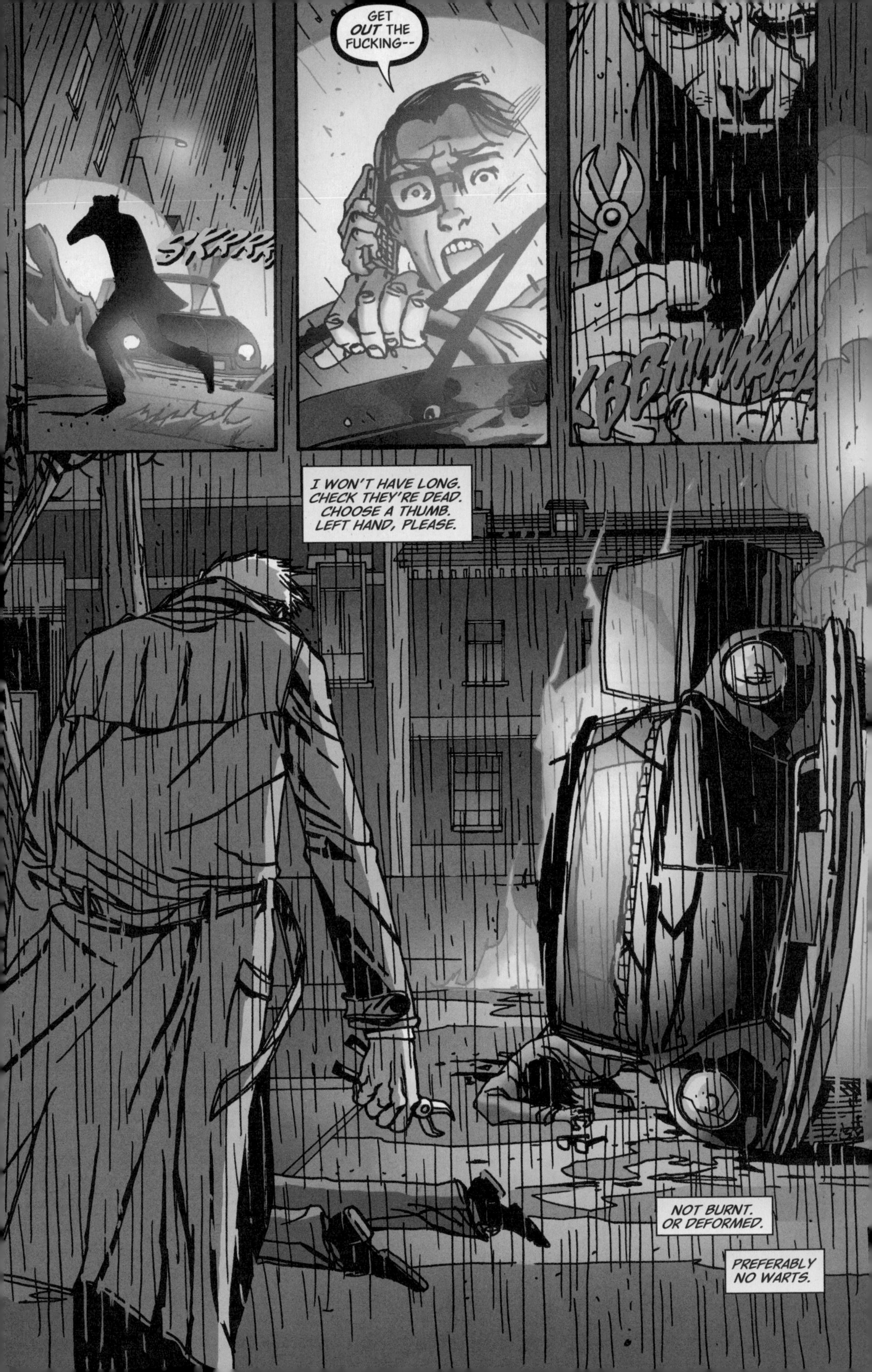
SKRRR
GET OUT THE FUCKING--
BBMMMAA
I WON'T HAVE LONG. CHECK THEY'RE DEAD. CHOOSE A THUMB. LEFT HAND, PLEASE.
NOT BURNT. OR DEFORMED.
PREFERABLY NO WARTS.

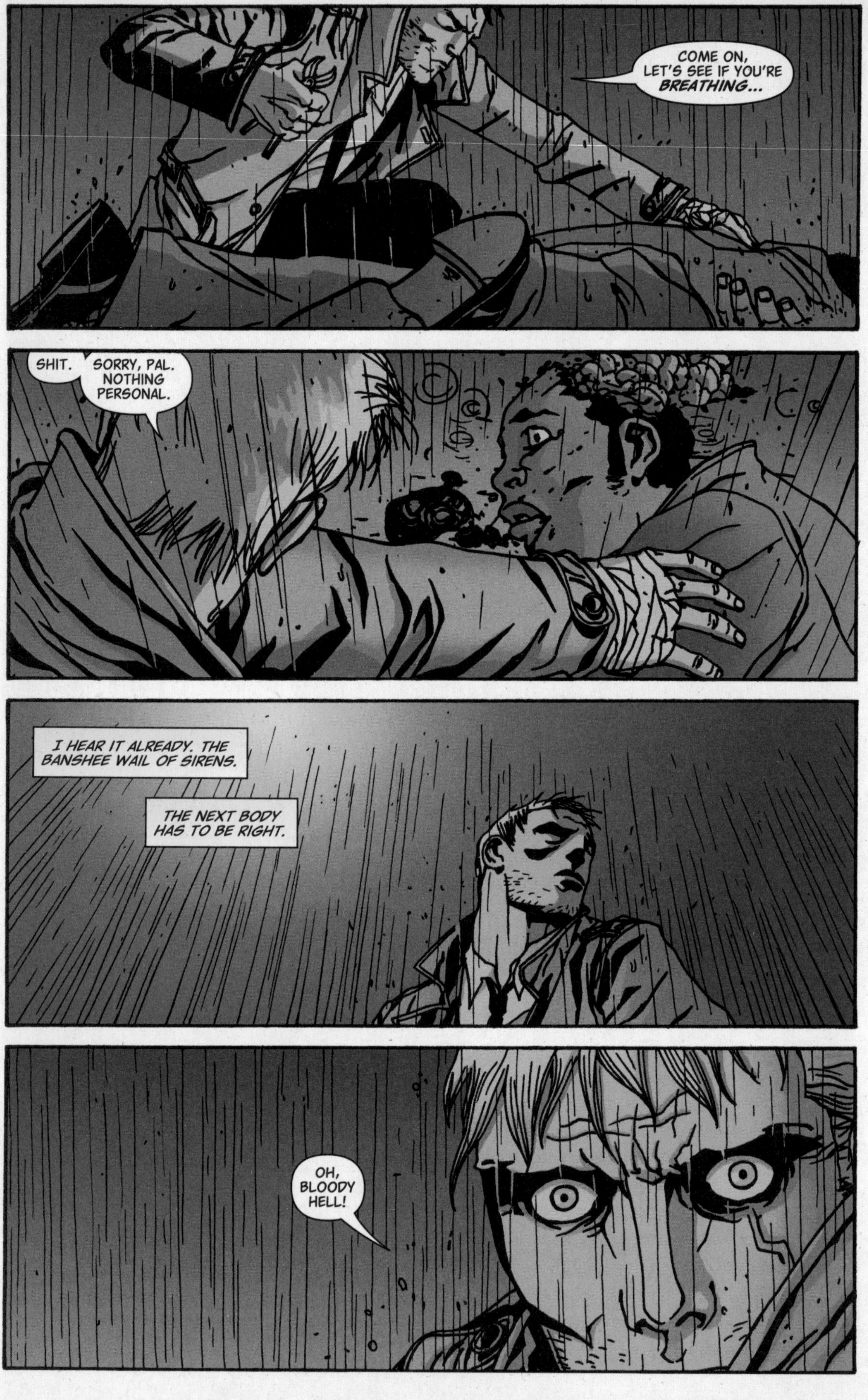
COME ON, LET'S SEE IF YOU'RE *BREATHING...*
SHIT.
SORRY, PAL. NOTHING PERSONAL.
I HEAR IT ALREADY. THE BANSHEE WAIL OF SIRENS.
THE NEXT BODY HAS TO BE RIGHT.
OH, BLOODY HELL!

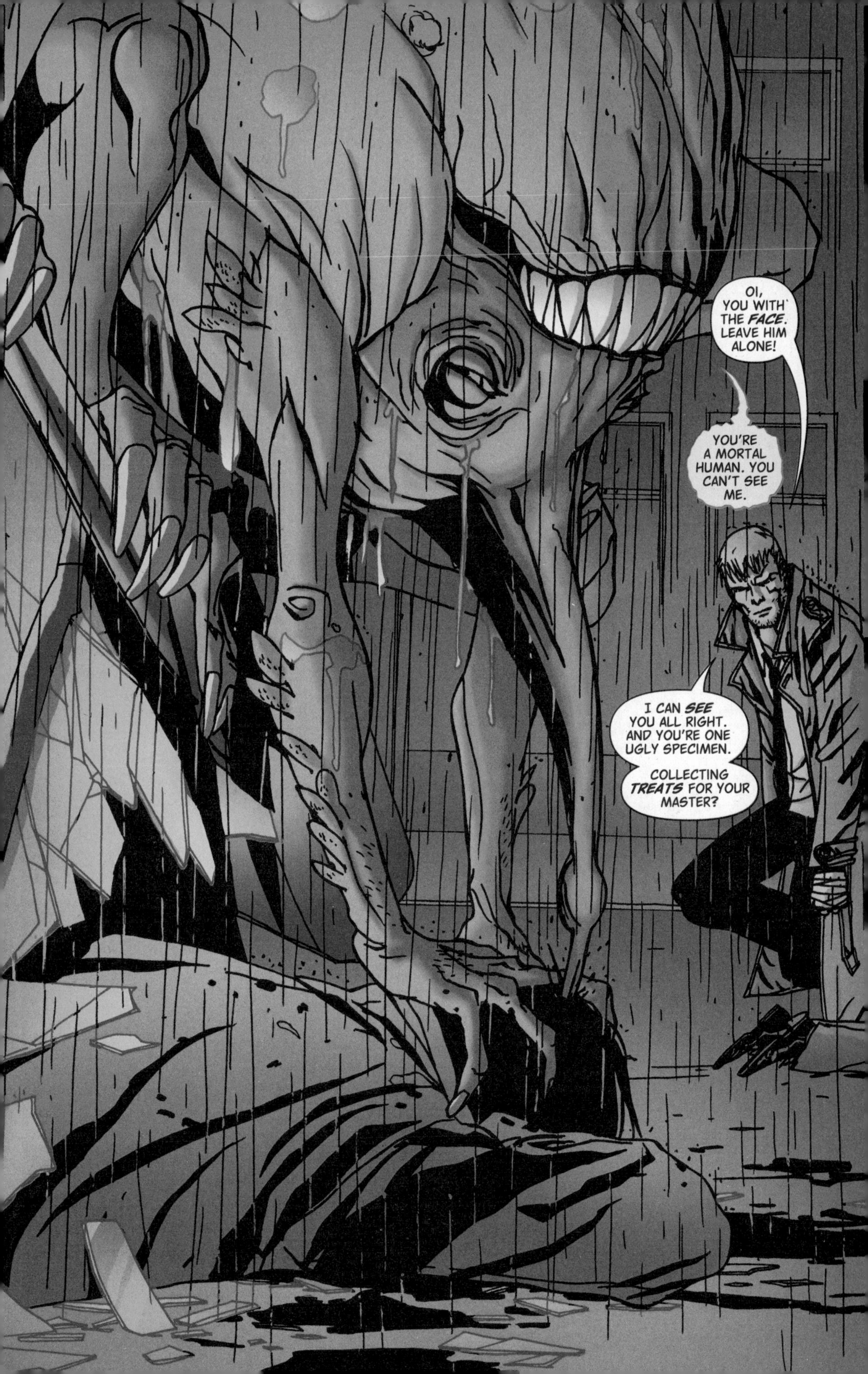
OI, YOU WITH THE *FACE*. LEAVE HIM ALONE!
YOU'RE A MORTAL HUMAN. YOU CAN'T SEE ME.
I CAN *SEE* YOU ALL RIGHT. AND YOU'RE ONE UGLY SPECIMEN.
COLLECTING *TREATS* FOR YOUR MASTER?

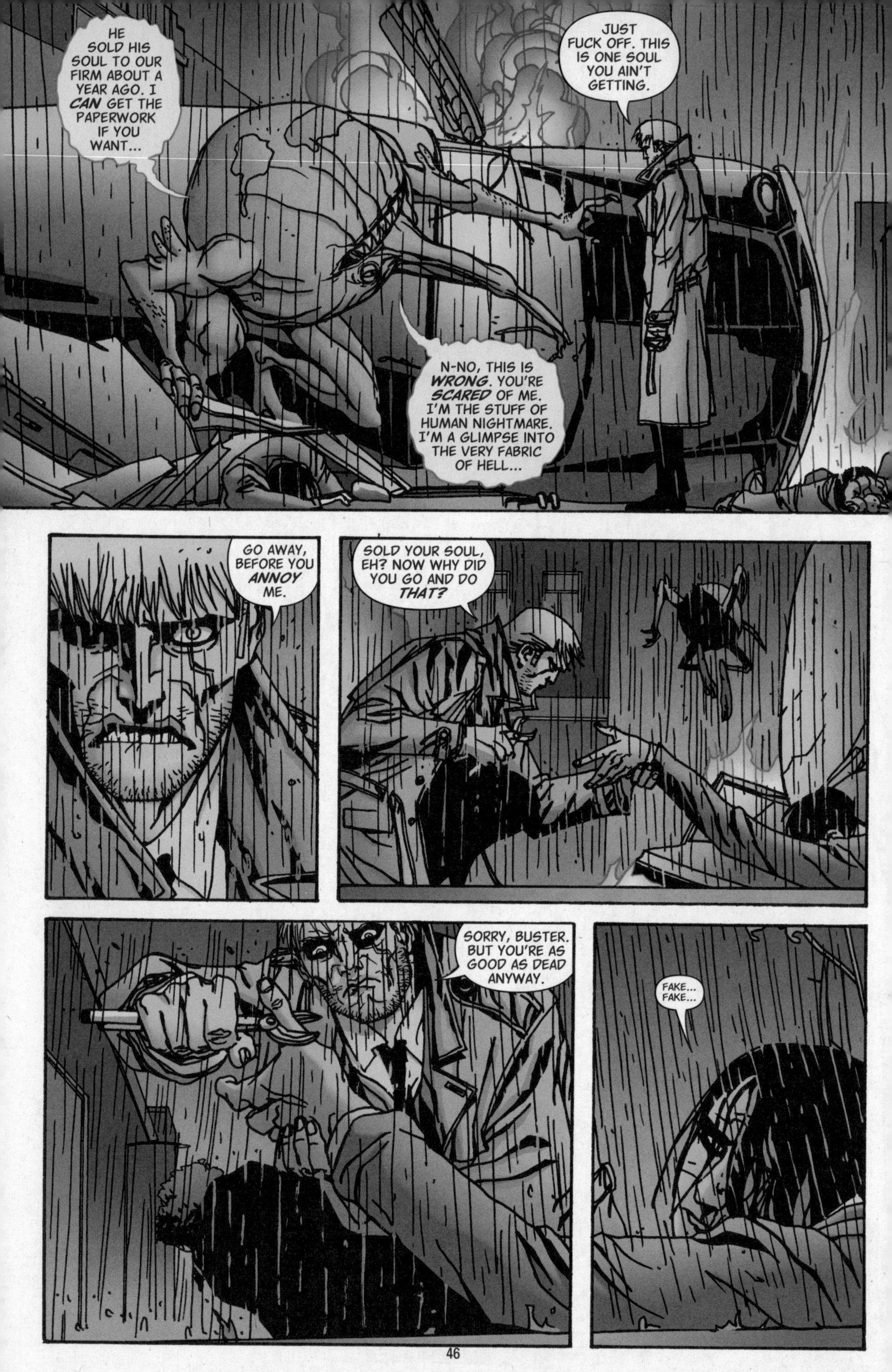
HE SOLD HIS SOUL TO OUR FIRM ABOUT A YEAR AGO. I CAN GET THE PAPERWORK IF YOU WANT...
JUST FUCK OFF. THIS IS ONE SOUL YOU AIN'T GETTING.
N-NO, THIS IS WRONG. YOU'RE SCARED OF ME. I'M THE STUFF OF HUMAN NIGHTMARE. I'M A GLIMPSE INTO THE VERY FABRIC OF HELL...
GO AWAY, BEFORE YOU ANNOY ME.
SOLD YOUR SOUL, EH? NOW WHY DID YOU GO AND DO THAT?
SORRY, BUSTER. BUT YOU'RE AS GOOD AS DEAD ANYWAY.
FAKE... FAKE...

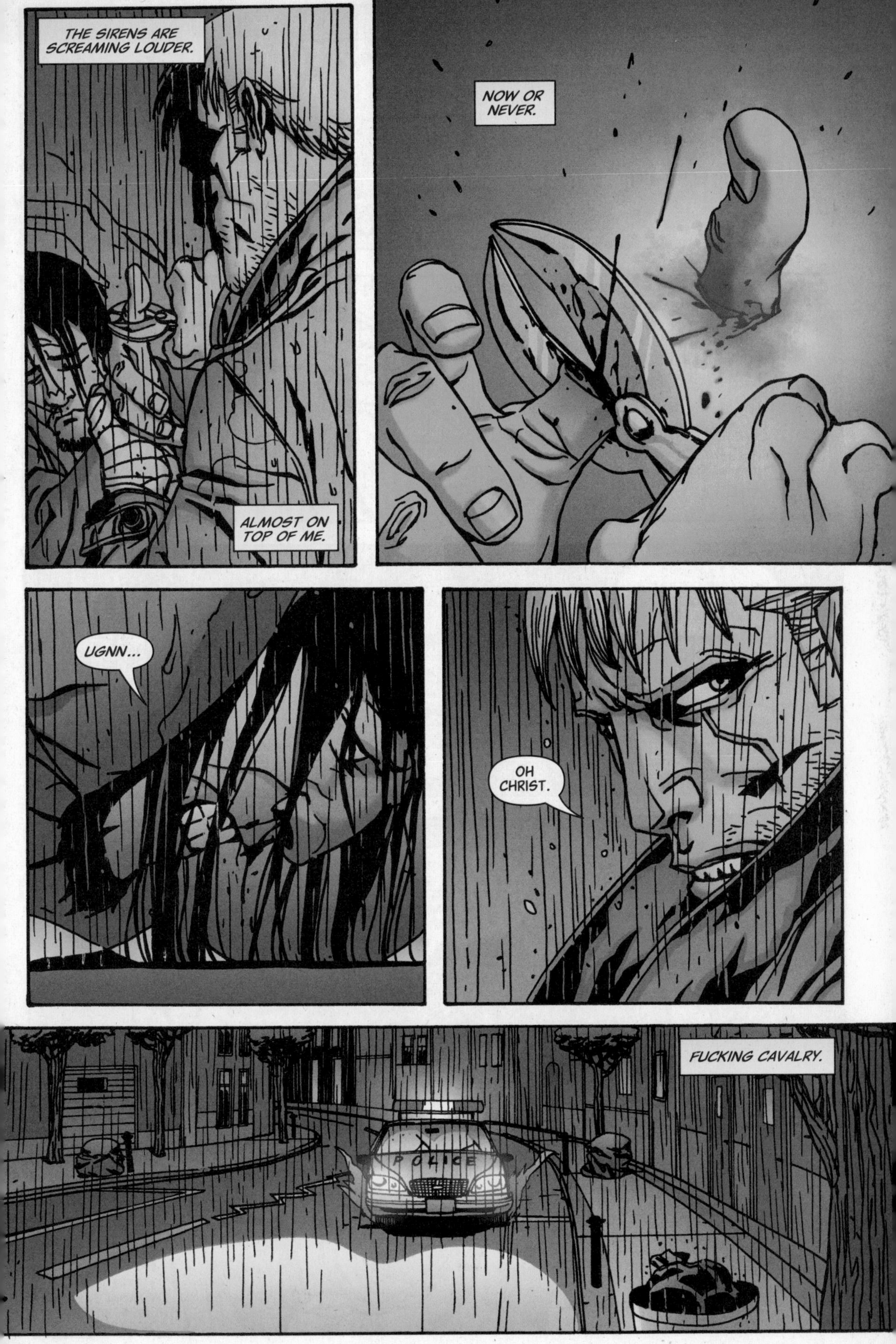
THE SIRENS ARE SCREAMING LOUDER.
ALMOST ON TOP OF ME.
NOW OR NEVER.
UGNN...
OH CHRIST.
P O L I C E
FUCKING CAVALRY.

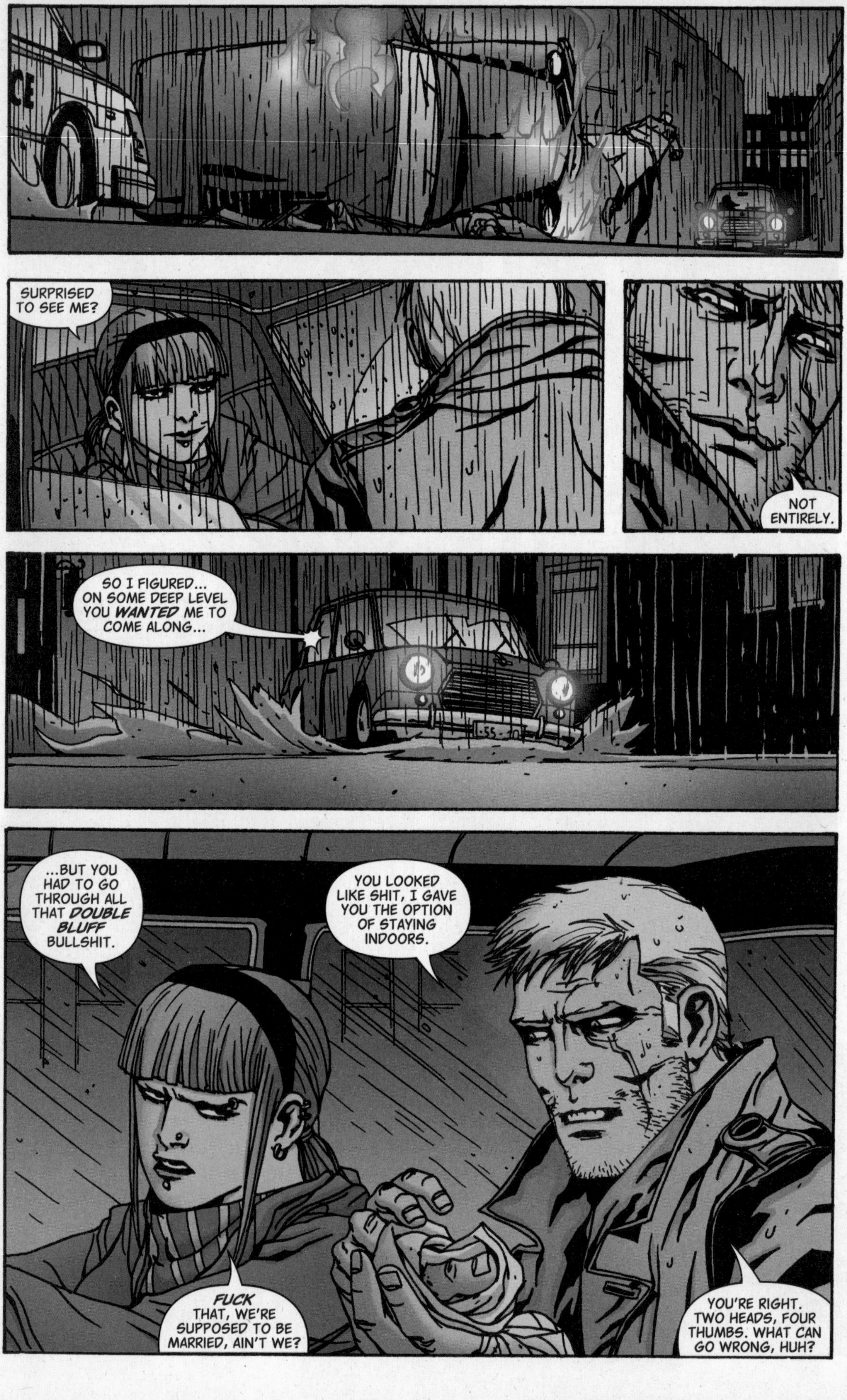
SURPRISED TO SEE ME?
NOT ENTIRELY.
SO I FIGURED... ON SOME DEEP LEVEL YOU *WANTED* ME TO COME ALONG...
...BUT YOU HAD TO GO THROUGH ALL THAT *DOUBLE BLUFF* BULLSHIT.
YOU LOOKED LIKE SHIT, I GAVE YOU THE OPTION OF STAYING INDOORS.
FUCK THAT, WE'RE SUPPOSED TO BE MARRIED, AIN'T WE?
YOU'RE RIGHT. TWO HEADS, FOUR THUMBS. WHAT CAN GO WRONG, HUH?

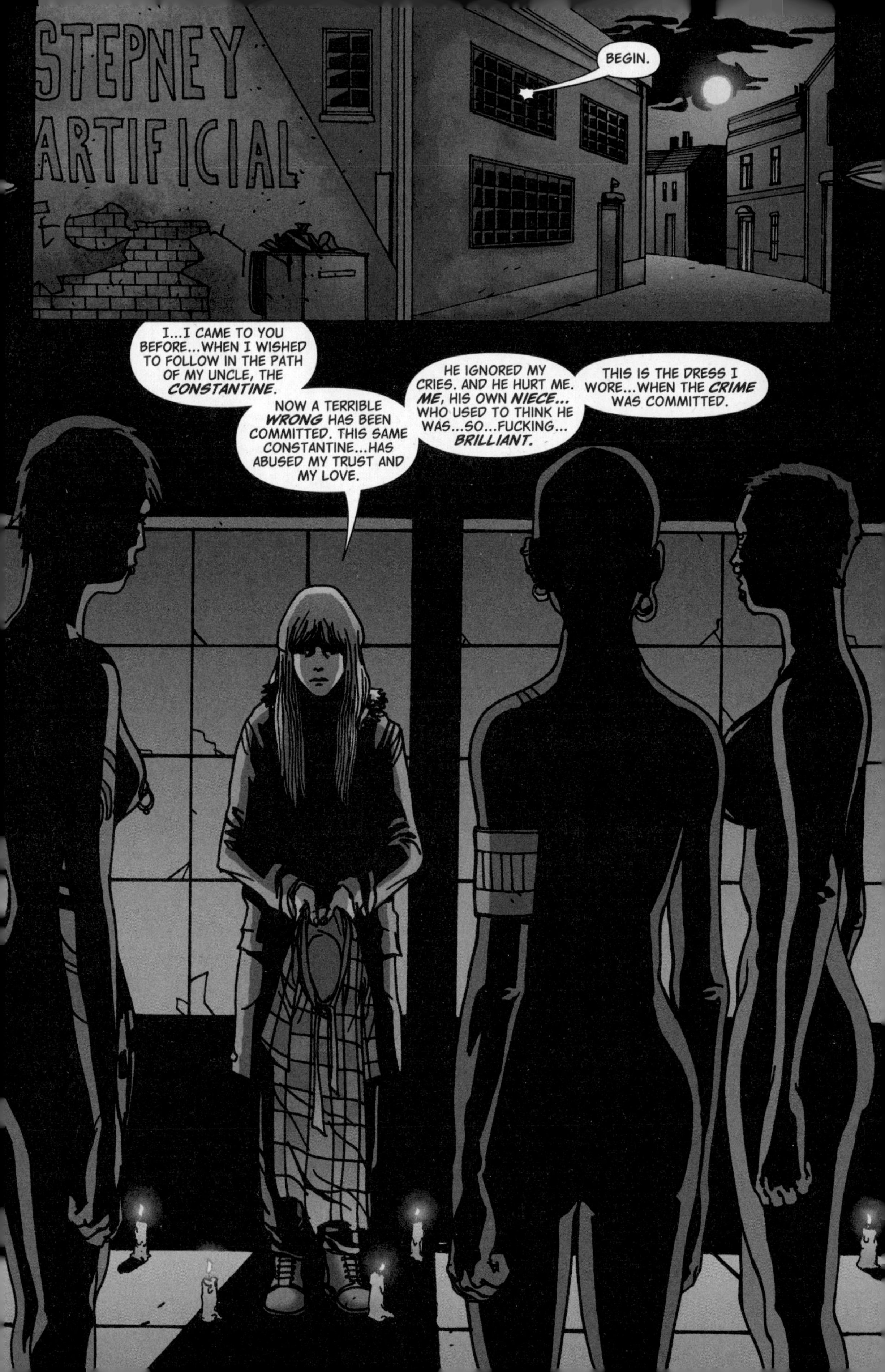
STEPNEY
ARTIFICIAL
BEGIN.
I...I CAME TO YOU BEFORE...WHEN I WISHED TO FOLLOW IN THE PATH OF MY UNCLE, THE CONSTANTINE.
NOW A TERRIBLE WRONG HAS BEEN COMMITTED. THIS SAME CONSTANTINE...HAS ABUSED MY TRUST AND MY LOVE.
HE IGNORED MY CRIES. AND HE HURT ME. ME, HIS OWN NIECE... WHO USED TO THINK HE WAS...SO...FUCKING... BRILLIANT.
THIS IS THE DRESS I WORE...WHEN THE CRIME WAS COMMITTED.

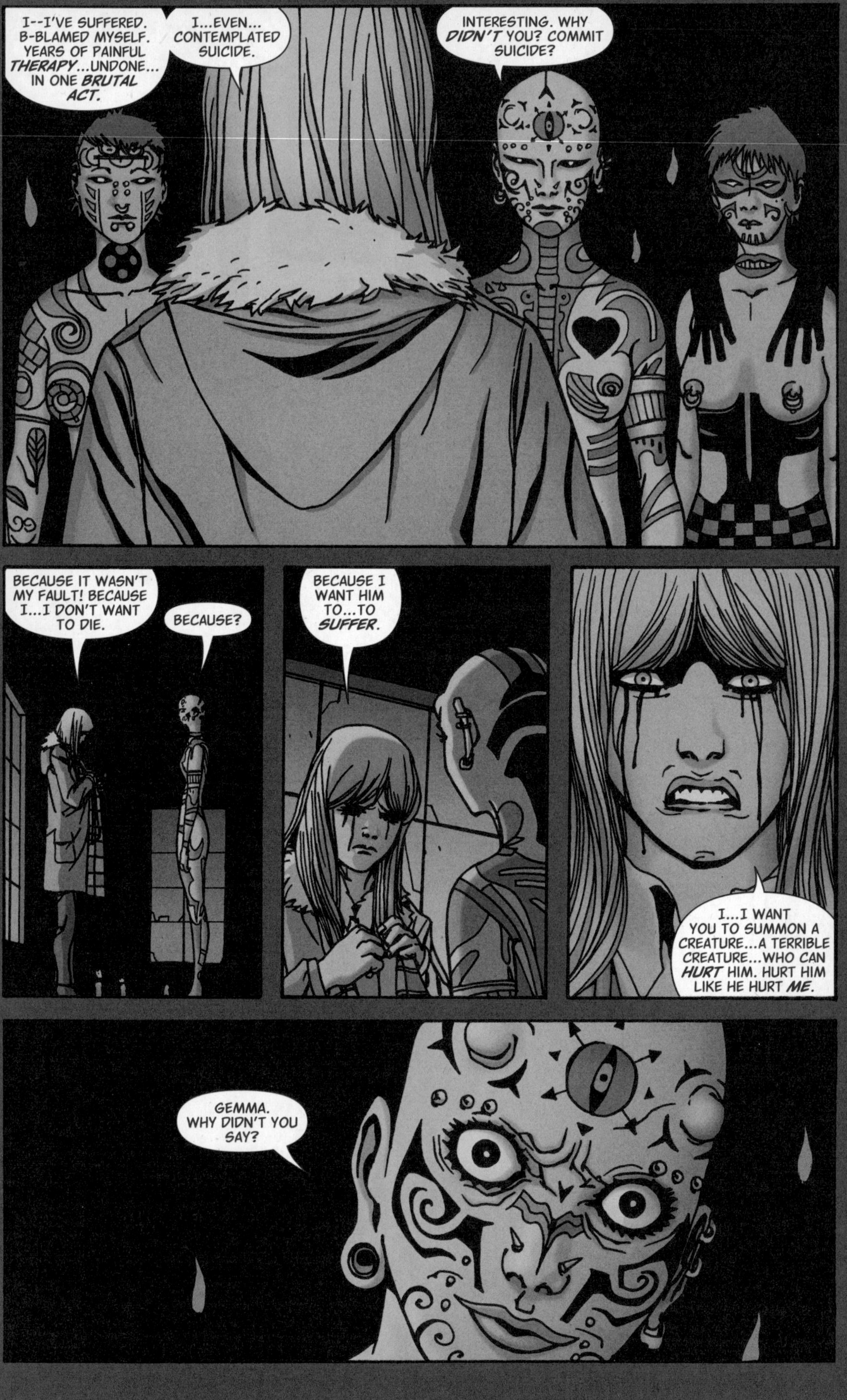
I--I'VE SUFFERED. B-BLAMED MYSELF. YEARS OF PAINFUL THERAPY...UNDONE... IN ONE BRUTAL ACT.
I...EVEN... CONTEMPLATED SUICIDE.
INTERESTING. WHY DIDN'T YOU? COMMIT SUICIDE?
BECAUSE IT WASN'T MY FAULT! BECAUSE I...I DON'T WANT TO DIE.
BECAUSE?
BECAUSE I WANT HIM TO...TO SUFFER.
I...I WANT YOU TO SUMMON A CREATURE...A TERRIBLE CREATURE...WHO CAN HURT HIM. HURT HIM LIKE HE HURT ME.
GEMMA. WHY DIDN'T YOU SAY?

Phantom Pains, Part Two
Lady Lazarus

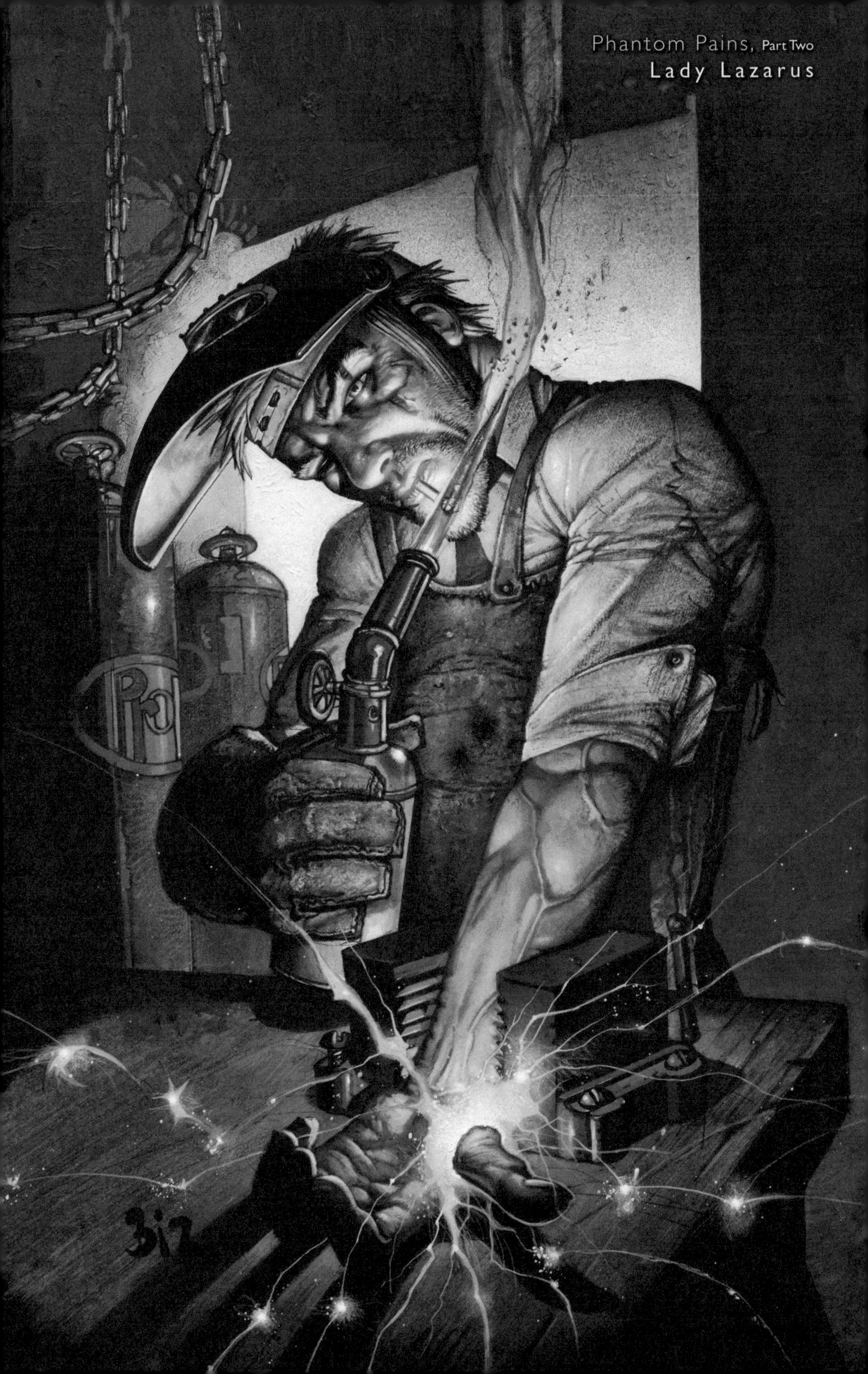

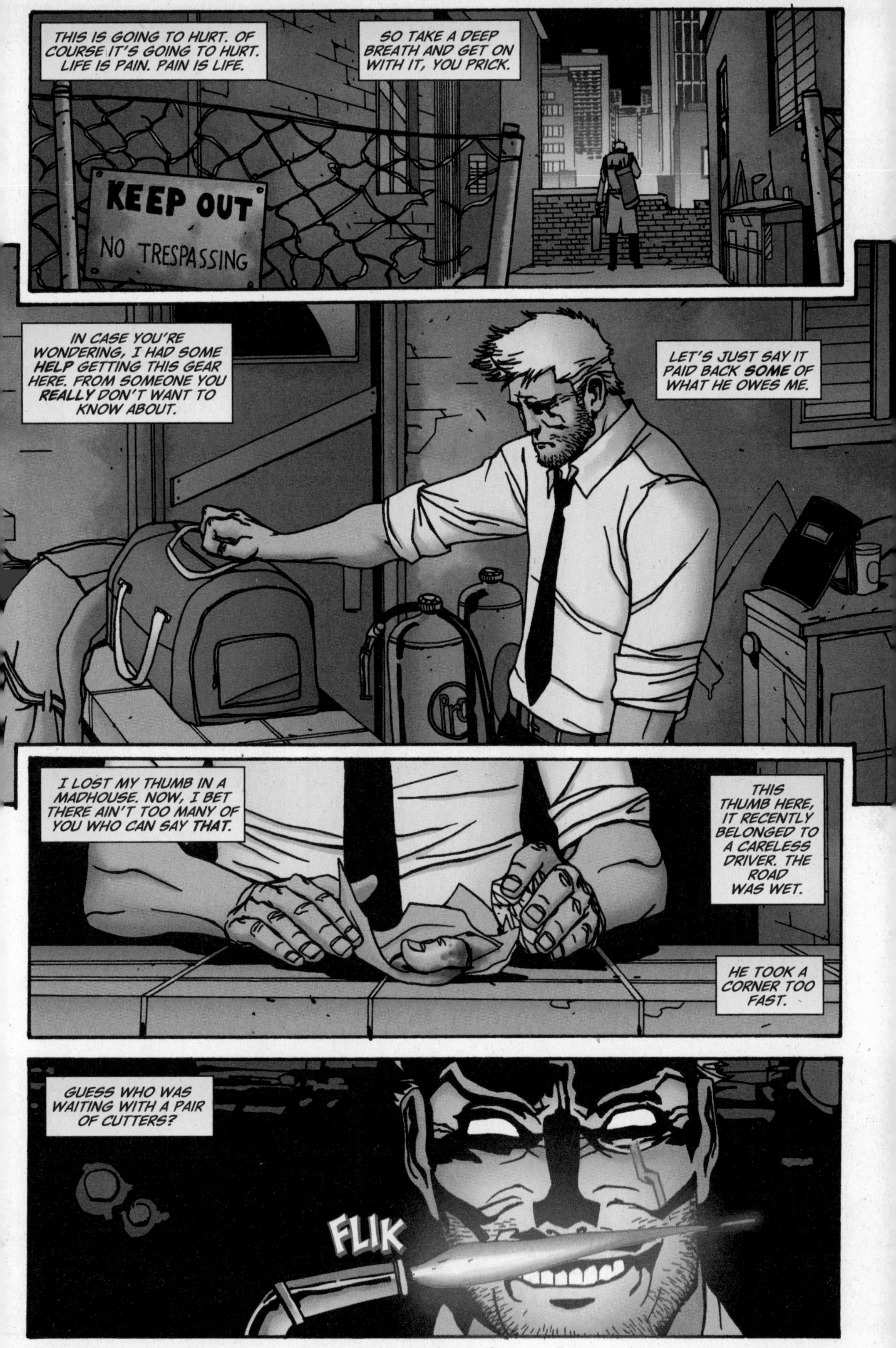
THIS IS GOING TO HURT. OF COURSE IT'S GOING TO HURT. LIFE IS PAIN. PAIN IS LIFE.
SO TAKE A DEEP BREATH AND GET ON WITH IT, YOU PRICK.
KEEP OUT
NO TRESPASSING
IN CASE YOU'RE WONDERING, I HAD SOME HELP GETTING THIS GEAR HERE. FROM SOMEONE YOU REALLY DON'T WANT TO KNOW ABOUT.
LET'S JUST SAY IT PAID BACK SOME OF WHAT HE OWES ME.
I LOST MY THUMB IN A MADHOUSE. NOW, I BET THERE AIN'T TOO MANY OF YOU WHO CAN SAY THAT.
THIS THUMB HERE, IT RECENTLY BELONGED TO A CARELESS DRIVER. THE ROAD WAS WET.
HE TOOK A CORNER TOO FAST.
GUESS WHO WAS WAITING WITH A PAIR OF CUTTERS?
FLIK

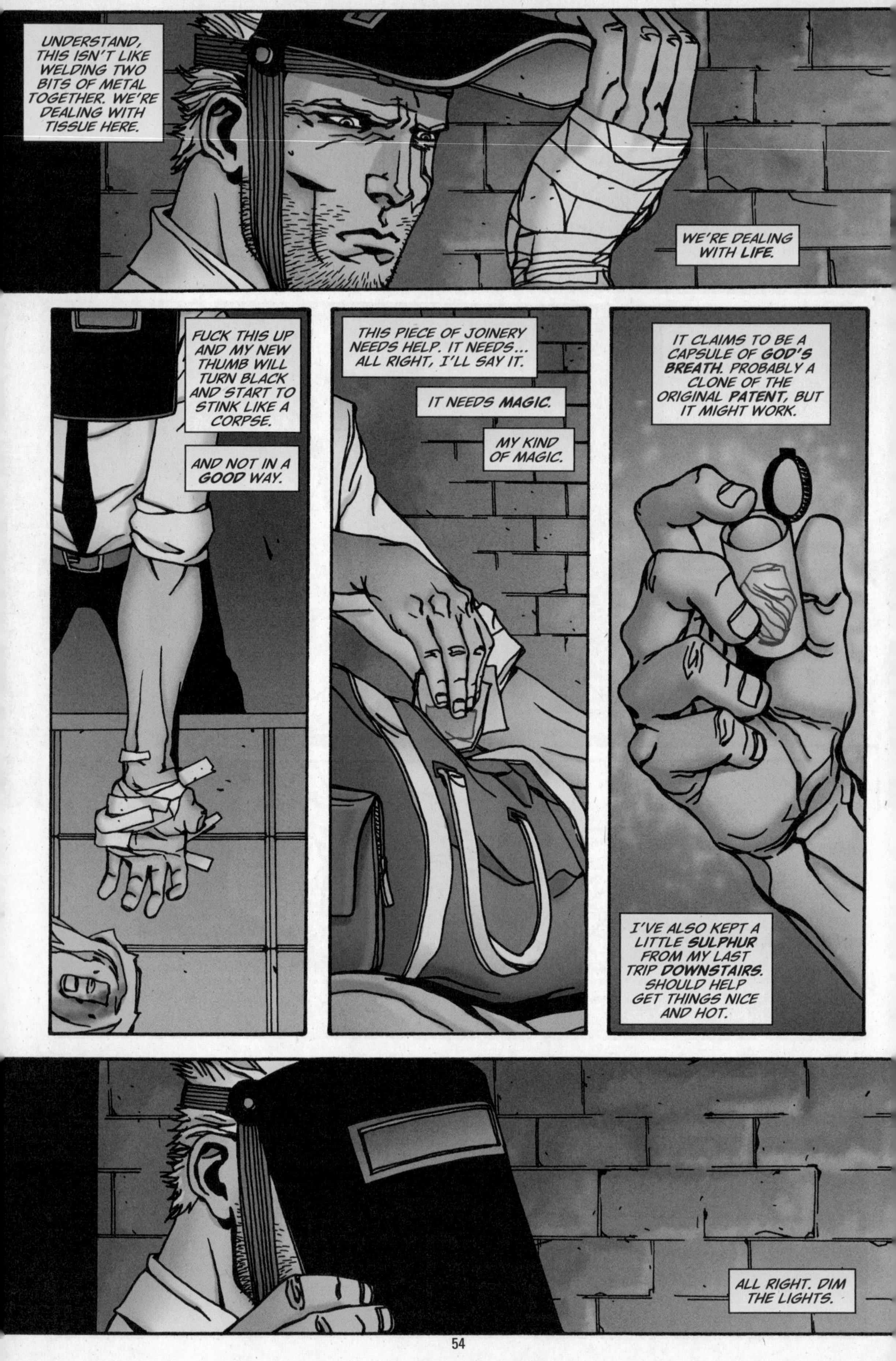
UNDERSTAND, THIS ISN'T LIKE WELDING TWO BITS OF METAL TOGETHER. WE'RE DEALING WITH TISSUE HERE.
WE'RE DEALING WITH LIFE.
FUCK THIS UP AND MY NEW THUMB WILL TURN BLACK AND START TO STINK LIKE A CORPSE.
AND NOT IN A GOOD WAY.
THIS PIECE OF JOINERY NEEDS HELP. IT NEEDS... ALL RIGHT, I'LL SAY IT.
IT NEEDS MAGIC.
MY KIND OF MAGIC.
IT CLAIMS TO BE A CAPSULE OF GOD'S BREATH. PROBABLY A CLONE OF THE ORIGINAL PATENT, BUT IT MIGHT WORK.
I'VE ALSO KEPT A LITTLE SULPHUR FROM MY LAST TRIP DOWNSTAIRS. SHOULD HELP GET THINGS NICE AND HOT.
ALL RIGHT. DIM THE LIGHTS.

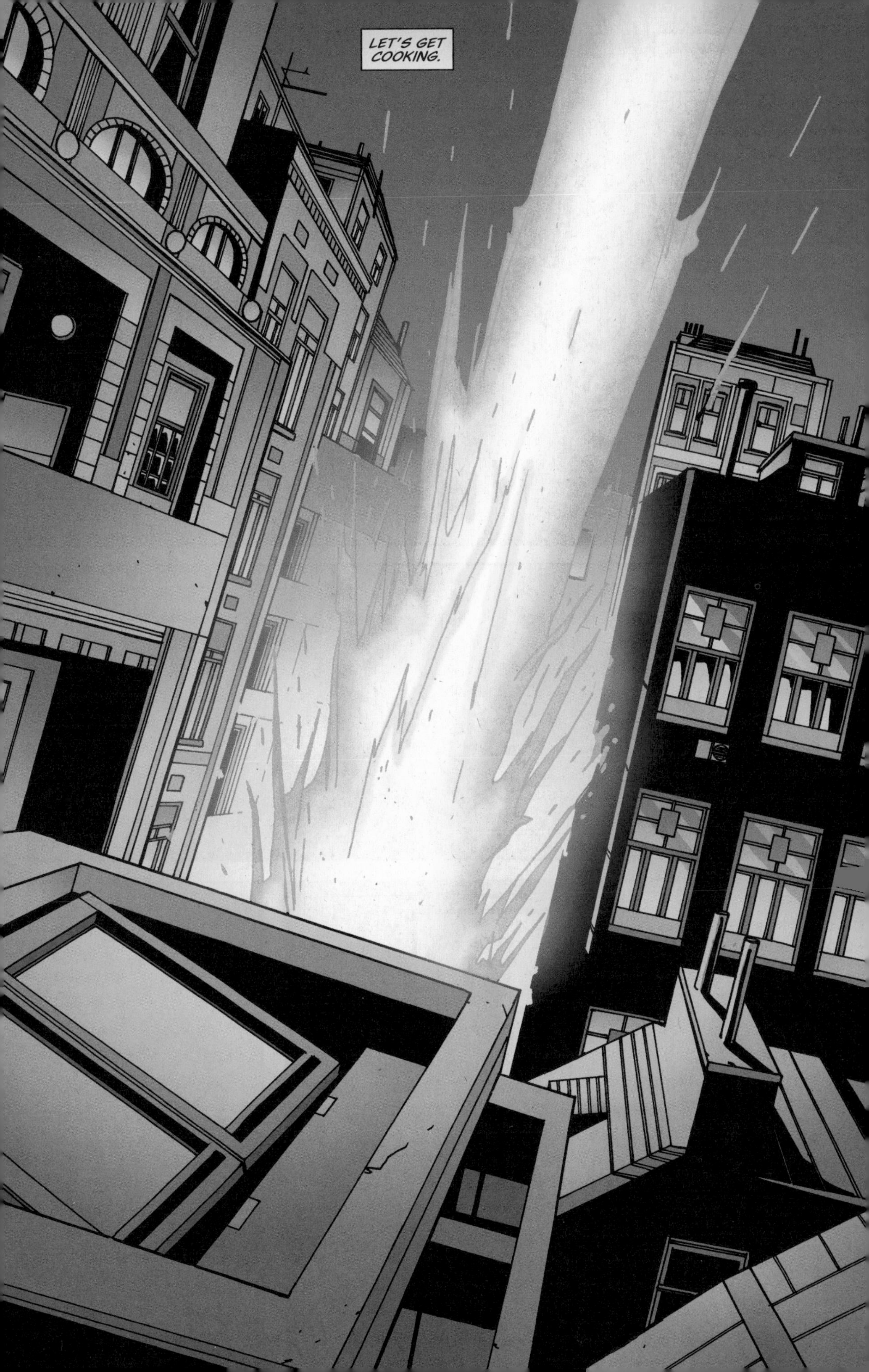
LET'S GET COOKING.

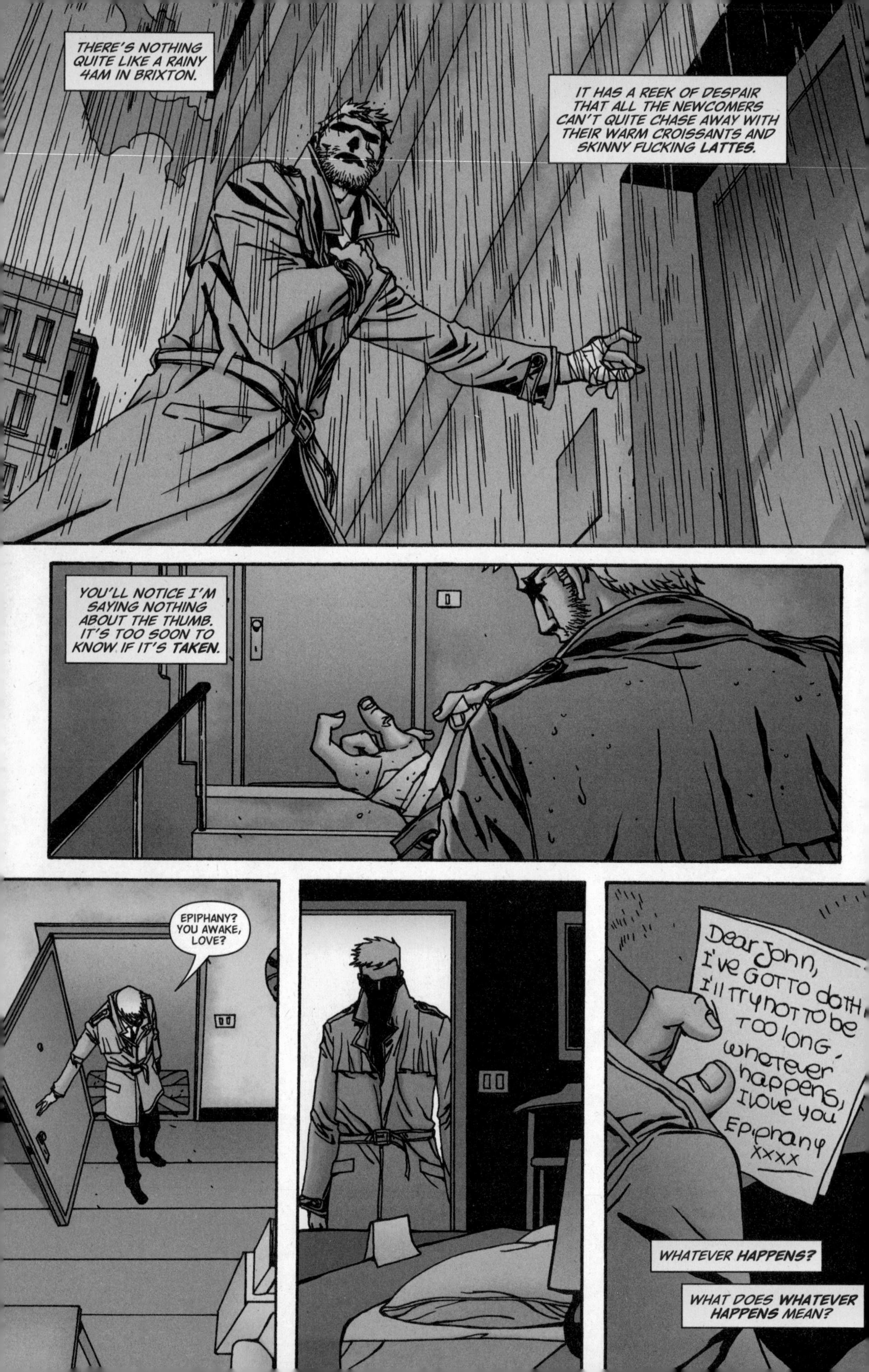

THERE'S NOTHING QUITE LIKE A RAINY 4AM IN BRIXTON.
IT HAS A REEK OF DESPAIR THAT ALL THE NEWCOMERS CAN'T QUITE CHASE AWAY WITH THEIR WARM CROISSANTS AND SKINNY FUCKING LATTES.
YOU'LL NOTICE I'M SAYING NOTHING ABOUT THE THUMB. IT'S TOO SOON TO KNOW IF IT'S TAKEN.
EPIPHANY? YOU AWAKE, LOVE?
Dear John, I've GOTTO do th. I'll try not to be too long. whatever happens, I love you Epiphany xxxx
WHATEVER HAPPENS?
WHAT DOES WHATEVER HAPPENS MEAN?

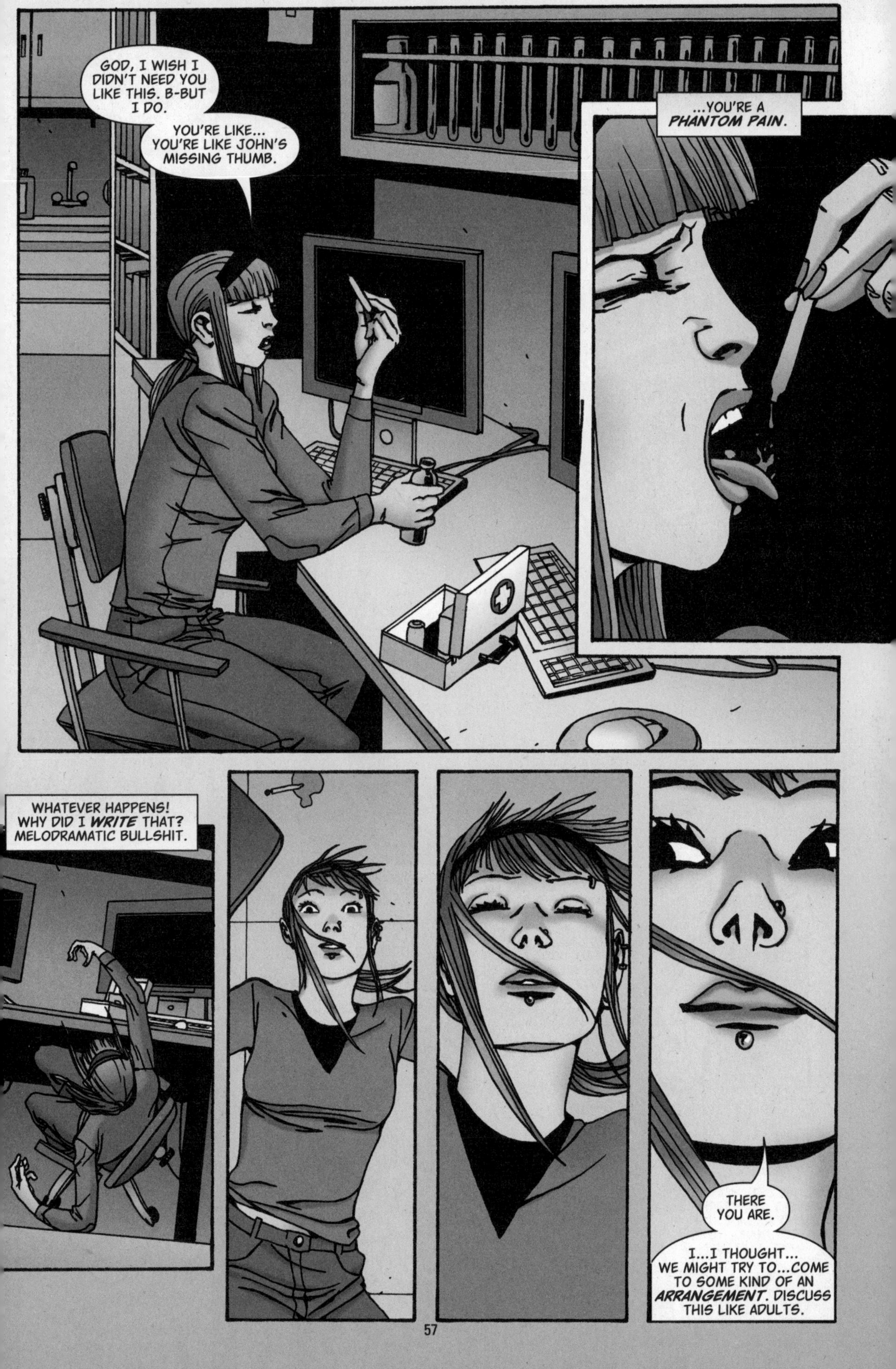
GOD, I WISH I DIDN'T NEED YOU LIKE THIS. B-BUT I DO.
YOU'RE LIKE... YOU'RE LIKE JOHN'S MISSING THUMB.
...YOU'RE A *PHANTOM PAIN*.
WHATEVER HAPPENS! WHY DID I *WRITE* THAT? MELODRAMATIC BULLSHIT.
THERE YOU ARE.
I...I THOUGHT... WE MIGHT TRY TO...COME TO SOME KIND OF AN *ARRANGEMENT*. DISCUSS THIS LIKE ADULTS.

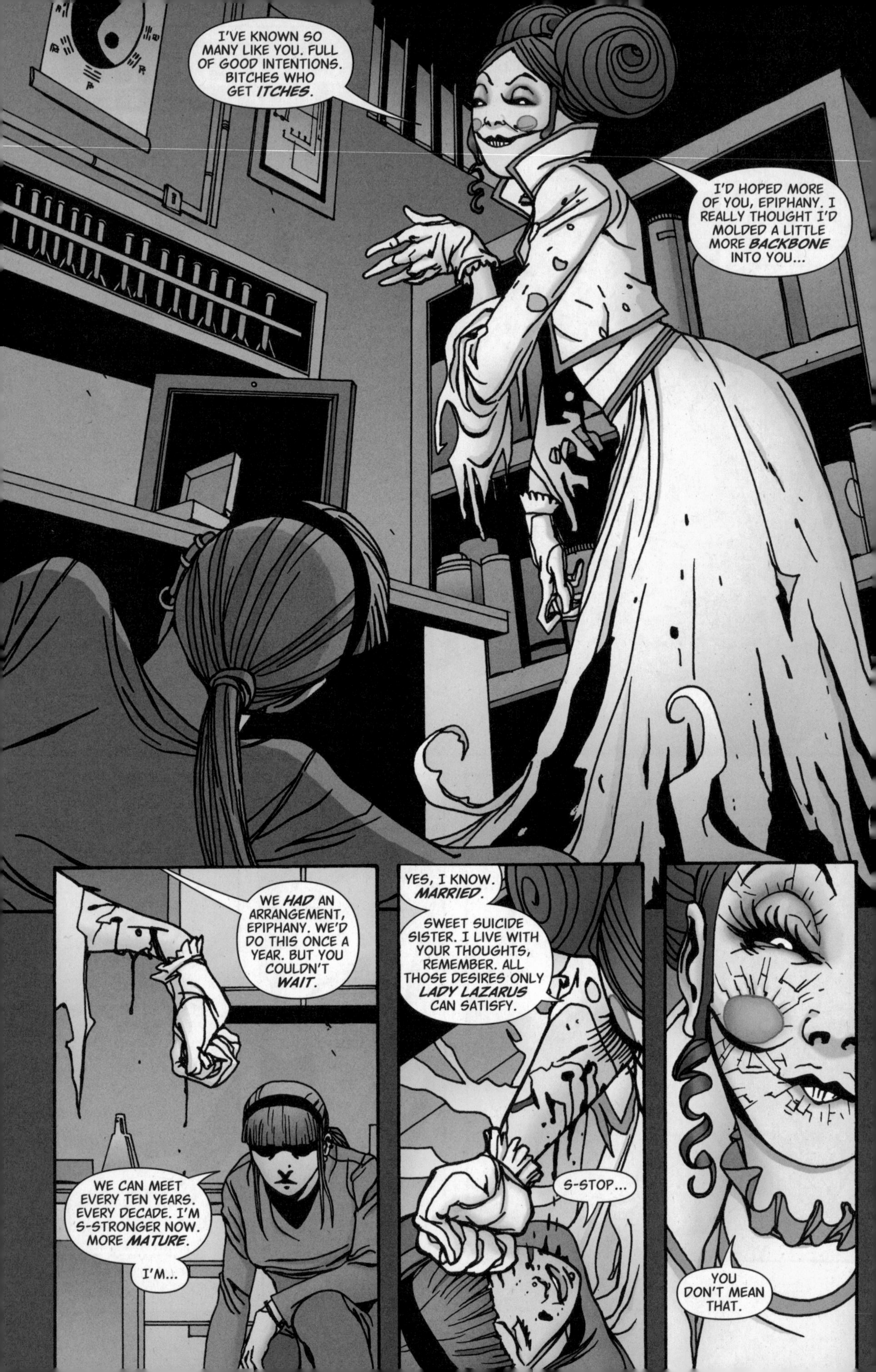
I'VE KNOWN SO MANY LIKE YOU. FULL OF GOOD INTENTIONS. BITCHES WHO GET *ITCHES*.
I'D HOPED MORE OF YOU, EPIPHANY. I REALLY THOUGHT I'D MOLDED A LITTLE MORE *BACKBONE* INTO YOU...
WE *HAD* AN ARRANGEMENT, EPIPHANY. WE'D DO THIS ONCE A YEAR. BUT YOU COULDN'T *WAIT*.
WE CAN MEET EVERY TEN YEARS. EVERY DECADE. I'M S-STRONGER NOW. MORE *MATURE*.
I'M...
YES, I KNOW. *MARRIED*.
SWEET SUICIDE SISTER. I LIVE WITH YOUR THOUGHTS, REMEMBER. ALL THOSE DESIRES ONLY *LADY LAZARUS* CAN SATISFY.
S-STOP...
YOU DON'T MEAN THAT.

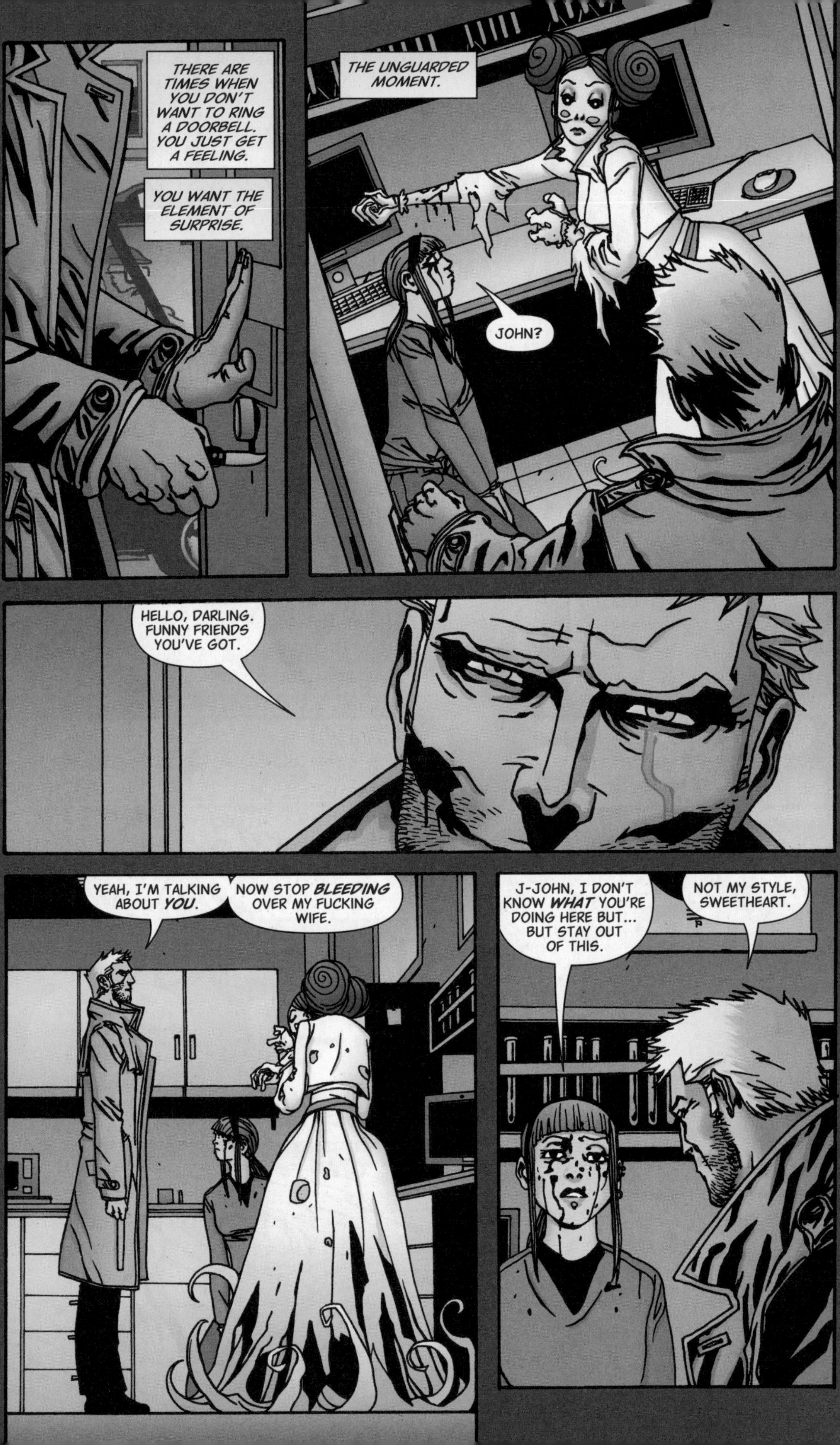
THERE ARE TIMES WHEN YOU DON'T WANT TO RING A DOORBELL. YOU JUST GET A FEELING.
YOU WANT THE ELEMENT OF SURPRISE.
THE UNGUARDED MOMENT.
JOHN?
HELLO, DARLING. FUNNY FRIENDS YOU'VE GOT.
YEAH, I'M TALKING ABOUT *YOU*.
NOW STOP *BLEEDING* OVER MY FUCKING WIFE.
J-JOHN, I DON'T KNOW *WHAT* YOU'RE DOING HERE BUT... BUT STAY OUT OF THIS.
NOT MY STYLE, SWEETHEART.

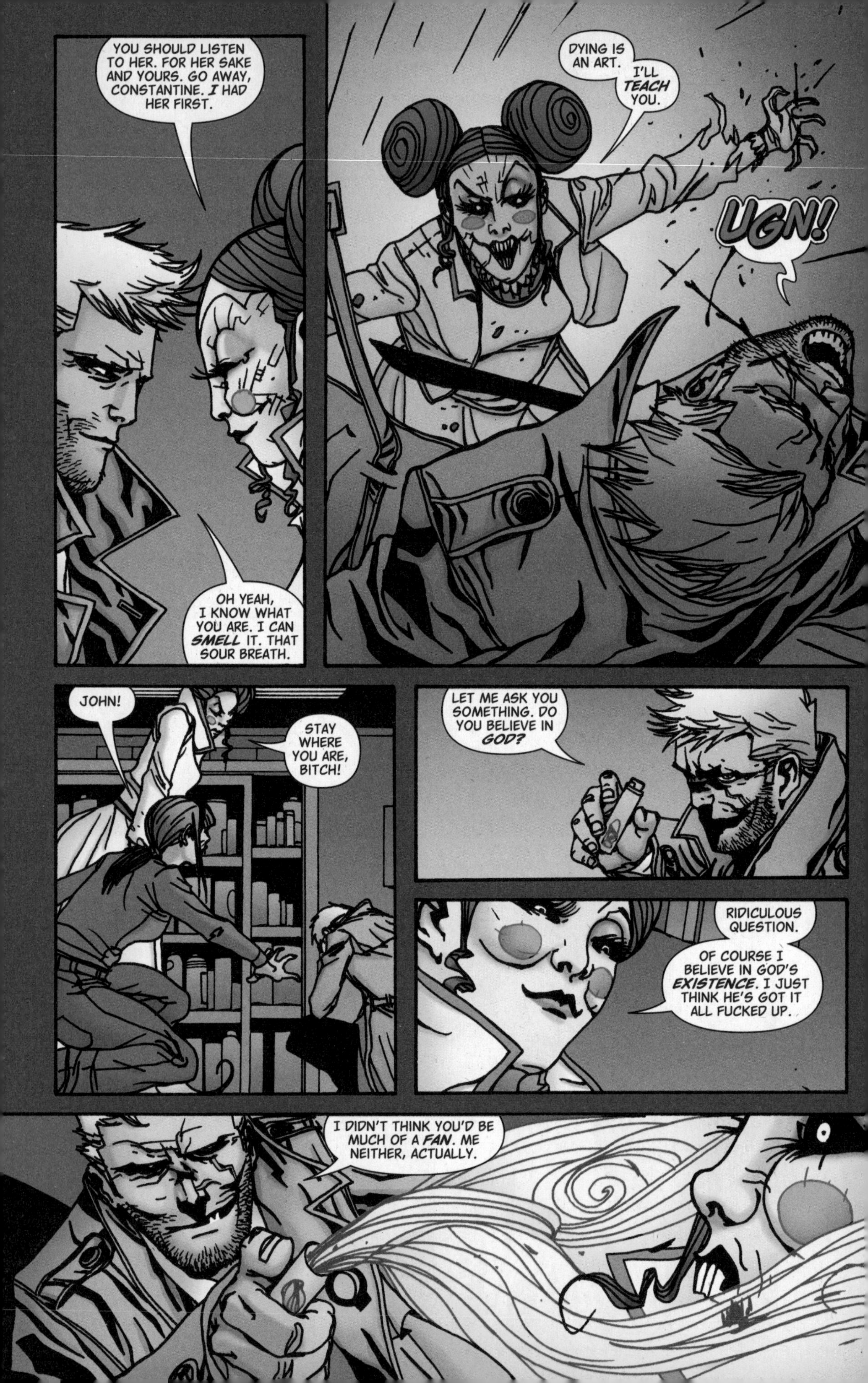
YOU SHOULD LISTEN TO HER. FOR HER SAKE AND YOURS. GO AWAY, CONSTANTINE. I HAD HER FIRST.
OH YEAH, I KNOW WHAT YOU ARE. I CAN SMELL IT. THAT SOUR BREATH.
DYING IS AN ART.
I'LL TEACH YOU.
UGN!
JOHN!
STAY WHERE YOU ARE, BITCH!
LET ME ASK YOU SOMETHING. DO YOU BELIEVE IN GOD?
RIDICULOUS QUESTION.
OF COURSE I BELIEVE IN GOD'S EXISTENCE. I JUST THINK HE'S GOT IT ALL FUCKED UP.
I DIDN'T THINK YOU'D BE MUCH OF A FAN. ME NEITHER, ACTUALLY.

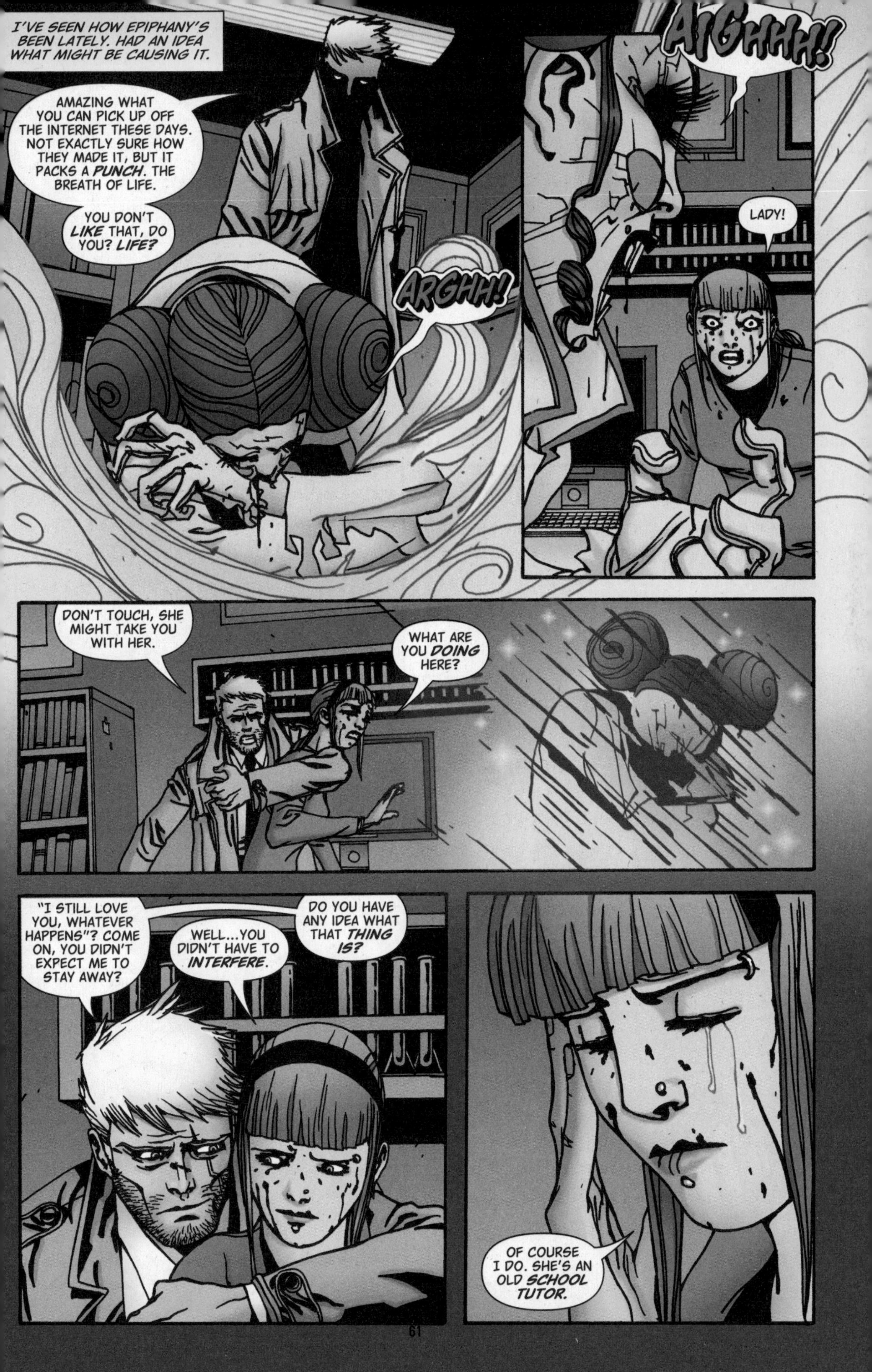
I'VE SEEN HOW EPIPHANY'S BEEN LATELY. HAD AN IDEA WHAT MIGHT BE CAUSING IT.
AMAZING WHAT YOU CAN PICK UP OFF THE INTERNET THESE DAYS. NOT EXACTLY SURE HOW THEY MADE IT, BUT IT PACKS A PUNCH. THE BREATH OF LIFE.
YOU DON'T LIKE THAT, DO YOU? LIFE?
ARGHH!
AIGHHH!
LADY!
DON'T TOUCH, SHE MIGHT TAKE YOU WITH HER.
WHAT ARE YOU DOING HERE?
"I STILL LOVE YOU, WHATEVER HAPPENS"? COME ON, YOU DIDN'T EXPECT ME TO STAY AWAY?
WELL...YOU DIDN'T HAVE TO INTERFERE.
DO YOU HAVE ANY IDEA WHAT THAT THING IS?
OF COURSE I DO. SHE'S AN OLD SCHOOL TUTOR.

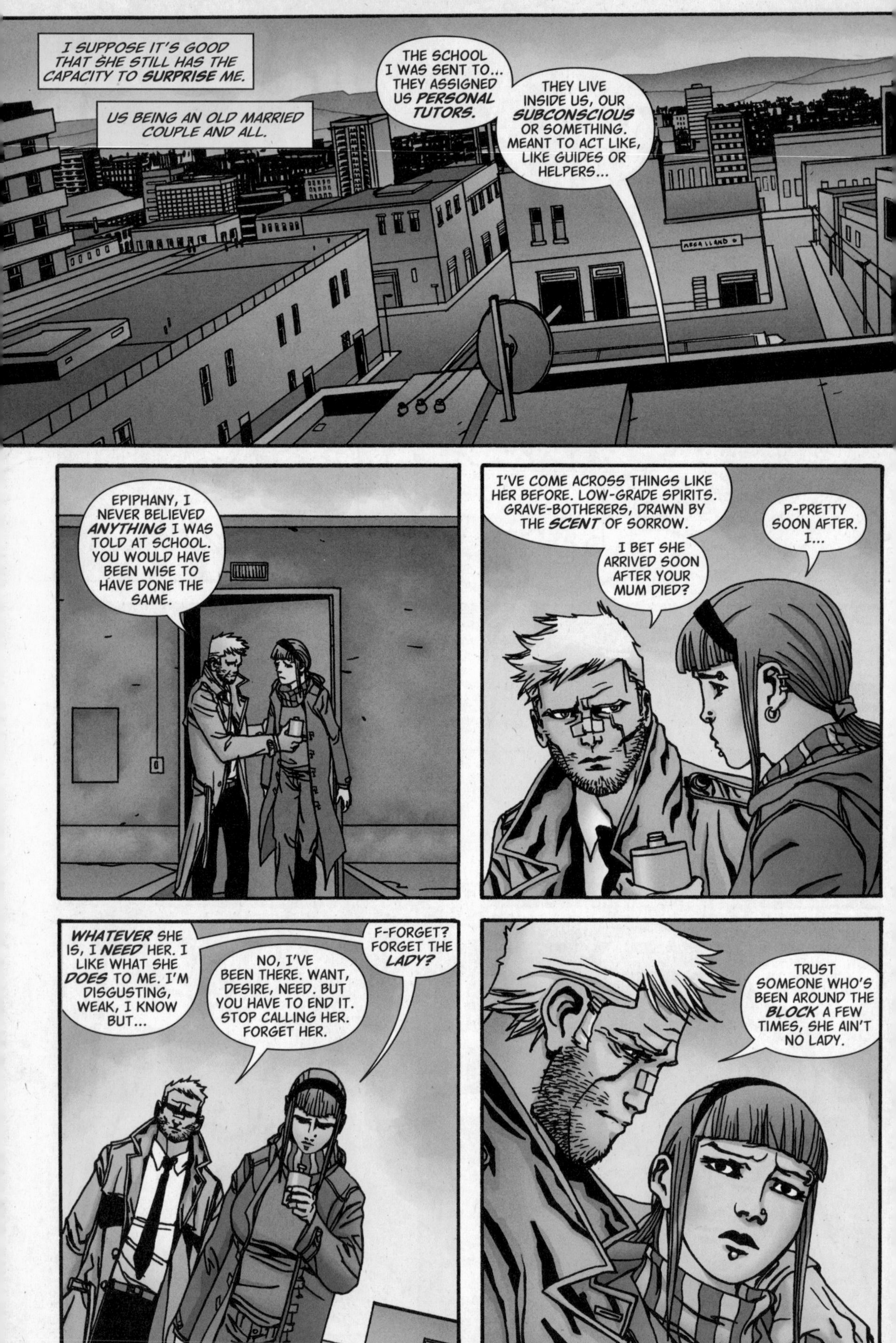

I SUPPOSE IT'S GOOD THAT SHE STILL HAS THE CAPACITY TO SURPRISE ME.
US BEING AN OLD MARRIED COUPLE AND ALL.
THE SCHOOL I WAS SENT TO... THEY ASSIGNED US PERSONAL TUTORS.
THEY LIVE INSIDE US, OUR SUBCONSCIOUS OR SOMETHING. MEANT TO ACT LIKE, LIKE GUIDES OR HELPERS...
EPIPHANY, I NEVER BELIEVED ANYTHING I WAS TOLD AT SCHOOL. YOU WOULD HAVE BEEN WISE TO HAVE DONE THE SAME.
I'VE COME ACROSS THINGS LIKE HER BEFORE. LOW-GRADE SPIRITS. GRAVE-BOTHERERS, DRAWN BY THE SCENT OF SORROW.
I BET SHE ARRIVED SOON AFTER YOUR MUM DIED?
P-PRETTY SOON AFTER. I...
WHATEVER SHE IS, I NEED HER. I LIKE WHAT SHE DOES TO ME. I'M DISGUSTING, WEAK, I KNOW BUT...
NO, I'VE BEEN THERE. WANT, DESIRE, NEED. BUT YOU HAVE TO END IT. STOP CALLING HER. FORGET HER.
F-FORGET? FORGET THE LADY?
TRUST SOMEONE WHO'S BEEN AROUND THE BLOCK A FEW TIMES, SHE AIN'T NO LADY.

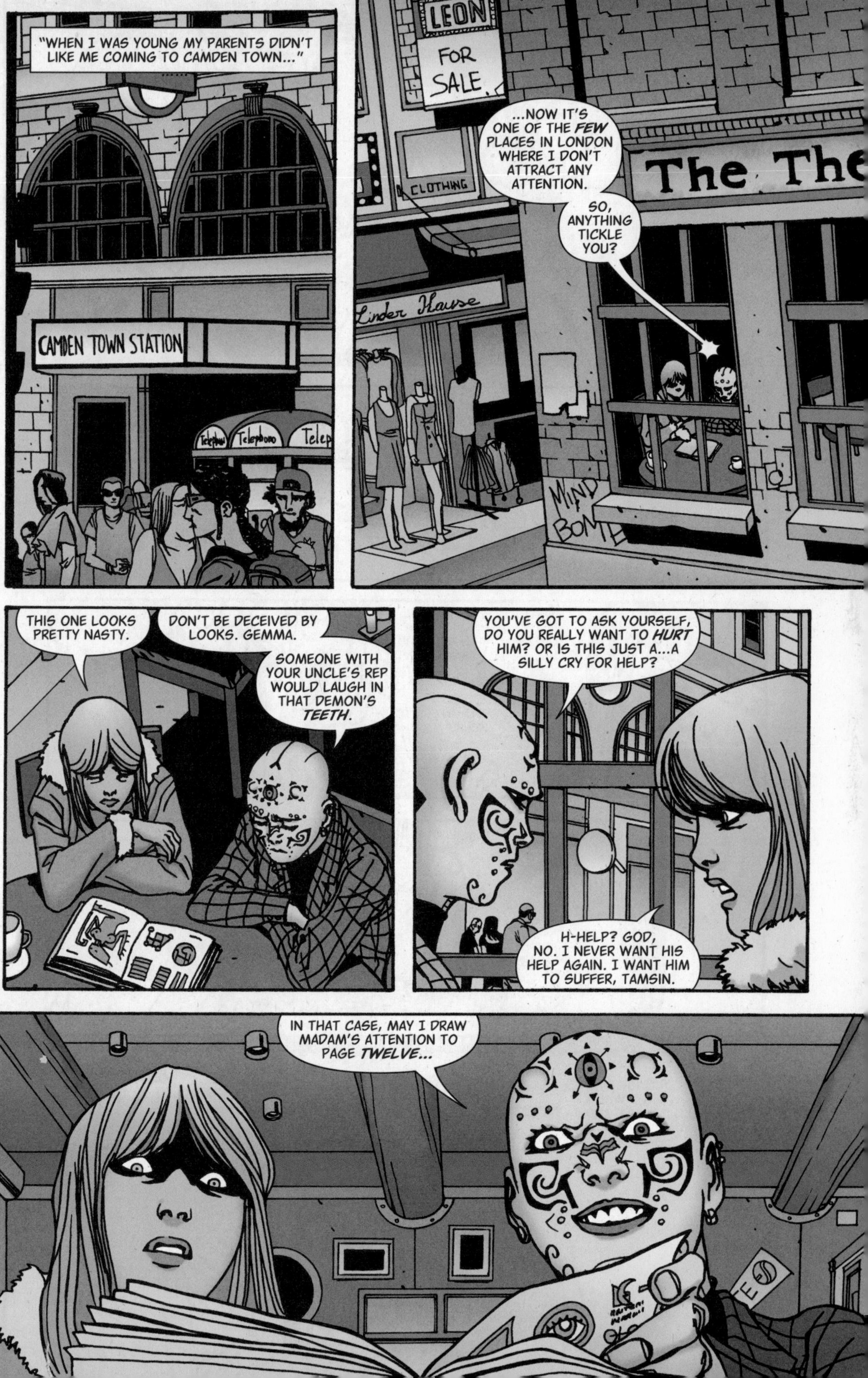
"WHEN I WAS YOUNG MY PARENTS DIDN'T LIKE ME COMING TO CAMDEN TOWN..."
CAMDEN TOWN STATION
LEON
FOR SALE
CLOTHING
...NOW IT'S ONE OF THE FEW PLACES IN LONDON WHERE I DON'T ATTRACT ANY ATTENTION.
SO, ANYTHING TICKLE YOU?
The The
MIND BOMB
THIS ONE LOOKS PRETTY NASTY.
DON'T BE DECEIVED BY LOOKS. GEMMA.
SOMEONE WITH YOUR UNCLE'S REP WOULD LAUGH IN THAT DEMON'S TEETH.
YOU'VE GOT TO ASK YOURSELF, DO YOU REALLY WANT TO HURT HIM? OR IS THIS JUST A...A SILLY CRY FOR HELP?
H-HELP? GOD, NO. I NEVER WANT HIS HELP AGAIN. I WANT HIM TO SUFFER, TAMSIN.
IN THAT CASE, MAY I DRAW MADAM'S ATTENTION TO PAGE TWELVE...

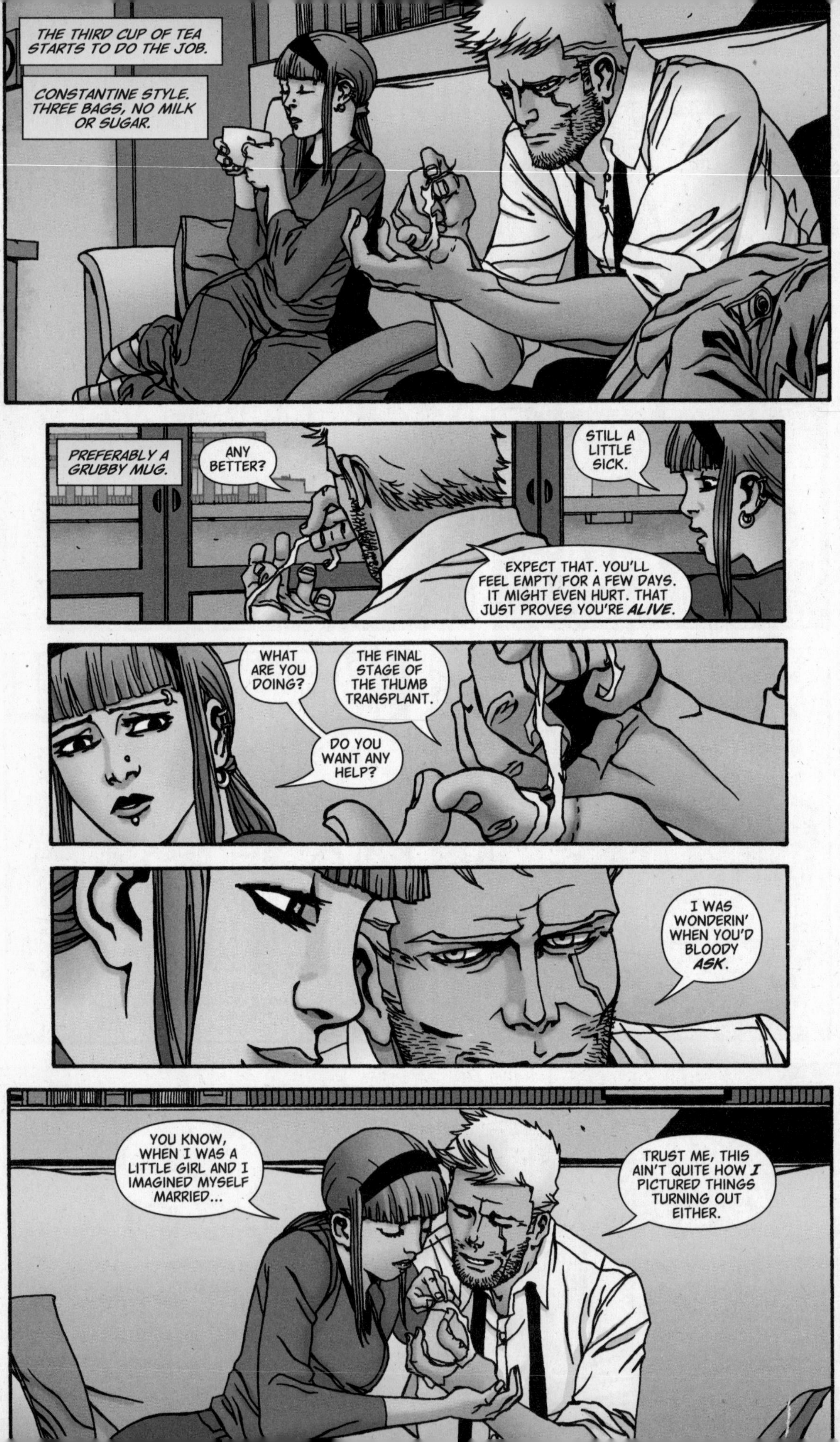
THE THIRD CUP OF TEA STARTS TO DO THE JOB.
CONSTANTINE STYLE. THREE BAGS, NO MILK OR SUGAR.
PREFERABLY A GRUBBY MUG.
ANY BETTER?
STILL A LITTLE SICK.
EXPECT THAT. YOU'LL FEEL EMPTY FOR A FEW DAYS. IT MIGHT EVEN HURT. THAT JUST PROVES YOU'RE ALIVE.
WHAT ARE YOU DOING?
THE FINAL STAGE OF THE THUMB TRANSPLANT.
DO YOU WANT ANY HELP?
I WAS WONDERIN' WHEN YOU'D BLOODY ASK.
YOU KNOW, WHEN I WAS A LITTLE GIRL AND I IMAGINED MYSELF MARRIED...
TRUST ME, THIS AIN'T QUITE HOW I PICTURED THINGS TURNING OUT EITHER.

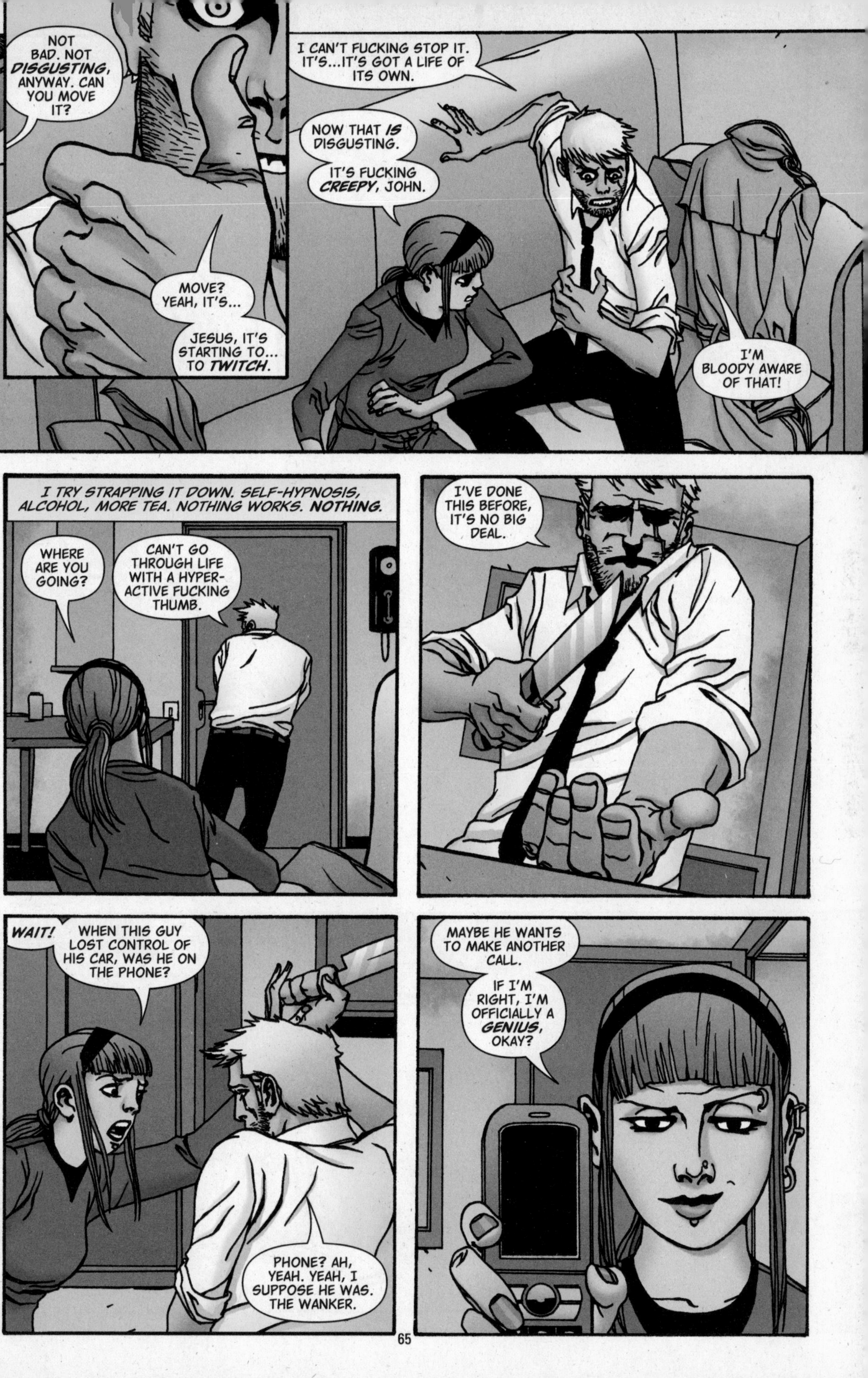
NOT BAD. NOT DISGUSTING, ANYWAY. CAN YOU MOVE IT?
I CAN'T FUCKING STOP IT. IT'S...IT'S GOT A LIFE OF ITS OWN.
NOW THAT IS DISGUSTING.
IT'S FUCKING CREEPY, JOHN.
MOVE? YEAH, IT'S...
JESUS, IT'S STARTING TO... TO TWITCH.
I'M BLOODY AWARE OF THAT!
I TRY STRAPPING IT DOWN. SELF-HYPNOSIS, ALCOHOL, MORE TEA. NOTHING WORKS. NOTHING.
WHERE ARE YOU GOING?
CAN'T GO THROUGH LIFE WITH A HYPER-ACTIVE FUCKING THUMB.
I'VE DONE THIS BEFORE, IT'S NO BIG DEAL.
WAIT!
WHEN THIS GUY LOST CONTROL OF HIS CAR, WAS HE ON THE PHONE?
PHONE? AH, YEAH. YEAH, I SUPPOSE HE WAS. THE WANKER.
MAYBE HE WANTS TO MAKE ANOTHER CALL.
IF I'M RIGHT, I'M OFFICIALLY A GENIUS, OKAY?

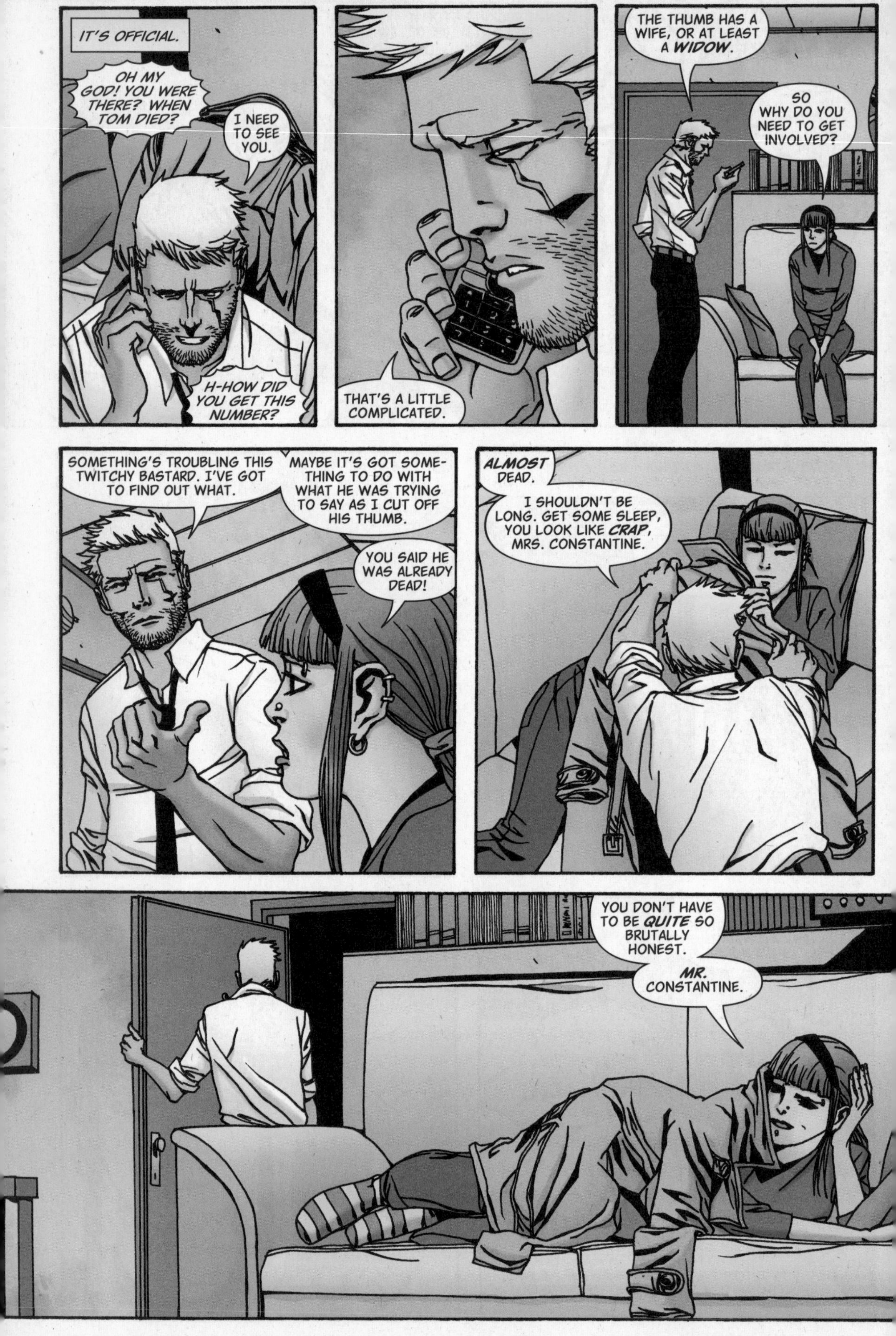
IT'S OFFICIAL.
OH MY GOD! YOU WERE THERE? WHEN TOM DIED?
I NEED TO SEE YOU.
H-HOW DID YOU GET THIS NUMBER?
THAT'S A LITTLE COMPLICATED.
THE THUMB HAS A WIFE, OR AT LEAST A WIDOW.
SO WHY DO YOU NEED TO GET INVOLVED?
SOMETHING'S TROUBLING THIS TWITCHY BASTARD. I'VE GOT TO FIND OUT WHAT.
MAYBE IT'S GOT SOMETHING TO DO WITH WHAT HE WAS TRYING TO SAY AS I CUT OFF HIS THUMB.
YOU SAID HE WAS ALREADY DEAD!
ALMOST DEAD.
I SHOULDN'T BE LONG. GET SOME SLEEP, YOU LOOK LIKE CRAP, MRS. CONSTANTINE.
YOU DON'T HAVE TO BE QUITE SO BRUTALLY HONEST.
MR. CONSTANTINE.

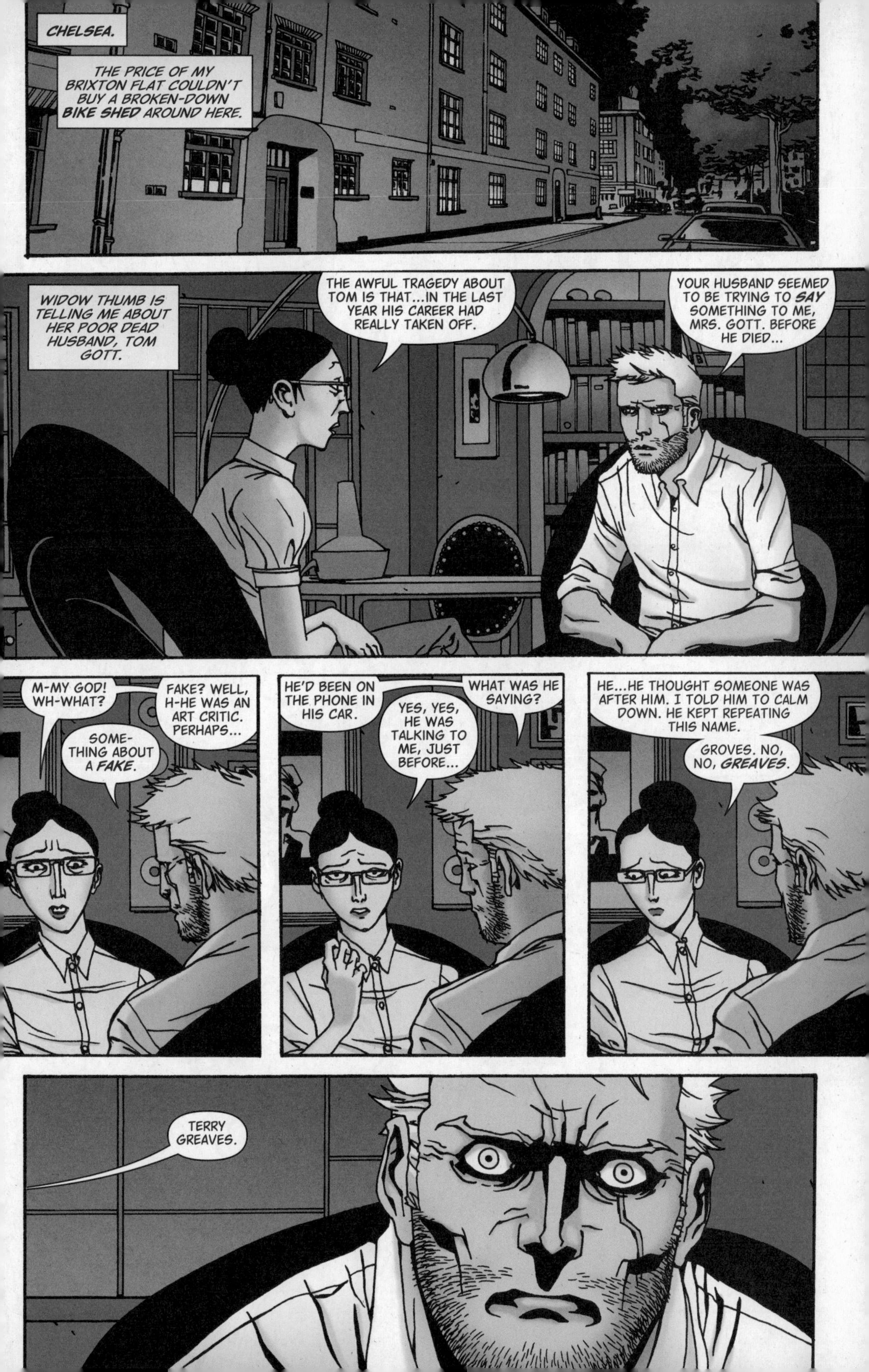
CHELSEA.
THE PRICE OF MY BRIXTON FLAT COULDN'T BUY A BROKEN-DOWN BIKE SHED AROUND HERE.
WIDOW THUMB IS TELLING ME ABOUT HER POOR DEAD HUSBAND, TOM GOTT.
THE AWFUL TRAGEDY ABOUT TOM IS THAT...IN THE LAST YEAR HIS CAREER HAD REALLY TAKEN OFF.
YOUR HUSBAND SEEMED TO BE TRYING TO SAY SOMETHING TO ME, MRS. GOTT. BEFORE HE DIED...
M-MY GOD! WH-WHAT?
FAKE? WELL, H-HE WAS AN ART CRITIC. PERHAPS...
SOME-THING ABOUT A FAKE.
HE'D BEEN ON THE PHONE IN HIS CAR.
WHAT WAS HE SAYING?
YES, YES, HE WAS TALKING TO ME, JUST BEFORE...
HE...HE THOUGHT SOMEONE WAS AFTER HIM. I TOLD HIM TO CALM DOWN. HE KEPT REPEATING THIS NAME.
GROVES. NO, NO, GREAVES.
TERRY GREAVES.

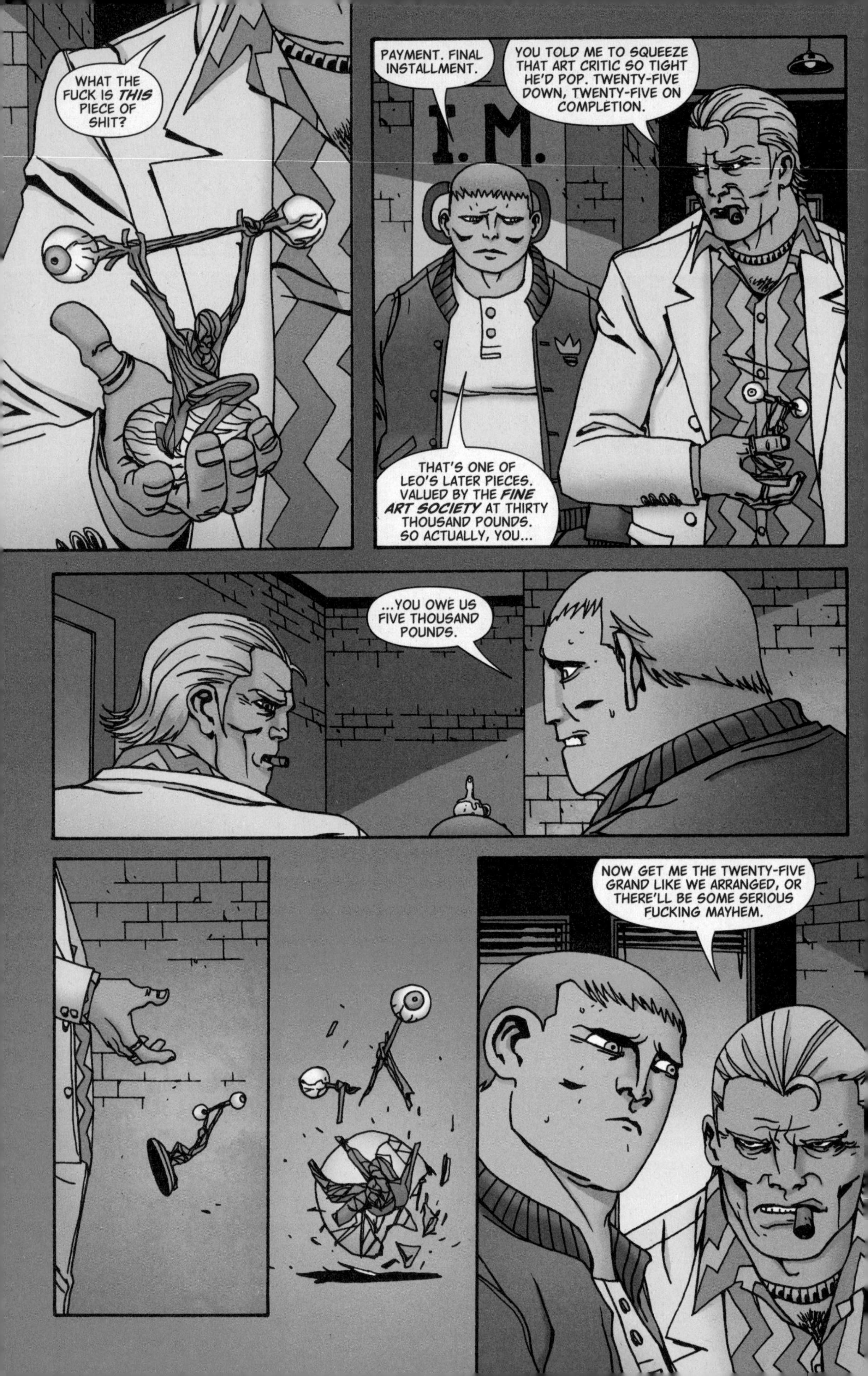
WHAT THE FUCK IS *THIS* PIECE OF SHIT?
PAYMENT. FINAL INSTALLMENT.
YOU TOLD ME TO SQUEEZE THAT ART CRITIC SO TIGHT HE'D POP. TWENTY-FIVE DOWN, TWENTY-FIVE ON COMPLETION.
I.M.
THAT'S ONE OF LEO'S LATER PIECES. VALUED BY THE *FINE ART SOCIETY* AT THIRTY THOUSAND POUNDS. SO ACTUALLY, YOU...
...YOU OWE US FIVE THOUSAND POUNDS.
NOW GET ME THE TWENTY-FIVE GRAND LIKE WE ARRANGED, OR THERE'LL BE SOME SERIOUS FUCKING MAYHEM.

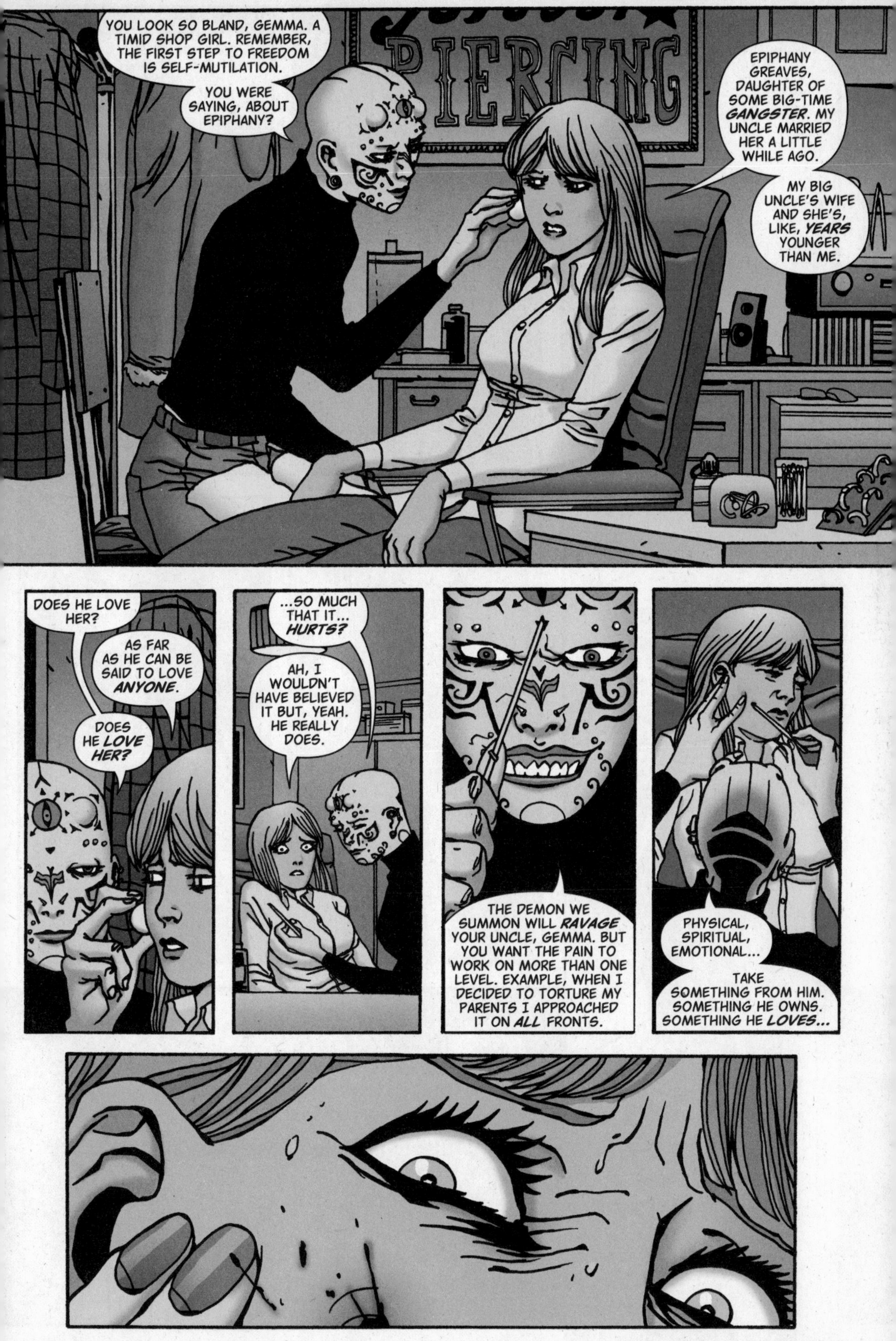
PIERCING
YOU LOOK SO BLAND, GEMMA. A TIMID SHOP GIRL. REMEMBER, THE FIRST STEP TO FREEDOM IS SELF-MUTILATION.
YOU WERE SAYING, ABOUT EPIPHANY?
EPIPHANY GREAVES, DAUGHTER OF SOME BIG-TIME GANGSTER. MY UNCLE MARRIED HER A LITTLE WHILE AGO.
MY BIG UNCLE'S WIFE AND SHE'S, LIKE, YEARS YOUNGER THAN ME.
DOES HE LOVE HER?
AS FAR AS HE CAN BE SAID TO LOVE ANYONE.
DOES HE LOVE HER?
...SO MUCH THAT IT... HURTS?
AH, I WOULDN'T HAVE BELIEVED IT BUT, YEAH. HE REALLY DOES.
THE DEMON WE SUMMON WILL RAVAGE YOUR UNCLE, GEMMA. BUT YOU WANT THE PAIN TO WORK ON MORE THAN ONE LEVEL. EXAMPLE, WHEN I DECIDED TO TORTURE MY PARENTS I APPROACHED IT ON ALL FRONTS.
PHYSICAL, SPIRITUAL, EMOTIONAL...
TAKE SOMETHING FROM HIM. SOMETHING HE OWNS. SOMETHING HE LOVES...

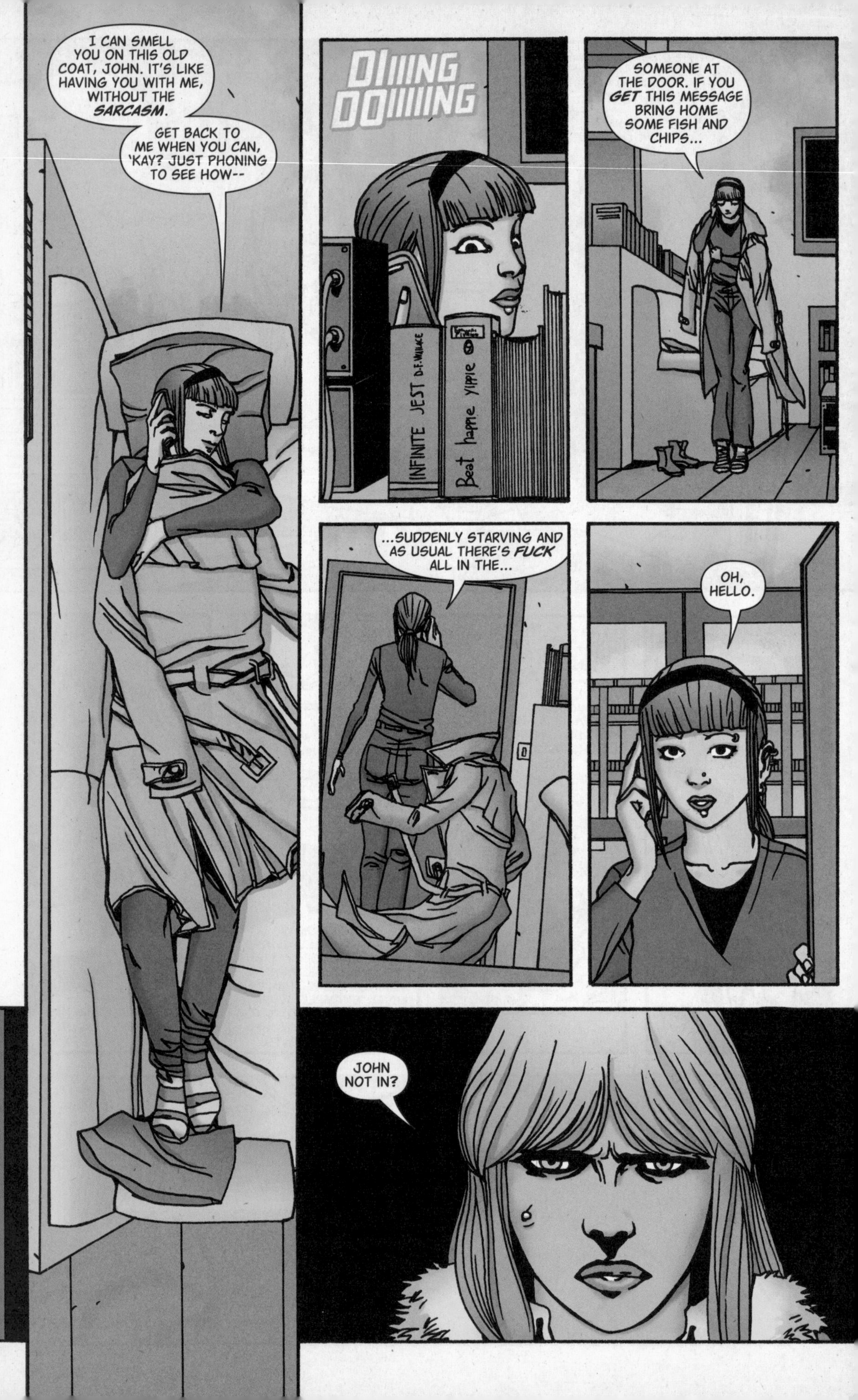
I CAN SMELL YOU ON THIS OLD COAT, JOHN. IT'S LIKE HAVING YOU WITH ME, WITHOUT THE *SARCASM*.
GET BACK TO ME WHEN YOU CAN, 'KAY? JUST PHONING TO SEE HOW--
DIIIIING DOIIIIING
INFINITE JEST D.F. WALLACE
Beat happie yippie
SOMEONE AT THE DOOR. IF YOU *GET* THIS MESSAGE BRING HOME SOME FISH AND CHIPS...
...SUDDENLY STARVING AND AS USUAL THERE'S *FUCK* ALL IN THE...
OH, HELLO.
JOHN NOT IN?

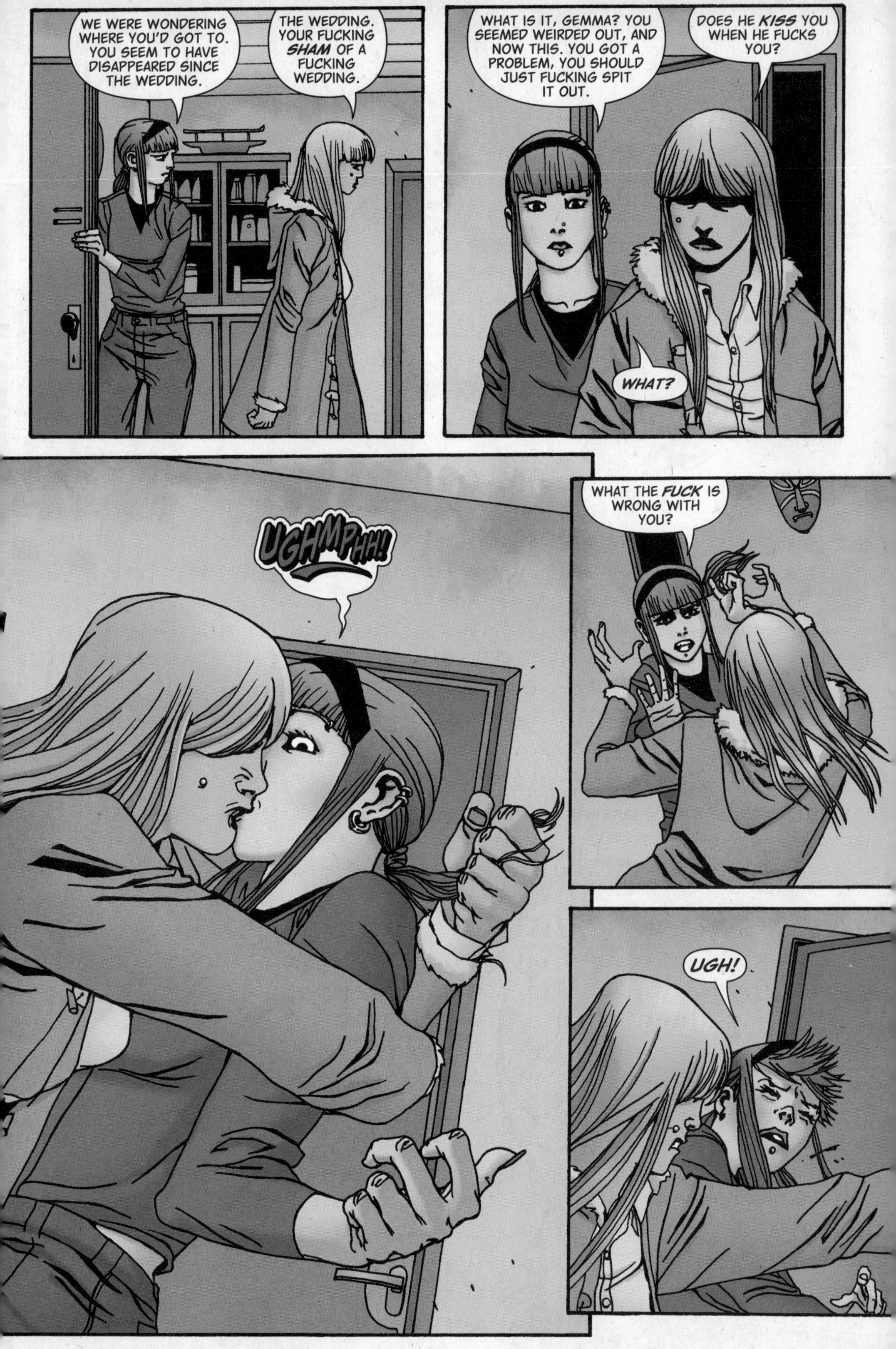
WE WERE WONDERING WHERE YOU'D GOT TO. YOU SEEM TO HAVE DISAPPEARED SINCE THE WEDDING.
THE WEDDING. YOUR FUCKING SHAM OF A FUCKING WEDDING.
WHAT IS IT, GEMMA? YOU SEEMED WEIRDED OUT, AND NOW THIS. YOU GOT A PROBLEM, YOU SHOULD JUST FUCKING SPIT IT OUT.
DOES HE KISS YOU WHEN HE FUCKS YOU?
WHAT?
UGHMPHH!!
WHAT THE FUCK IS WRONG WITH YOU?
UGH!

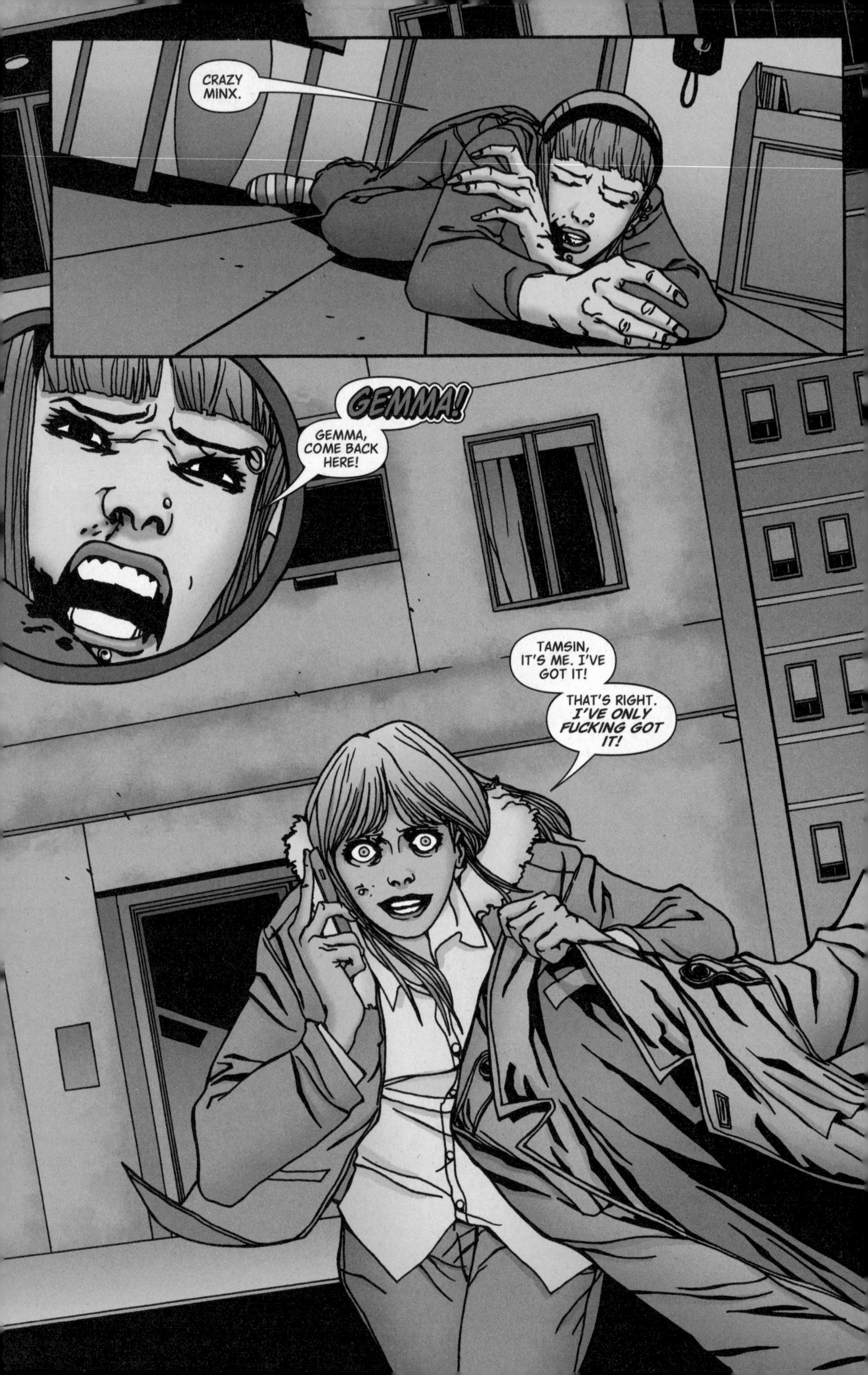
CRAZY MINX.
GEMMA!
GEMMA, COME BACK HERE!
TAMSIN, IT'S ME. I'VE GOT IT!
THAT'S RIGHT. *I'VE ONLY FUCKING GOT IT!*

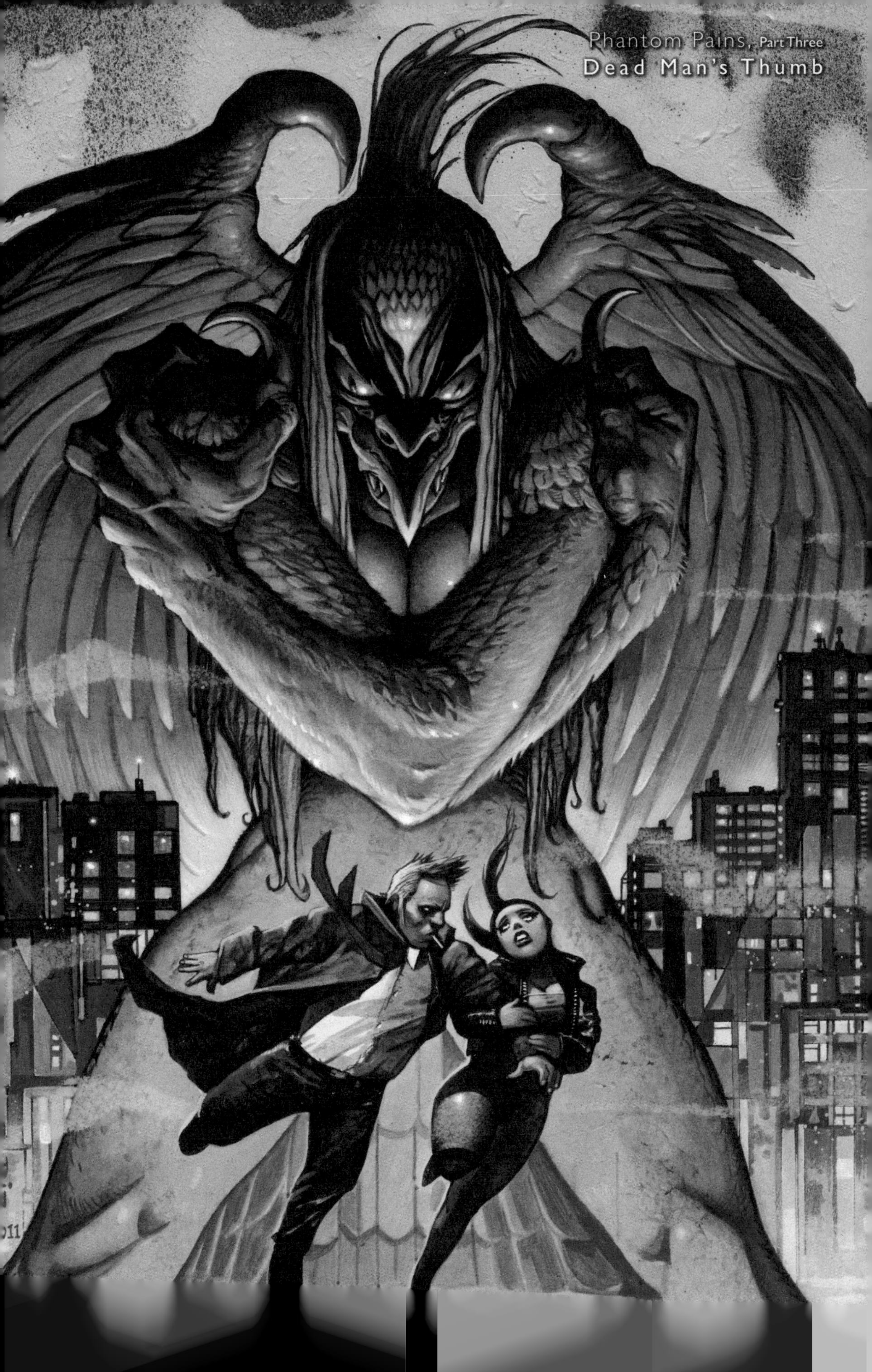
Phantom Pains, Part Three
Dead Man's Thumb

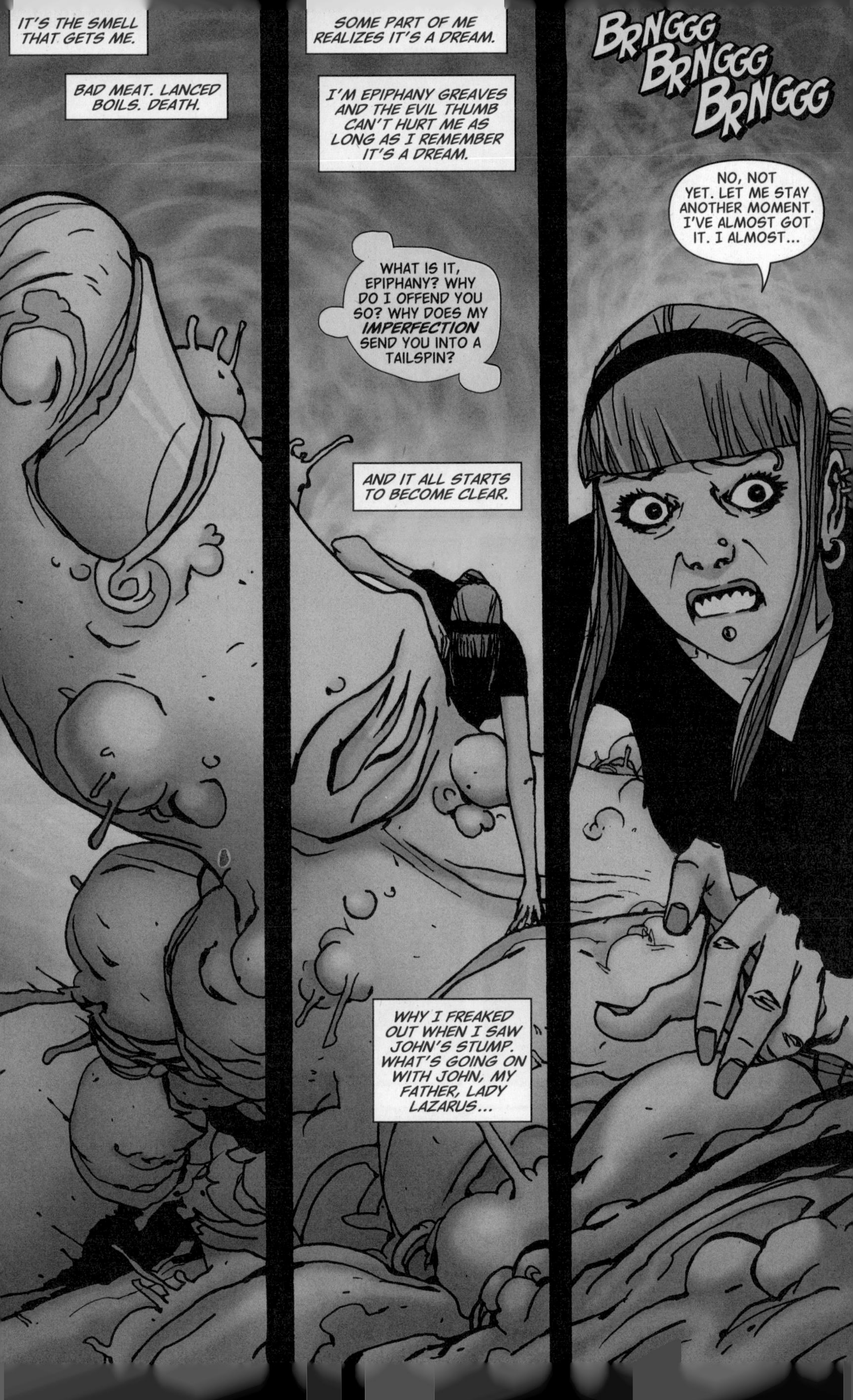
IT'S THE SMELL THAT GETS ME.
BAD MEAT. LANCED BOILS. DEATH.
SOME PART OF ME REALIZES IT'S A DREAM.
I'M EPIPHANY GREAVES AND THE EVIL THUMB CAN'T HURT ME AS LONG AS I REMEMBER IT'S A DREAM.
WHAT IS IT, EPIPHANY? WHY DO I OFFEND YOU SO? WHY DOES MY IMPERFECTION SEND YOU INTO A TAILSPIN?
AND IT ALL STARTS TO BECOME CLEAR.
WHY I FREAKED OUT WHEN I SAW JOHN'S STUMP. WHAT'S GOING ON WITH JOHN, MY FATHER, LADY LAZARUS...
BRNGGG BRNGGG BRNGGG
NO, NOT YET. LET ME STAY ANOTHER MOMENT. I'VE ALMOST GOT IT. I ALMOST...

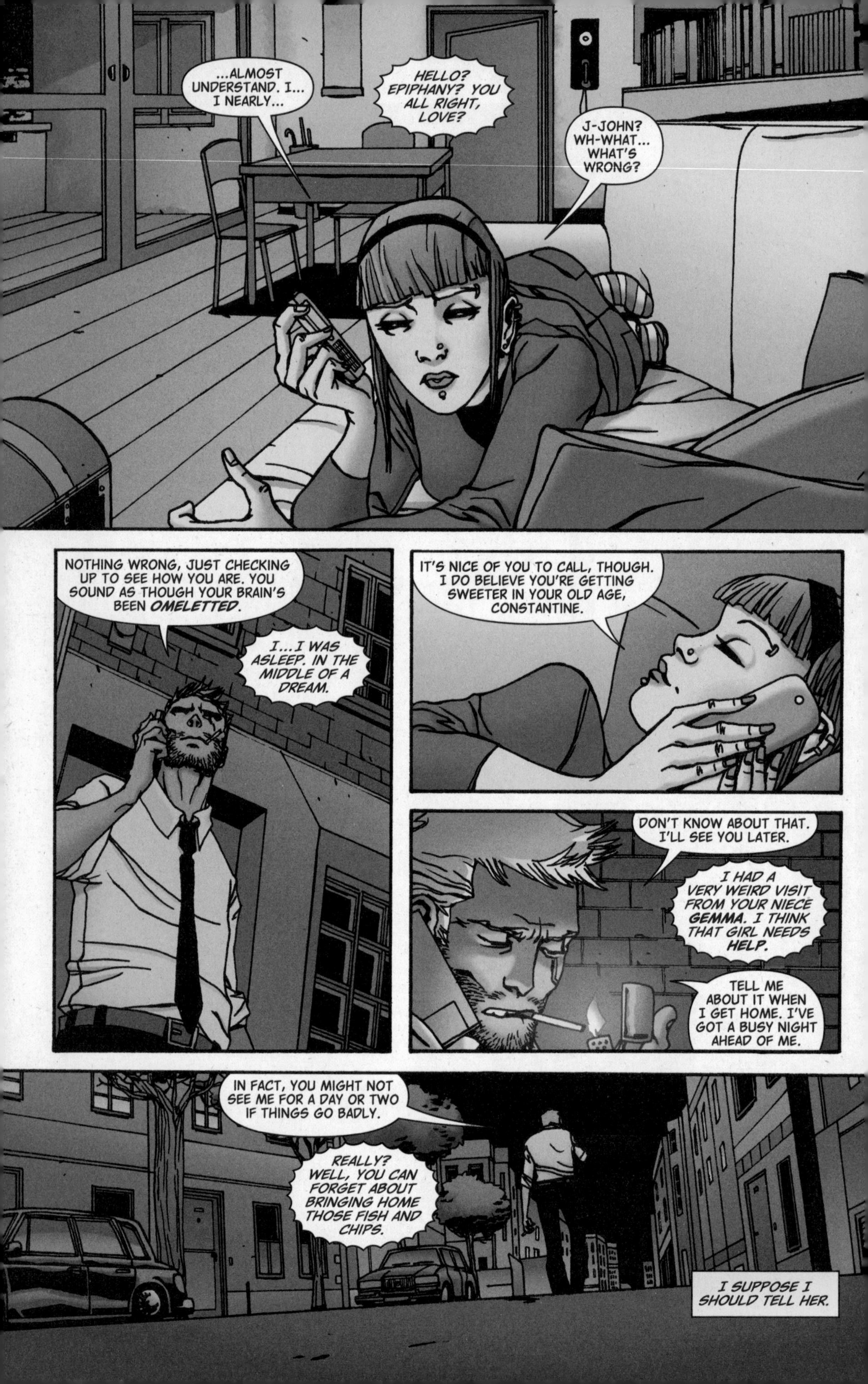
...ALMOST UNDERSTAND. I... I NEARLY...
HELLO? EPIPHANY? YOU ALL RIGHT, LOVE?
J-JOHN? WH-WHAT... WHAT'S WRONG?
NOTHING WRONG, JUST CHECKING UP TO SEE HOW YOU ARE. YOU SOUND AS THOUGH YOUR BRAIN'S BEEN OMELETTED.
I...I WAS ASLEEP. IN THE MIDDLE OF A DREAM.
IT'S NICE OF YOU TO CALL, THOUGH. I DO BELIEVE YOU'RE GETTING SWEETER IN YOUR OLD AGE, CONSTANTINE.
DON'T KNOW ABOUT THAT. I'LL SEE YOU LATER.
I HAD A VERY WEIRD VISIT FROM YOUR NIECE GEMMA. I THINK THAT GIRL NEEDS HELP.
TELL ME ABOUT IT WHEN I GET HOME. I'VE GOT A BUSY NIGHT AHEAD OF ME.
IN FACT, YOU MIGHT NOT SEE ME FOR A DAY OR TWO IF THINGS GO BADLY.
REALLY? WELL, YOU CAN FORGET ABOUT BRINGING HOME THOSE FISH AND CHIPS.
I SUPPOSE I SHOULD TELL HER.

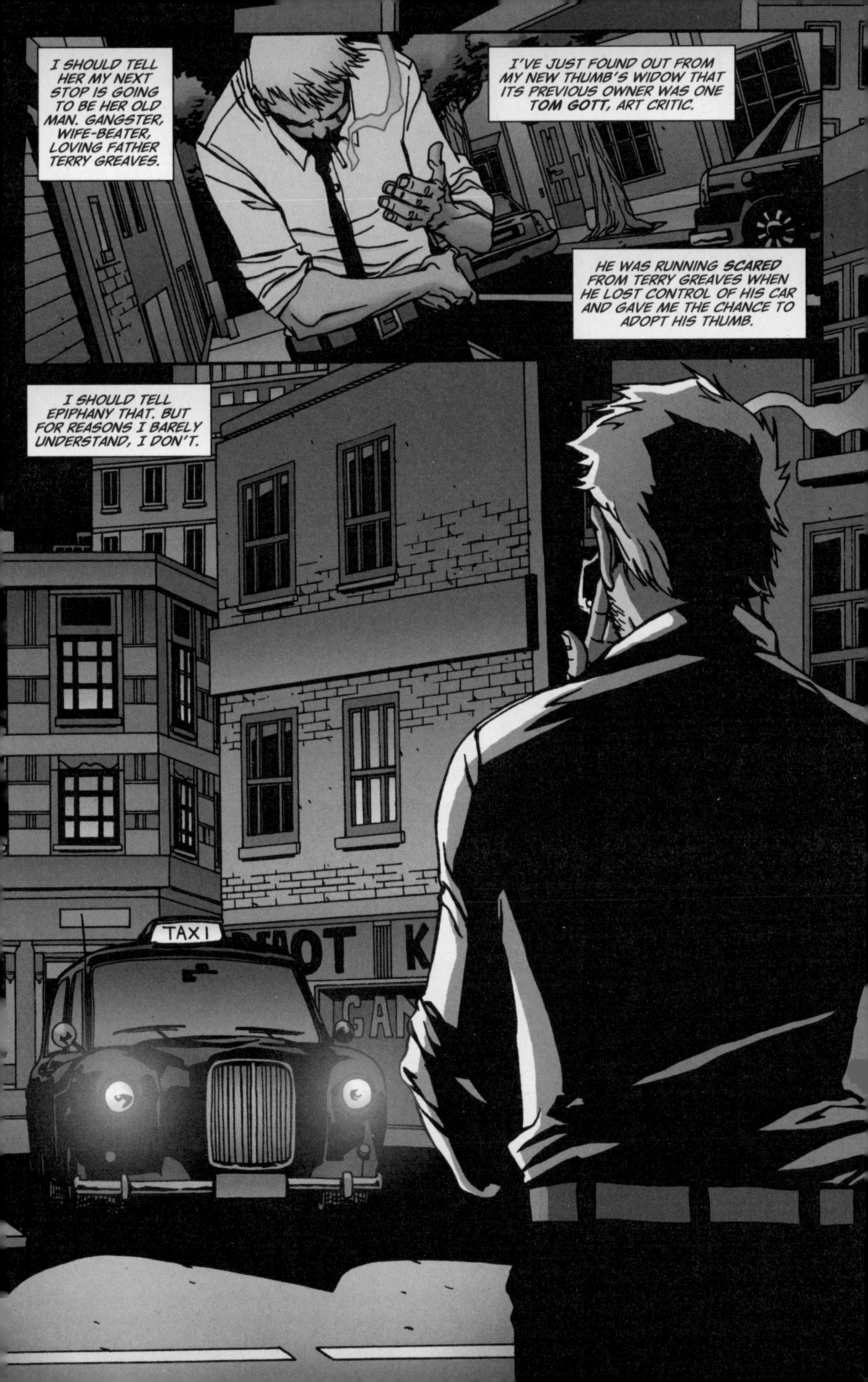
I SHOULD TELL HER MY NEXT STOP IS GOING TO BE HER OLD MAN. GANGSTER, WIFE-BEATER, LOVING FATHER TERRY GREAVES.
I'VE JUST FOUND OUT FROM MY NEW THUMB'S WIDOW THAT ITS PREVIOUS OWNER WAS ONE TOM GOTT, ART CRITIC.
HE WAS RUNNING SCARED FROM TERRY GREAVES WHEN HE LOST CONTROL OF HIS CAR AND GAVE ME THE CHANCE TO ADOPT HIS THUMB.
I SHOULD TELL EPIPHANY THAT. BUT FOR REASONS I BARELY UNDERSTAND, I DON'T.
TAXI

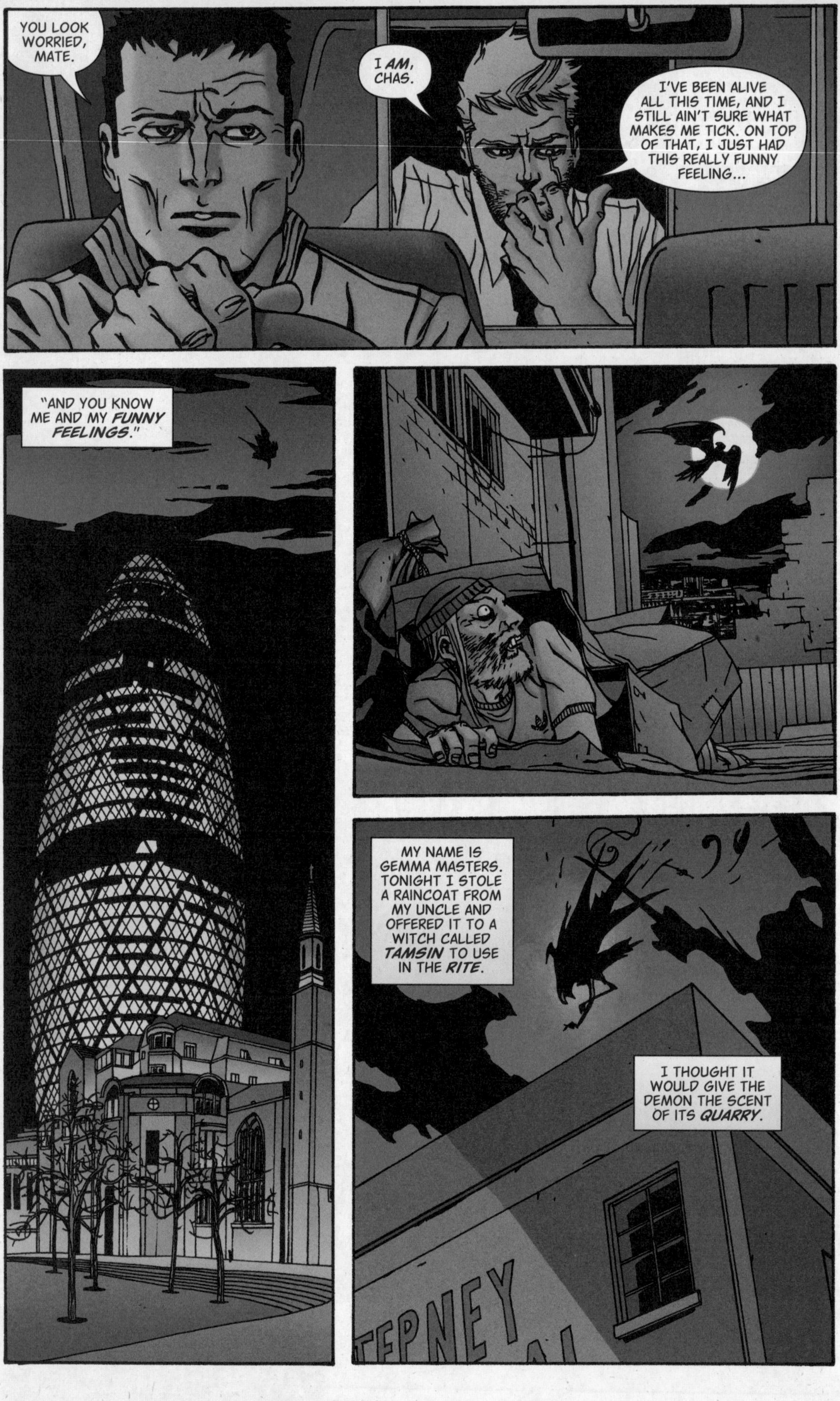

YOU LOOK WORRIED, MATE.
I AM, CHAS.
I'VE BEEN ALIVE ALL THIS TIME, AND I STILL AIN'T SURE WHAT MAKES ME TICK. ON TOP OF THAT, I JUST HAD THIS REALLY FUNNY FEELING...
"AND YOU KNOW ME AND MY FUNNY FEELINGS."
MY NAME IS GEMMA MASTERS. TONIGHT I STOLE A RAINCOAT FROM MY UNCLE AND OFFERED IT TO A WITCH CALLED TAMSIN TO USE IN THE RITE.
I THOUGHT IT WOULD GIVE THE DEMON THE SCENT OF ITS QUARRY.
TEPNEY

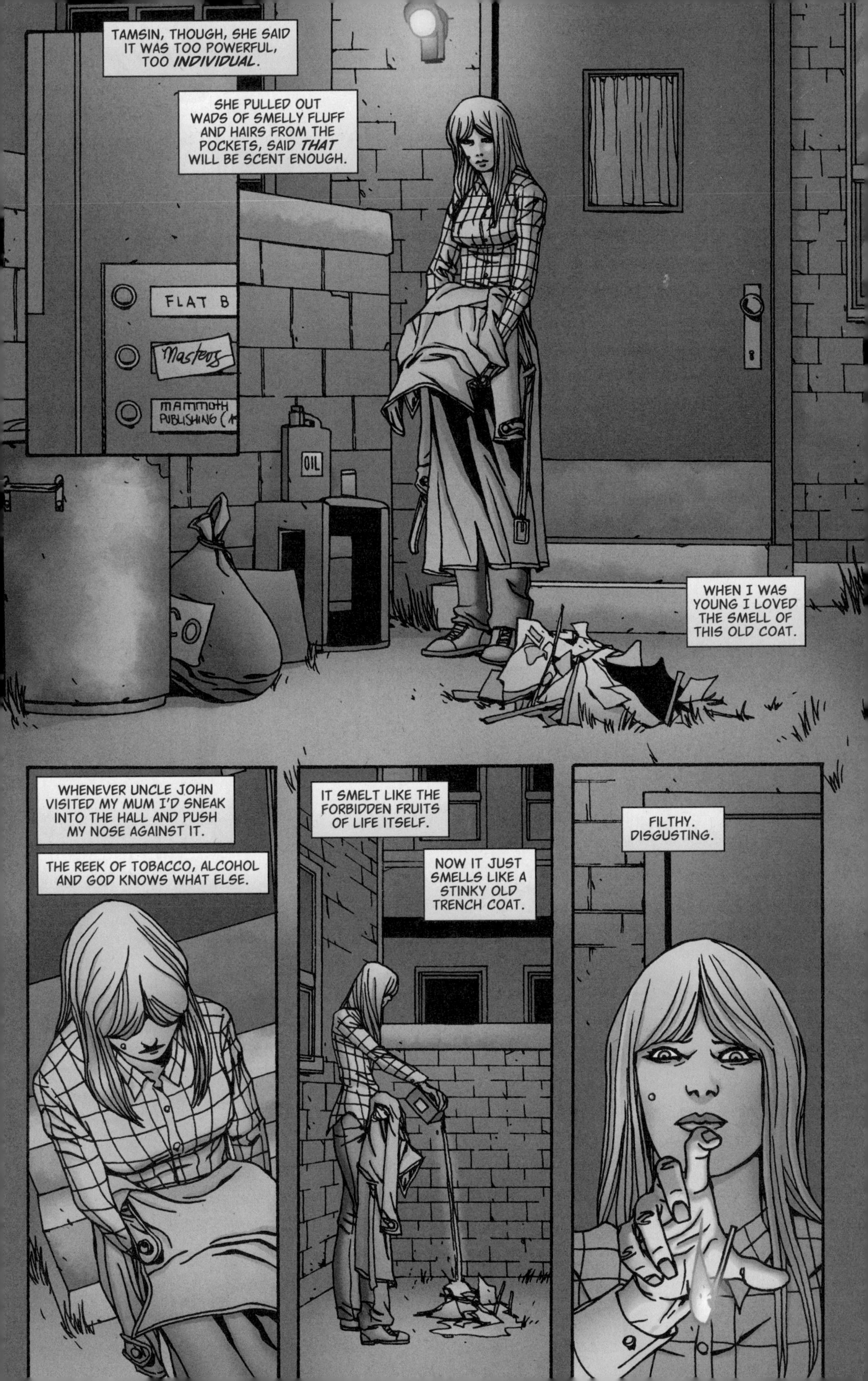

TAMSIN, THOUGH, SHE SAID IT WAS TOO POWERFUL, TOO *INDIVIDUAL*.
SHE PULLED OUT WADS OF SMELLY FLUFF AND HAIRS FROM THE POCKETS, SAID *THAT* WILL BE SCENT ENOUGH.
FLAT B
Masters
MAMMOTH PUBLISHING
OIL
WHEN I WAS YOUNG I LOVED THE SMELL OF THIS OLD COAT.
WHENEVER UNCLE JOHN VISITED MY MUM I'D SNEAK INTO THE HALL AND PUSH MY NOSE AGAINST IT.
THE REEK OF TOBACCO, ALCOHOL AND GOD KNOWS WHAT ELSE.
IT SMELT LIKE THE FORBIDDEN FRUITS OF LIFE ITSELF.
NOW IT JUST SMELLS LIKE A STINKY OLD TRENCH COAT.
FILTHY. DISGUSTING.

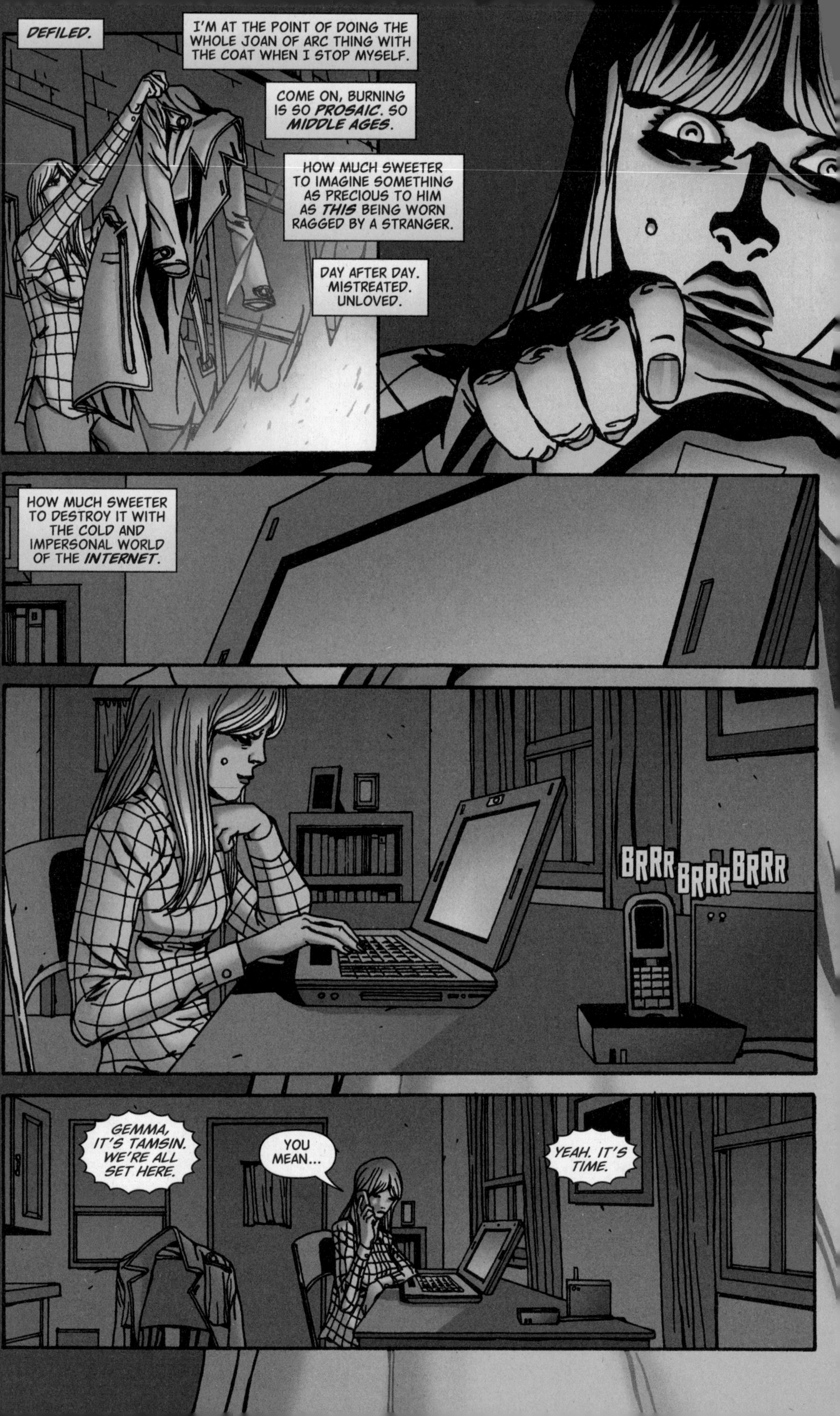
DEFILED.
I'M AT THE POINT OF DOING THE WHOLE JOAN OF ARC THING WITH THE COAT WHEN I STOP MYSELF.
COME ON, BURNING IS SO PROSAIC. SO MIDDLE AGES.
HOW MUCH SWEETER TO IMAGINE SOMETHING AS PRECIOUS TO HIM AS THIS BEING WORN RAGGED BY A STRANGER.
DAY AFTER DAY. MISTREATED. UNLOVED.
HOW MUCH SWEETER TO DESTROY IT WITH THE COLD AND IMPERSONAL WORLD OF THE INTERNET.
BRRR BRRR BRRR
GEMMA, IT'S TAMSIN. WE'RE ALL SET HERE.
YOU MEAN...
YEAH. IT'S TIME.

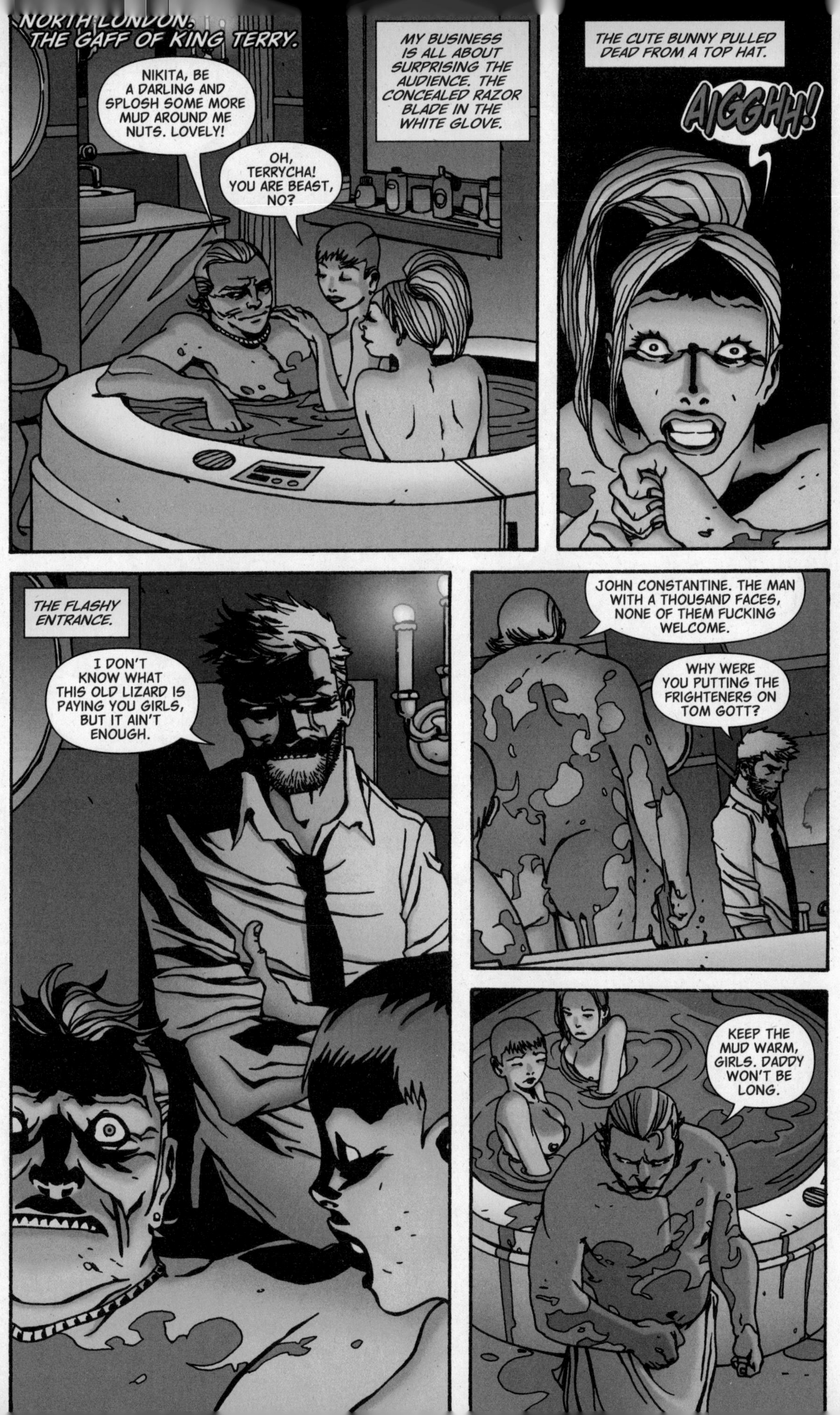
NORTH LONDON. THE GAFF OF KING TERRY.
NIKITA, BE A DARLING AND SPLOSH SOME MORE MUD AROUND ME NUTS. LOVELY!
OH, TERRYCHA! YOU ARE BEAST, NO?
MY BUSINESS IS ALL ABOUT SURPRISING THE AUDIENCE. THE CONCEALED RAZOR BLADE IN THE WHITE GLOVE.
THE CUTE BUNNY PULLED DEAD FROM A TOP HAT.
AIGGHH!
THE FLASHY ENTRANCE.
I DON'T KNOW WHAT THIS OLD LIZARD IS PAYING YOU GIRLS, BUT IT AIN'T ENOUGH.
JOHN CONSTANTINE. THE MAN WITH A THOUSAND FACES, NONE OF THEM FUCKING WELCOME.
WHY WERE YOU PUTTING THE FRIGHTENERS ON TOM GOTT?
KEEP THE MUD WARM, GIRLS. DADDY WON'T BE LONG.

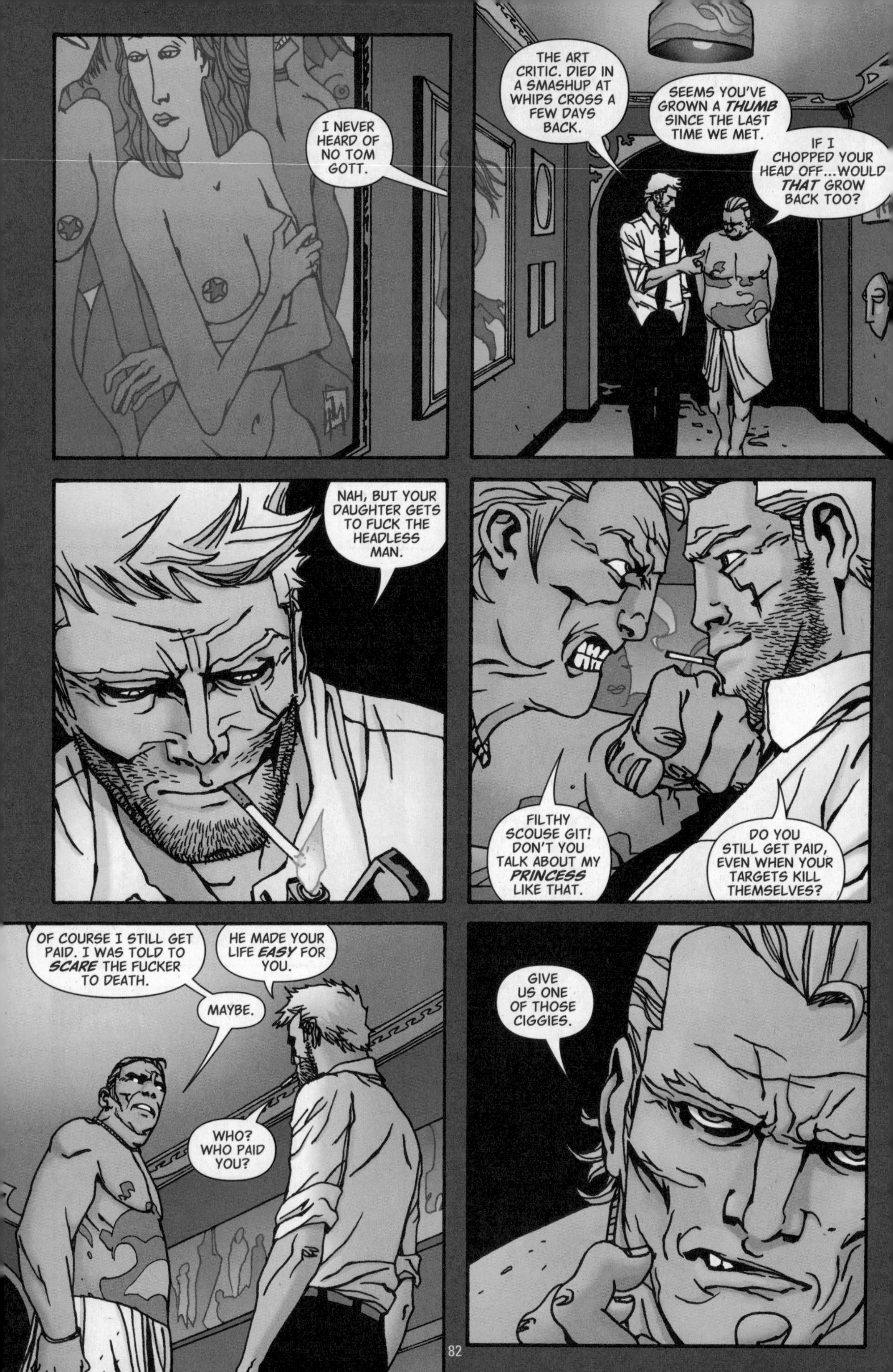
I NEVER HEARD OF NO TOM GOTT.
THE ART CRITIC. DIED IN A SMASHUP AT WHIPS CROSS A FEW DAYS BACK.
SEEMS YOU'VE GROWN A THUMB SINCE THE LAST TIME WE MET.
IF I CHOPPED YOUR HEAD OFF...WOULD THAT GROW BACK TOO?
NAH, BUT YOUR DAUGHTER GETS TO FUCK THE HEADLESS MAN.
FILTHY SCOUSE GIT! DON'T YOU TALK ABOUT MY PRINCESS LIKE THAT.
DO YOU STILL GET PAID, EVEN WHEN YOUR TARGETS KILL THEMSELVES?
OF COURSE I STILL GET PAID. I WAS TOLD TO SCARE THE FUCKER TO DEATH.
HE MADE YOUR LIFE EASY FOR YOU.
MAYBE.
WHO? WHO PAID YOU?
GIVE US ONE OF THOSE CIGGIES.

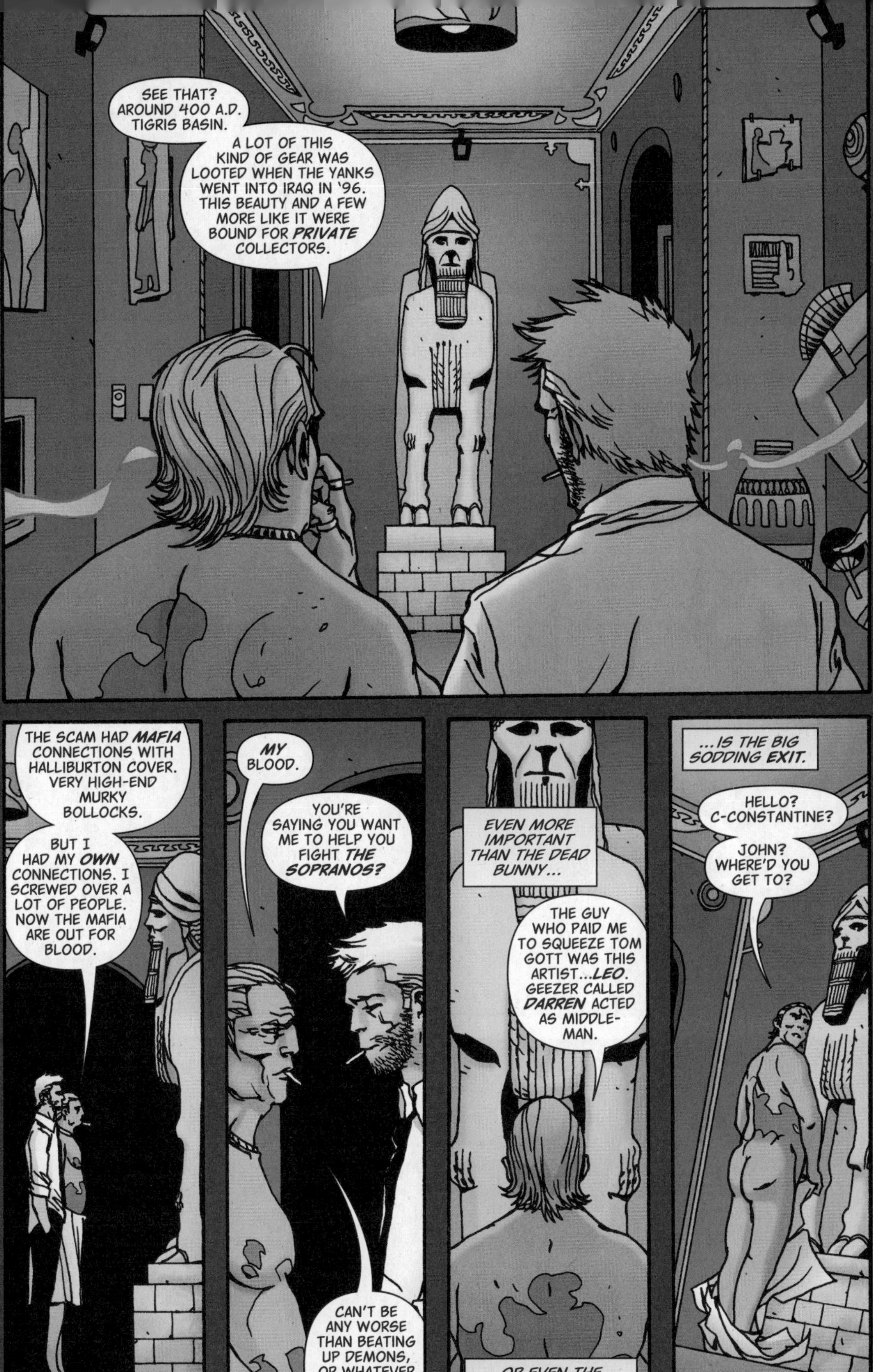
SEE THAT? AROUND 400 A.D. TIGRIS BASIN.
A LOT OF THIS KIND OF GEAR WAS LOOTED WHEN THE YANKS WENT INTO IRAQ IN '96. THIS BEAUTY AND A FEW MORE LIKE IT WERE BOUND FOR PRIVATE COLLECTORS.
THE SCAM HAD MAFIA CONNECTIONS WITH HALLIBURTON COVER. VERY HIGH-END MURKY BOLLOCKS.
BUT I HAD MY OWN CONNECTIONS. I SCREWED OVER A LOT OF PEOPLE. NOW THE MAFIA ARE OUT FOR BLOOD.
MY BLOOD.
YOU'RE SAYING YOU WANT ME TO HELP YOU FIGHT THE SOPRANOS?
CAN'T BE ANY WORSE THAN BEATING UP DEMONS, OR WHATEVER THE FUCK IT IS YOU DO.
EVEN MORE IMPORTANT THAN THE DEAD BUNNY...
THE GUY WHO PAID ME TO SQUEEZE TOM GOTT WAS THIS ARTIST...LEO. GEEZER CALLED DARREN ACTED AS MIDDLE-MAN.
OR EVEN THE FLASHY ENTRANCE...
...IS THE BIG SODDING EXIT.
HELLO? C-CONSTANTINE?
JOHN? WHERE'D YOU GET TO?

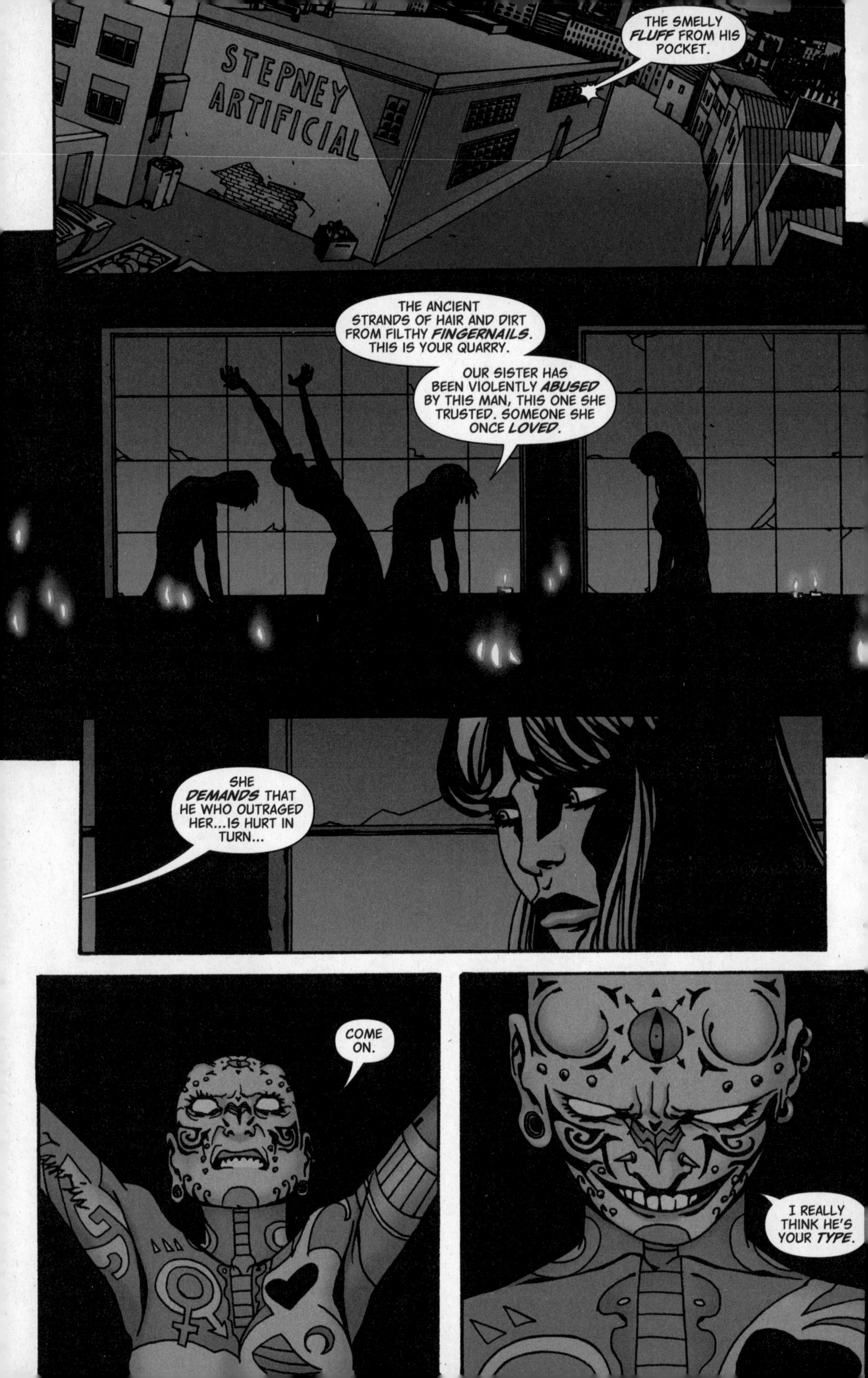
THE SMELLY FLUFF FROM HIS POCKET.
STEPNEY ARTIFICIAL
THE ANCIENT STRANDS OF HAIR AND DIRT FROM FILTHY FINGERNAILS. THIS IS YOUR QUARRY.
OUR SISTER HAS BEEN VIOLENTLY ABUSED BY THIS MAN, THIS ONE SHE TRUSTED. SOMEONE SHE ONCE LOVED.
SHE DEMANDS THAT HE WHO OUTRAGED HER...IS HURT IN TURN...
COME ON.
I REALLY THINK HE'S YOUR TYPE.

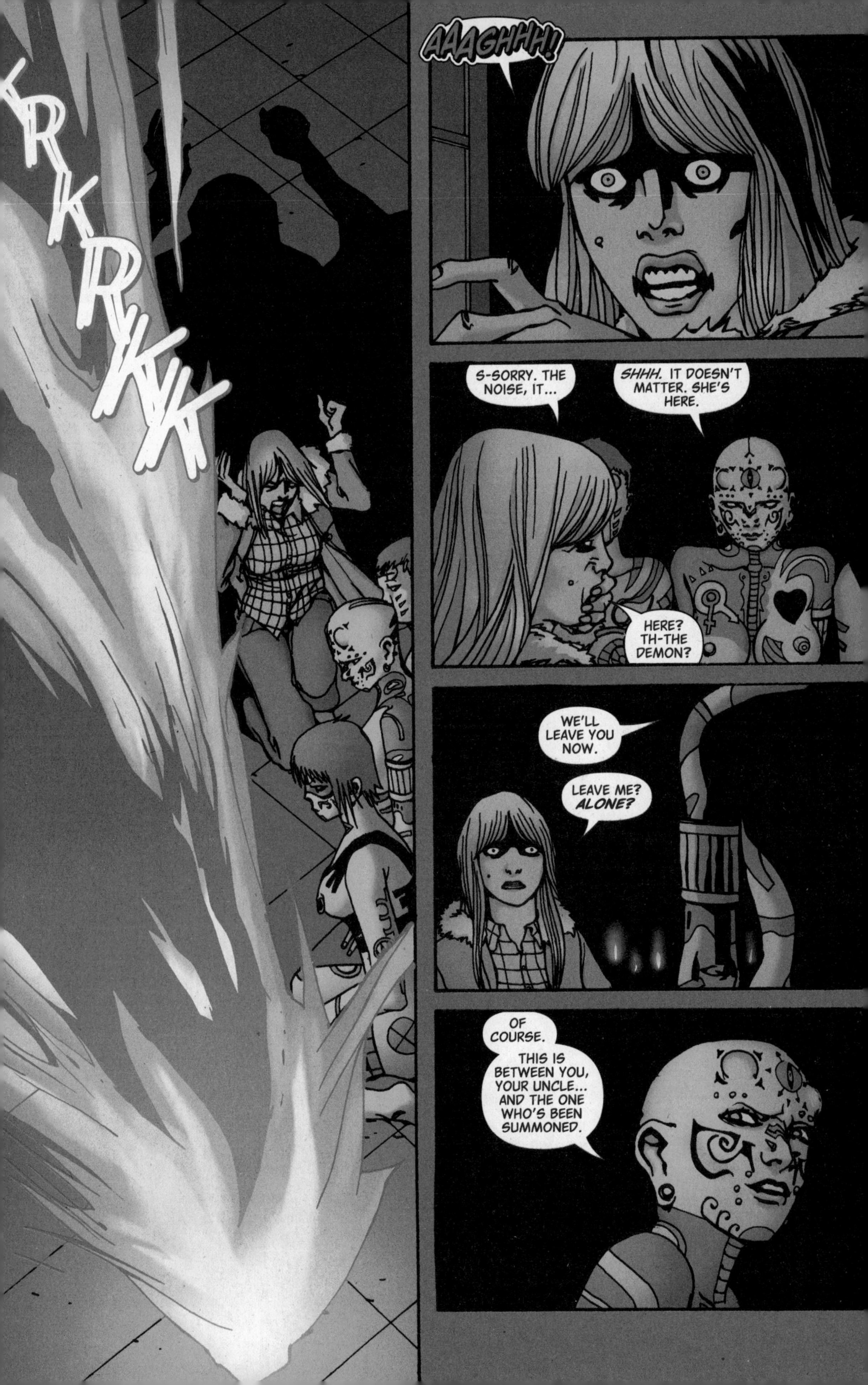
KRKRKKKK
AAAGHHH!
S-SORRY. THE NOISE, IT...
SHHH. IT DOESN'T MATTER. SHE'S HERE.
HERE? TH-THE DEMON?
WE'LL LEAVE YOU NOW.
LEAVE ME? ALONE?
OF COURSE.
THIS IS BETWEEN YOU, YOUR UNCLE... AND THE ONE WHO'S BEEN SUMMONED.

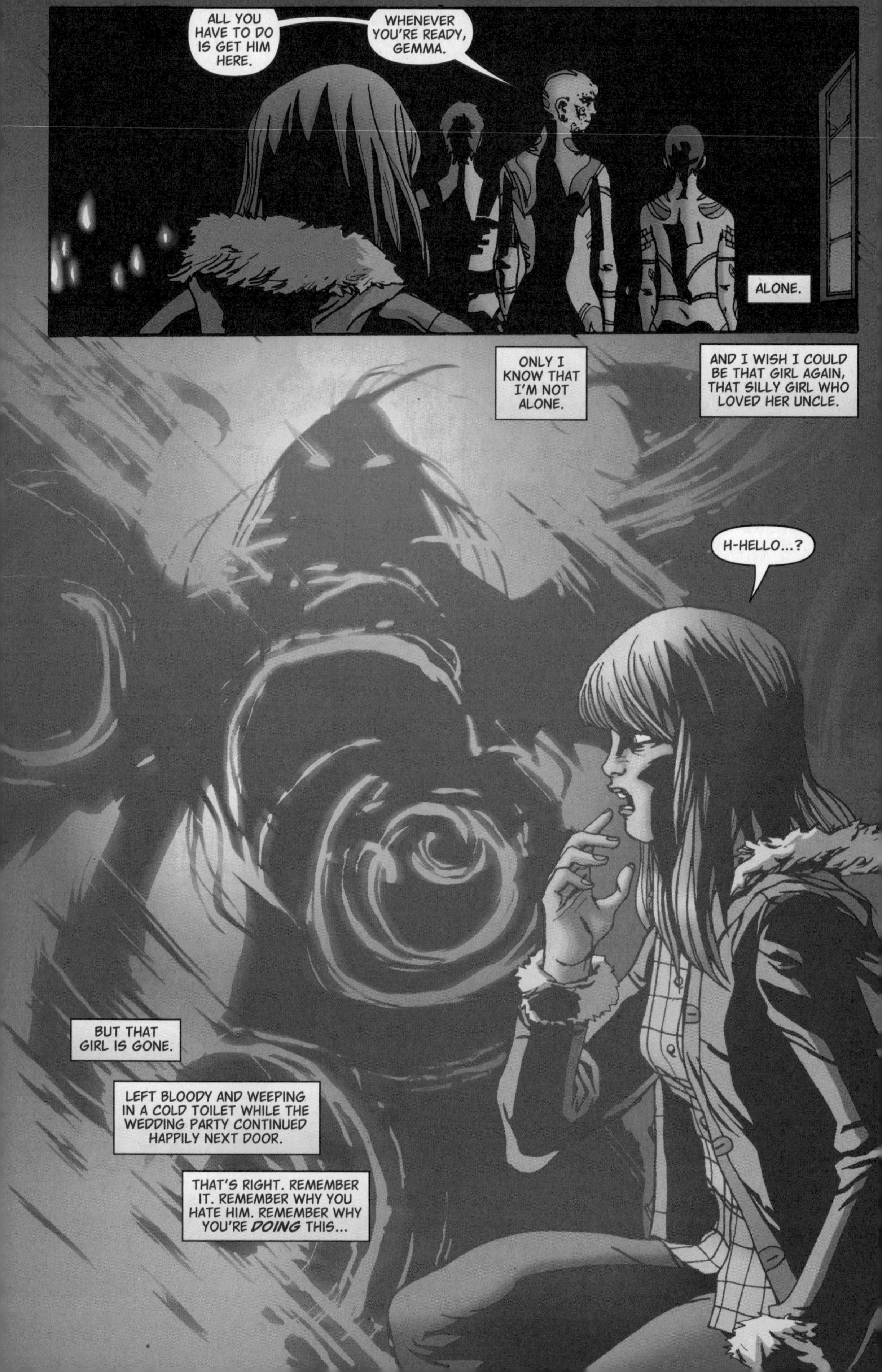
ALL YOU HAVE TO DO IS GET HIM HERE.
WHENEVER YOU'RE READY, GEMMA.
ALONE.
ONLY I KNOW THAT I'M NOT ALONE.
AND I WISH I COULD BE THAT GIRL AGAIN, THAT SILLY GIRL WHO LOVED HER UNCLE.
H-HELLO...?
BUT THAT GIRL IS GONE.
LEFT BLOODY AND WEEPING IN A COLD TOILET WHILE THE WEDDING PARTY CONTINUED HAPPILY NEXT DOOR.
THAT'S RIGHT. REMEMBER IT. REMEMBER WHY YOU HATE HIM. REMEMBER WHY YOU'RE *DOING* THIS...

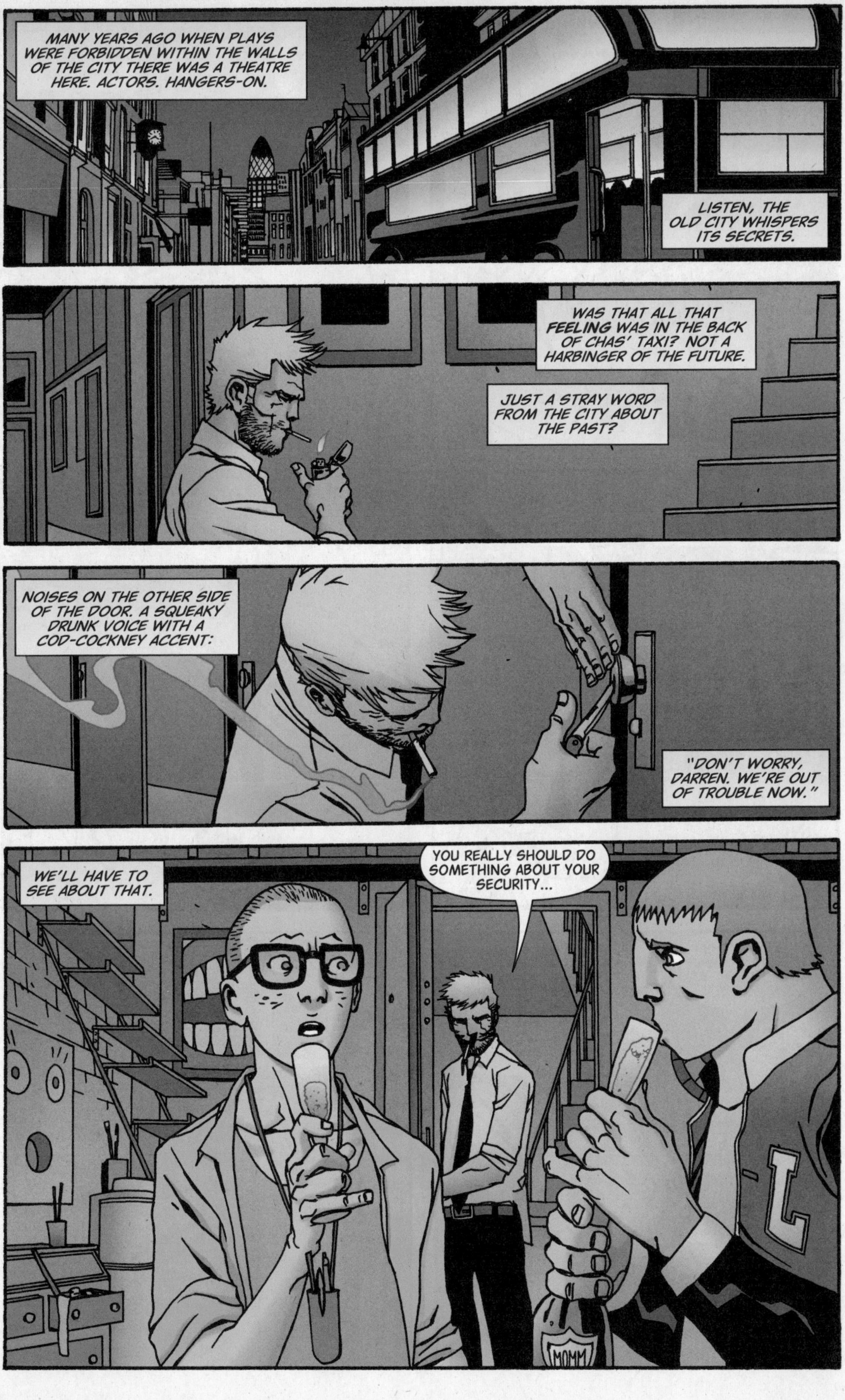
MANY YEARS AGO WHEN PLAYS WERE FORBIDDEN WITHIN THE WALLS OF THE CITY THERE WAS A THEATRE HERE. ACTORS. HANGERS-ON.
LISTEN, THE OLD CITY WHISPERS ITS SECRETS.
WAS THAT ALL THAT FEELING WAS IN THE BACK OF CHAS' TAXI? NOT A HARBINGER OF THE FUTURE.
JUST A STRAY WORD FROM THE CITY ABOUT THE PAST?
NOISES ON THE OTHER SIDE OF THE DOOR. A SQUEAKY DRUNK VOICE WITH A COD-COCKNEY ACCENT:
"DON'T WORRY, DARREN. WE'RE OUT OF TROUBLE NOW."
WE'LL HAVE TO SEE ABOUT THAT.
YOU REALLY SHOULD DO SOMETHING ABOUT YOUR SECURITY...
MOMM

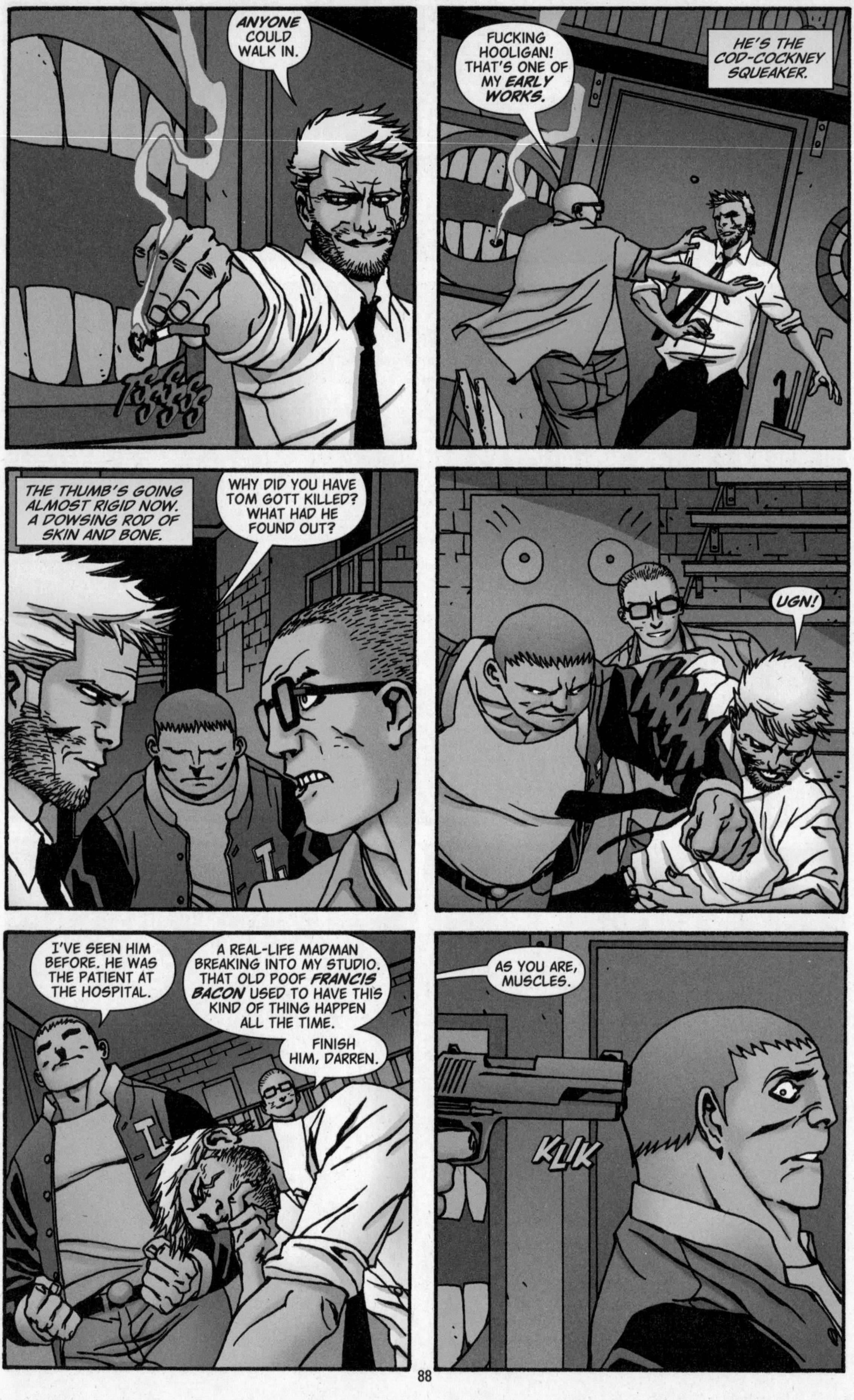
ANYONE COULD WALK IN.
FUCKING HOOLIGAN! THAT'S ONE OF MY EARLY WORKS.
HE'S THE COD-COCKNEY SQUEAKER.
THE THUMB'S GOING ALMOST RIGID NOW. A DOWSING ROD OF SKIN AND BONE.
WHY DID YOU HAVE TOM GOTT KILLED? WHAT HAD HE FOUND OUT?
UGN!
I'VE SEEN HIM BEFORE. HE WAS THE PATIENT AT THE HOSPITAL.
A REAL-LIFE MADMAN BREAKING INTO MY STUDIO. THAT OLD POOF FRANCIS BACON USED TO HAVE THIS KIND OF THING HAPPEN ALL THE TIME.
FINISH HIM, DARREN.
AS YOU ARE, MUSCLES.
KLIK

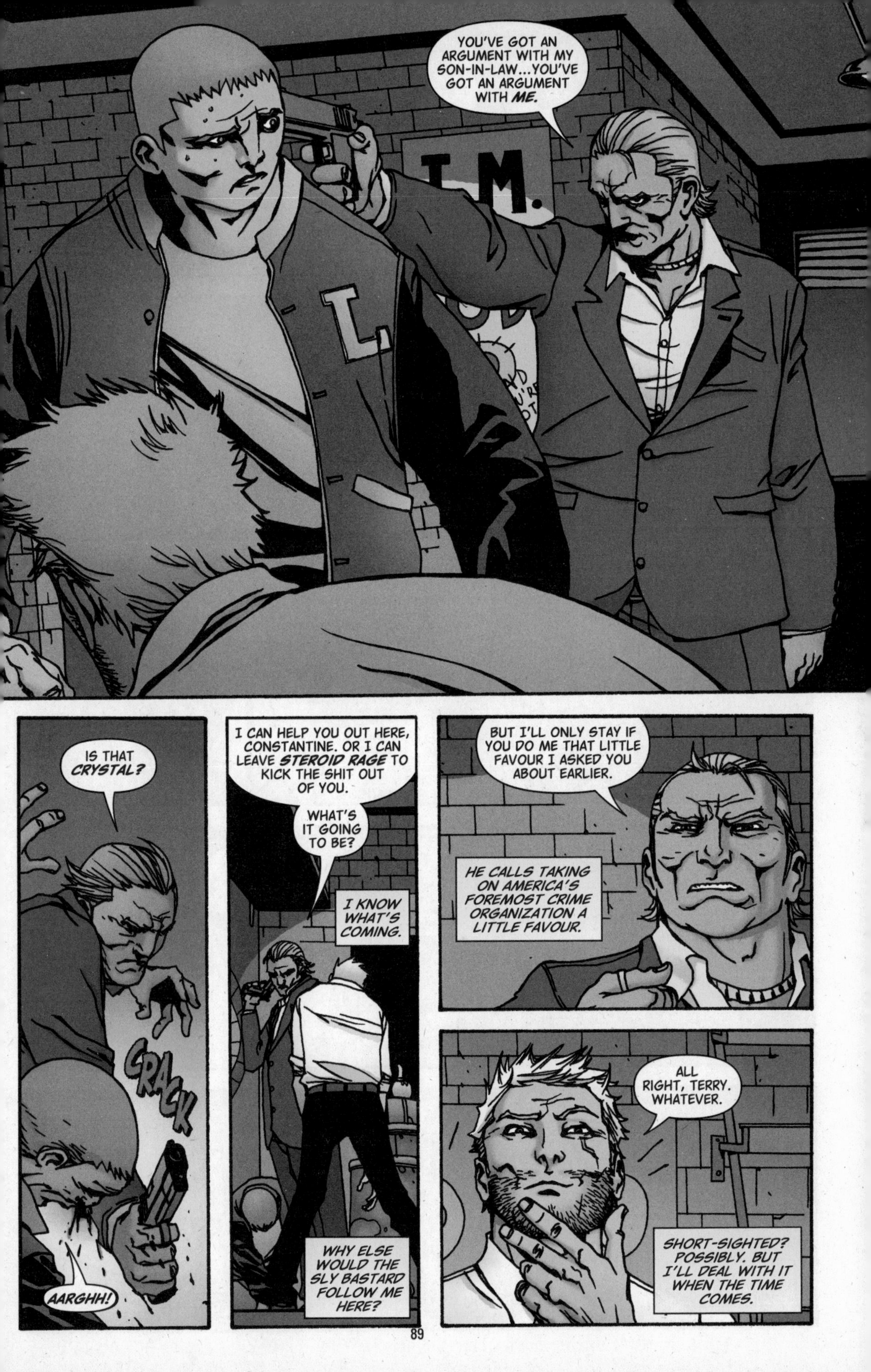
YOU'VE GOT AN ARGUMENT WITH MY SON-IN-LAW...YOU'VE GOT AN ARGUMENT WITH *ME.*
I.M.
L
IS THAT *CRYSTAL?*
CRACK
AARGHH!
I CAN HELP YOU OUT HERE, CONSTANTINE. OR I CAN LEAVE *STEROID RAGE* TO KICK THE SHIT OUT OF YOU.
WHAT'S IT GOING TO BE?
I KNOW WHAT'S COMING.
WHY ELSE WOULD THE SLY BASTARD FOLLOW ME HERE?
BUT I'LL ONLY STAY IF YOU DO ME THAT LITTLE FAVOUR I ASKED YOU ABOUT EARLIER.
HE CALLS TAKING ON AMERICA'S FOREMOST CRIME ORGANIZATION A LITTLE FAVOUR.
ALL RIGHT, TERRY. WHATEVER.
SHORT-SIGHTED? POSSIBLY. BUT I'LL DEAL WITH IT WHEN THE TIME COMES.

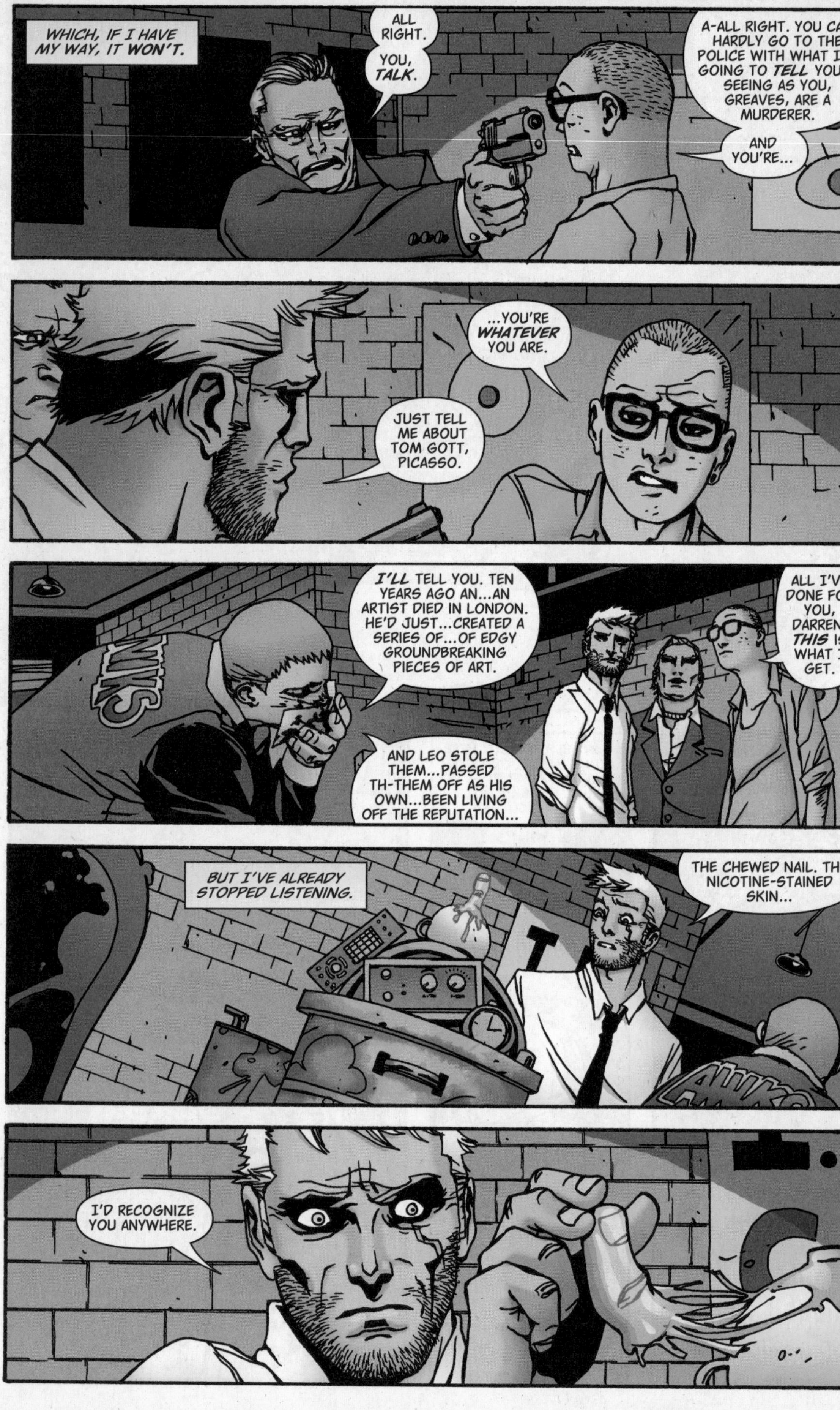

WHICH, IF I HAVE MY WAY, IT WON'T.
ALL RIGHT.
YOU, TALK.
A-ALL RIGHT. YOU CAN HARDLY GO TO THE POLICE WITH WHAT I'M GOING TO TELL YOU... SEEING AS YOU, GREAVES, ARE A MURDERER.
AND YOU'RE...
...YOU'RE WHATEVER YOU ARE.
JUST TELL ME ABOUT TOM GOTT, PICASSO.
I'LL TELL YOU. TEN YEARS AGO AN...AN ARTIST DIED IN LONDON. HE'D JUST...CREATED A SERIES OF...OF EDGY GROUNDBREAKING PIECES OF ART.
AND LEO STOLE THEM...PASSED TH-THEM OFF AS HIS OWN...BEEN LIVING OFF THE REPUTATION...
ALL I'VE DONE FOR YOU, DARREN. THIS IS WHAT I GET.
BUT I'VE ALREADY STOPPED LISTENING.
THE CHEWED NAIL. THE NICOTINE-STAINED SKIN...
I'D RECOGNIZE YOU ANYWHERE.

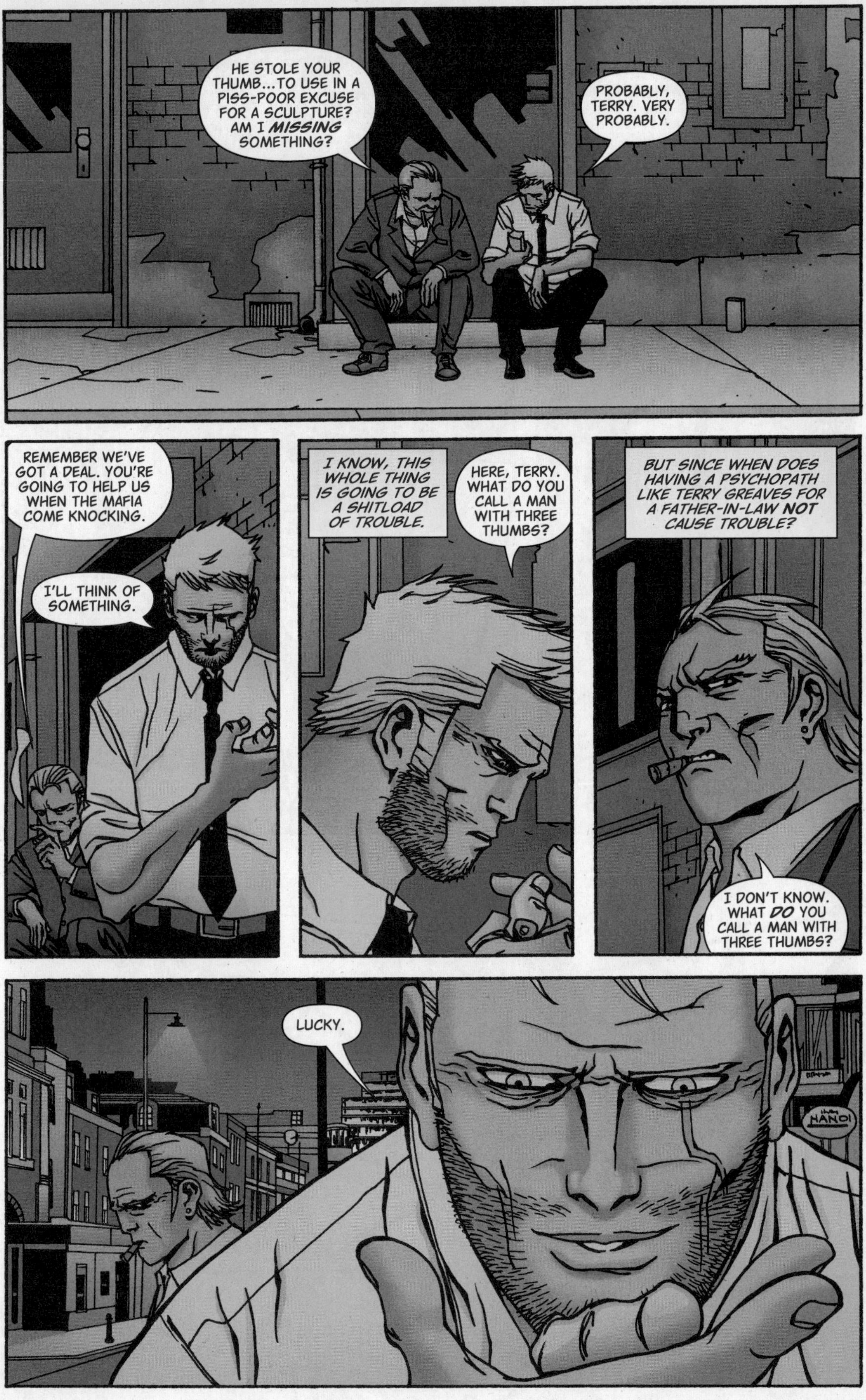
HE STOLE YOUR THUMB...TO USE IN A PISS-POOR EXCUSE FOR A SCULPTURE? AM I *MISSING* SOMETHING?
PROBABLY, TERRY. VERY PROBABLY.
REMEMBER WE'VE GOT A DEAL. YOU'RE GOING TO HELP US WHEN THE MAFIA COME KNOCKING.
I'LL THINK OF SOMETHING.
I KNOW, THIS WHOLE THING IS GOING TO BE A SHITLOAD OF TROUBLE.
HERE, TERRY. WHAT DO YOU CALL A MAN WITH THREE THUMBS?
BUT SINCE WHEN DOES HAVING A PSYCHOPATH LIKE TERRY GREAVES FOR A FATHER-IN-LAW ***NOT*** *CAUSE TROUBLE?*
I DON'T KNOW. WHAT ***DO*** YOU CALL A MAN WITH THREE THUMBS?
LUCKY.
HANOI

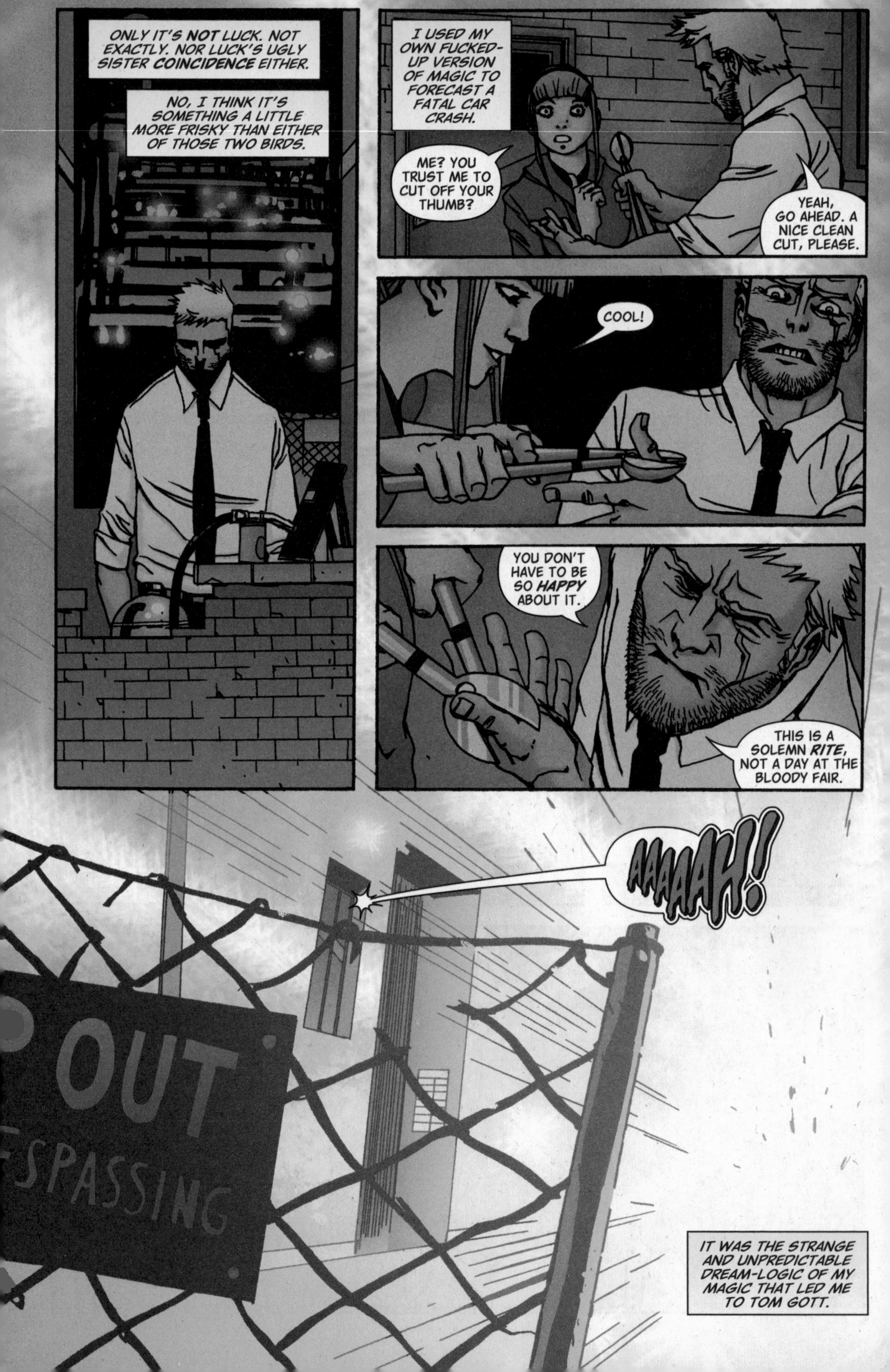
ONLY IT'S NOT LUCK. NOT EXACTLY. NOR LUCK'S UGLY SISTER COINCIDENCE EITHER.
NO, I THINK IT'S SOMETHING A LITTLE MORE FRISKY THAN EITHER OF THOSE TWO BIRDS.
I USED MY OWN FUCKED-UP VERSION OF MAGIC TO FORECAST A FATAL CAR CRASH.
ME? YOU TRUST ME TO CUT OFF YOUR THUMB?
YEAH, GO AHEAD. A NICE CLEAN CUT, PLEASE.
COOL!
YOU DON'T HAVE TO BE SO HAPPY ABOUT IT.
THIS IS A SOLEMN RITE, NOT A DAY AT THE BLOODY FAIR.
AAAAAH!
OUT
SPASSING
IT WAS THE STRANGE AND UNPREDICTABLE DREAM-LOGIC OF MY MAGIC THAT LED ME TO TOM GOTT.

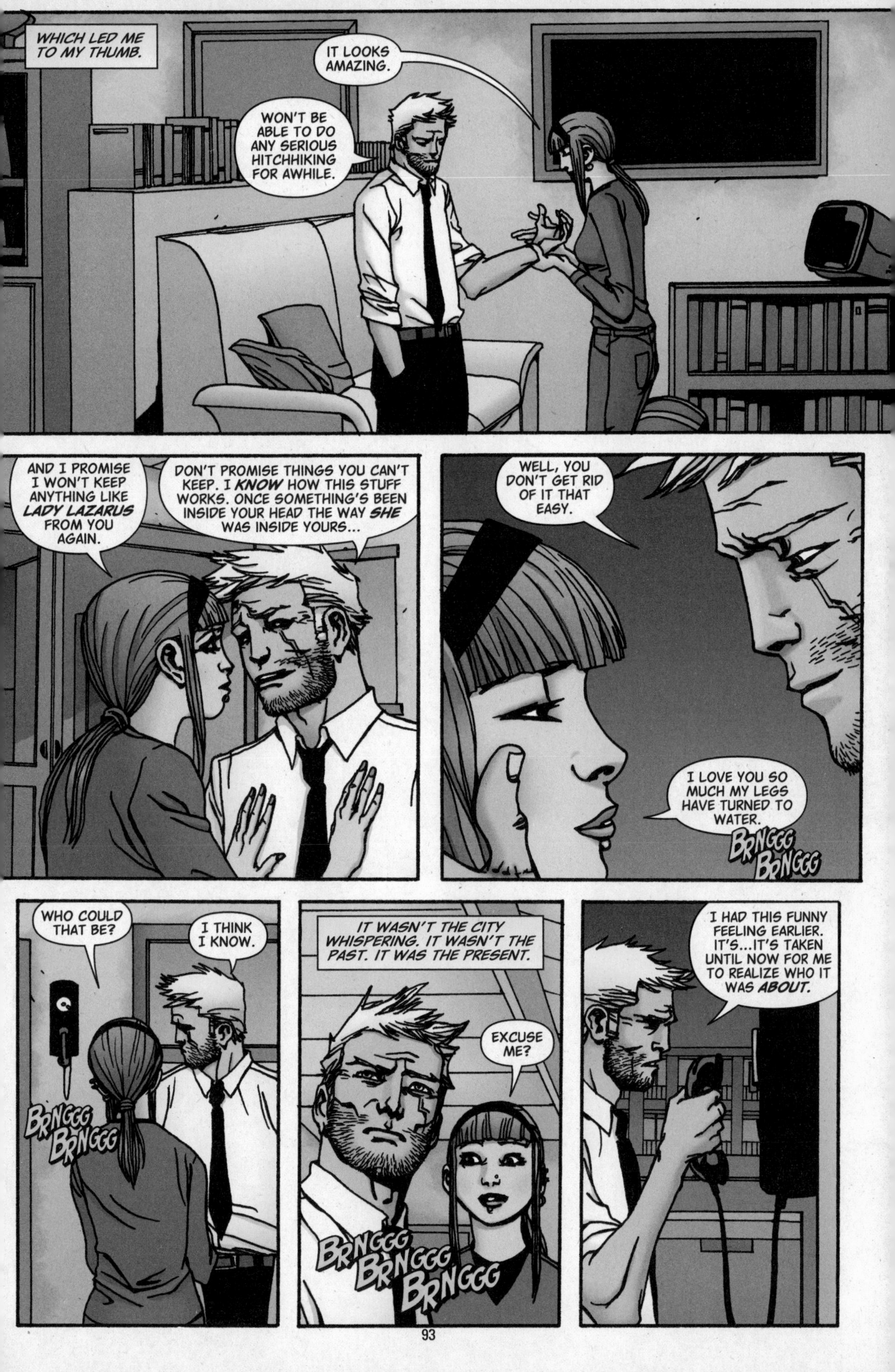
WHICH LED ME TO MY THUMB.
IT LOOKS AMAZING.
WON'T BE ABLE TO DO ANY SERIOUS HITCHHIKING FOR AWHILE.
AND I PROMISE I WON'T KEEP ANYTHING LIKE LADY LAZARUS FROM YOU AGAIN.
DON'T PROMISE THINGS YOU CAN'T KEEP. I KNOW HOW THIS STUFF WORKS. ONCE SOMETHING'S BEEN INSIDE YOUR HEAD THE WAY SHE WAS INSIDE YOURS...
WELL, YOU DON'T GET RID OF IT THAT EASY.
I LOVE YOU SO MUCH MY LEGS HAVE TURNED TO WATER.
BRNGGG BRNGGG
WHO COULD THAT BE?
I THINK I KNOW.
BRNGGG BRNGGG
IT WASN'T THE CITY WHISPERING. IT WASN'T THE PAST. IT WAS THE PRESENT.
EXCUSE ME?
BRNGGG BRNGGG BRNGGG
I HAD THIS FUNNY FEELING EARLIER. IT'S...IT'S TAKEN UNTIL NOW FOR ME TO REALIZE WHO IT WAS ABOUT.

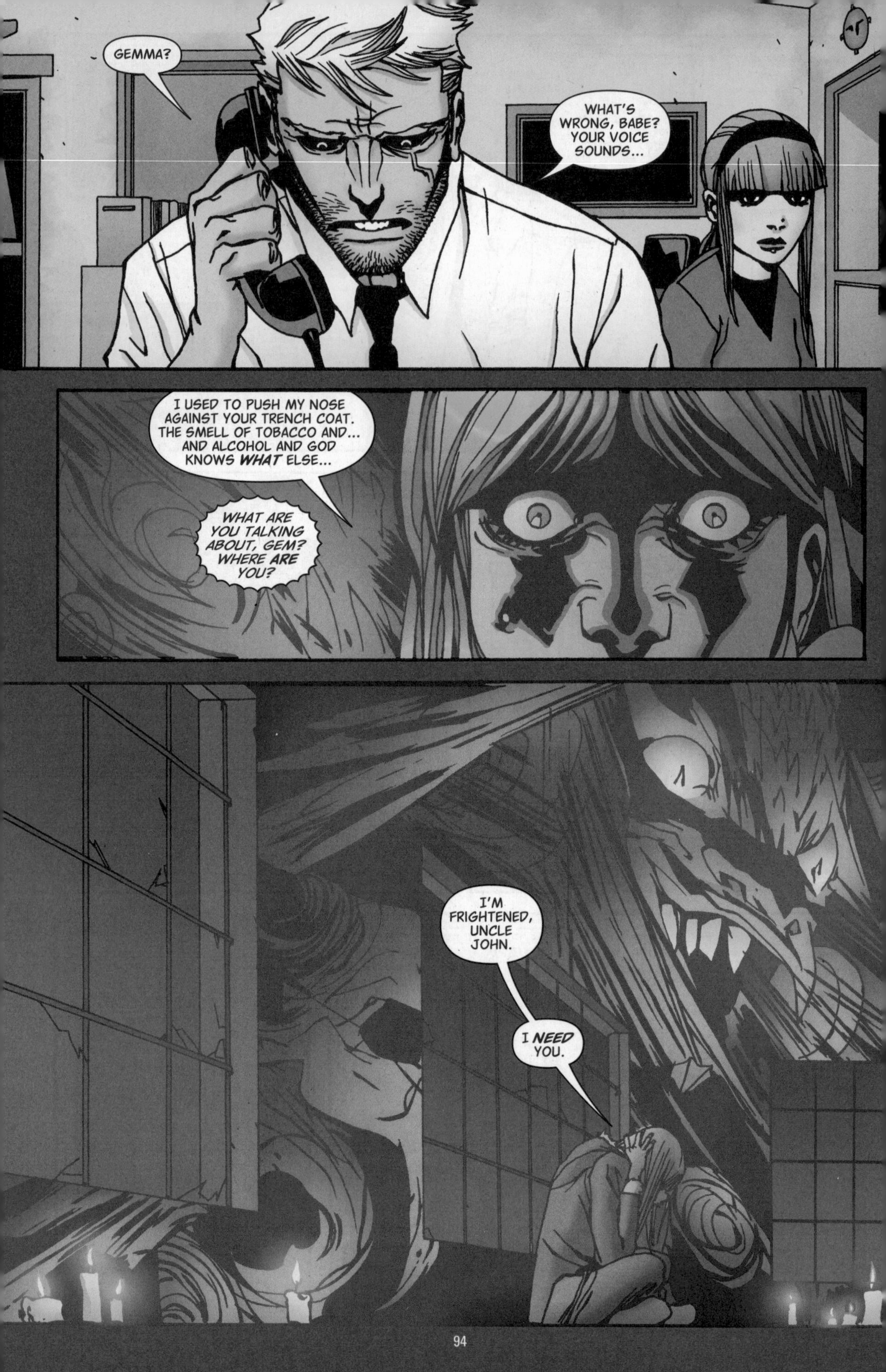
GEMMA?
WHAT'S WRONG, BABE? YOUR VOICE SOUNDS...
I USED TO PUSH MY NOSE AGAINST YOUR TRENCH COAT. THE SMELL OF TOBACCO AND... AND ALCOHOL AND GOD KNOWS *WHAT* ELSE...
WHAT ARE YOU TALKING ABOUT, GEM? WHERE *ARE* YOU?
I'M FRIGHTENED, UNCLE JOHN.
I *NEED* YOU.

Phantom Pains, Part Four
Gemma's Story

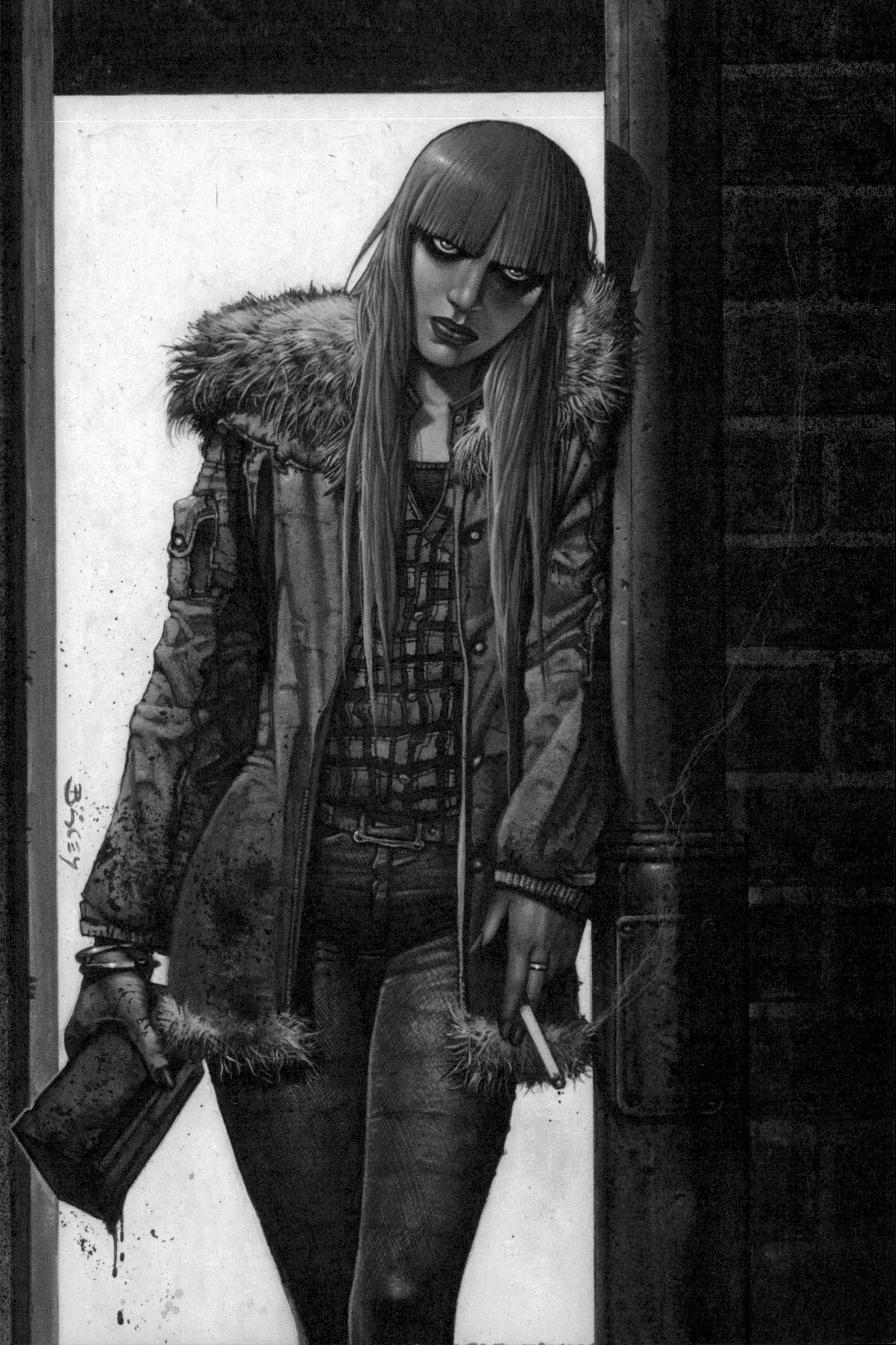

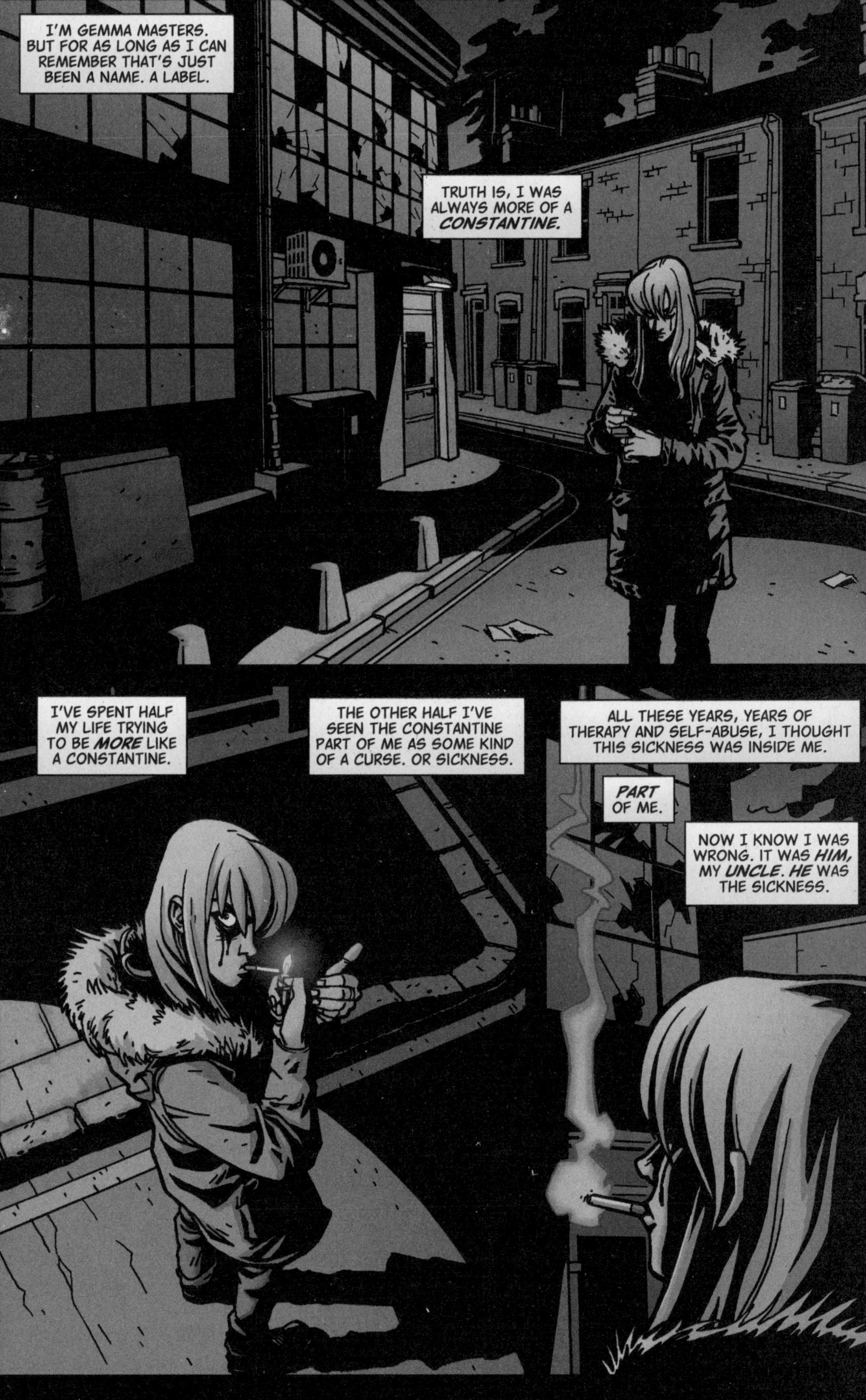
I'M GEMMA MASTERS. BUT FOR AS LONG AS I CAN REMEMBER THAT'S JUST BEEN A NAME. A LABEL.
TRUTH IS, I WAS ALWAYS MORE OF A *CONSTANTINE.*
I'VE SPENT HALF MY LIFE TRYING TO BE *MORE* LIKE A CONSTANTINE.
THE OTHER HALF I'VE SEEN THE CONSTANTINE PART OF ME AS SOME KIND OF A CURSE. OR SICKNESS.
ALL THESE YEARS, YEARS OF THERAPY AND SELF-ABUSE, I THOUGHT THIS SICKNESS WAS INSIDE ME.
PART OF ME.
NOW I KNOW I WAS WRONG. IT WAS *HIM,* MY *UNCLE*. *HE* WAS THE SICKNESS.

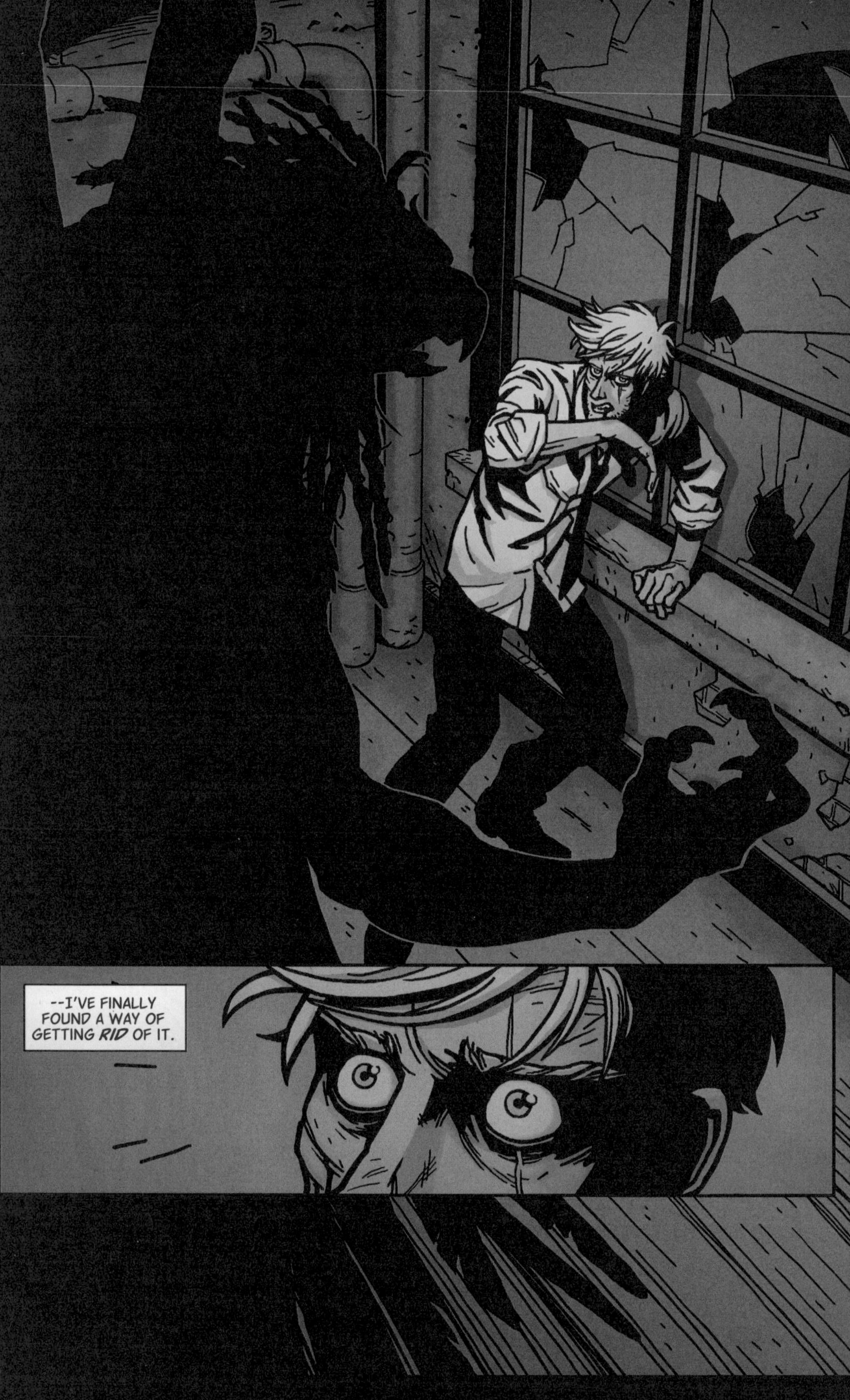
--I'VE FINALLY FOUND A WAY OF GETTING *RID* OF IT.

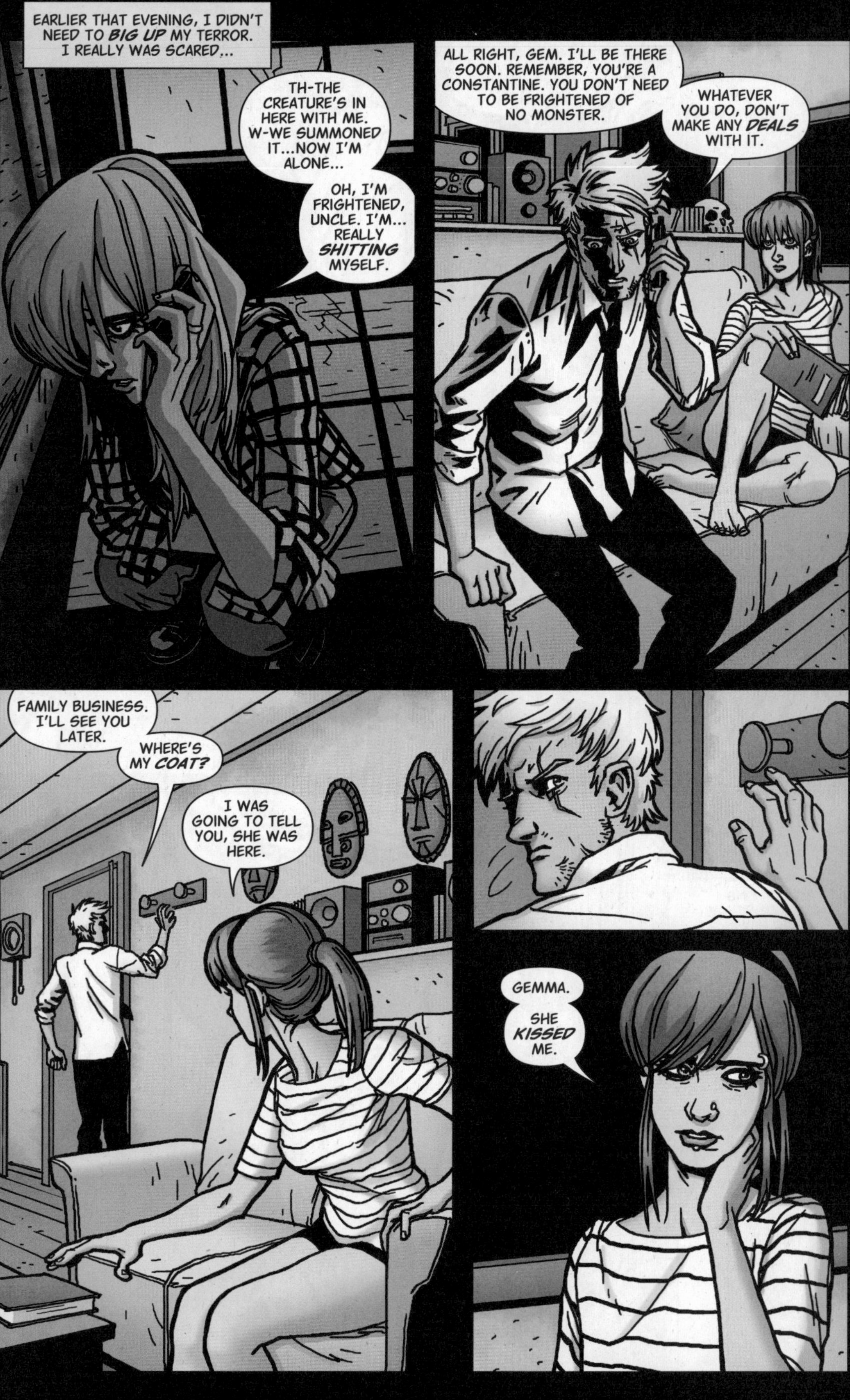
EARLIER THAT EVENING, I DIDN'T NEED TO *BIG UP* MY TERROR. I REALLY WAS SCARED...
TH-THE CREATURE'S IN HERE WITH ME. W-WE SUMMONED IT...NOW I'M ALONE...
OH, I'M FRIGHTENED, UNCLE. I'M... REALLY *SHITTING* MYSELF.
ALL RIGHT, GEM. I'LL BE THERE SOON. REMEMBER, YOU'RE A CONSTANTINE. YOU DON'T NEED TO BE FRIGHTENED OF NO MONSTER.
WHATEVER YOU DO, DON'T MAKE ANY *DEALS* WITH IT.
FAMILY BUSINESS. I'LL SEE YOU LATER.
WHERE'S MY *COAT?*
I WAS GOING TO TELL YOU, SHE WAS HERE.
GEMMA.
SHE *KISSED* ME.

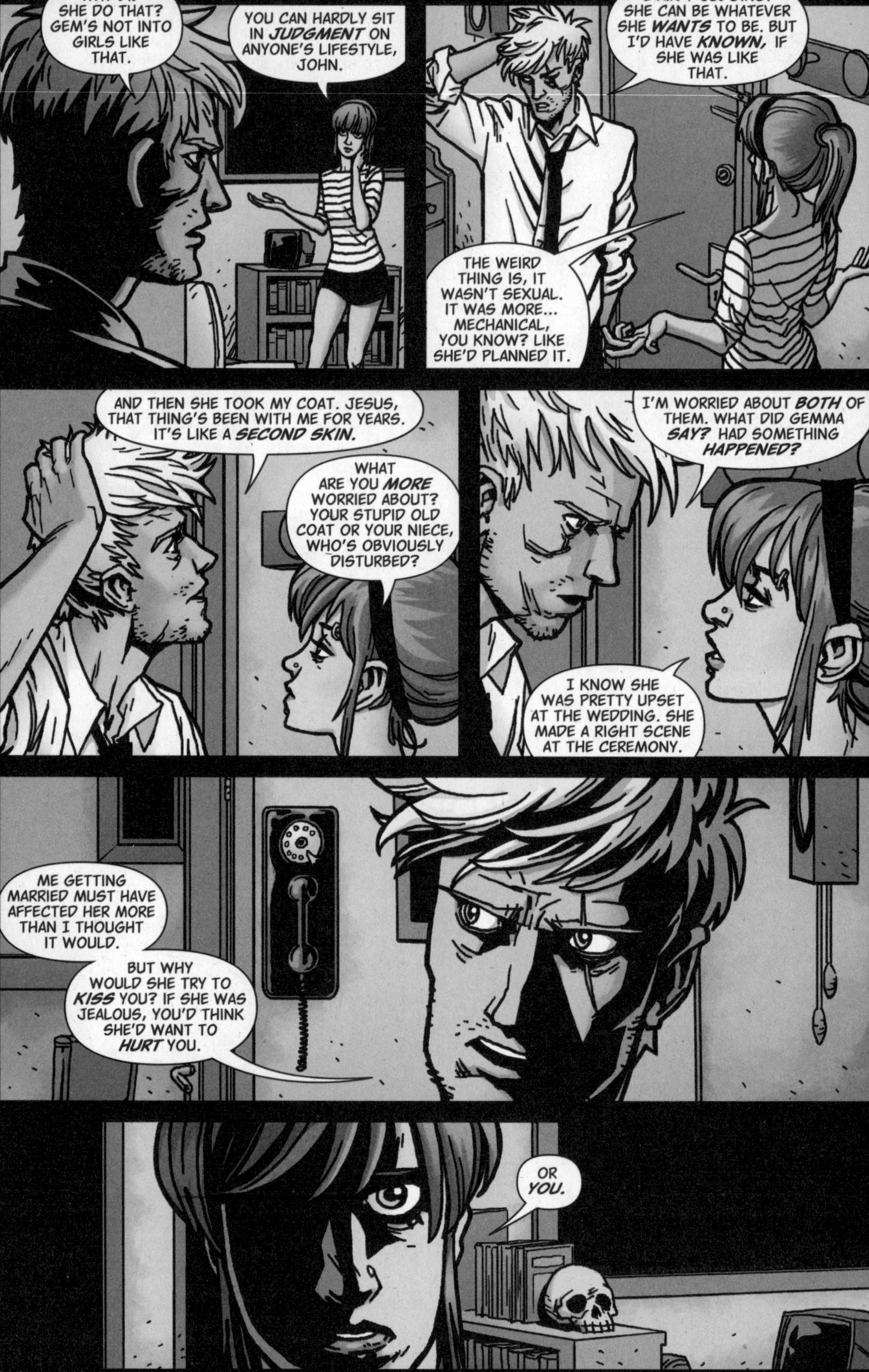
WHY DID SHE DO THAT? GEM'S NOT INTO GIRLS LIKE THAT.
YOU CAN HARDLY SIT IN JUDGMENT ON ANYONE'S LIFESTYLE, JOHN.
I AIN'T JUDGING. SHE CAN BE WHATEVER SHE WANTS TO BE. BUT I'D HAVE KNOWN, IF SHE WAS LIKE THAT.
THE WEIRD THING IS, IT WASN'T SEXUAL. IT WAS MORE... MECHANICAL, YOU KNOW? LIKE SHE'D PLANNED IT.
AND THEN SHE TOOK MY COAT. JESUS, THAT THING'S BEEN WITH ME FOR YEARS. IT'S LIKE A SECOND SKIN.
WHAT ARE YOU MORE WORRIED ABOUT? YOUR STUPID OLD COAT OR YOUR NIECE, WHO'S OBVIOUSLY DISTURBED?
I'M WORRIED ABOUT BOTH OF THEM. WHAT DID GEMMA SAY? HAD SOMETHING HAPPENED?
I KNOW SHE WAS PRETTY UPSET AT THE WEDDING. SHE MADE A RIGHT SCENE AT THE CEREMONY.
ME GETTING MARRIED MUST HAVE AFFECTED HER MORE THAN I THOUGHT IT WOULD.
BUT WHY WOULD SHE TRY TO KISS YOU? IF SHE WAS JEALOUS, YOU'D THINK SHE'D WANT TO HURT YOU.
OR YOU.

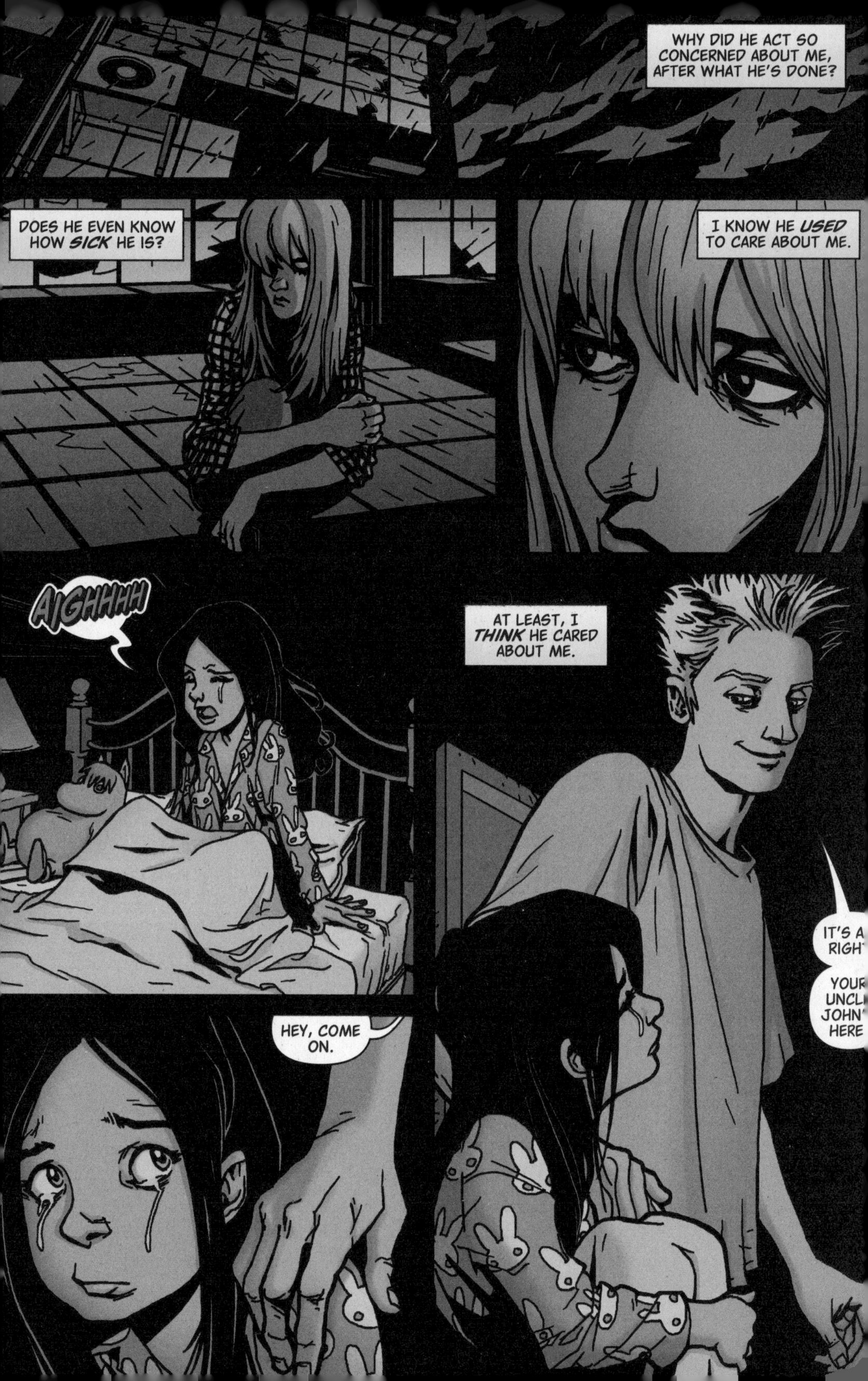
WHY DID HE ACT SO CONCERNED ABOUT ME, AFTER WHAT HE'S DONE?
DOES HE EVEN KNOW HOW SICK HE IS?
I KNOW HE USED TO CARE ABOUT ME.
AIGHHHH
AT LEAST, I THINK HE CARED ABOUT ME.
HEY, COME ON.

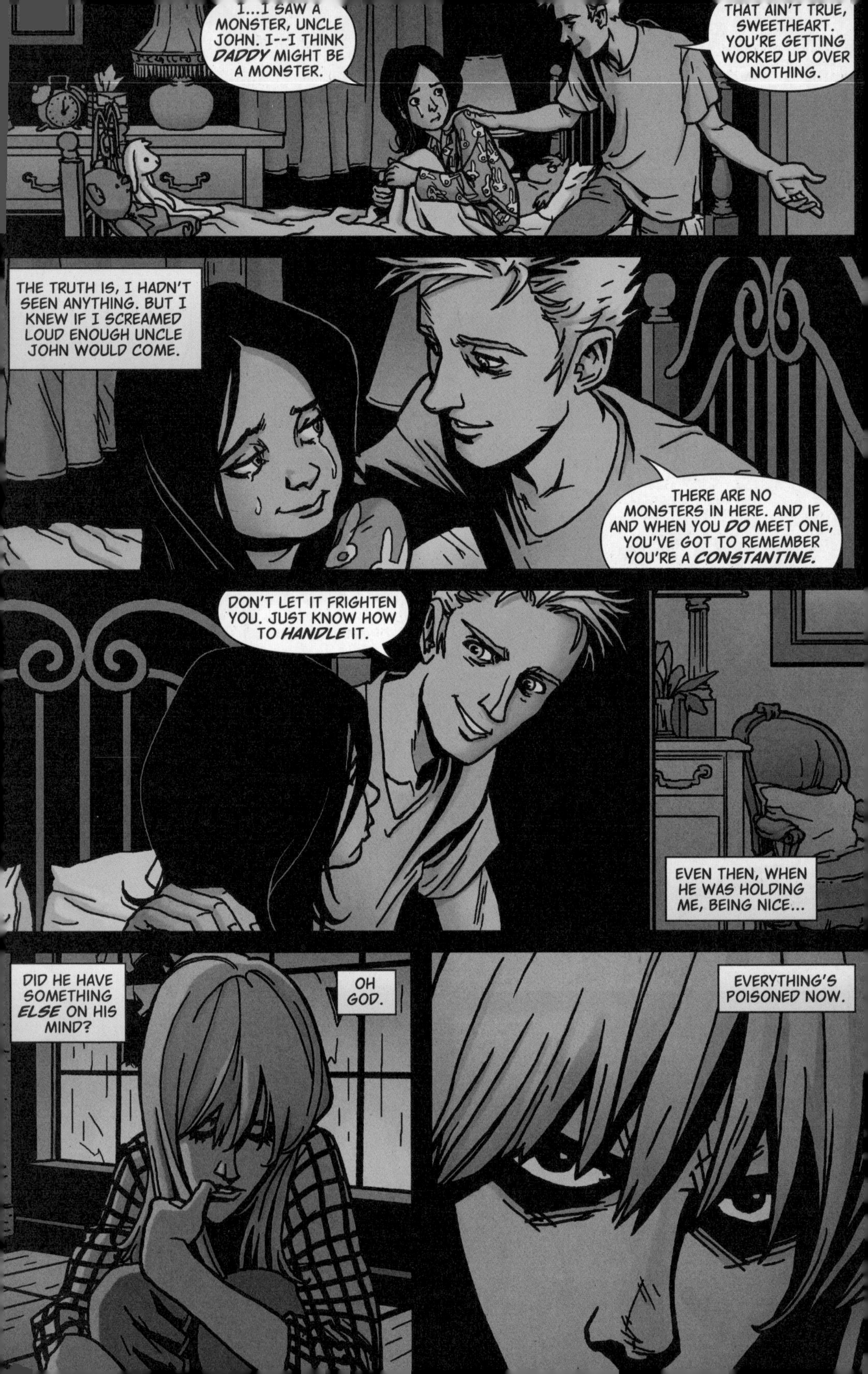
I...I SAW A MONSTER, UNCLE JOHN. I--I THINK DADDY MIGHT BE A MONSTER.
THAT AIN'T TRUE, SWEETHEART. YOU'RE GETTING WORKED UP OVER NOTHING.
THE TRUTH IS, I HADN'T SEEN ANYTHING. BUT I KNEW IF I SCREAMED LOUD ENOUGH UNCLE JOHN WOULD COME.
THERE ARE NO MONSTERS IN HERE. AND IF AND WHEN YOU DO MEET ONE, YOU'VE GOT TO REMEMBER YOU'RE A CONSTANTINE.
DON'T LET IT FRIGHTEN YOU. JUST KNOW HOW TO HANDLE IT.
EVEN THEN, WHEN HE WAS HOLDING ME, BEING NICE...
DID HE HAVE SOMETHING ELSE ON HIS MIND?
OH GOD.
EVERYTHING'S POISONED NOW.

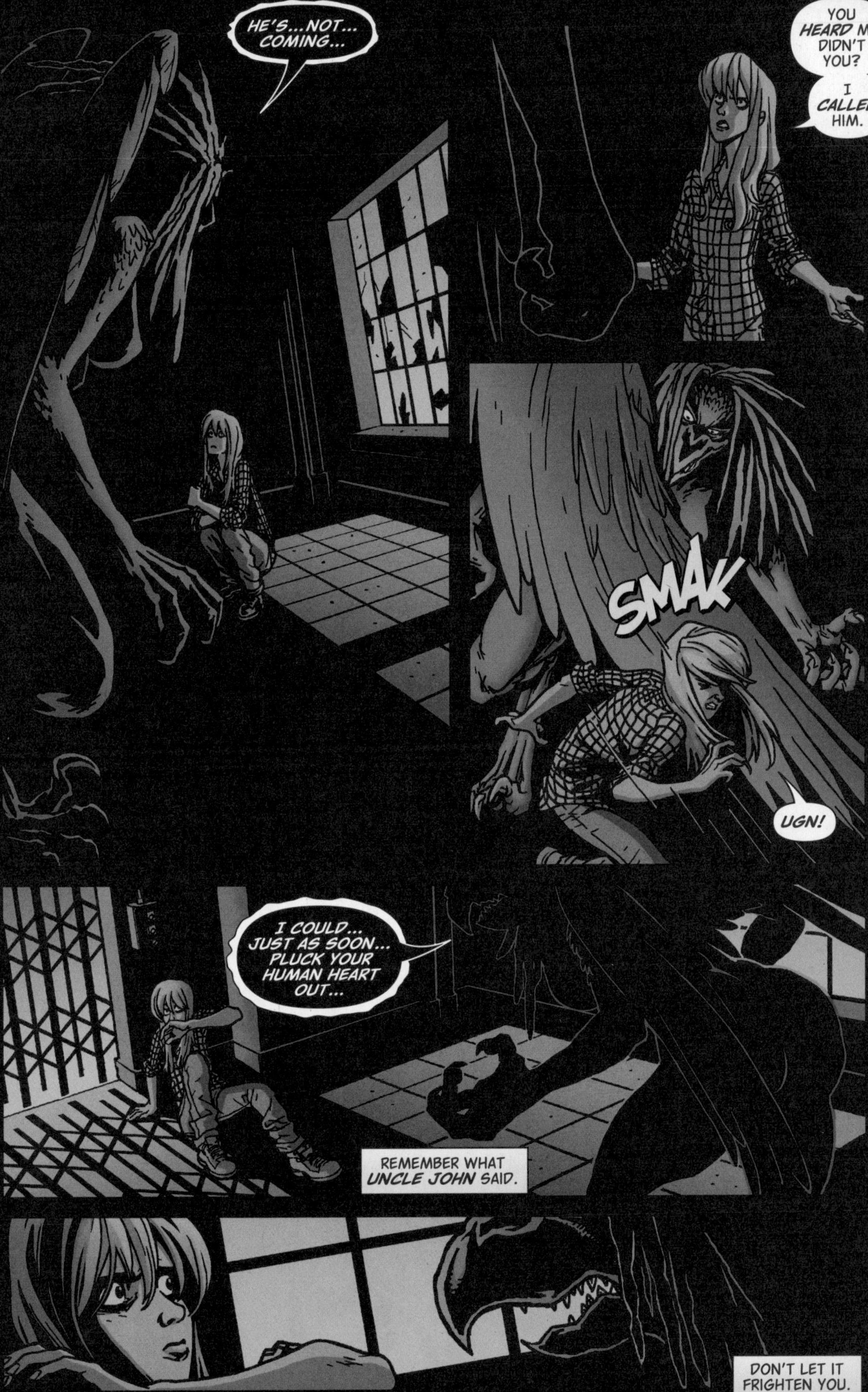
HE'S...NOT... COMING...
YOU HEARD ME, DIDN'T YOU?
I CALLED HIM.
SMAK
UGN!
I COULD... JUST AS SOON... PLUCK YOUR HUMAN HEART OUT...
REMEMBER WHAT UNCLE JOHN SAID.
DON'T LET IT FRIGHTEN YOU.

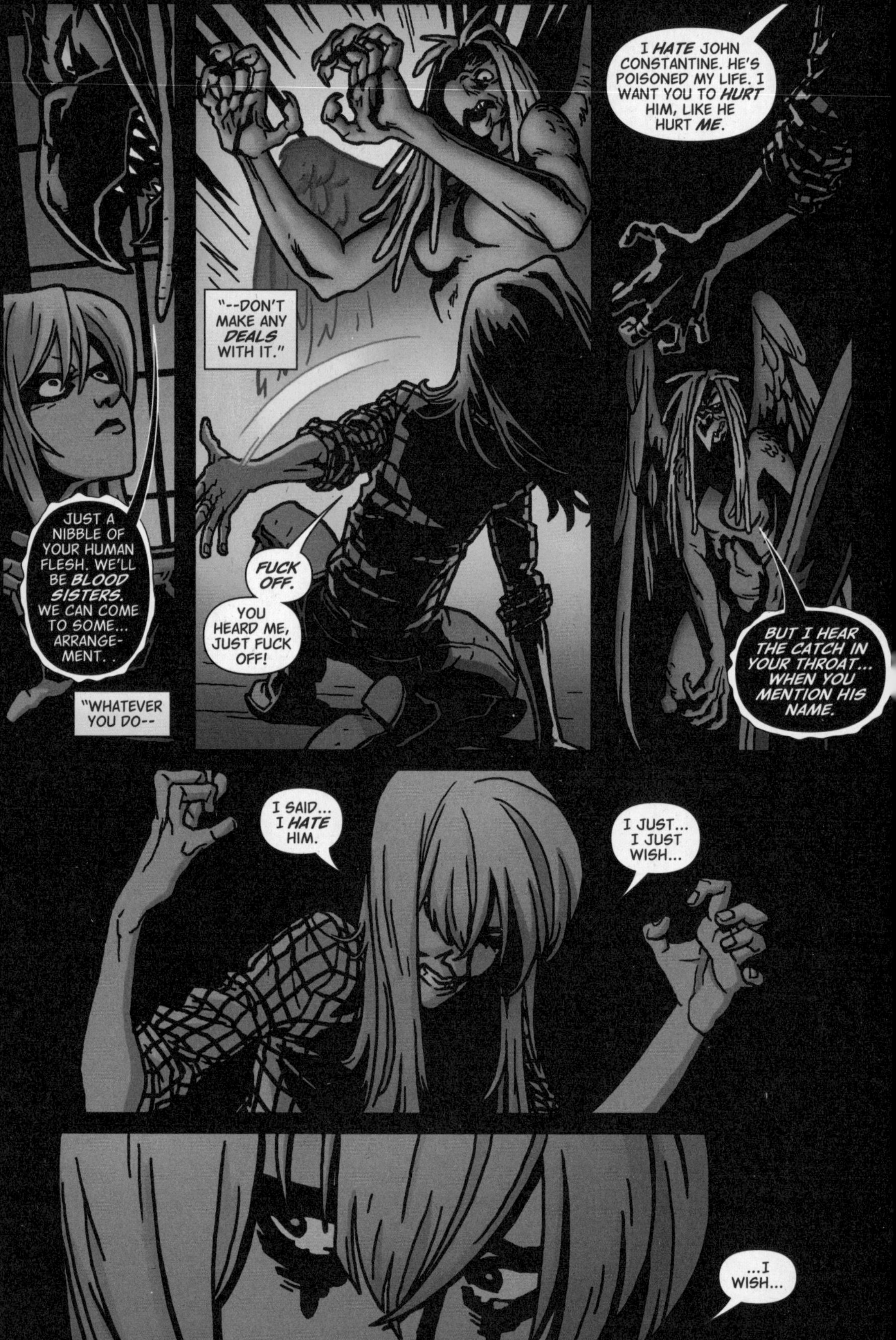
JUST A NIBBLE OF YOUR HUMAN FLESH. WE'LL BE BLOOD SISTERS. WE CAN COME TO SOME... ARRANGE-MENT. .
"WHATEVER YOU DO--
"--DON'T MAKE ANY DEALS WITH IT."
FUCK OFF.
YOU HEARD ME, JUST FUCK OFF!
I HATE JOHN CONSTANTINE. HE'S POISONED MY LIFE. I WANT YOU TO HURT HIM, LIKE HE HURT ME.
BUT I HEAR THE CATCH IN YOUR THROAT... WHEN YOU MENTION HIS NAME.
I SAID... I HATE HIM.
I JUST... I JUST WISH...
...I WISH...

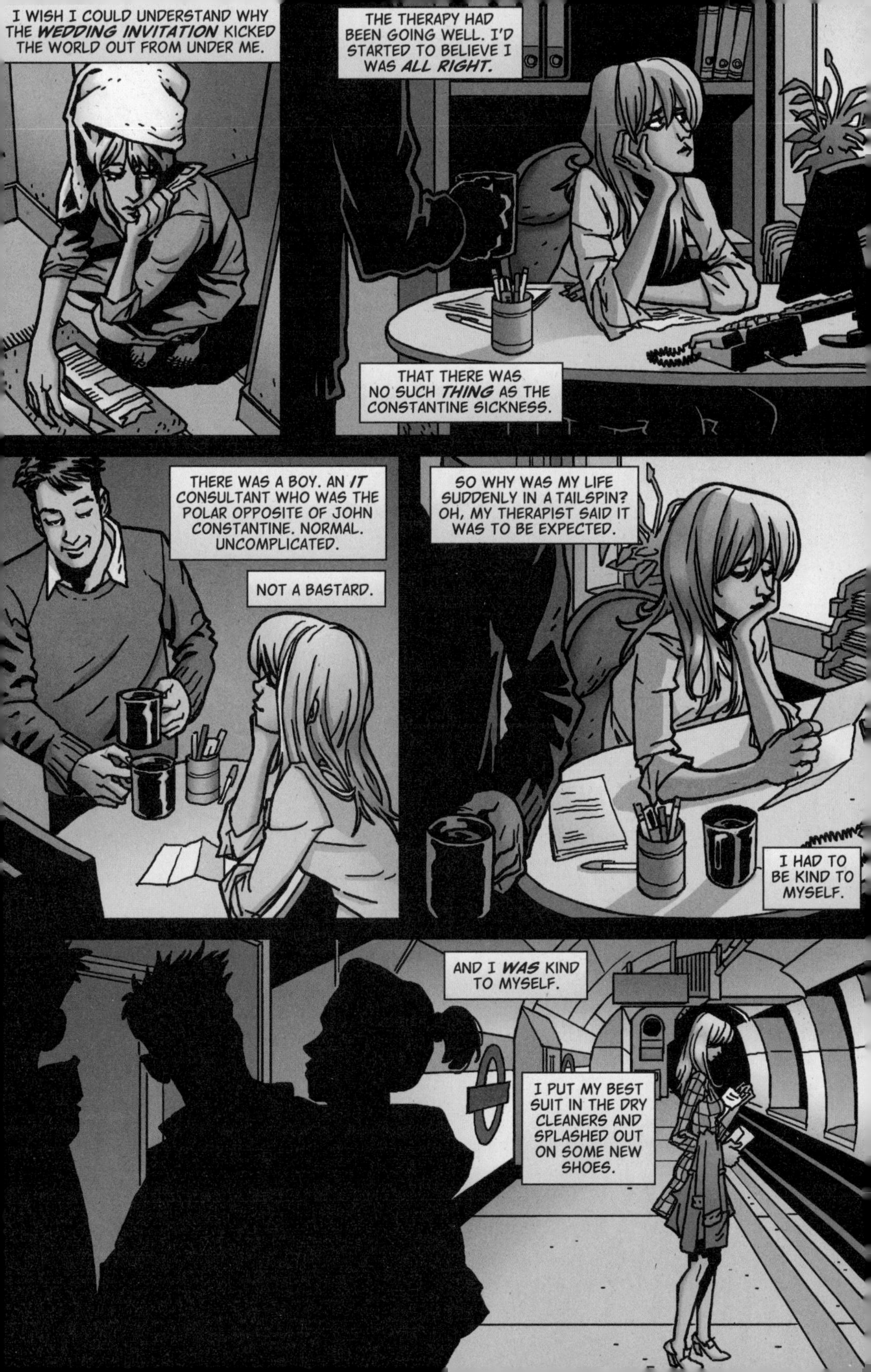
I WISH I COULD UNDERSTAND WHY THE ***WEDDING INVITATION*** KICKED THE WORLD OUT FROM UNDER ME.
THE THERAPY HAD BEEN GOING WELL. I'D STARTED TO BELIEVE I WAS ***ALL RIGHT.***
THAT THERE WAS NO SUCH ***THING*** AS THE CONSTANTINE SICKNESS.
THERE WAS A BOY. AN *IT* CONSULTANT WHO WAS THE POLAR OPPOSITE OF JOHN CONSTANTINE. NORMAL. UNCOMPLICATED.
NOT A BASTARD.
SO WHY WAS MY LIFE SUDDENLY IN A TAILSPIN? OH, MY THERAPIST SAID IT WAS TO BE EXPECTED.
I HAD TO BE KIND TO MYSELF.
AND I ***WAS*** KIND TO MYSELF.
I PUT MY BEST SUIT IN THE DRY CLEANERS AND SPLASHED OUT ON SOME NEW SHOES.

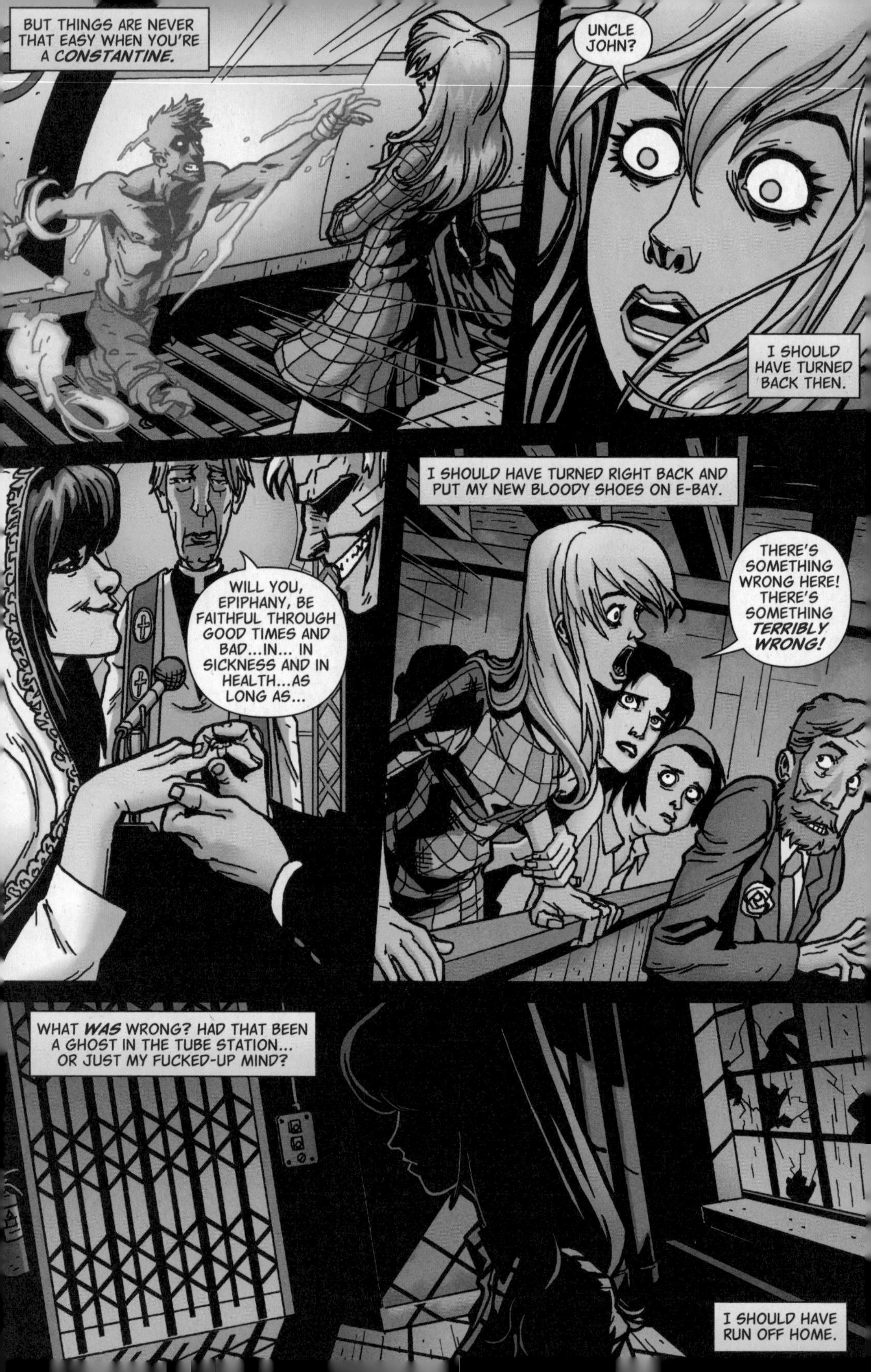
BUT THINGS ARE NEVER THAT EASY WHEN YOU'RE A *CONSTANTINE.*
UNCLE JOHN?
I SHOULD HAVE TURNED BACK THEN.
WILL YOU, EPIPHANY, BE FAITHFUL THROUGH GOOD TIMES AND BAD...IN... IN SICKNESS AND IN HEALTH...AS LONG AS...
I SHOULD HAVE TURNED RIGHT BACK AND PUT MY NEW BLOODY SHOES ON E-BAY.
THERE'S SOMETHING WRONG HERE! THERE'S SOMETHING *TERRIBLY WRONG!*
WHAT *WAS* WRONG? HAD THAT BEEN A GHOST IN THE TUBE STATION... OR JUST MY FUCKED-UP MIND?
I SHOULD HAVE RUN OFF HOME.

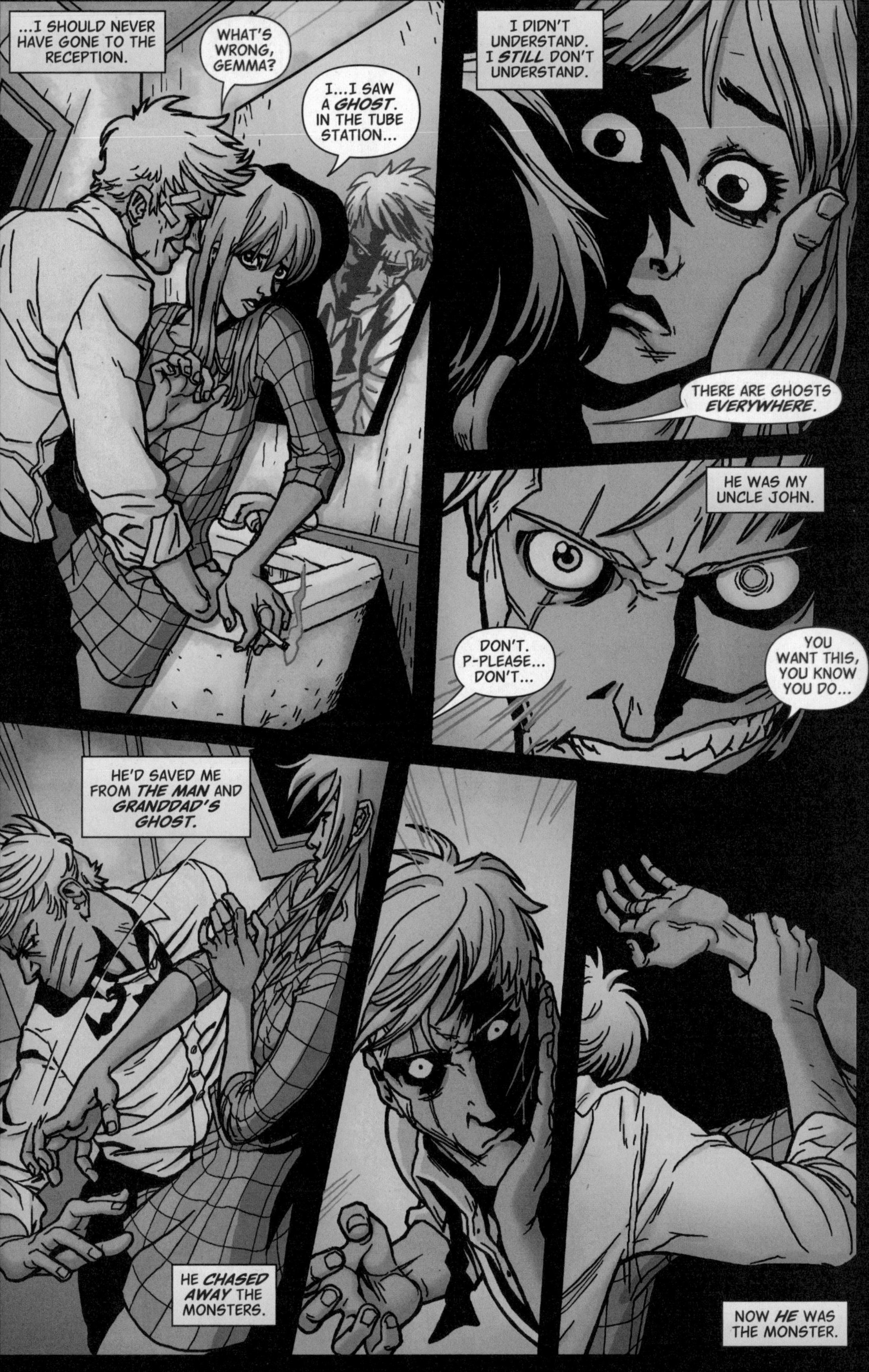
...I SHOULD NEVER HAVE GONE TO THE RECEPTION.
WHAT'S WRONG, GEMMA?
I...I SAW A *GHOST*. IN THE TUBE STATION...
I DIDN'T UNDERSTAND. I *STILL* DON'T UNDERSTAND.
THERE ARE GHOSTS *EVERYWHERE*.
HE WAS MY UNCLE JOHN.
DON'T. P-PLEASE... DON'T...
YOU WANT THIS, YOU KNOW YOU DO...
HE'D SAVED ME FROM *THE MAN* AND *GRANDDAD'S GHOST*.
HE *CHASED AWAY* THE MONSTERS.
NOW *HE* WAS THE MONSTER.

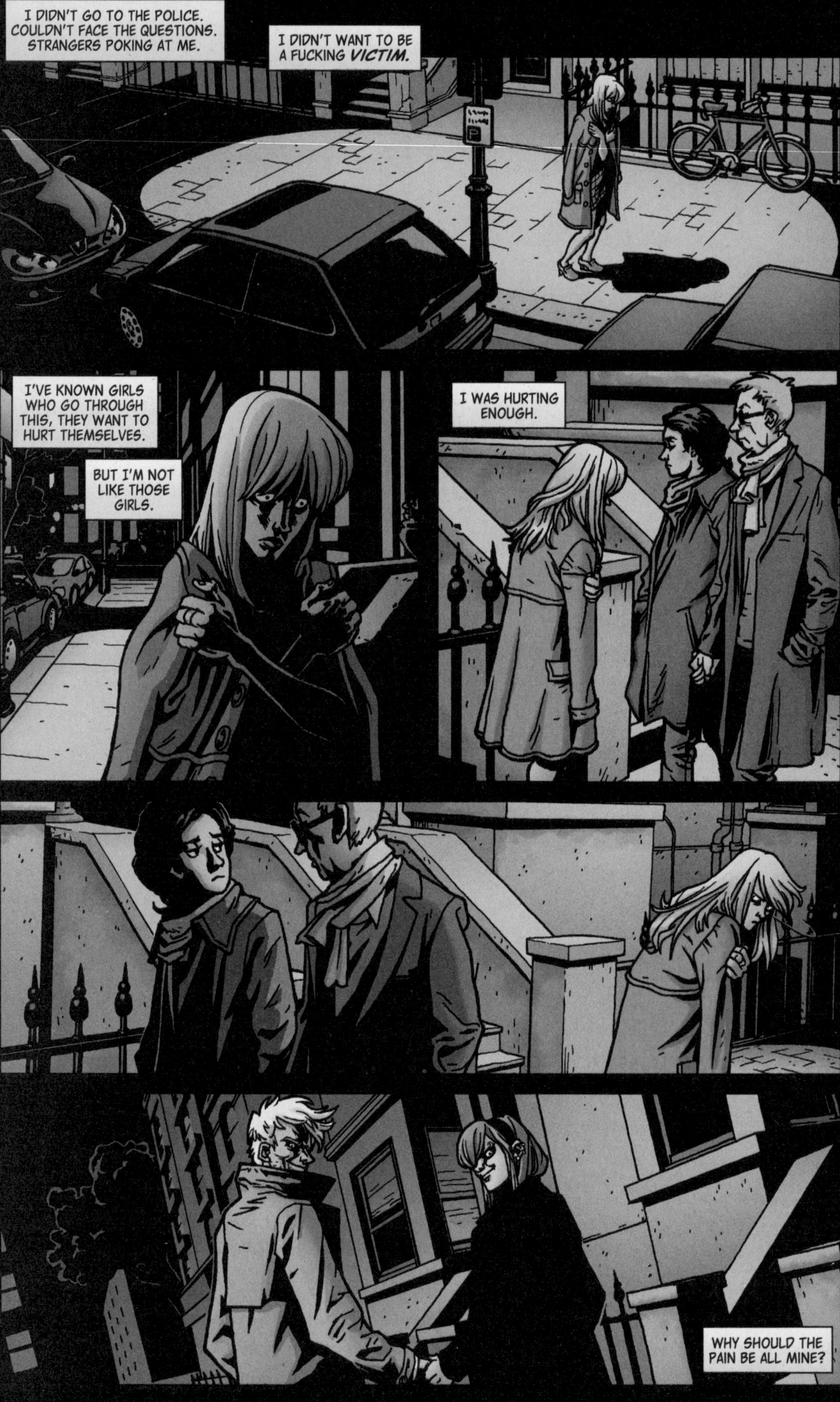
I DIDN'T GO TO THE POLICE. COULDN'T FACE THE QUESTIONS. STRANGERS POKING AT ME.
I DIDN'T WANT TO BE A FUCKING *VICTIM.*
I'VE KNOWN GIRLS WHO GO THROUGH THIS, THEY WANT TO HURT THEMSELVES.
BUT I'M NOT LIKE THOSE GIRLS.
I WAS HURTING ENOUGH.
WHY SHOULD THE PAIN BE ALL MINE?

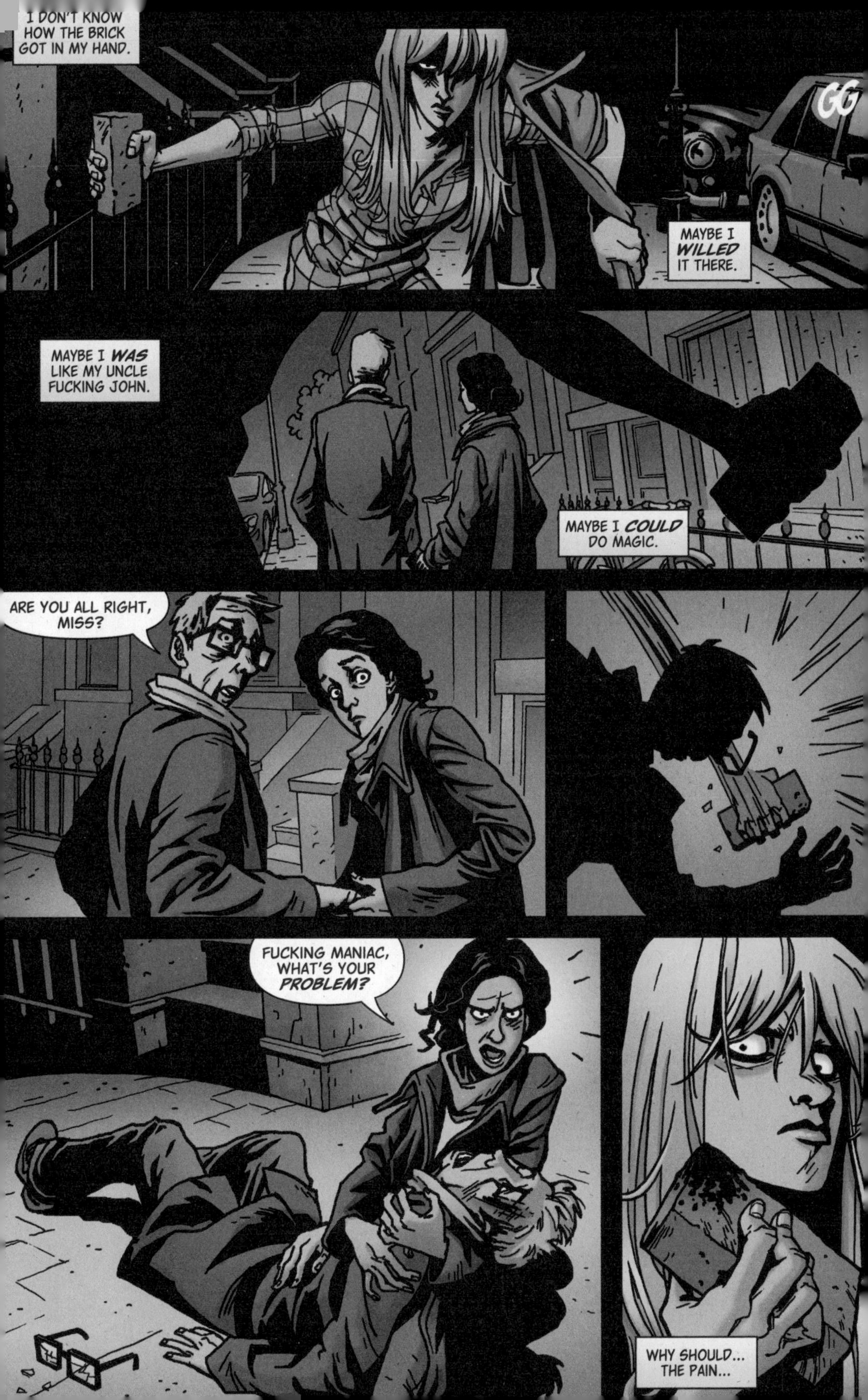
I DON'T KNOW HOW THE BRICK GOT IN MY HAND.
GG
MAYBE I WILLED IT THERE.
MAYBE I WAS LIKE MY UNCLE FUCKING JOHN.
MAYBE I COULD DO MAGIC.
ARE YOU ALL RIGHT, MISS?
FUCKING MANIAC, WHAT'S YOUR PROBLEM?
WHY SHOULD... THE PAIN...

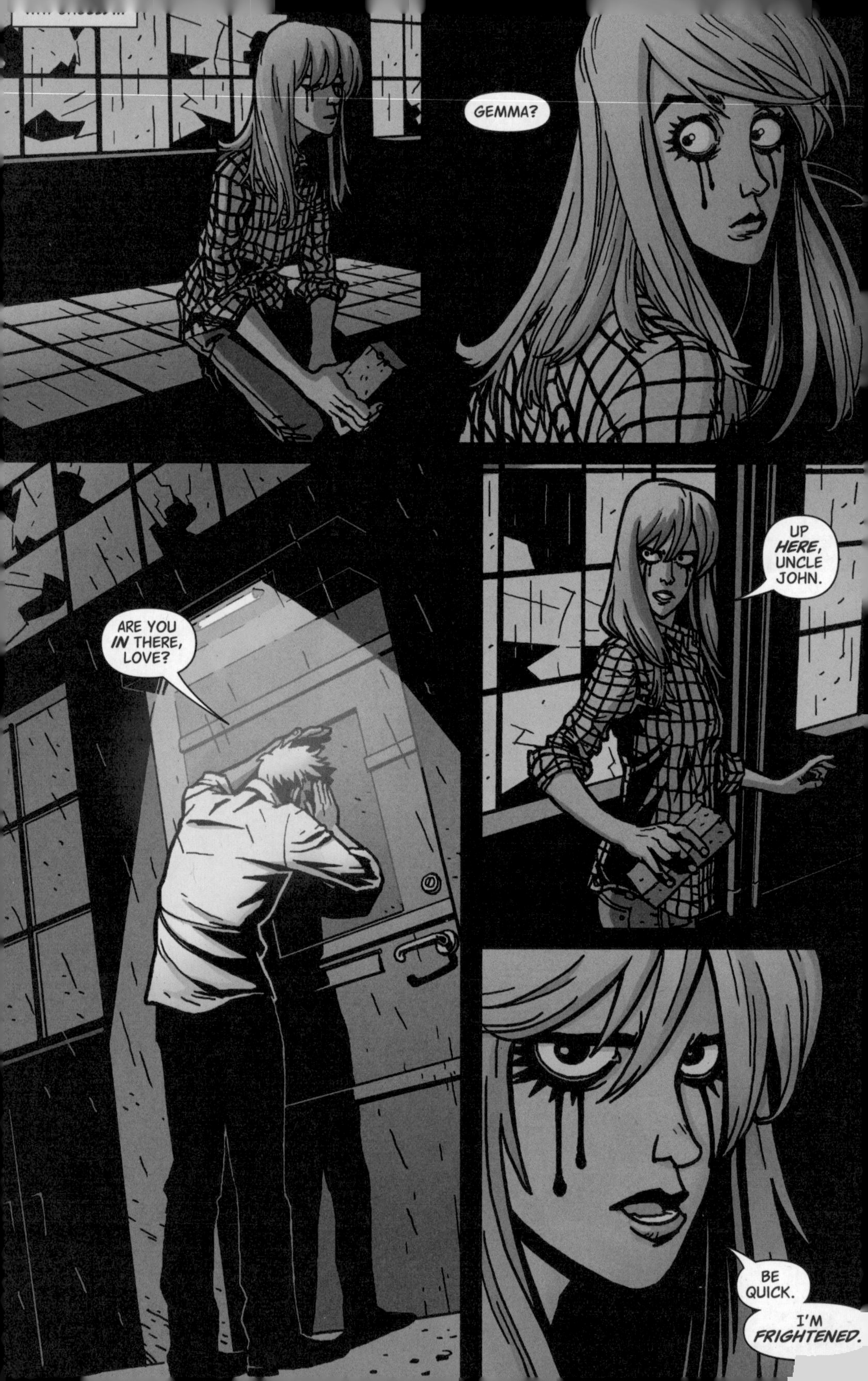
GEMMA?
ARE YOU IN THERE, LOVE?
UP HERE, UNCLE JOHN.
BE QUICK.
I'M FRIGHTENED.

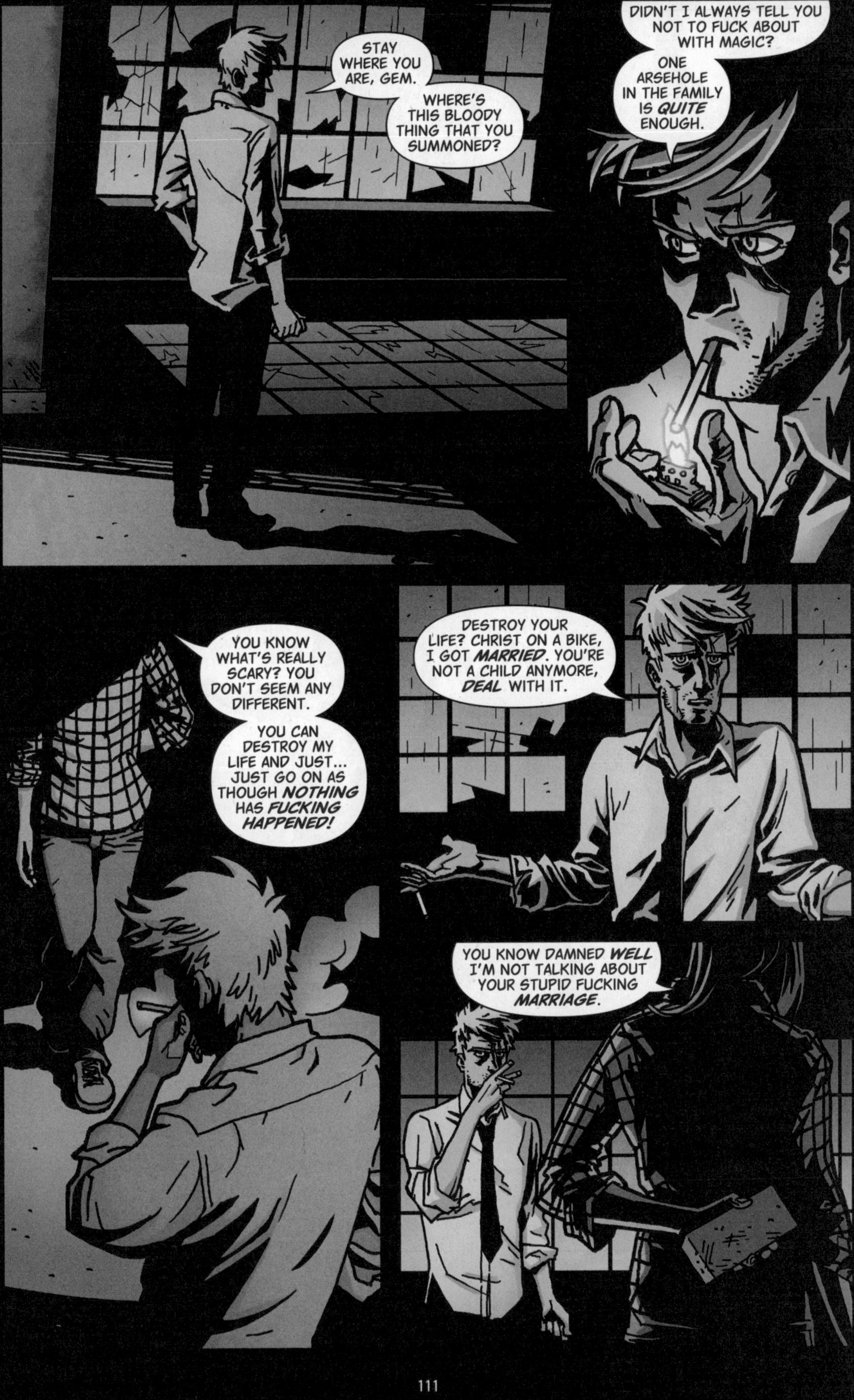
STAY WHERE YOU ARE, GEM.
WHERE'S THIS BLOODY THING THAT YOU SUMMONED?
DIDN'T I ALWAYS TELL YOU NOT TO FUCK ABOUT WITH MAGIC?
ONE ARSEHOLE IN THE FAMILY IS *QUITE* ENOUGH.
YOU KNOW WHAT'S REALLY SCARY? YOU DON'T SEEM ANY DIFFERENT.
YOU CAN DESTROY MY LIFE AND JUST... JUST GO ON AS THOUGH *NOTHING* HAS *FUCKING HAPPENED!*
DESTROY YOUR LIFE? CHRIST ON A BIKE, I GOT *MARRIED*. YOU'RE NOT A CHILD ANYMORE, *DEAL* WITH IT.
YOU KNOW DAMNED *WELL* I'M NOT TALKING ABOUT YOUR STUPID FUCKING *MARRIAGE*.

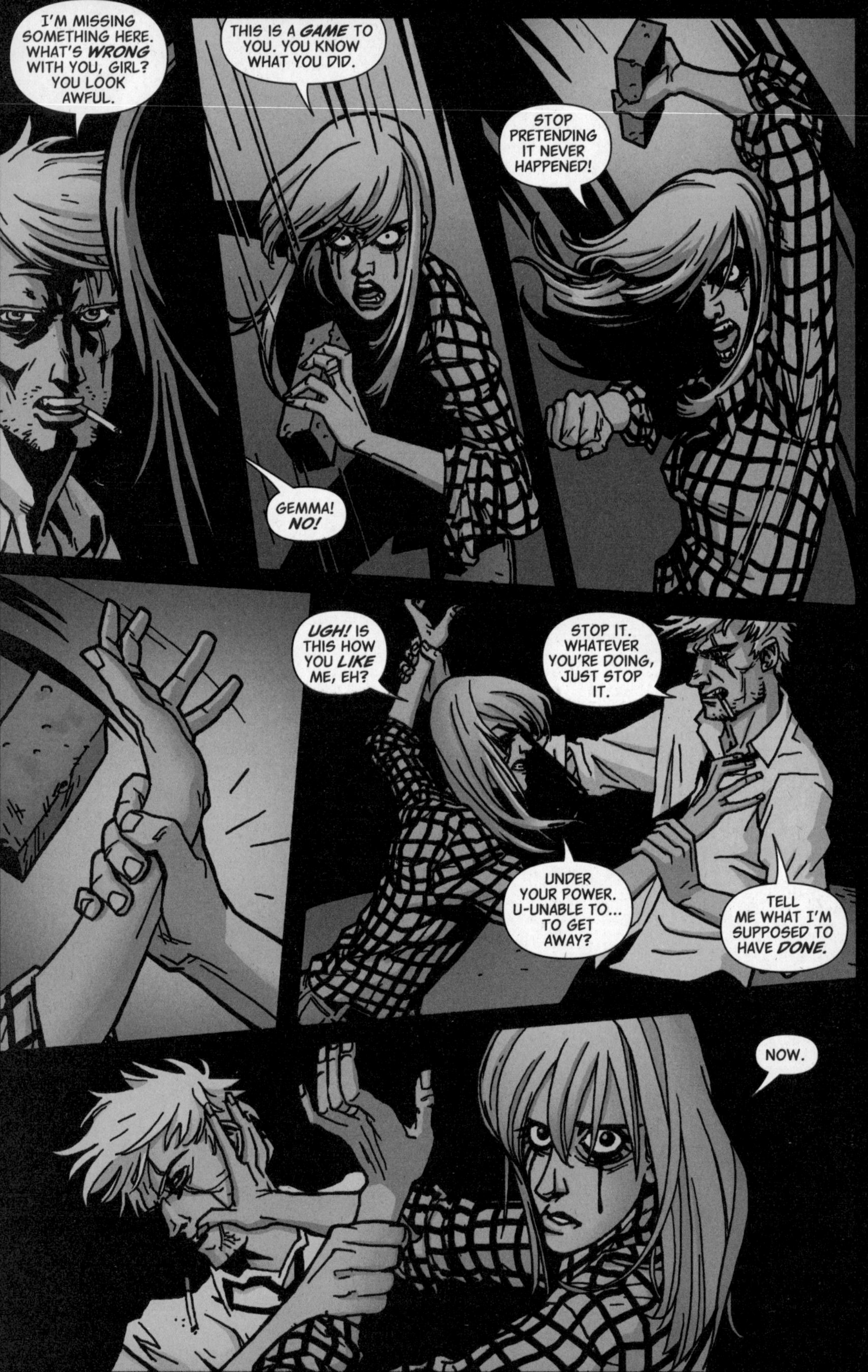

I'M MISSING SOMETHING HERE. WHAT'S *WRONG* WITH YOU, GIRL? YOU LOOK AWFUL.
THIS IS A *GAME* TO YOU. YOU KNOW WHAT YOU DID.
GEMMA! *NO!*
STOP PRETENDING IT NEVER HAPPENED!
UGH! IS THIS HOW YOU *LIKE* ME, EH?
STOP IT. WHATEVER YOU'RE DOING, JUST STOP IT.
UNDER YOUR POWER. U-UNABLE TO... TO GET AWAY?
TELL ME WHAT I'M SUPPOSED TO HAVE *DONE.*
NOW.

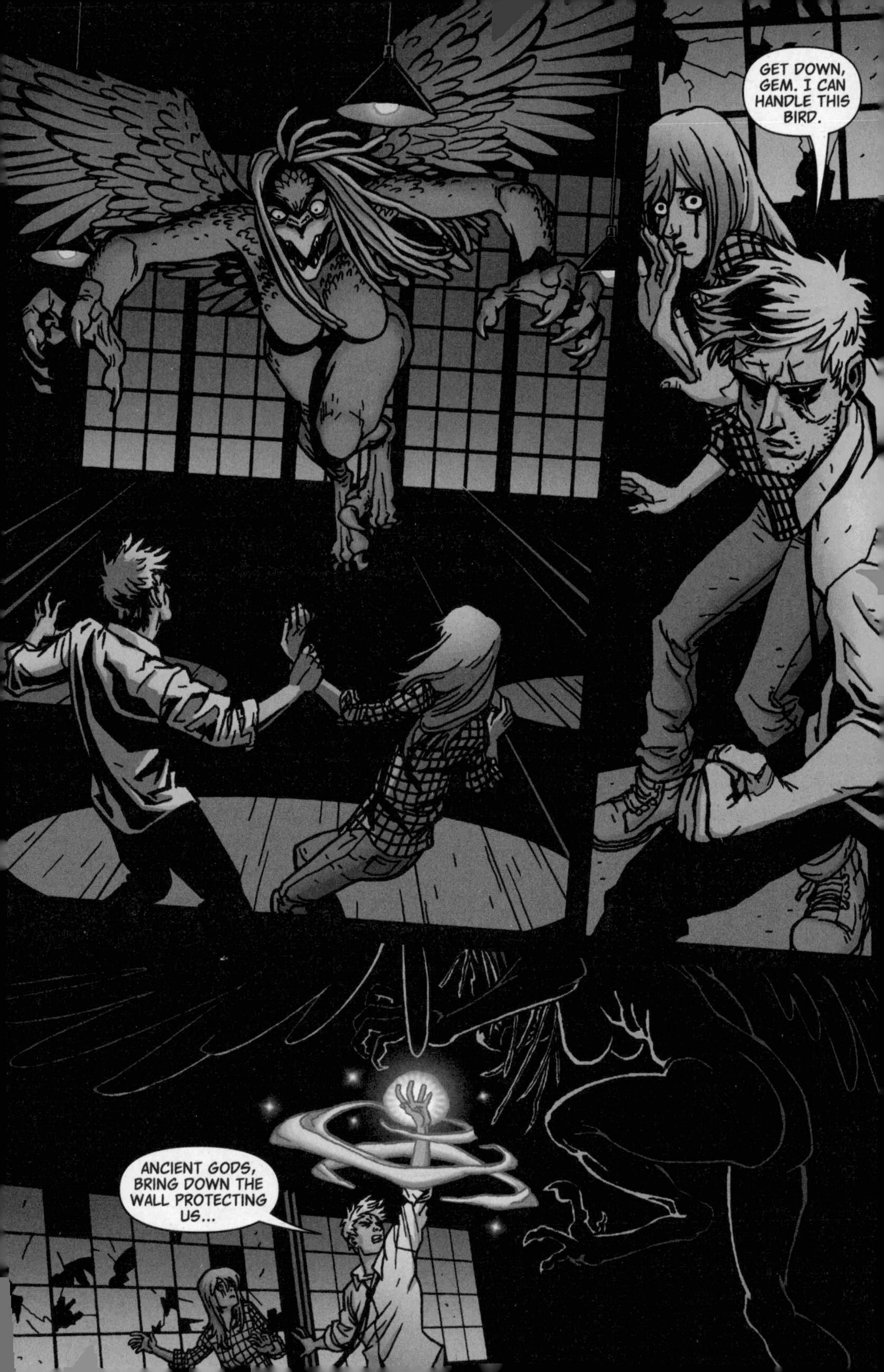
GET DOWN, GEM. I CAN HANDLE THIS BIRD.
ANCIENT GODS, BRING DOWN THE WALL PROTECTING US...

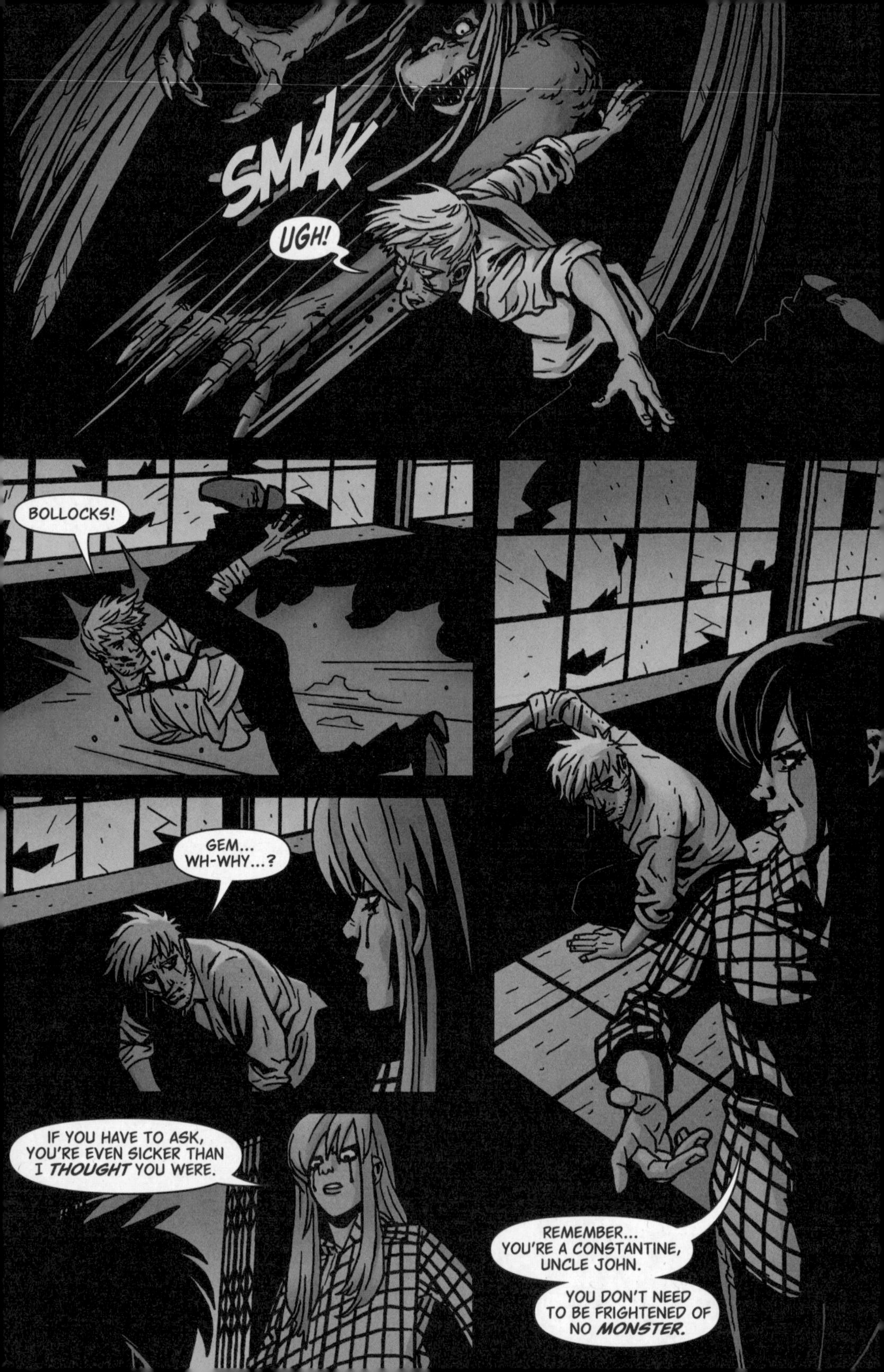
SMAK
UGH!
BOLLOCKS!
GEM... WH-WHY...?
IF YOU HAVE TO ASK, YOU'RE EVEN SICKER THAN I THOUGHT YOU WERE.
REMEMBER... YOU'RE A CONSTANTINE, UNCLE JOHN.
YOU DON'T NEED TO BE FRIGHTENED OF NO MONSTER.

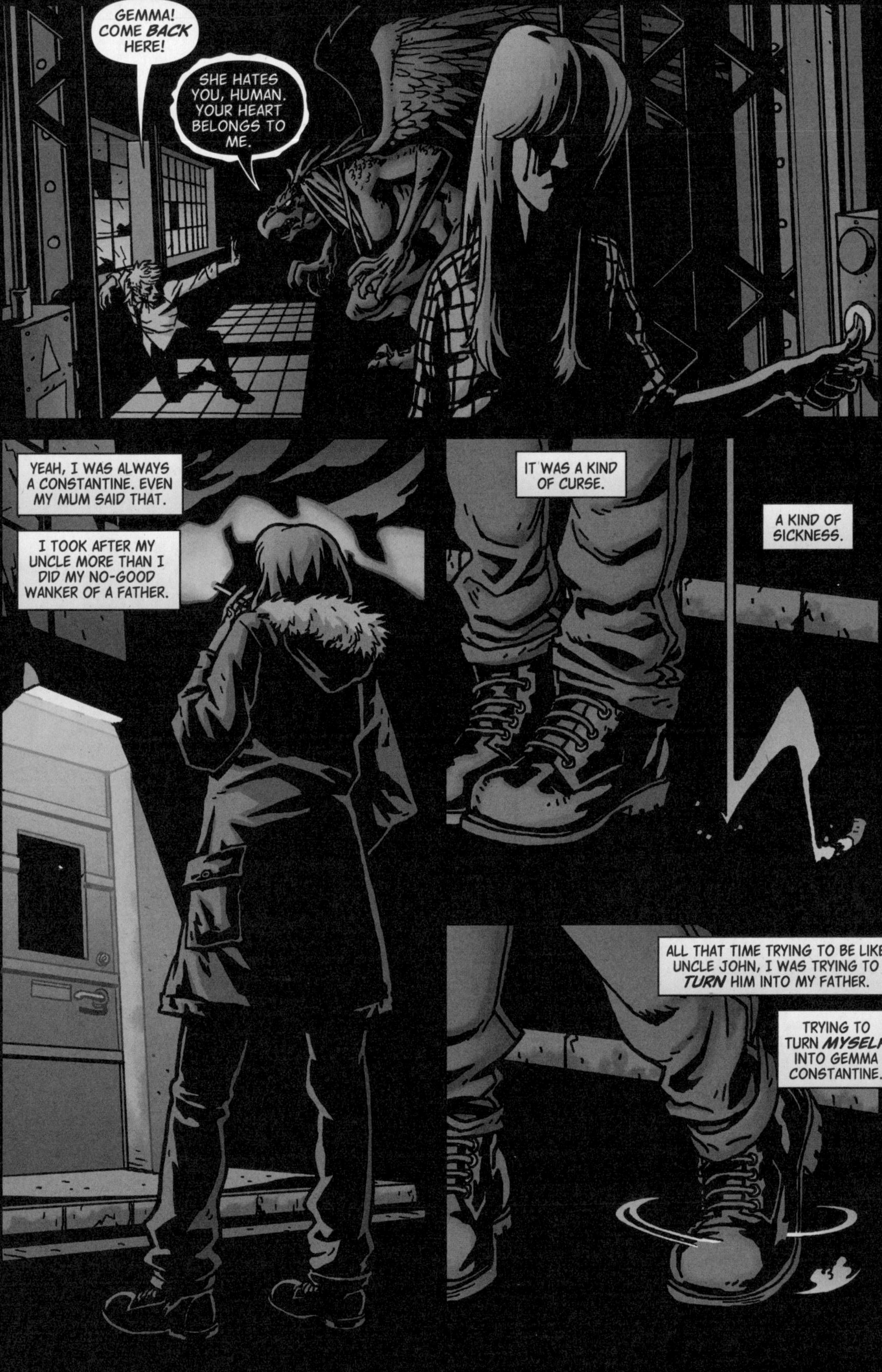
GEMMA! COME *BACK* HERE!
SHE HATES YOU, HUMAN. YOUR HEART BELONGS TO ME.
YEAH, I WAS ALWAYS A CONSTANTINE. EVEN MY MUM SAID THAT.
I TOOK AFTER MY UNCLE MORE THAN I DID MY NO-GOOD WANKER OF A FATHER.
IT WAS A KIND OF CURSE.
A KIND OF SICKNESS.
ALL THAT TIME TRYING TO BE LIKE UNCLE JOHN, I WAS TRYING TO *TURN* HIM INTO MY FATHER.
TRYING TO TURN *MYSELF* INTO GEMMA CONSTANTINE.

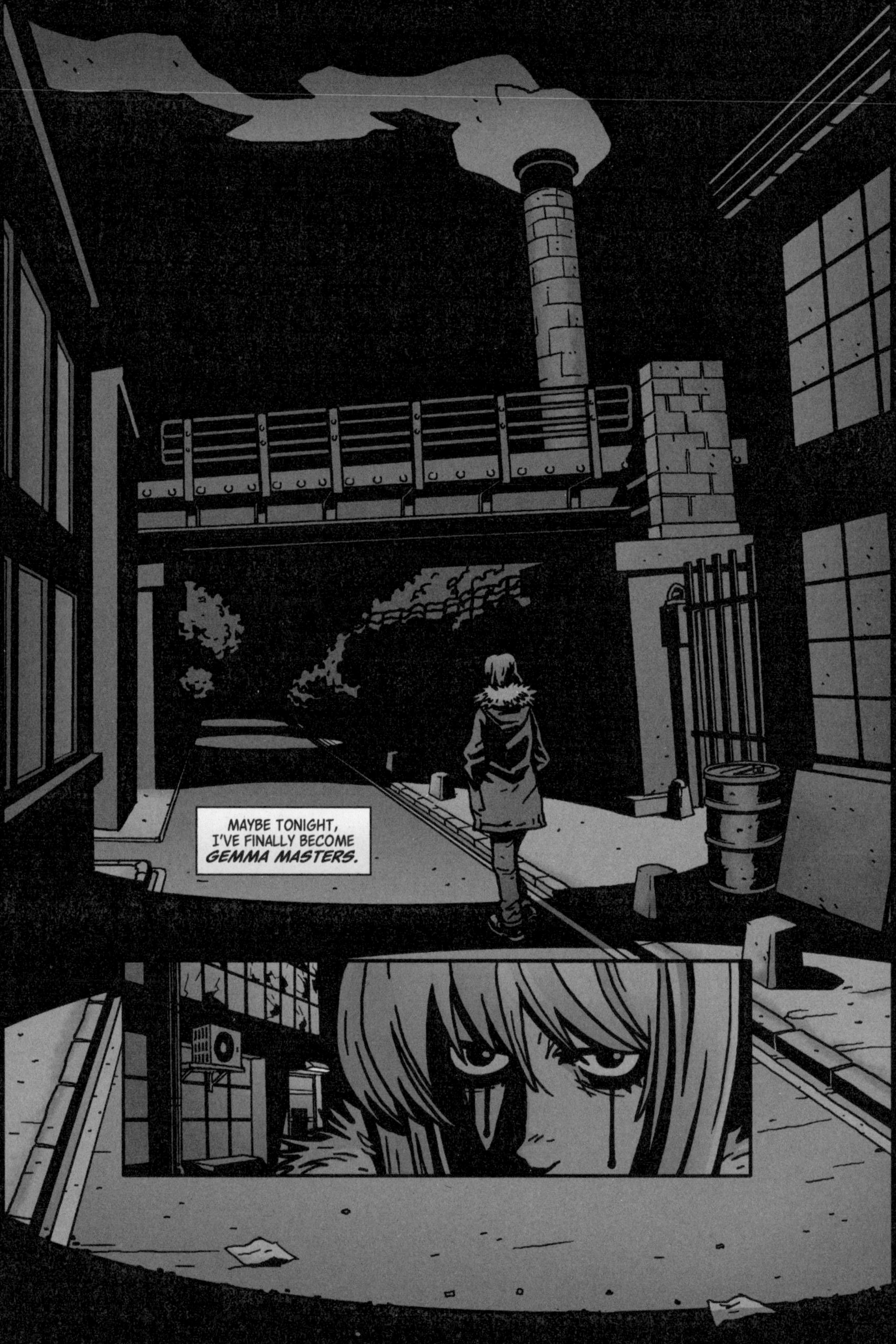
MAYBE TONIGHT, I'VE FINALLY BECOME GEMMA MASTERS.

Phantom Pains, Part Five

Choke

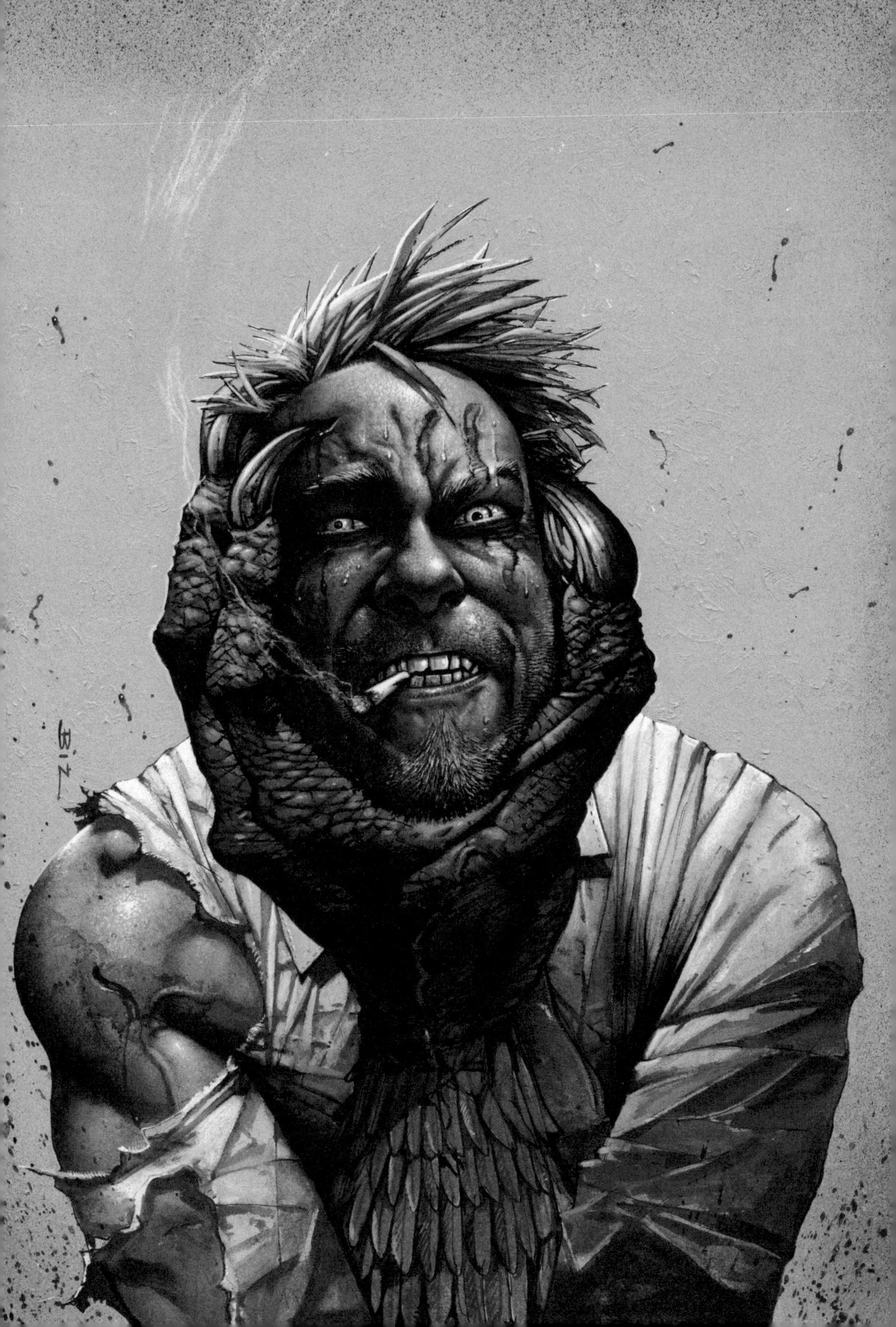

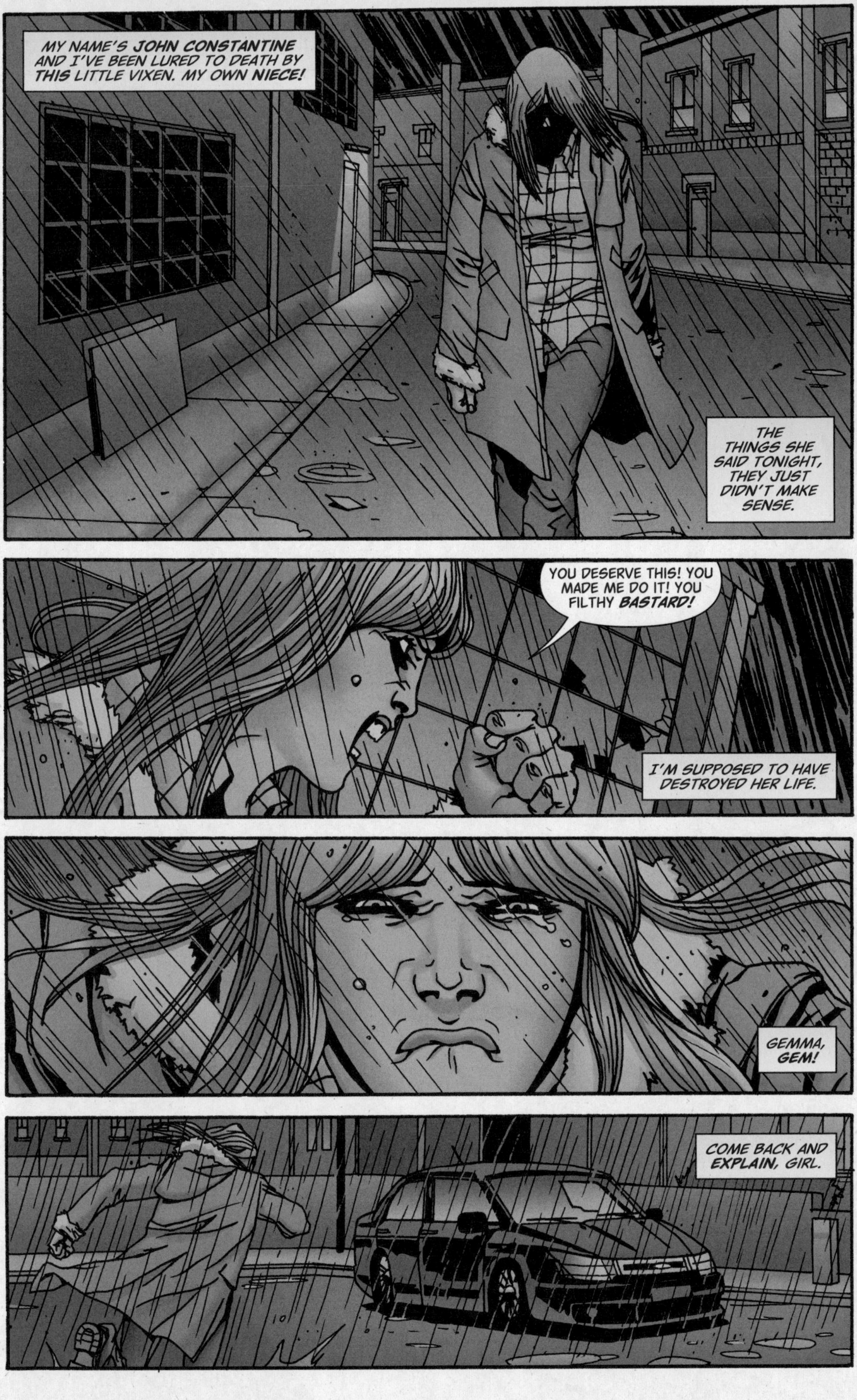
MY NAME'S JOHN CONSTANTINE AND I'VE BEEN LURED TO DEATH BY THIS LITTLE VIXEN. MY OWN NIECE!
THE THINGS SHE SAID TONIGHT, THEY JUST DIDN'T MAKE SENSE.
YOU DESERVE THIS! YOU MADE ME DO IT! YOU FILTHY BASTARD!
I'M SUPPOSED TO HAVE DESTROYED HER LIFE.
GEMMA, GEM!
COME BACK AND EXPLAIN, GIRL.

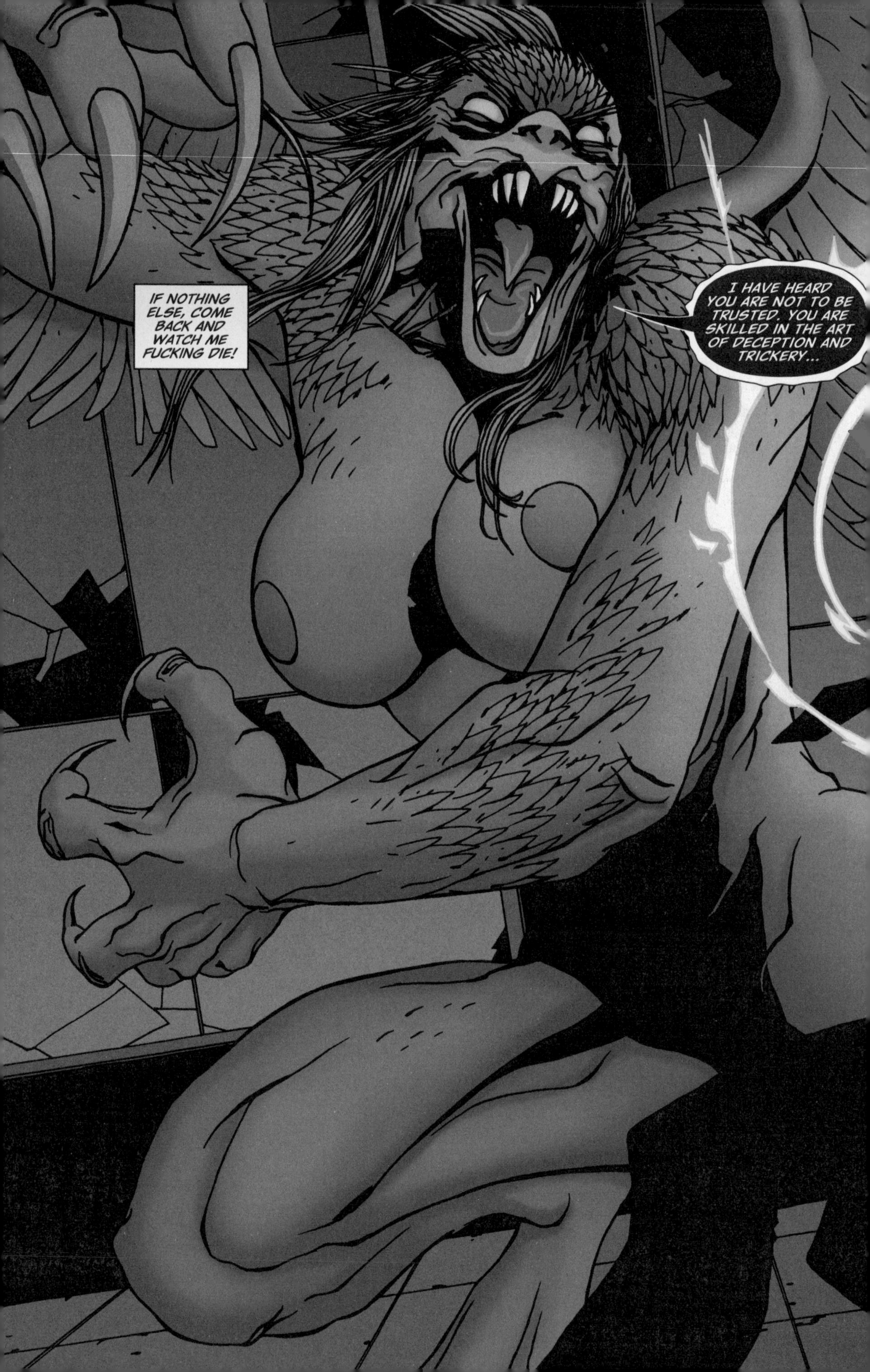
IF NOTHING ELSE, COME BACK AND WATCH ME FUCKING DIE!
I HAVE HEARD YOU ARE NOT TO BE TRUSTED. YOU ARE SKILLED IN THE ART OF DECEPTION AND TRICKERY...

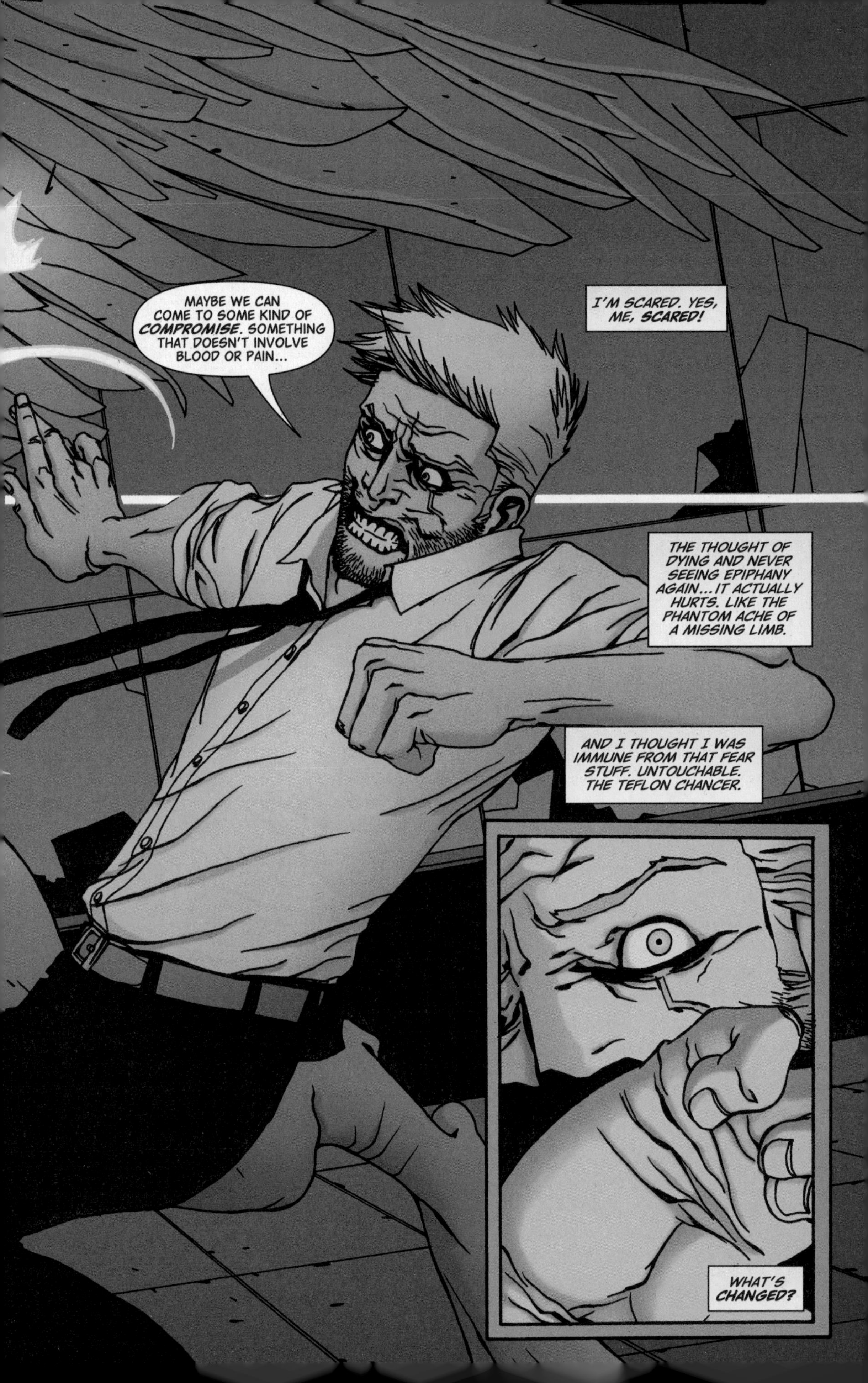
MAYBE WE CAN COME TO SOME KIND OF COMPROMISE. SOMETHING THAT DOESN'T INVOLVE BLOOD OR PAIN...
I'M SCARED. YES, ME, SCARED!
THE THOUGHT OF DYING AND NEVER SEEING EPIPHANY AGAIN...IT ACTUALLY HURTS. LIKE THE PHANTOM ACHE OF A MISSING LIMB.
AND I THOUGHT I WAS IMMUNE FROM THAT FEAR STUFF. UNTOUCHABLE. THE TEFLON CHANCER.
WHAT'S CHANGED?

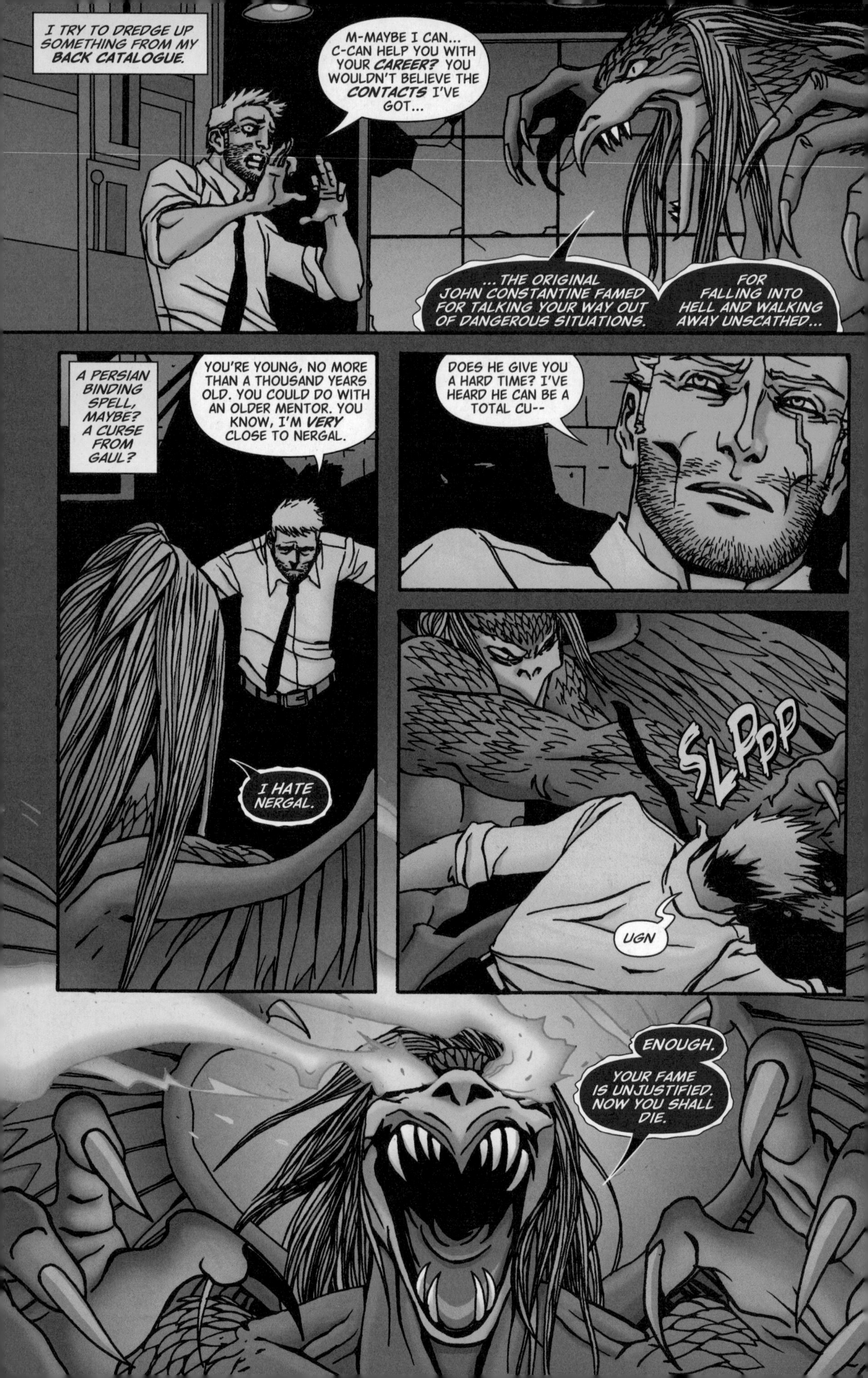
I TRY TO DREDGE UP SOMETHING FROM MY BACK CATALOGUE.
M-MAYBE I CAN... C-CAN HELP YOU WITH YOUR CAREER? YOU WOULDN'T BELIEVE THE CONTACTS I'VE GOT...
...THE ORIGINAL JOHN CONSTANTINE FAMED FOR TALKING YOUR WAY OUT OF DANGEROUS SITUATIONS.
FOR FALLING INTO HELL AND WALKING AWAY UNSCATHED...
A PERSIAN BINDING SPELL, MAYBE? A CURSE FROM GAUL?
YOU'RE YOUNG, NO MORE THAN A THOUSAND YEARS OLD. YOU COULD DO WITH AN OLDER MENTOR. YOU KNOW, I'M VERY CLOSE TO NERGAL.
I HATE NERGAL.
DOES HE GIVE YOU A HARD TIME? I'VE HEARD HE CAN BE A TOTAL CU--
SLPPP
UGN
ENOUGH.
YOUR FAME IS UNJUSTIFIED. NOW YOU SHALL DIE.

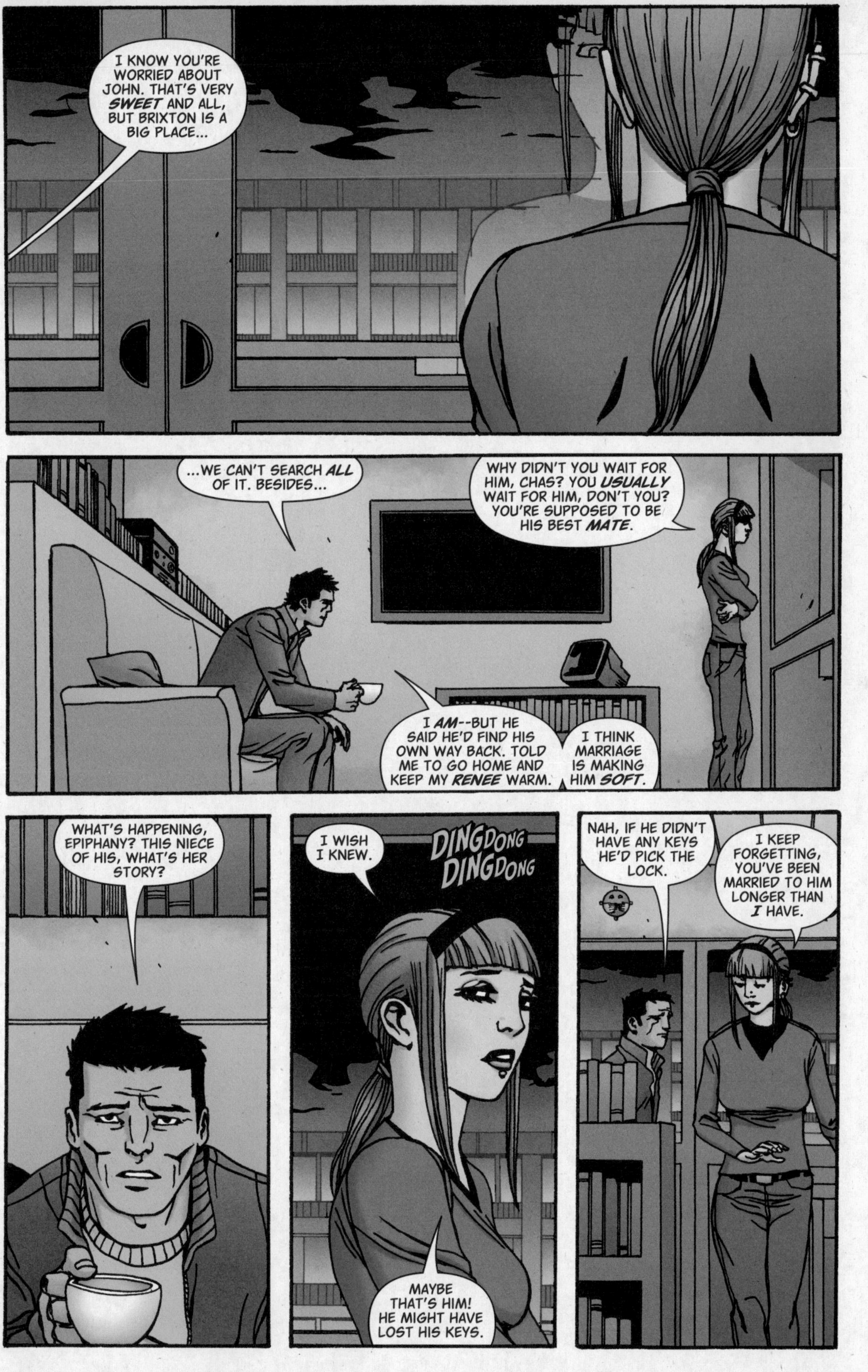
I KNOW YOU'RE WORRIED ABOUT JOHN. THAT'S VERY SWEET AND ALL, BUT BRIXTON IS A BIG PLACE...
...WE CAN'T SEARCH ALL OF IT. BESIDES...
WHY DIDN'T YOU WAIT FOR HIM, CHAS? YOU USUALLY WAIT FOR HIM, DON'T YOU? YOU'RE SUPPOSED TO BE HIS BEST MATE.
I AM--BUT HE SAID HE'D FIND HIS OWN WAY BACK. TOLD ME TO GO HOME AND KEEP MY RENEE WARM.
I THINK MARRIAGE IS MAKING HIM SOFT.
WHAT'S HAPPENING, EPIPHANY? THIS NIECE OF HIS, WHAT'S HER STORY?
I WISH I KNEW.
DINGDONG DINGDONG
MAYBE THAT'S HIM! HE MIGHT HAVE LOST HIS KEYS.
NAH, IF HE DIDN'T HAVE ANY KEYS HE'D PICK THE LOCK.
I KEEP FORGETTING, YOU'VE BEEN MARRIED TO HIM LONGER THAN I HAVE.

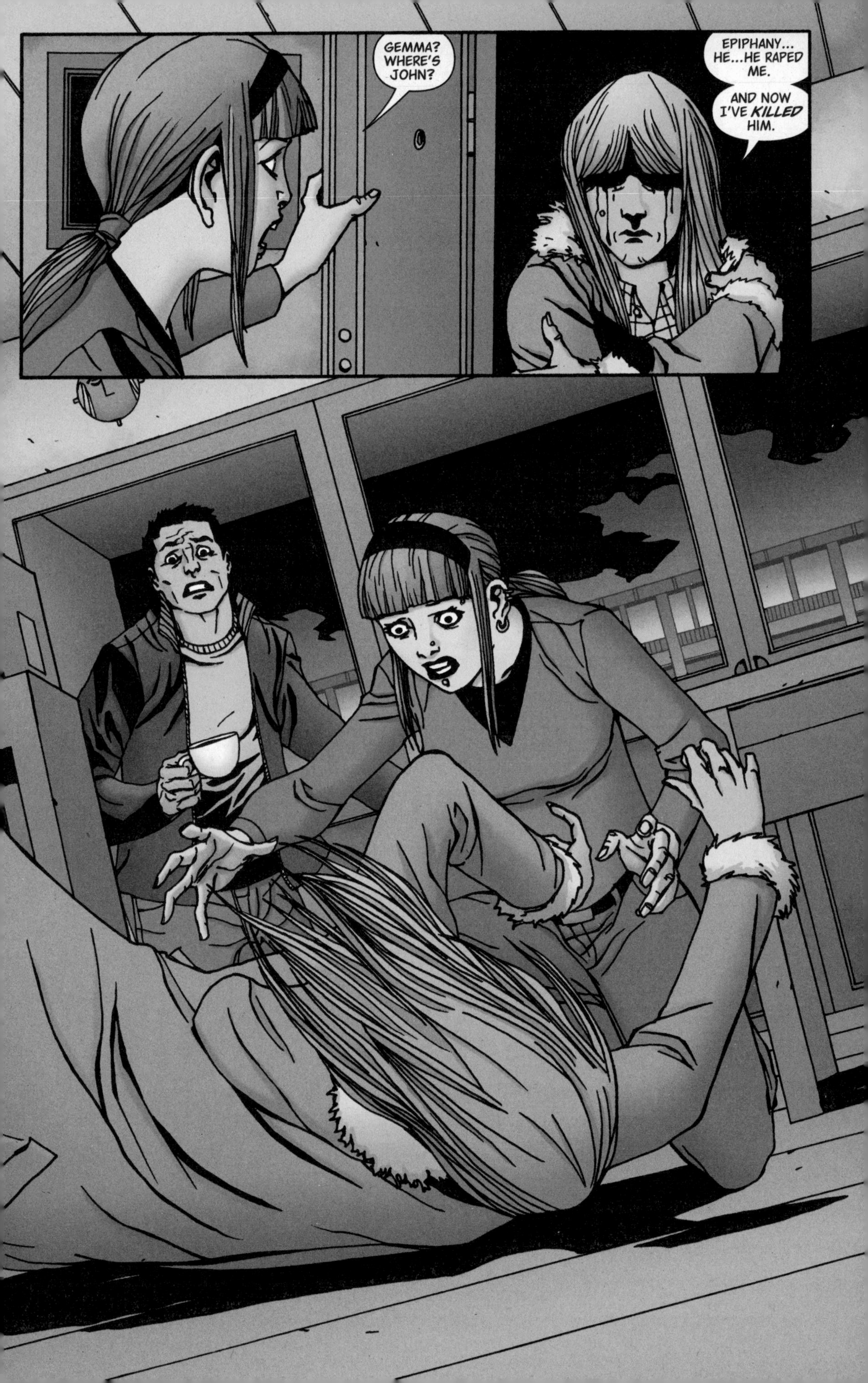
GEMMA? WHERE'S JOHN?
EPIPHANY... HE...HE RAPED ME.
AND NOW I'VE KILLED HIM.

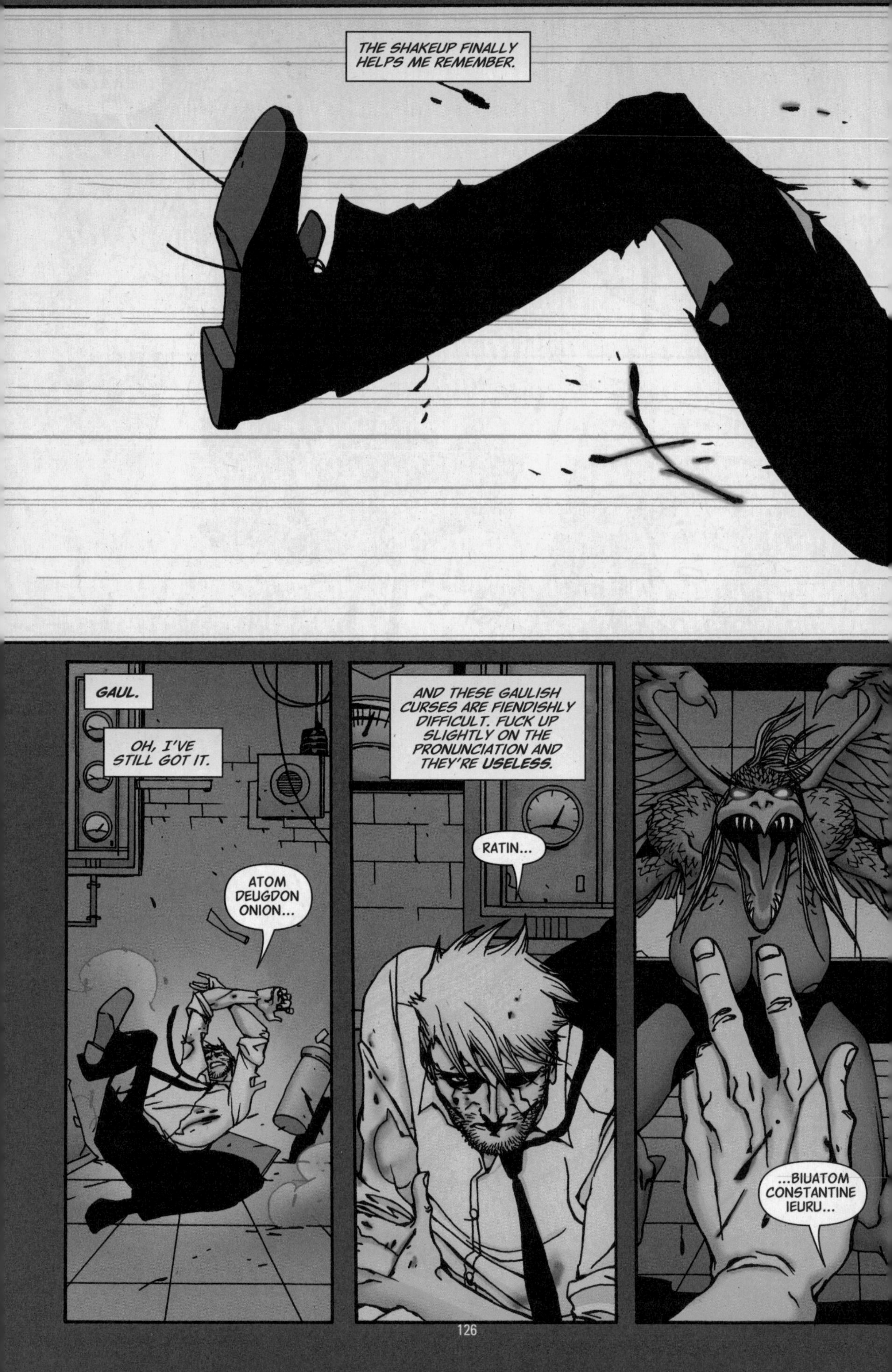

THE SHAKEUP FINALLY HELPS ME REMEMBER.
GAUL.
OH, I'VE STILL GOT IT.
ATOM DEUGDON ONION...
AND THESE GAULISH CURSES ARE FIENDISHLY DIFFICULT. FUCK UP SLIGHTLY ON THE PRONUNCIATION AND THEY'RE USELESS.
RATIN...
...BIUATOM CONSTANTINE IEURU...

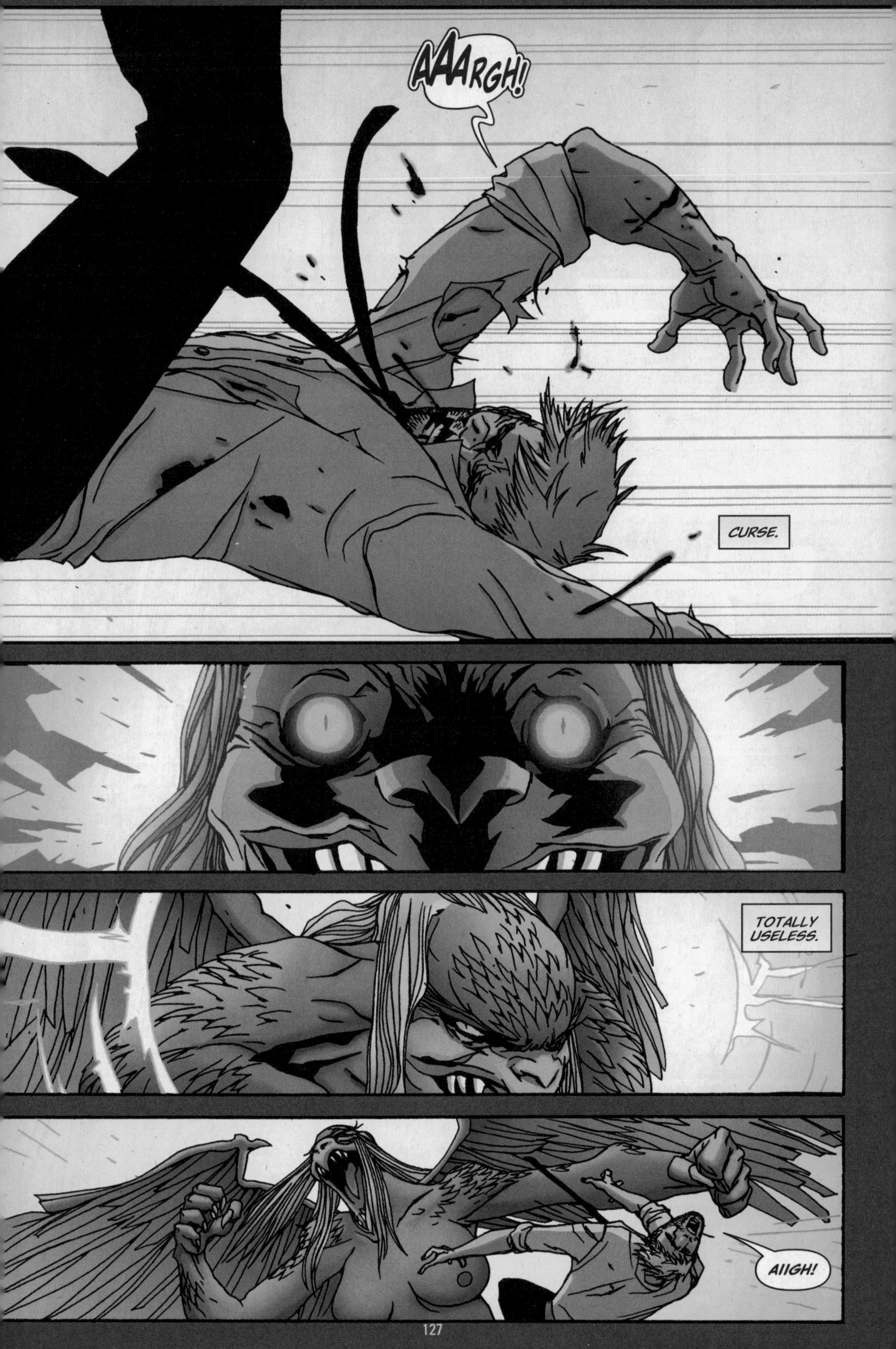
AAARGH!
CURSE.
TOTALLY USELESS.
AIIGH!

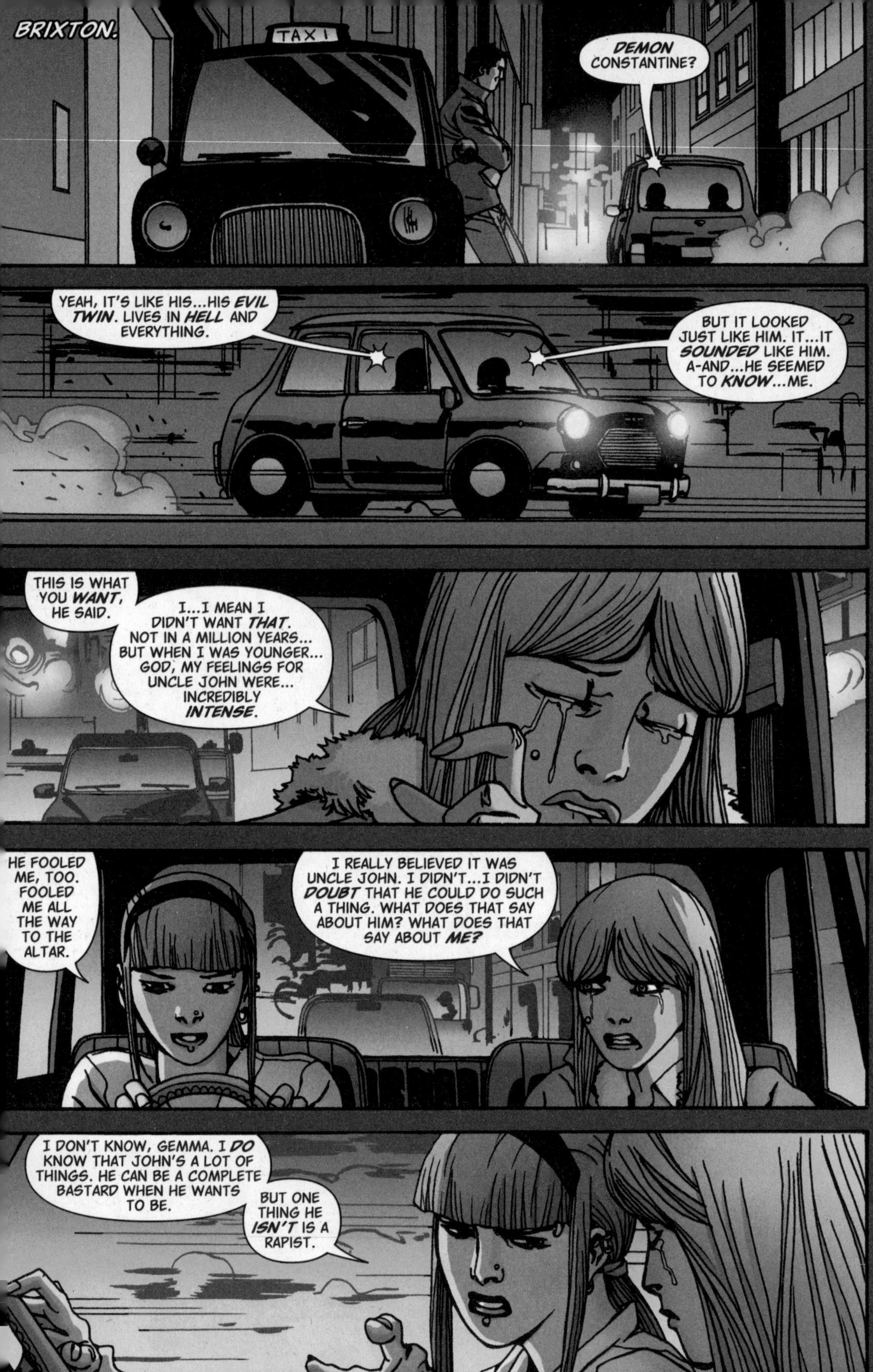
BRIXTON.
TAXI
DEMON CONSTANTINE?
YEAH, IT'S LIKE HIS...HIS EVIL TWIN. LIVES IN HELL AND EVERYTHING.
BUT IT LOOKED JUST LIKE HIM. IT...IT SOUNDED LIKE HIM. A-AND...HE SEEMED TO KNOW...ME.
THIS IS WHAT YOU WANT, HE SAID.
I...I MEAN I DIDN'T WANT THAT. NOT IN A MILLION YEARS... BUT WHEN I WAS YOUNGER... GOD, MY FEELINGS FOR UNCLE JOHN WERE... INCREDIBLY INTENSE.
HE FOOLED ME, TOO. FOOLED ME ALL THE WAY TO THE ALTAR.
I REALLY BELIEVED IT WAS UNCLE JOHN. I DIDN'T...I DIDN'T DOUBT THAT HE COULD DO SUCH A THING. WHAT DOES THAT SAY ABOUT HIM? WHAT DOES THAT SAY ABOUT ME?
I DON'T KNOW, GEMMA. I DO KNOW THAT JOHN'S A LOT OF THINGS. HE CAN BE A COMPLETE BASTARD WHEN HE WANTS TO BE.
BUT ONE THING HE ISN'T IS A RAPIST.

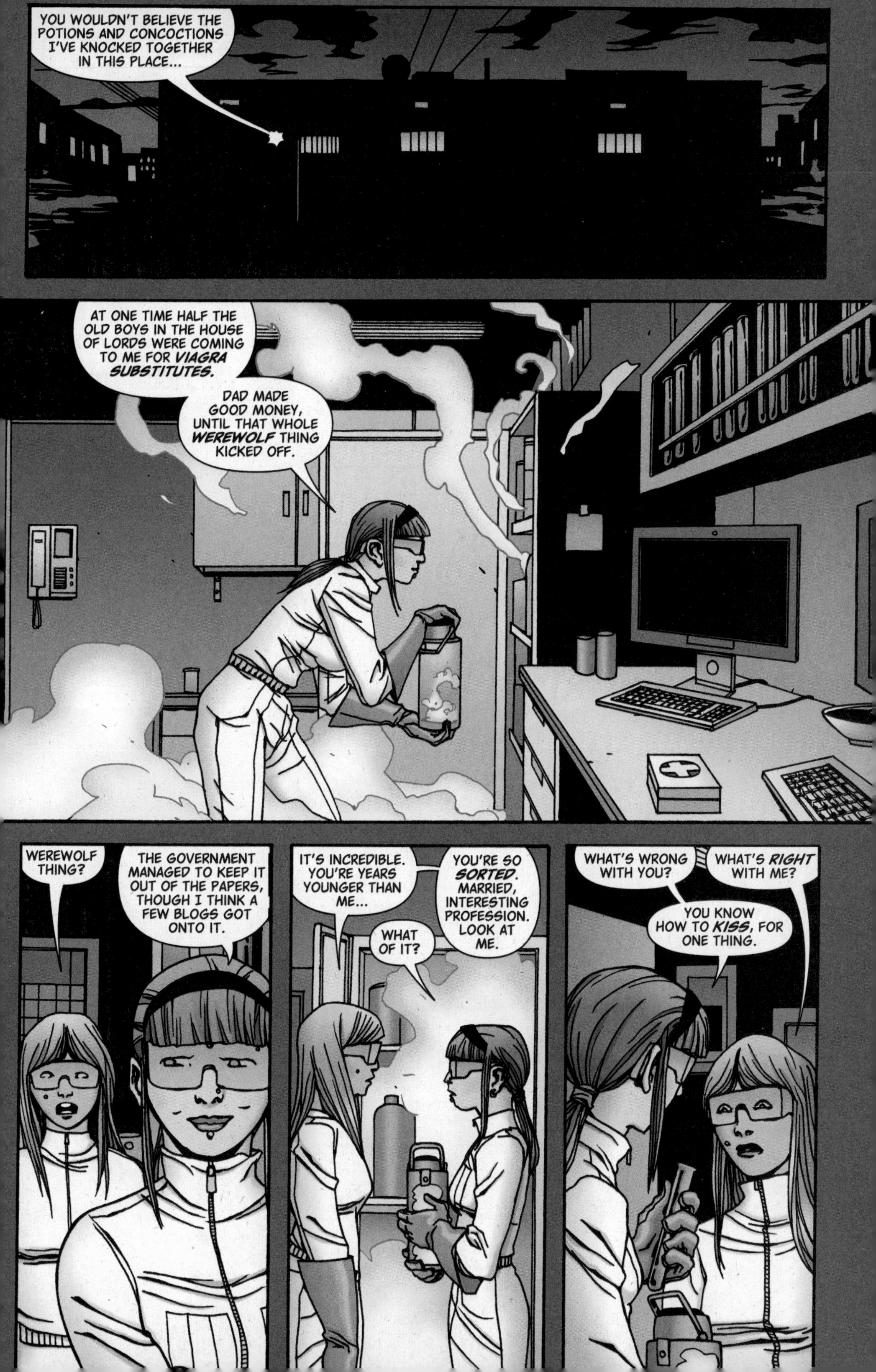
YOU WOULDN'T BELIEVE THE POTIONS AND CONCOCTIONS I'VE KNOCKED TOGETHER IN THIS PLACE...
AT ONE TIME HALF THE OLD BOYS IN THE HOUSE OF LORDS WERE COMING TO ME FOR *VIAGRA SUBSTITUTES.*
DAD MADE GOOD MONEY, UNTIL THAT WHOLE *WEREWOLF* THING KICKED OFF.
WEREWOLF THING?
THE GOVERNMENT MANAGED TO KEEP IT OUT OF THE PAPERS, THOUGH I THINK A FEW BLOGS GOT ONTO IT.
IT'S INCREDIBLE. YOU'RE YEARS YOUNGER THAN ME...
WHAT OF IT?
YOU'RE SO *SORTED*. MARRIED, INTERESTING PROFESSION. LOOK AT ME.
WHAT'S WRONG WITH YOU?
WHAT'S *RIGHT* WITH ME?
YOU KNOW HOW TO *KISS*, FOR ONE THING.

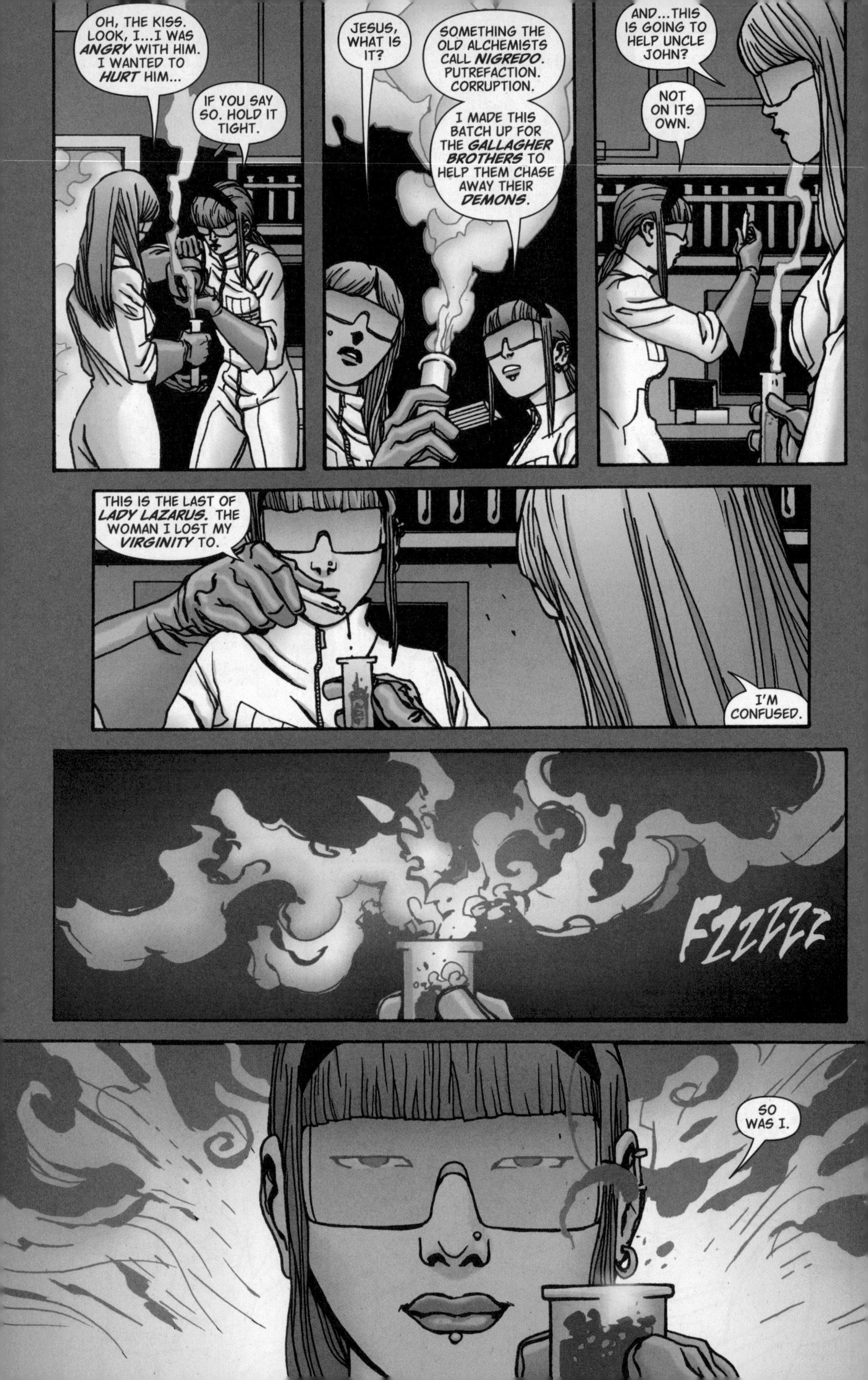
OH, THE KISS. LOOK, I...I WAS ANGRY WITH HIM. I WANTED TO HURT HIM...
IF YOU SAY SO. HOLD IT TIGHT.
JESUS, WHAT IS IT?
SOMETHING THE OLD ALCHEMISTS CALL NIGREDO. PUTREFACTION. CORRUPTION.
I MADE THIS BATCH UP FOR THE GALLAGHER BROTHERS TO HELP THEM CHASE AWAY THEIR DEMONS.
AND...THIS IS GOING TO HELP UNCLE JOHN?
NOT ON ITS OWN.
THIS IS THE LAST OF LADY LAZARUS. THE WOMAN I LOST MY VIRGINITY TO.
I'M CONFUSED.
FZZZZZ
SO WAS I.

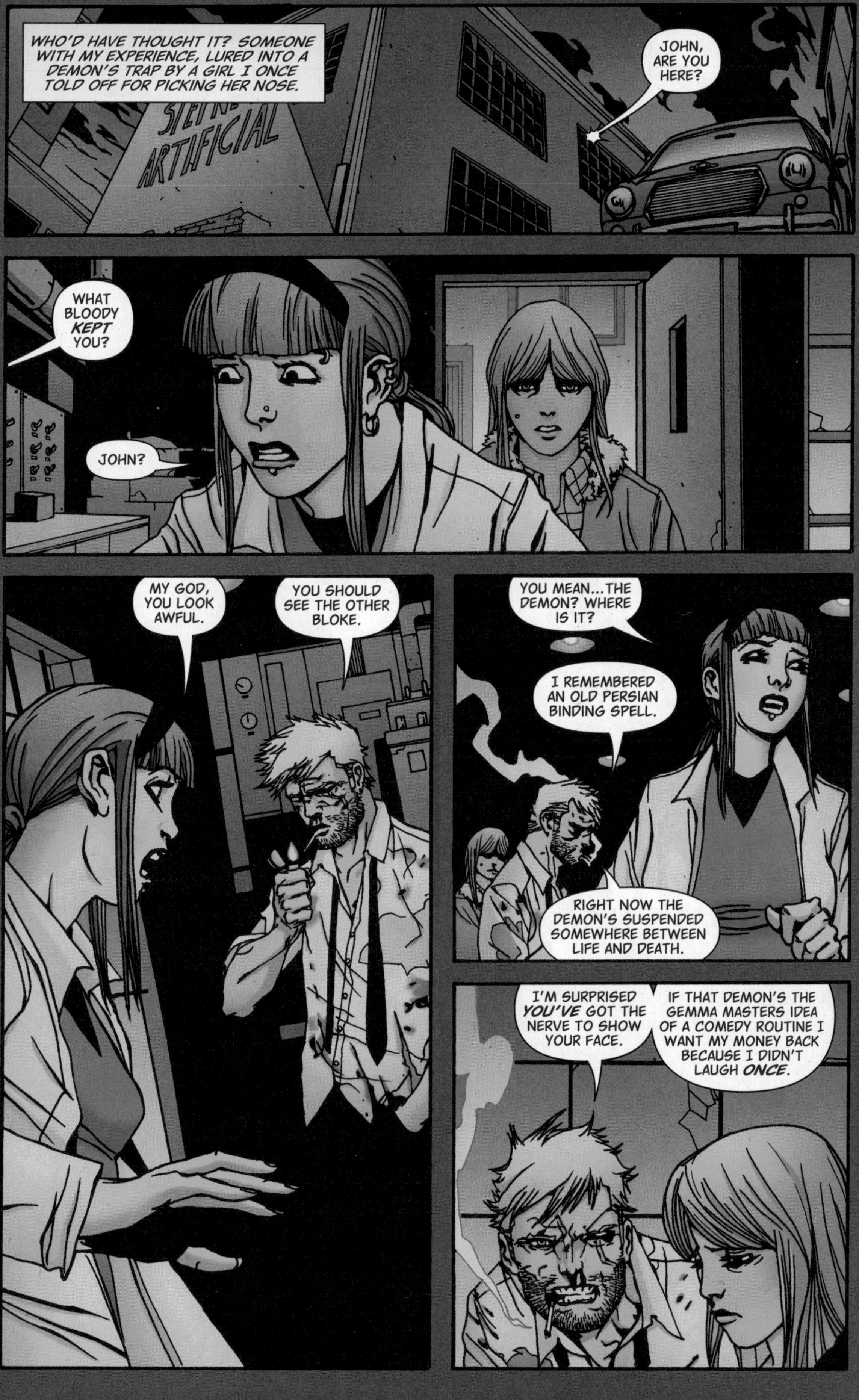
WHO'D HAVE THOUGHT IT? SOMEONE WITH MY EXPERIENCE, LURED INTO A DEMON'S TRAP BY A GIRL I ONCE TOLD OFF FOR PICKING HER NOSE.
ARTIFICIAL
JOHN, ARE YOU HERE?
WHAT BLOODY KEPT YOU?
JOHN?
MY GOD, YOU LOOK AWFUL.
YOU SHOULD SEE THE OTHER BLOKE.
YOU MEAN...THE DEMON? WHERE IS IT?
I REMEMBERED AN OLD PERSIAN BINDING SPELL.
RIGHT NOW THE DEMON'S SUSPENDED SOMEWHERE BETWEEN LIFE AND DEATH.
I'M SURPRISED YOU'VE GOT THE NERVE TO SHOW YOUR FACE.
IF THAT DEMON'S THE GEMMA MASTERS IDEA OF A COMEDY ROUTINE I WANT MY MONEY BACK BECAUSE I DIDN'T LAUGH ONCE.

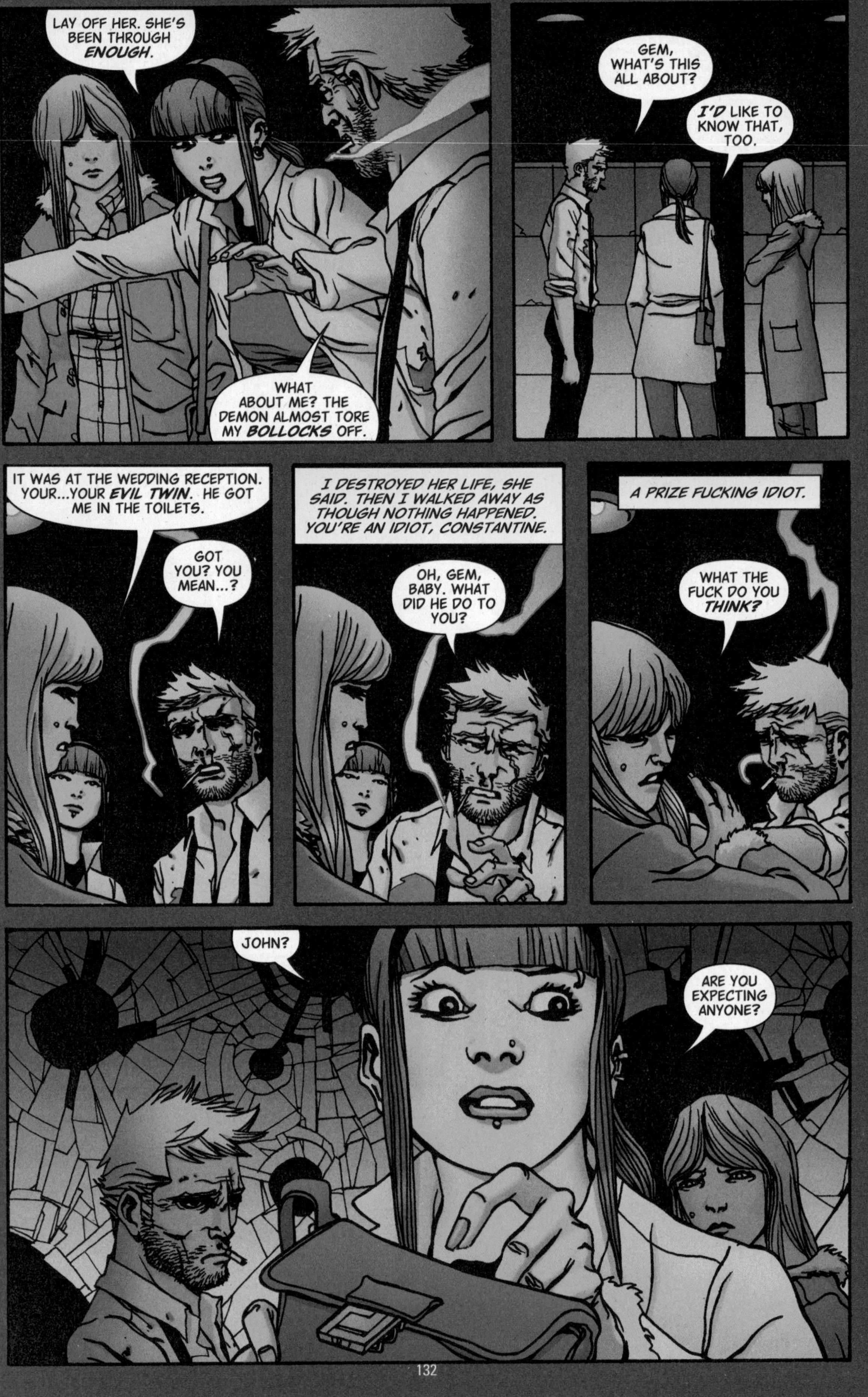
LAY OFF HER. SHE'S BEEN THROUGH ENOUGH.
WHAT ABOUT ME? THE DEMON ALMOST TORE MY BOLLOCKS OFF.
GEM, WHAT'S THIS ALL ABOUT?
I'D LIKE TO KNOW THAT, TOO.
IT WAS AT THE WEDDING RECEPTION. YOUR...YOUR EVIL TWIN. HE GOT ME IN THE TOILETS.
GOT YOU? YOU MEAN...?
I DESTROYED HER LIFE, SHE SAID. THEN I WALKED AWAY AS THOUGH NOTHING HAPPENED. YOU'RE AN IDIOT, CONSTANTINE.
OH, GEM, BABY. WHAT DID HE DO TO YOU?
A PRIZE FUCKING IDIOT.
WHAT THE FUCK DO YOU THINK?
JOHN?
ARE YOU EXPECTING ANYONE?

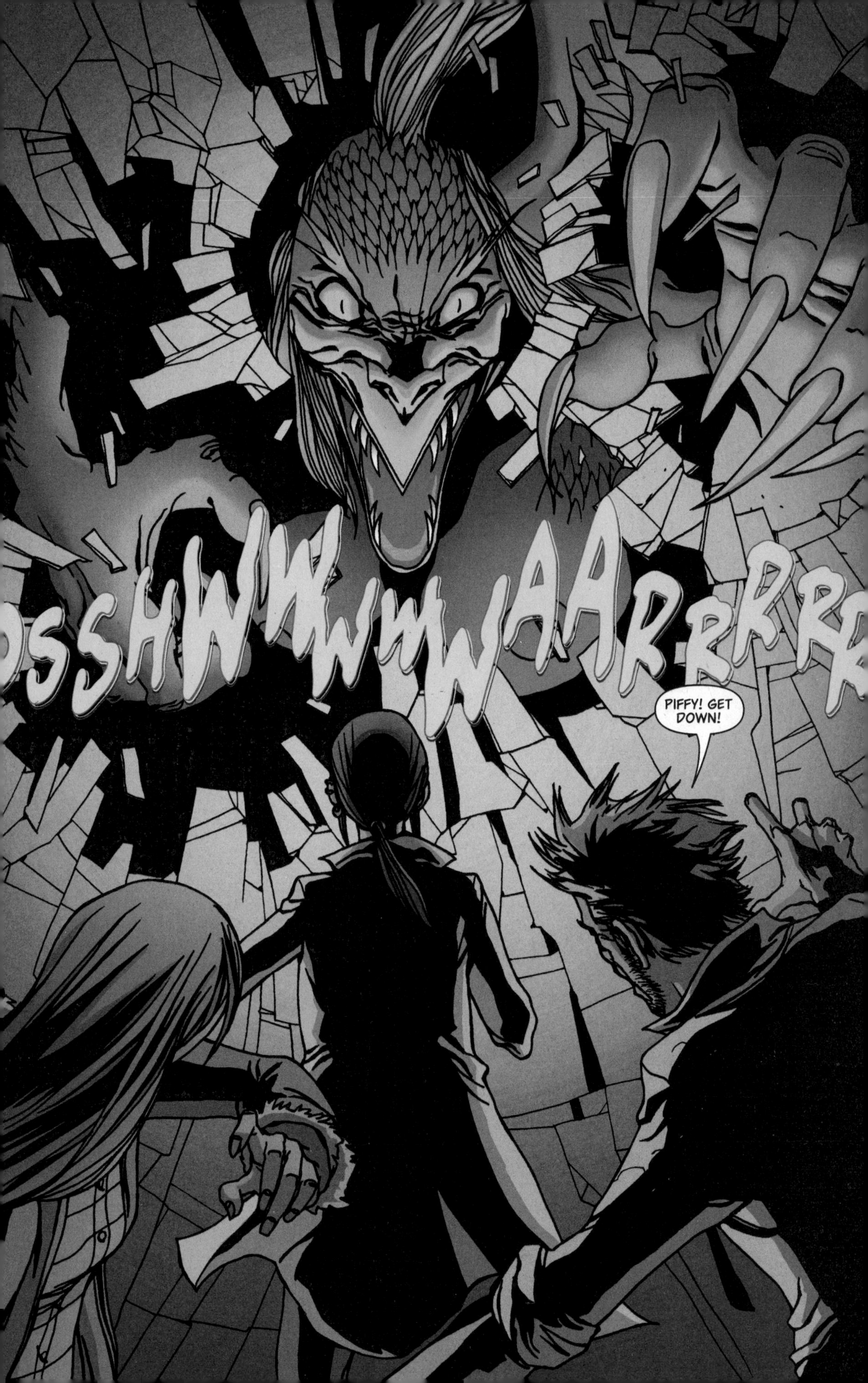
SSHWWWWWAARRRR
PIFFY! GET DOWN!

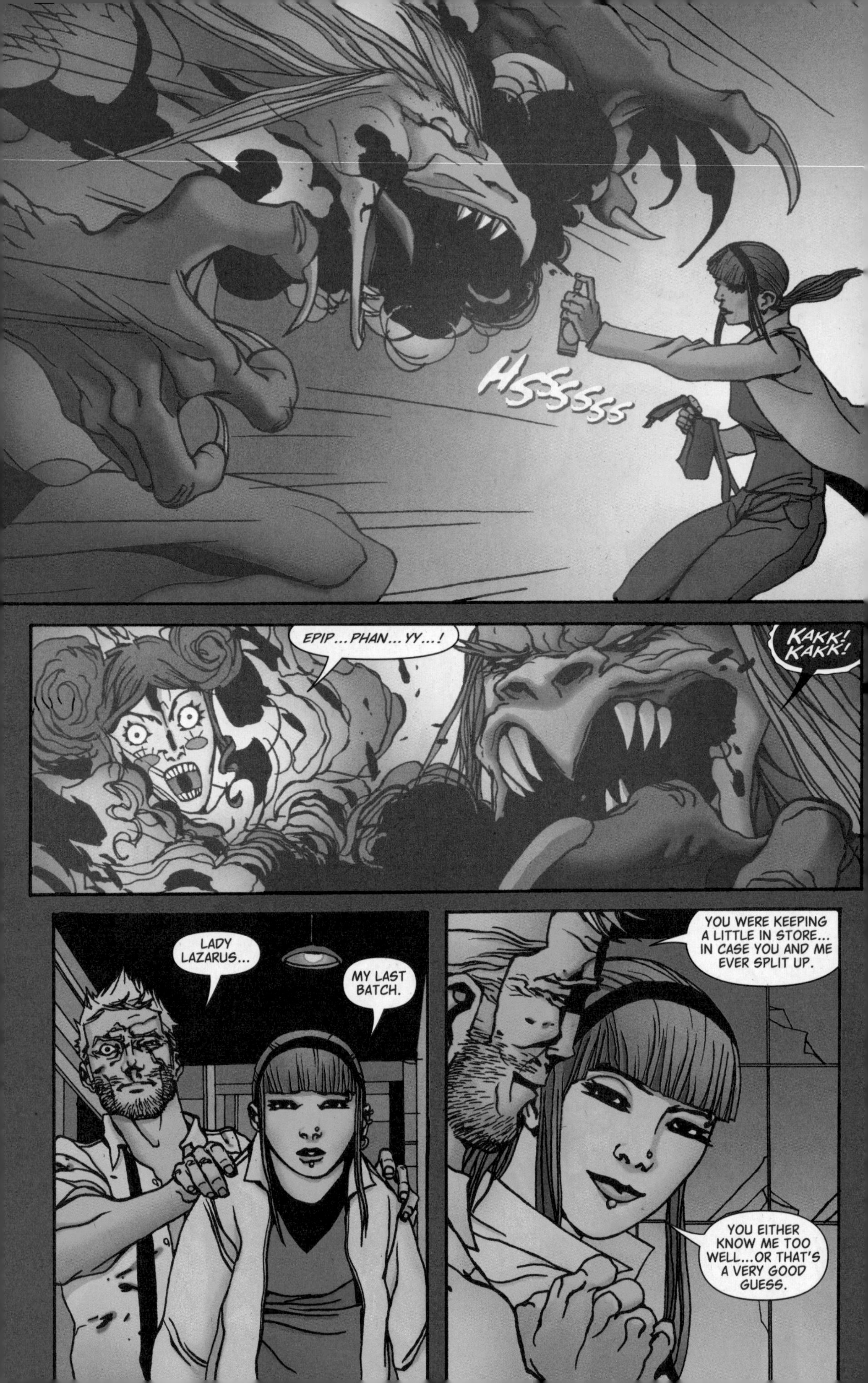
HSSSSSS
EPIP...PHAN...YY...!
KAKK! KAKK!
LADY LAZARUS...
MY LAST BATCH.
YOU WERE KEEPING A LITTLE IN STORE... IN CASE YOU AND ME EVER SPLIT UP.
YOU EITHER KNOW ME TOO WELL...OR THAT'S A VERY GOOD GUESS.

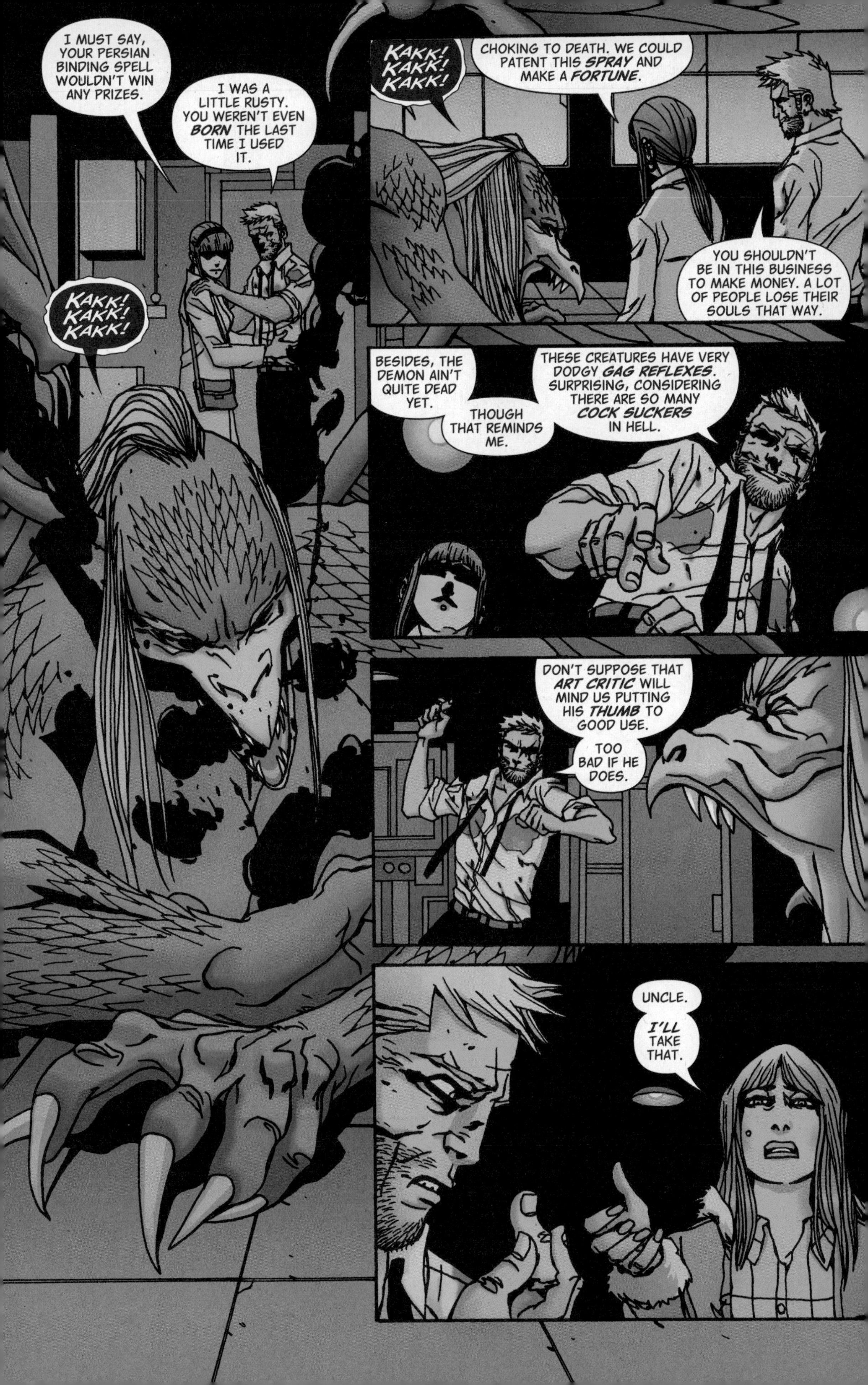
I MUST SAY, YOUR PERSIAN BINDING SPELL WOULDN'T WIN ANY PRIZES.
I WAS A LITTLE RUSTY. YOU WEREN'T EVEN BORN THE LAST TIME I USED IT.
KAKK! KAKK! KAKK!
KAKK! KAKK! KAKK!
CHOKING TO DEATH. WE COULD PATENT THIS SPRAY AND MAKE A FORTUNE.
YOU SHOULDN'T BE IN THIS BUSINESS TO MAKE MONEY. A LOT OF PEOPLE LOSE THEIR SOULS THAT WAY.
BESIDES, THE DEMON AIN'T QUITE DEAD YET.
THOUGH THAT REMINDS ME.
THESE CREATURES HAVE VERY DODGY GAG REFLEXES. SURPRISING, CONSIDERING THERE ARE SO MANY COCK SUCKERS IN HELL.
DON'T SUPPOSE THAT ART CRITIC WILL MIND US PUTTING HIS THUMB TO GOOD USE.
TOO BAD IF HE DOES.
UNCLE.
I'LL TAKE THAT.

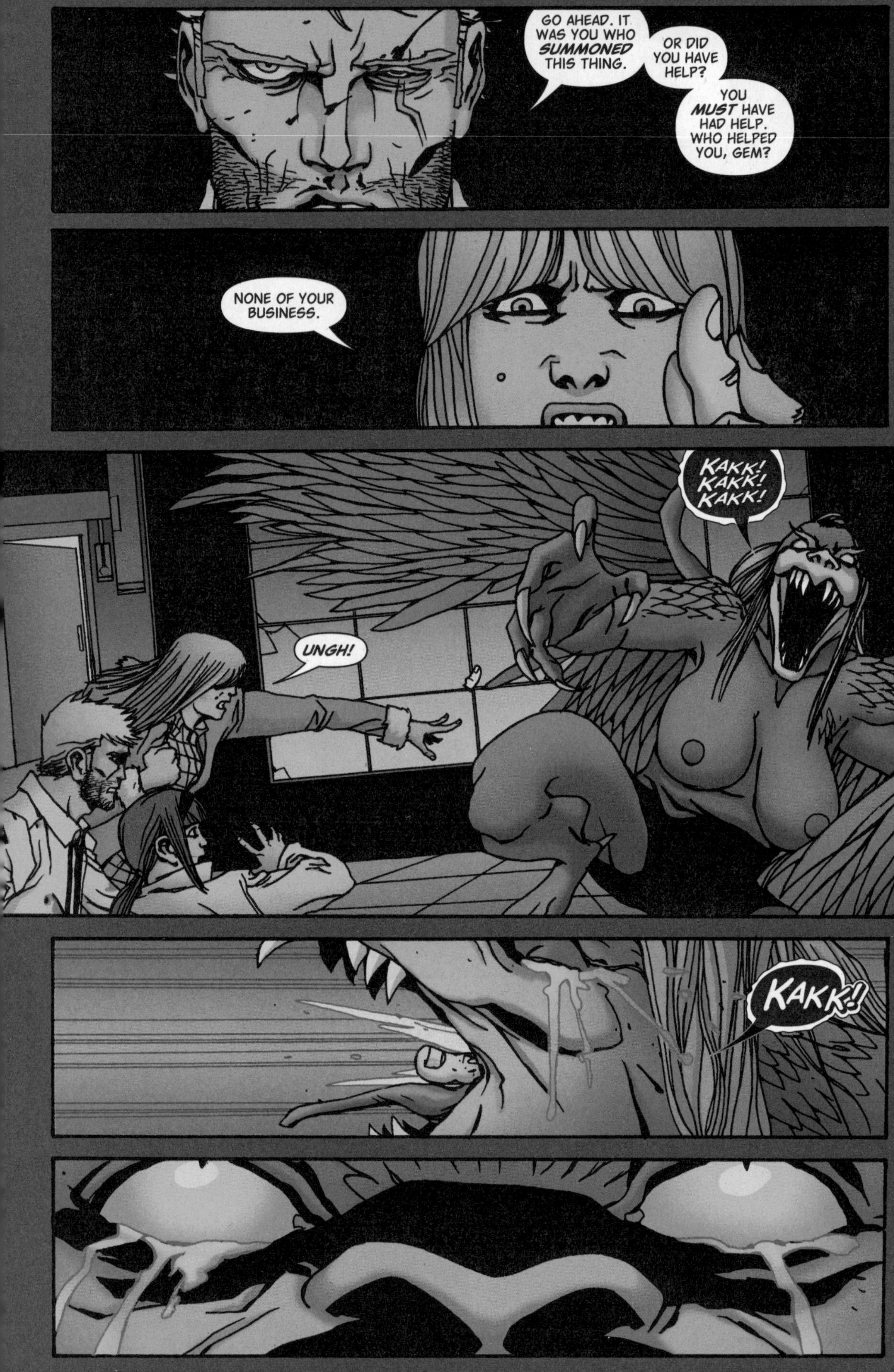
GO AHEAD. IT WAS YOU WHO *SUMMONED* THIS THING.
OR DID YOU HAVE HELP?
YOU **MUST** HAVE HAD HELP. WHO HELPED YOU, GEM?
NONE OF YOUR BUSINESS.
KAKK! KAKK! KAKK!
UNGH!
KAKK!

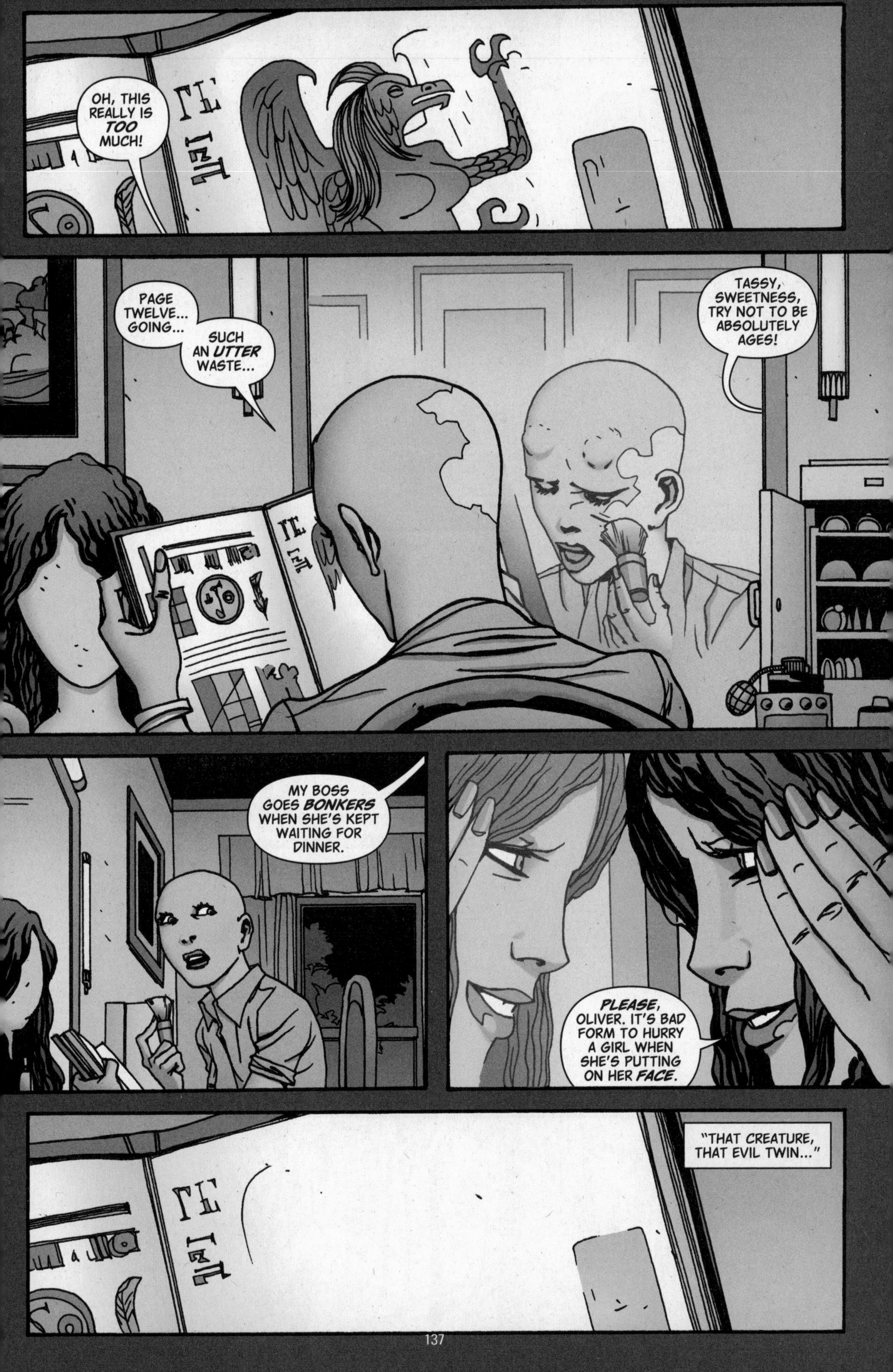
OH, THIS REALLY IS *TOO* MUCH!
PAGE TWELVE... GOING...
SUCH AN *UTTER* WASTE...
TASSY, SWEETNESS, TRY NOT TO BE ABSOLUTELY AGES!
MY BOSS GOES *BONKERS* WHEN SHE'S KEPT WAITING FOR DINNER.
PLEASE, OLIVER. IT'S BAD FORM TO HURRY A GIRL WHEN SHE'S PUTTING ON HER *FACE*.
"THAT CREATURE, THAT EVIL TWIN..."

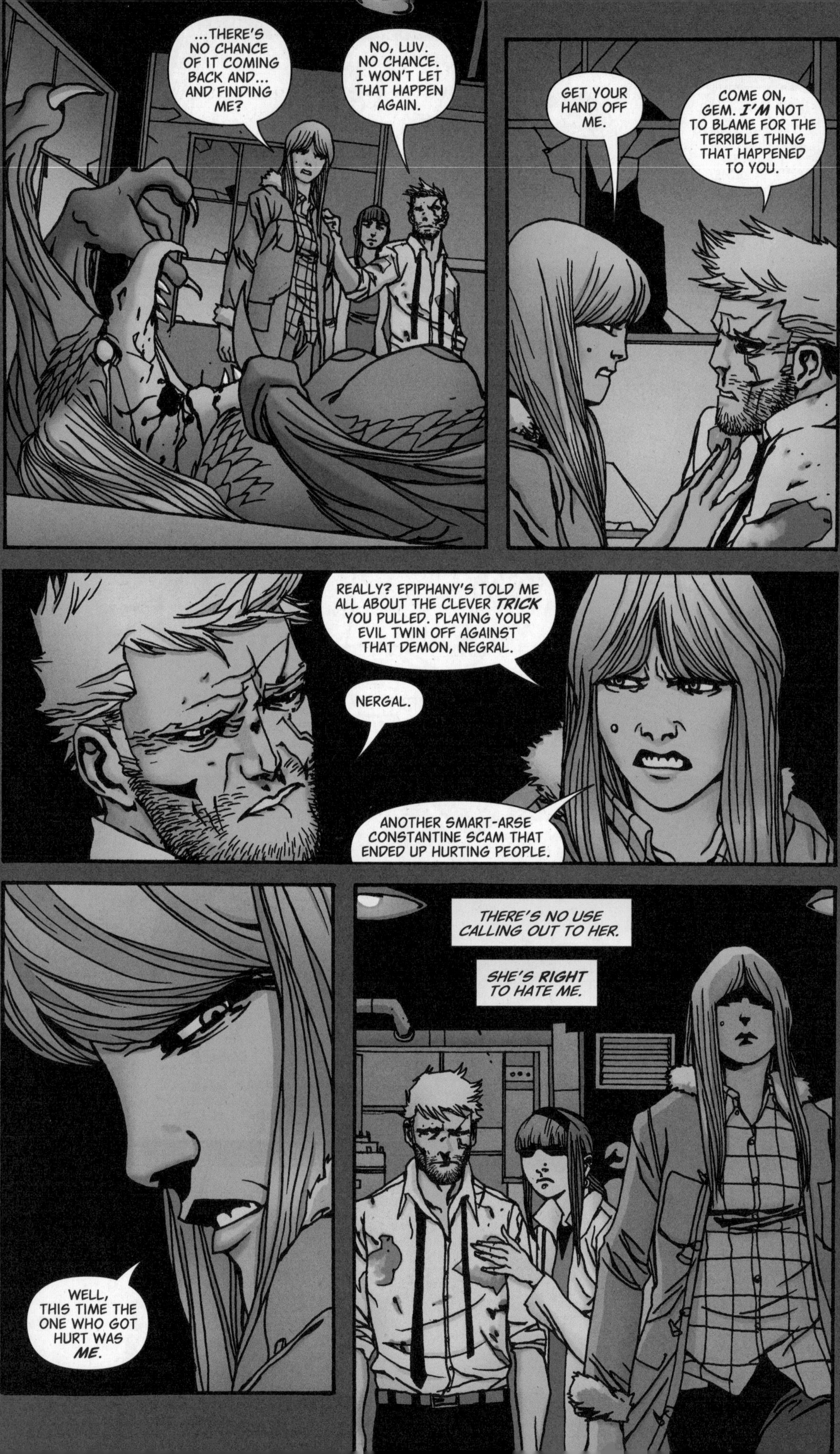
...THERE'S NO CHANCE OF IT COMING BACK AND... AND FINDING ME?
NO, LUV. NO CHANCE. I WON'T LET THAT HAPPEN AGAIN.
GET YOUR HAND OFF ME.
COME ON, GEM. I'M NOT TO BLAME FOR THE TERRIBLE THING THAT HAPPENED TO YOU.
REALLY? EPIPHANY'S TOLD ME ALL ABOUT THE CLEVER TRICK YOU PULLED. PLAYING YOUR EVIL TWIN OFF AGAINST THAT DEMON, NEGRAL.
NERGAL.
ANOTHER SMART-ARSE CONSTANTINE SCAM THAT ENDED UP HURTING PEOPLE.
WELL, THIS TIME THE ONE WHO GOT HURT WAS ME.
THERE'S NO USE CALLING OUT TO HER.
SHE'S RIGHT TO HATE ME.

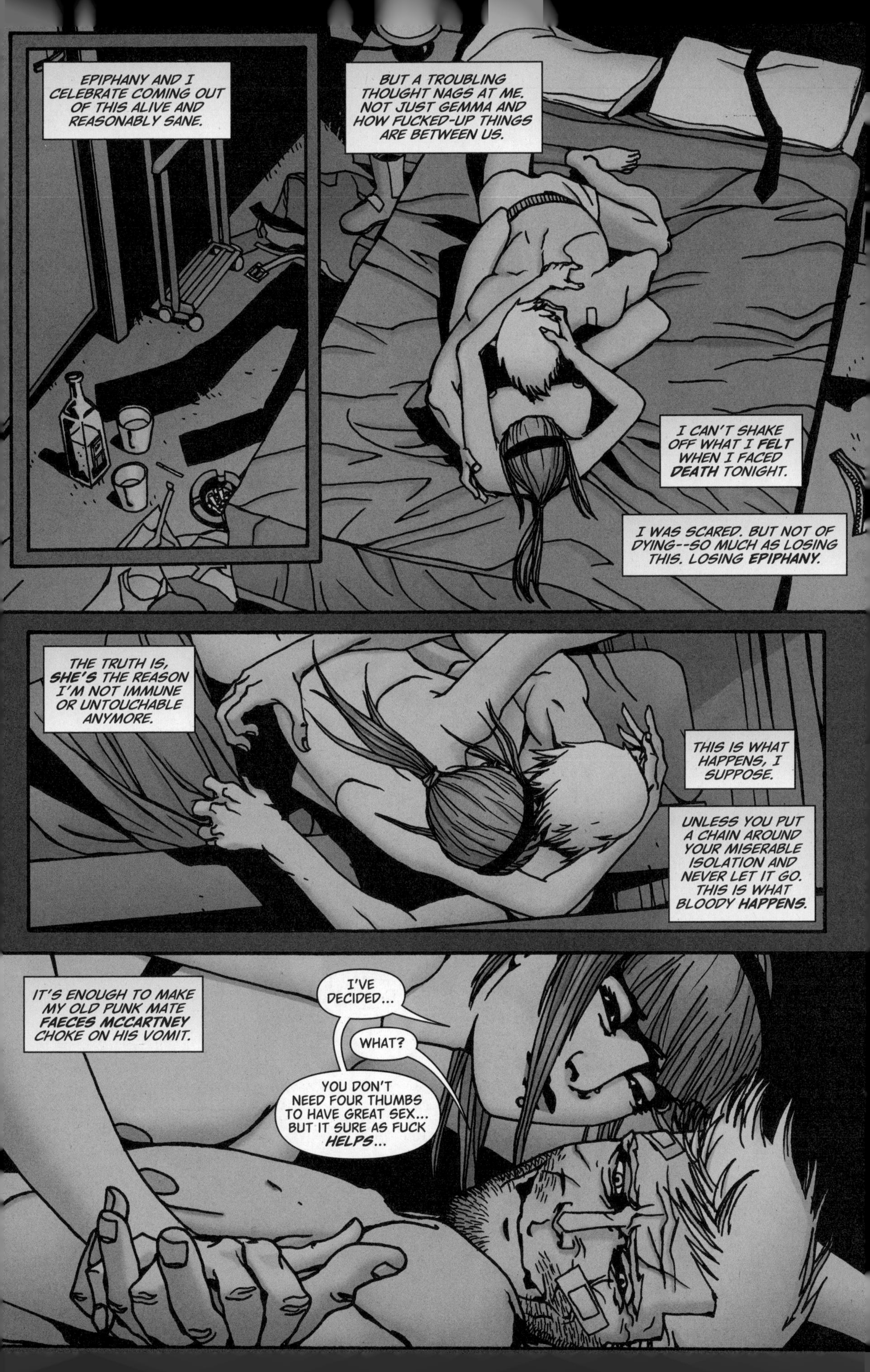
EPIPHANY AND I CELEBRATE COMING OUT OF THIS ALIVE AND REASONABLY SANE.
BUT A TROUBLING THOUGHT NAGS AT ME. NOT JUST GEMMA AND HOW FUCKED-UP THINGS ARE BETWEEN US.
I CAN'T SHAKE OFF WHAT I FELT WHEN I FACED DEATH TONIGHT.
I WAS SCARED. BUT NOT OF DYING--SO MUCH AS LOSING THIS. LOSING EPIPHANY.
THE TRUTH IS, SHE'S THE REASON I'M NOT IMMUNE OR UNTOUCHABLE ANYMORE.
THIS IS WHAT HAPPENS, I SUPPOSE.
UNLESS YOU PUT A CHAIN AROUND YOUR MISERABLE ISOLATION AND NEVER LET IT GO. THIS IS WHAT BLOODY HAPPENS.
IT'S ENOUGH TO MAKE MY OLD PUNK MATE FAECES MCCARTNEY CHOKE ON HIS VOMIT.
I'VE DECIDED...
WHAT?
YOU DON'T NEED FOUR THUMBS TO HAVE GREAT SEX... BUT IT SURE AS FUCK HELPS...

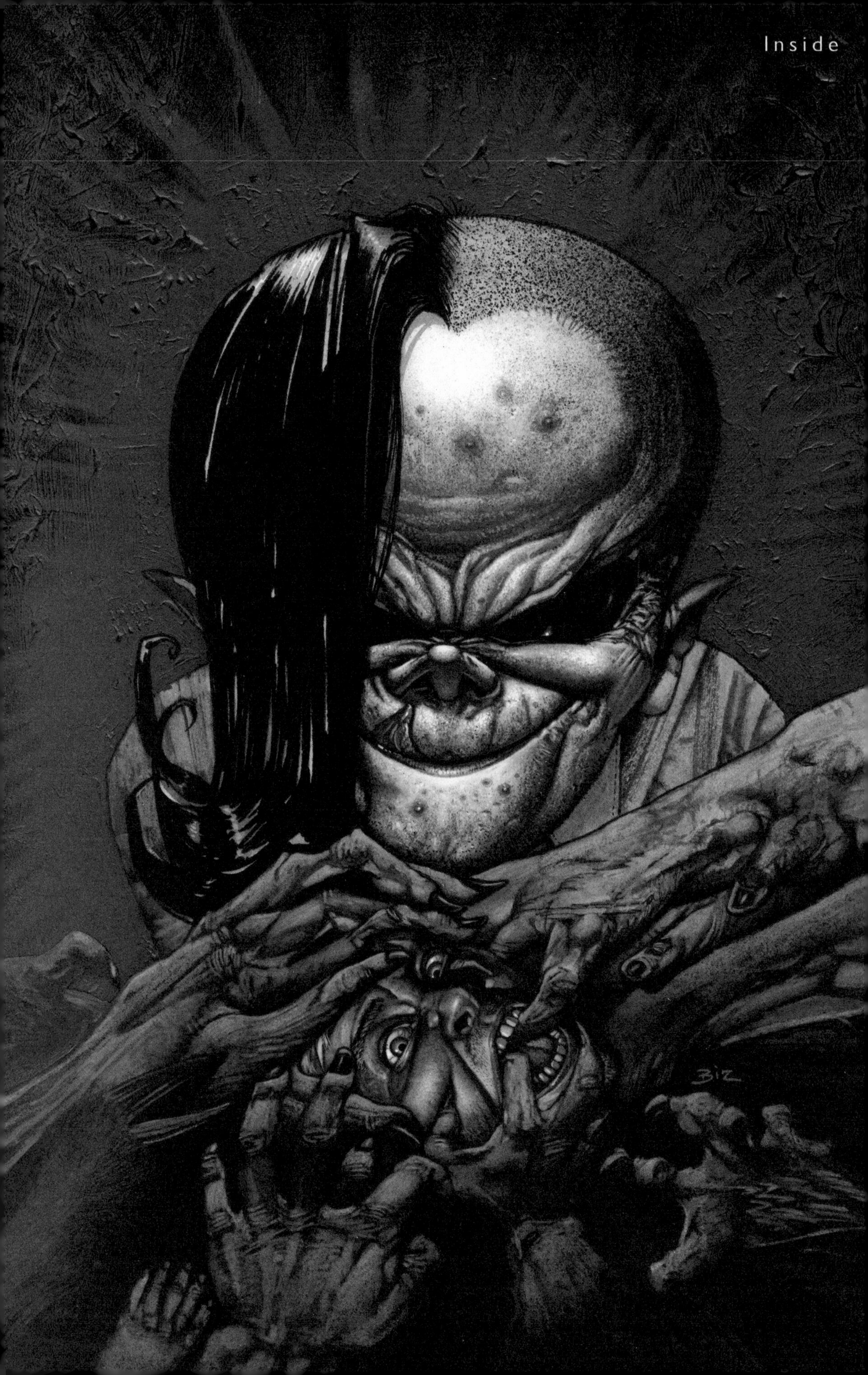
BIZ

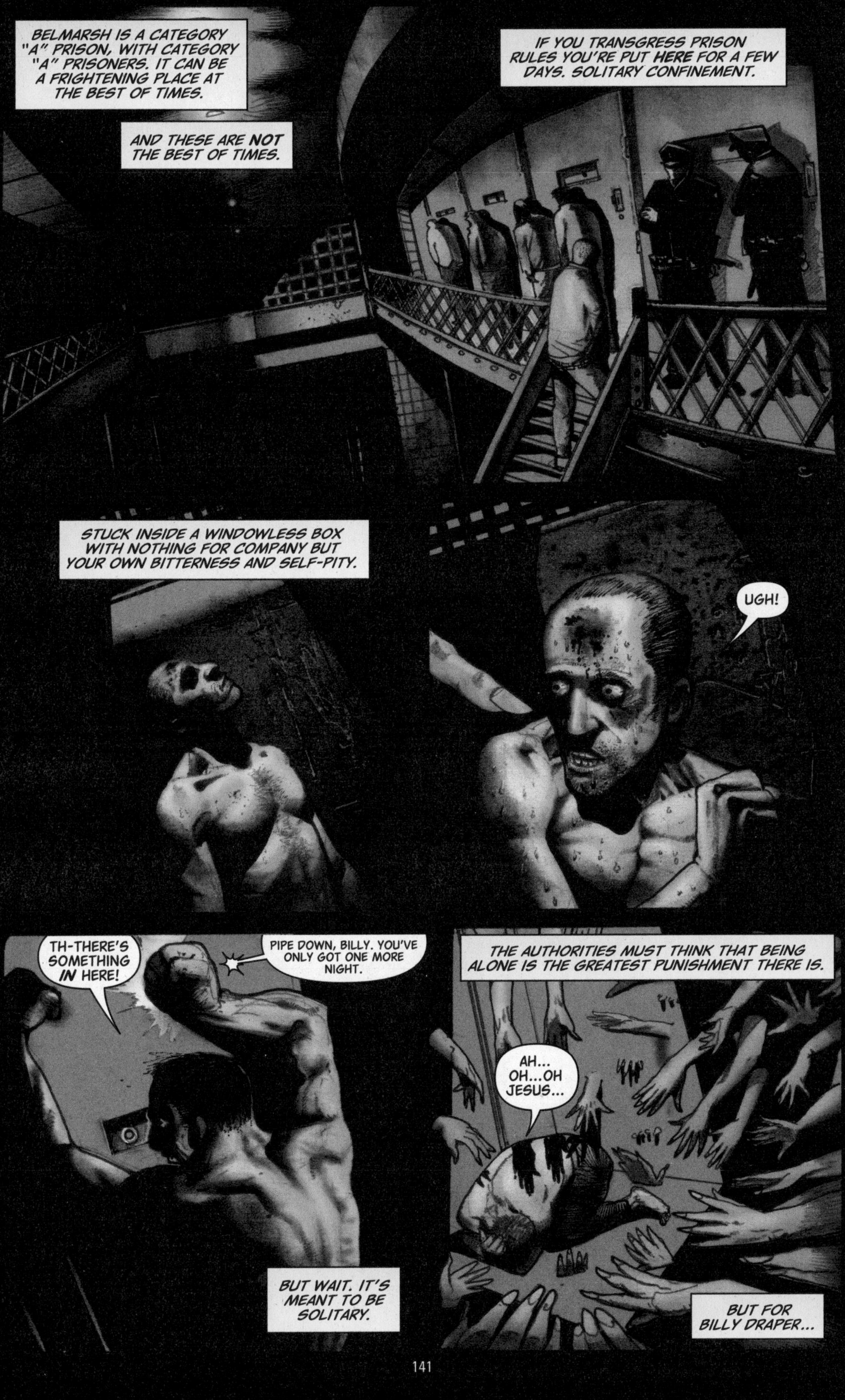
BELMARSH IS A CATEGORY "A" PRISON, WITH CATEGORY "A" PRISONERS. IT CAN BE A FRIGHTENING PLACE AT THE BEST OF TIMES.
AND THESE ARE NOT THE BEST OF TIMES.
IF YOU TRANSGRESS PRISON RULES YOU'RE PUT HERE FOR A FEW DAYS. SOLITARY CONFINEMENT.
STUCK INSIDE A WINDOWLESS BOX WITH NOTHING FOR COMPANY BUT YOUR OWN BITTERNESS AND SELF-PITY.
UGH!
TH-THERE'S SOMETHING IN HERE!
PIPE DOWN, BILLY. YOU'VE ONLY GOT ONE MORE NIGHT.
BUT WAIT. IT'S MEANT TO BE SOLITARY.
THE AUTHORITIES MUST THINK THAT BEING ALONE IS THE GREATEST PUNISHMENT THERE IS.
AH... OH...OH JESUS...
BUT FOR BILLY DRAPER...

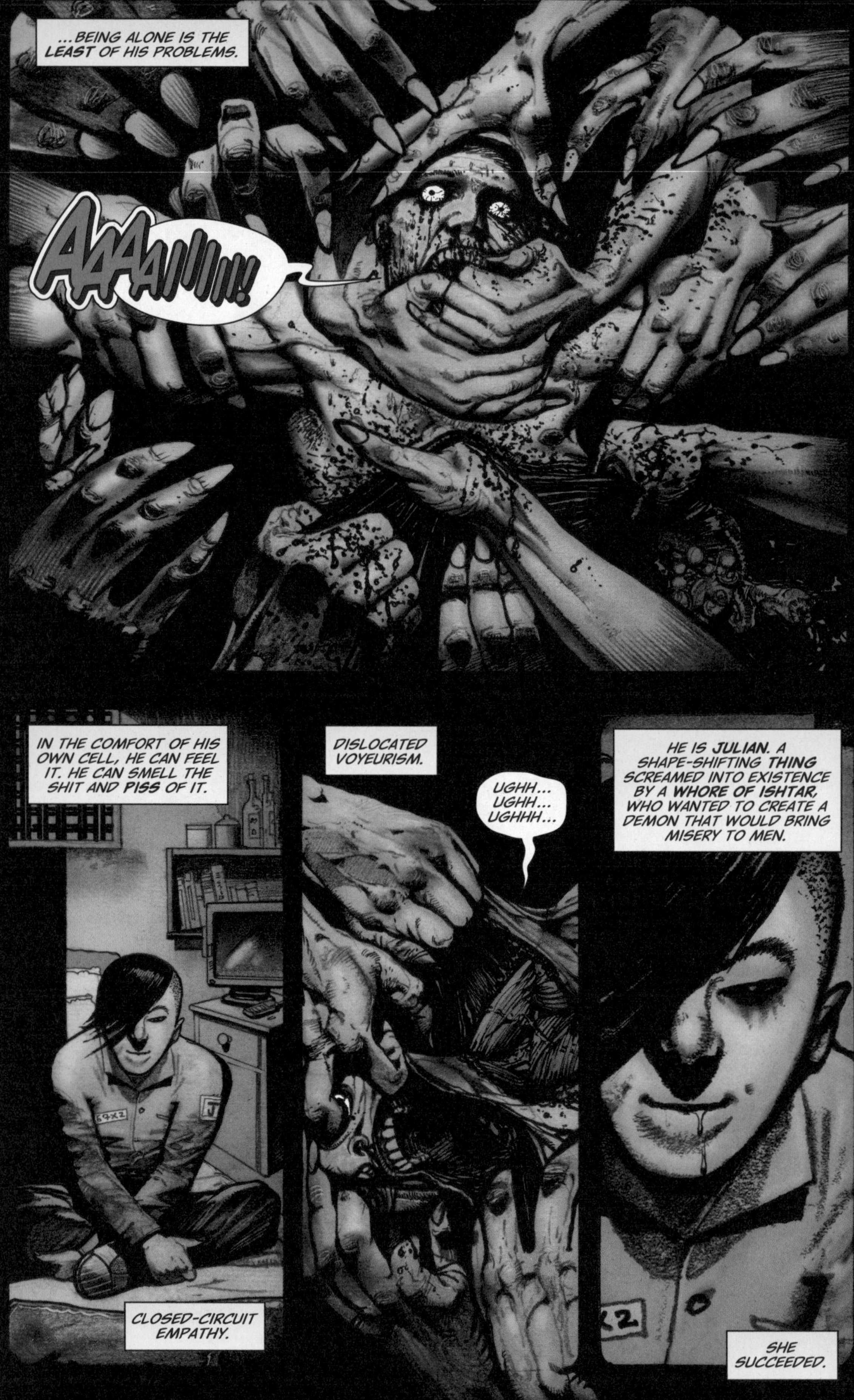
...BEING ALONE IS THE LEAST OF HIS PROBLEMS.
AAAAIIIIIII!
IN THE COMFORT OF HIS OWN CELL, HE CAN FEEL IT. HE CAN SMELL THE SHIT AND PISS OF IT.
CLOSED-CIRCUIT EMPATHY.
DISLOCATED VOYEURISM.
UGHH... UGHH... UGHHH...
HE IS JULIAN. A SHAPE-SHIFTING THING SCREAMED INTO EXISTENCE BY A WHORE OF ISHTAR, WHO WANTED TO CREATE A DEMON THAT WOULD BRING MISERY TO MEN.
SHE SUCCEEDED.

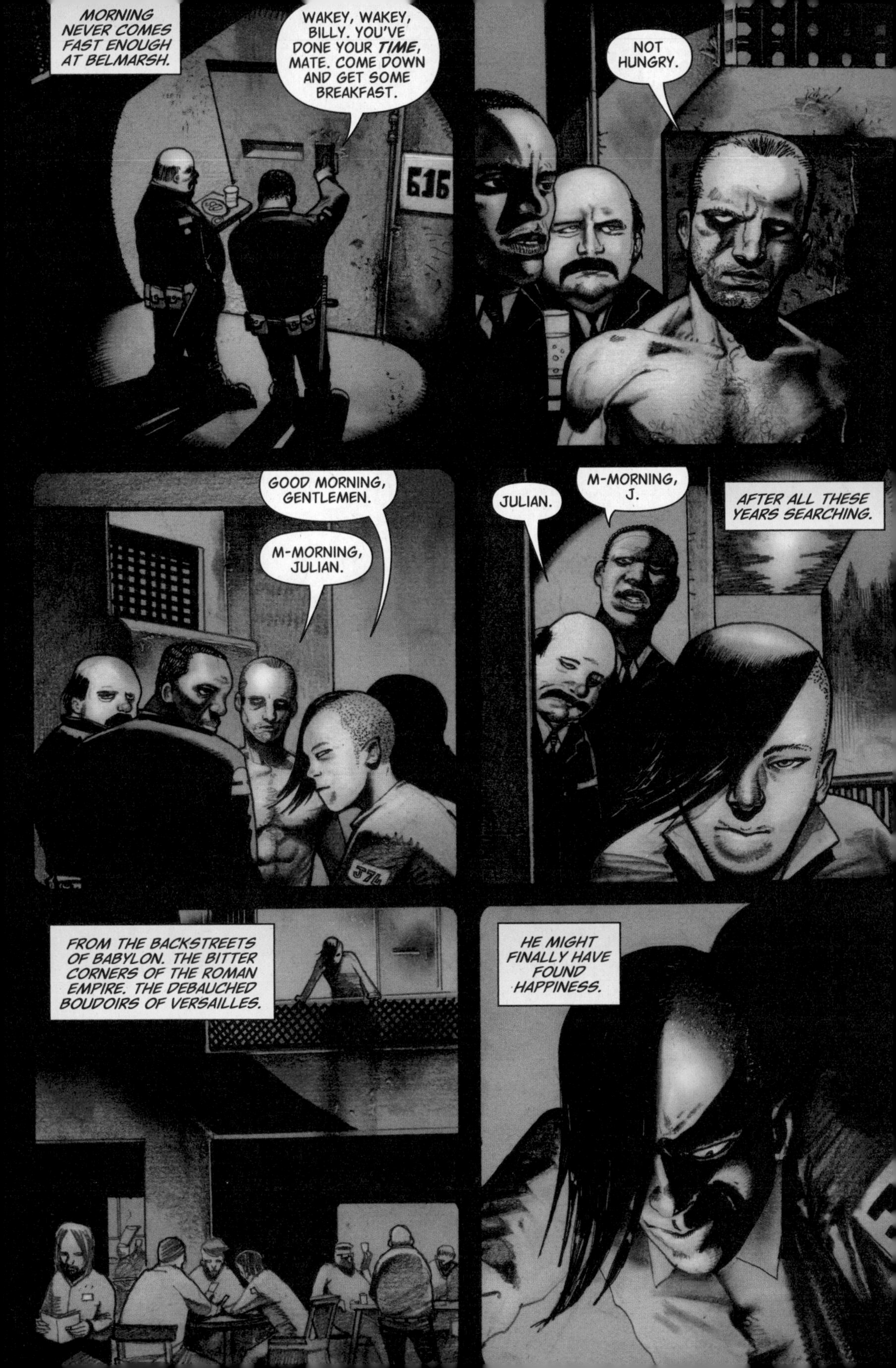
MORNING NEVER COMES FAST ENOUGH AT BELMARSH.
WAKEY, WAKEY, BILLY. YOU'VE DONE YOUR *TIME*, MATE. COME DOWN AND GET SOME BREAKFAST.
NOT HUNGRY.
GOOD MORNING, GENTLEMEN.
M-MORNING, JULIAN.
JULIAN.
M-MORNING, J.
AFTER ALL THESE YEARS SEARCHING.
FROM THE BACKSTREETS OF BABYLON. THE BITTER CORNERS OF THE ROMAN EMPIRE. THE DEBAUCHED BOUDOIRS OF VERSAILLES.
HE MIGHT FINALLY HAVE FOUND HAPPINESS.

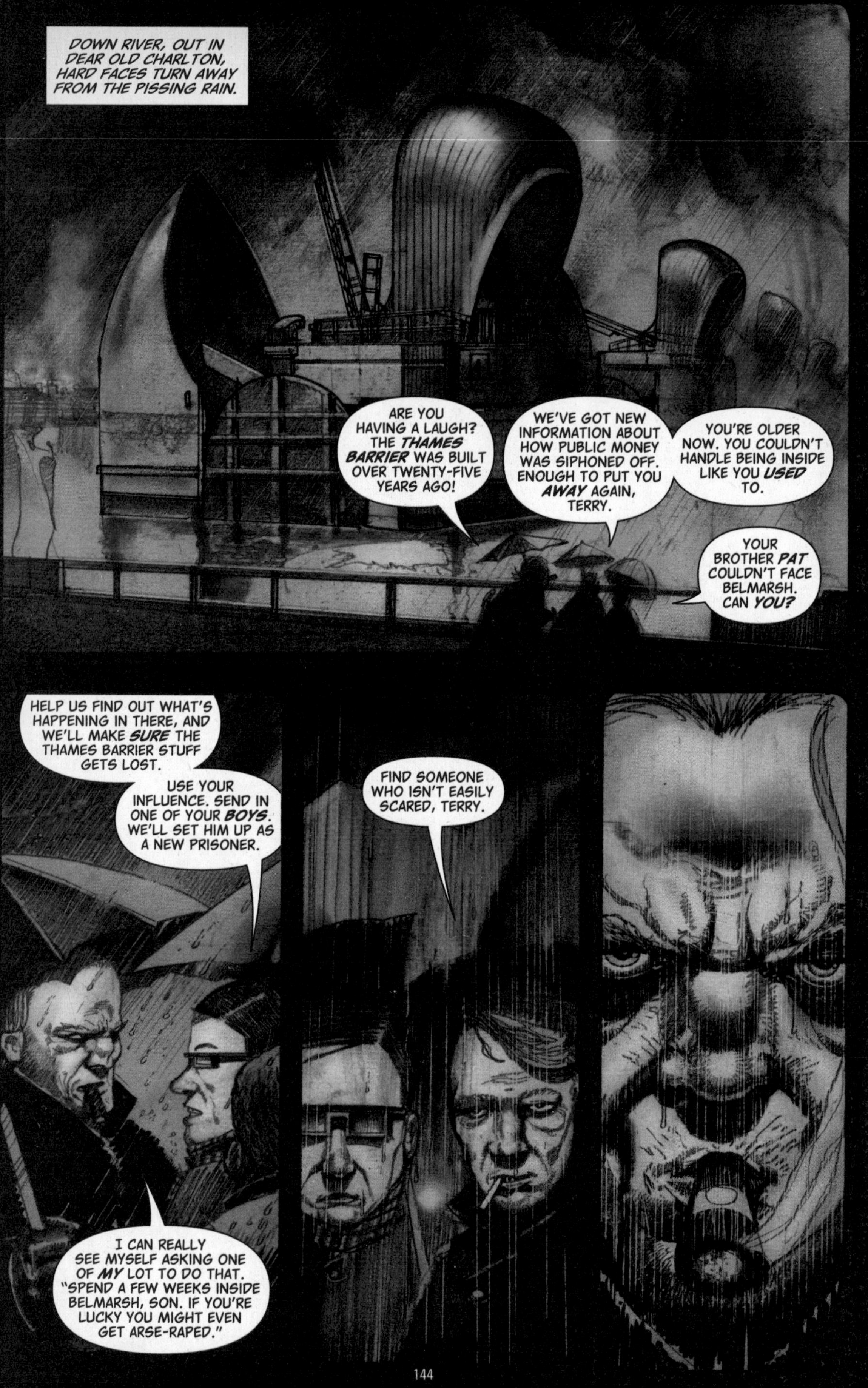
DOWN RIVER, OUT IN DEAR OLD CHARLTON, HARD FACES TURN AWAY FROM THE PISSING RAIN.
ARE YOU HAVING A LAUGH? THE THAMES BARRIER WAS BUILT OVER TWENTY-FIVE YEARS AGO!
WE'VE GOT NEW INFORMATION ABOUT HOW PUBLIC MONEY WAS SIPHONED OFF. ENOUGH TO PUT YOU AWAY AGAIN, TERRY.
YOU'RE OLDER NOW. YOU COULDN'T HANDLE BEING INSIDE LIKE YOU USED TO.
YOUR BROTHER PAT COULDN'T FACE BELMARSH. CAN YOU?
HELP US FIND OUT WHAT'S HAPPENING IN THERE, AND WE'LL MAKE SURE THE THAMES BARRIER STUFF GETS LOST.
USE YOUR INFLUENCE. SEND IN ONE OF YOUR BOYS. WE'LL SET HIM UP AS A NEW PRISONER.
I CAN REALLY SEE MYSELF ASKING ONE OF MY LOT TO DO THAT. "SPEND A FEW WEEKS INSIDE BELMARSH, SON. IF YOU'RE LUCKY YOU MIGHT EVEN GET ARSE-RAPED."
FIND SOMEONE WHO ISN'T EASILY SCARED, TERRY.

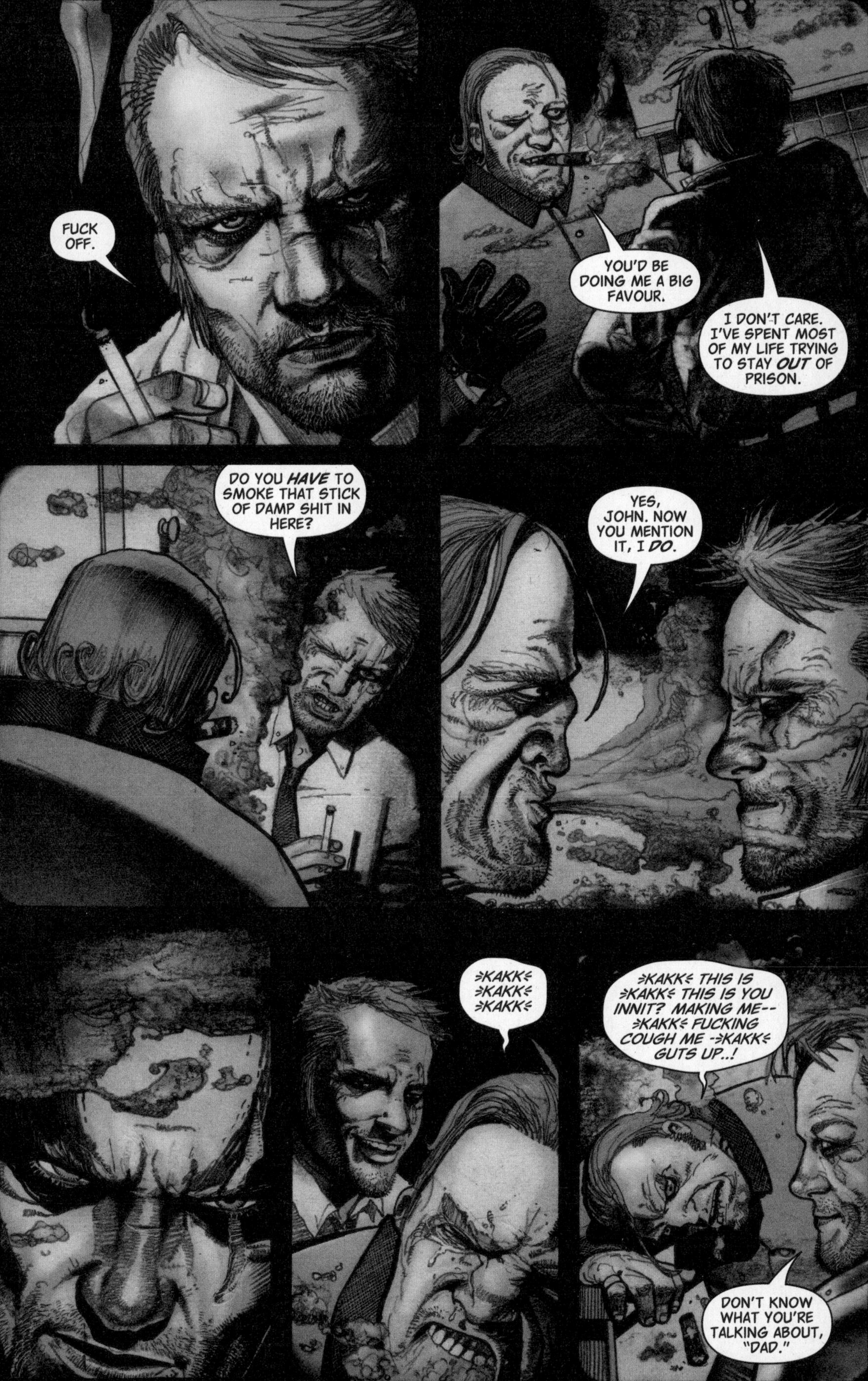
FUCK OFF.
YOU'D BE DOING ME A BIG FAVOUR.
I DON'T CARE. I'VE SPENT MOST OF MY LIFE TRYING TO STAY OUT OF PRISON.
DO YOU HAVE TO SMOKE THAT STICK OF DAMP SHIT IN HERE?
YES, JOHN. NOW YOU MENTION IT, I DO.
KAKK KAKK KAKK
KAKK THIS IS KAKK THIS IS YOU INNIT? MAKING ME-- KAKK FUCKING COUGH ME -KAKK GUTS UP..!
DON'T KNOW WHAT YOU'RE TALKING ABOUT, "DAD."

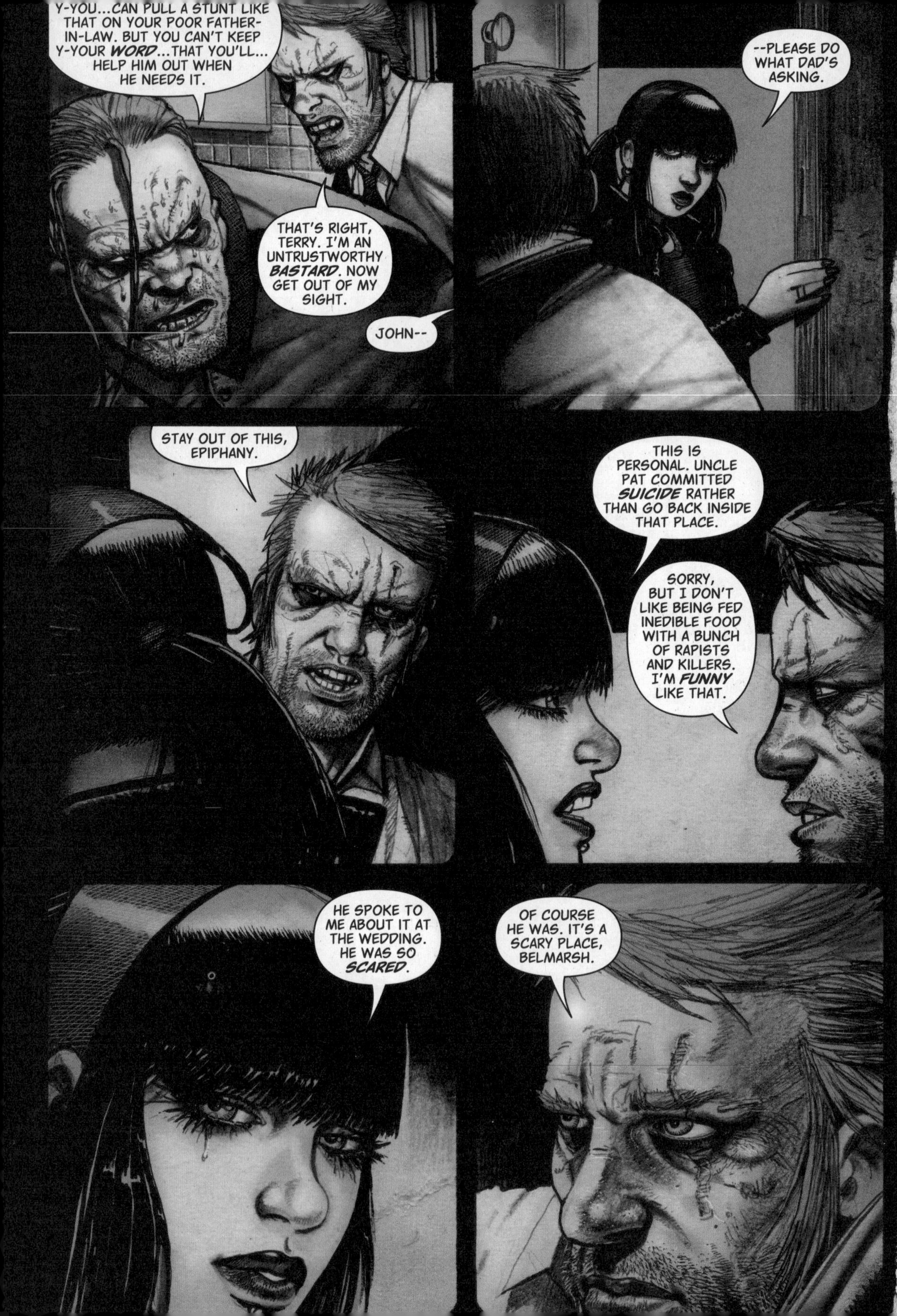
Y-YOU...CAN PULL A STUNT LIKE THAT ON YOUR POOR FATHER-IN-LAW. BUT YOU CAN'T KEEP Y-YOUR WORD...THAT YOU'LL... HELP HIM OUT WHEN HE NEEDS IT.
THAT'S RIGHT, TERRY. I'M AN UNTRUSTWORTHY BASTARD. NOW GET OUT OF MY SIGHT.
JOHN--
--PLEASE DO WHAT DAD'S ASKING.
STAY OUT OF THIS, EPIPHANY.
THIS IS PERSONAL. UNCLE PAT COMMITTED SUICIDE RATHER THAN GO BACK INSIDE THAT PLACE.
SORRY, BUT I DON'T LIKE BEING FED INEDIBLE FOOD WITH A BUNCH OF RAPISTS AND KILLERS. I'M FUNNY LIKE THAT.
HE SPOKE TO ME ABOUT IT AT THE WEDDING. HE WAS SO SCARED.
OF COURSE HE WAS. IT'S A SCARY PLACE, BELMARSH.

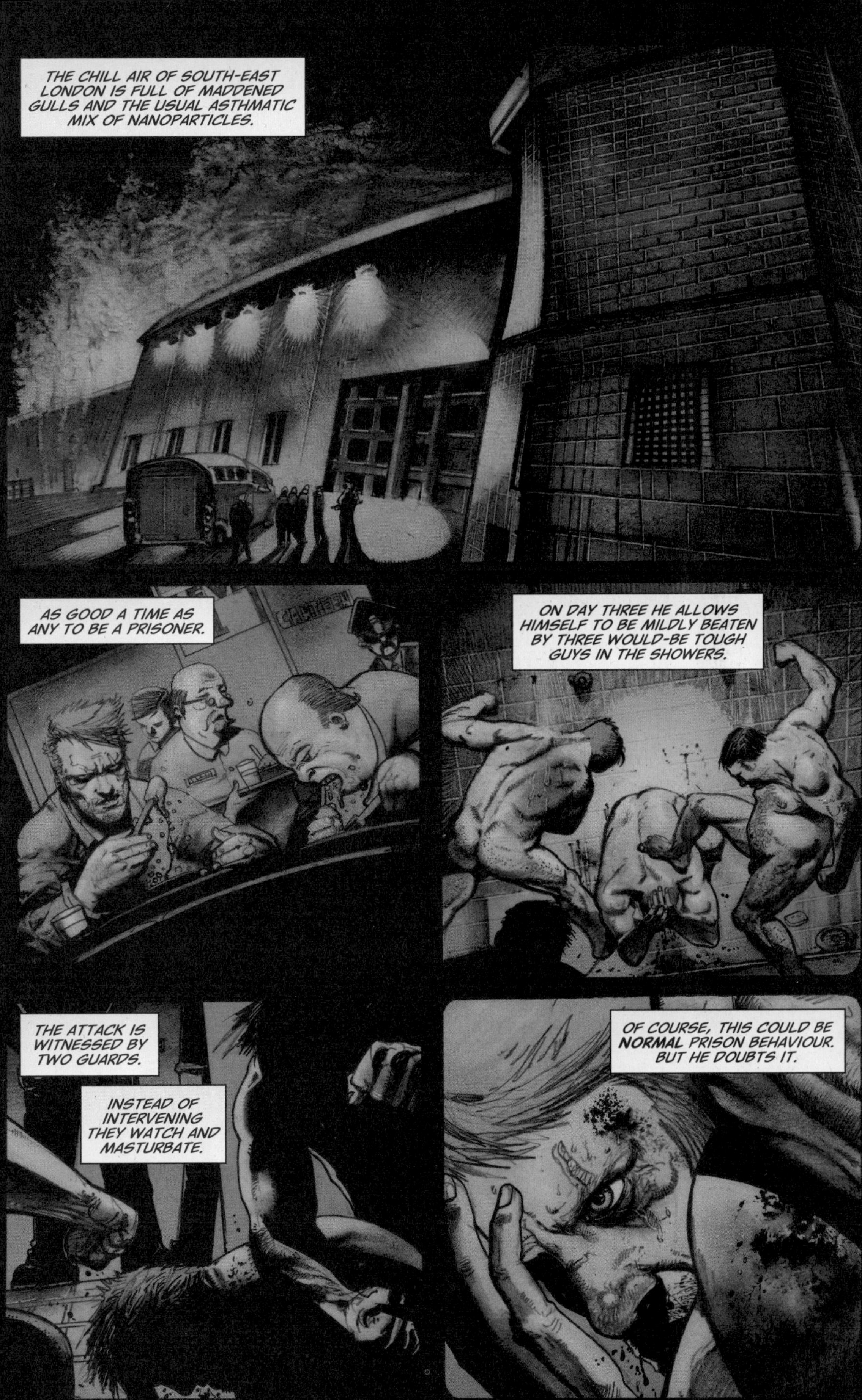
THE CHILL AIR OF SOUTH-EAST LONDON IS FULL OF MADDENED GULLS AND THE USUAL ASTHMATIC MIX OF NANOPARTICLES.
AS GOOD A TIME AS ANY TO BE A PRISONER.
ON DAY THREE HE ALLOWS HIMSELF TO BE MILDLY BEATEN BY THREE WOULD-BE TOUGH GUYS IN THE SHOWERS.
THE ATTACK IS WITNESSED BY TWO GUARDS.
INSTEAD OF INTERVENING THEY WATCH AND MASTURBATE.
OF COURSE, THIS COULD BE **NORMAL** PRISON BEHAVIOUR. BUT HE DOUBTS IT.

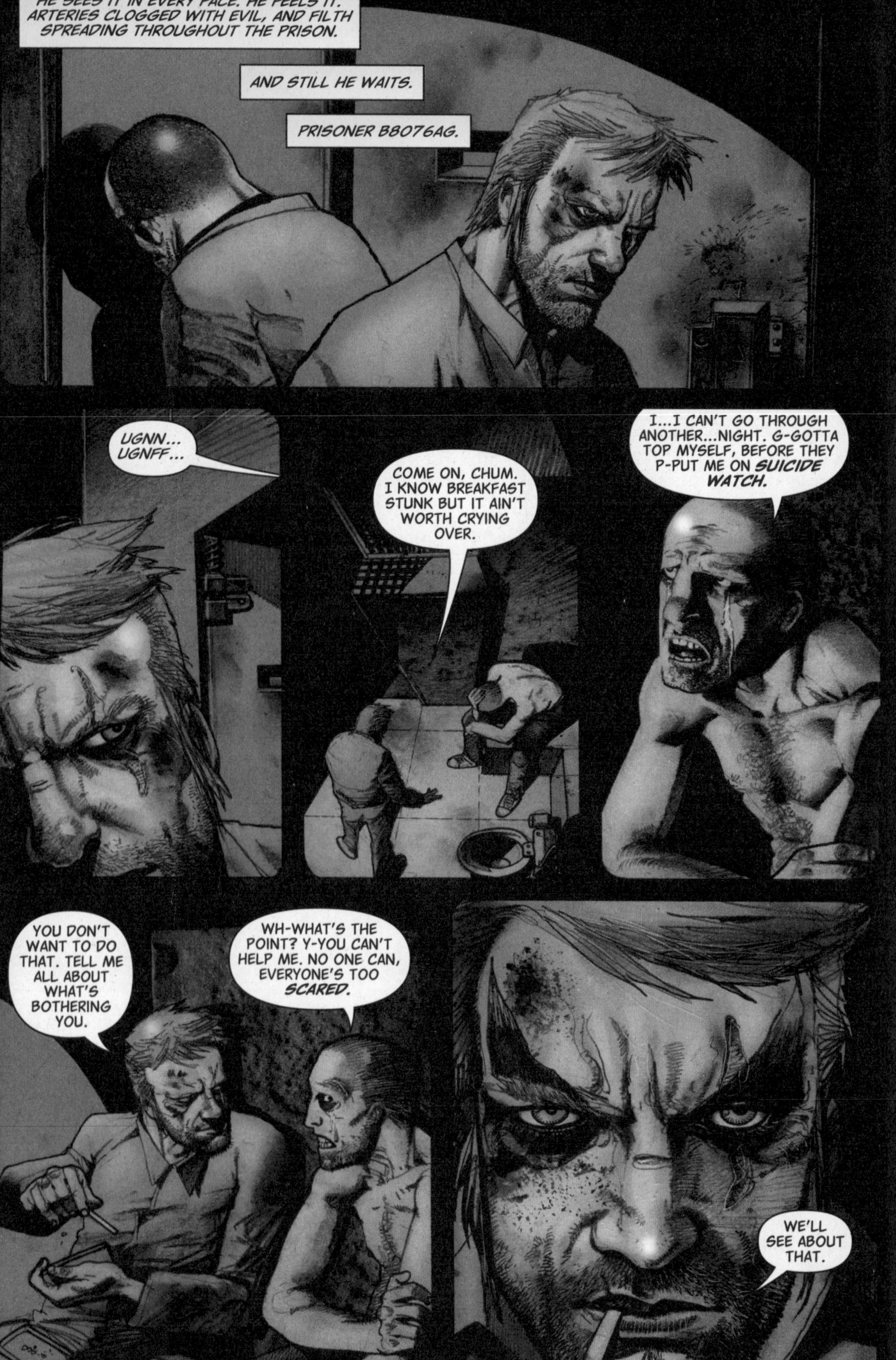
HE SEES IT IN EVERY FACE. HE FEELS IT. ARTERIES CLOGGED WITH EVIL, AND FILTH SPREADING THROUGHOUT THE PRISON.
AND STILL HE WAITS.
PRISONER B8076AG.
UGNN... UGNFF...
COME ON, CHUM. I KNOW BREAKFAST STUNK BUT IT AIN'T WORTH CRYING OVER.
I...I CAN'T GO THROUGH ANOTHER...NIGHT. G-GOTTA TOP MYSELF, BEFORE THEY P-PUT ME ON SUICIDE WATCH.
YOU DON'T WANT TO DO THAT. TELL ME ALL ABOUT WHAT'S BOTHERING YOU.
WH-WHAT'S THE POINT? Y-YOU CAN'T HELP ME. NO ONE CAN, EVERYONE'S TOO SCARED.
WE'LL SEE ABOUT THAT.

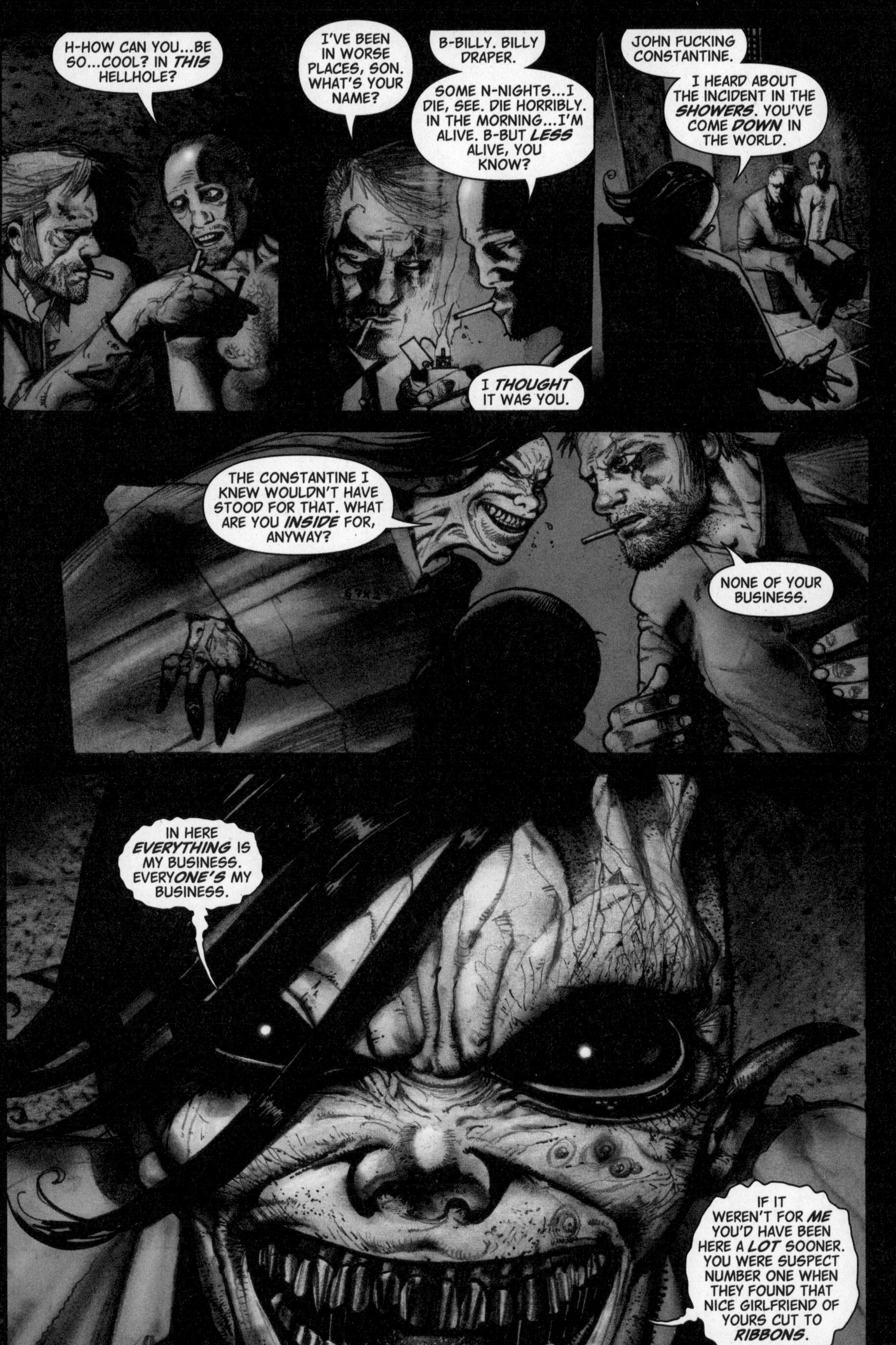
H-HOW CAN YOU...BE SO...COOL? IN THIS HELLHOLE?
I'VE BEEN IN WORSE PLACES, SON. WHAT'S YOUR NAME?
B-BILLY. BILLY DRAPER.
SOME N-NIGHTS...I DIE, SEE. DIE HORRIBLY. IN THE MORNING...I'M ALIVE. B-BUT LESS ALIVE, YOU KNOW?
I THOUGHT IT WAS YOU.
JOHN FUCKING CONSTANTINE.
I HEARD ABOUT THE INCIDENT IN THE SHOWERS. YOU'VE COME DOWN IN THE WORLD.
THE CONSTANTINE I KNEW WOULDN'T HAVE STOOD FOR THAT. WHAT ARE YOU INSIDE FOR, ANYWAY?
NONE OF YOUR BUSINESS.
IN HERE EVERYTHING IS MY BUSINESS. EVERYONE'S MY BUSINESS.
IF IT WEREN'T FOR ME YOU'D HAVE BEEN HERE A LOT SOONER. YOU WERE SUSPECT NUMBER ONE WHEN THEY FOUND THAT NICE GIRLFRIEND OF YOURS CUT TO RIBBONS.

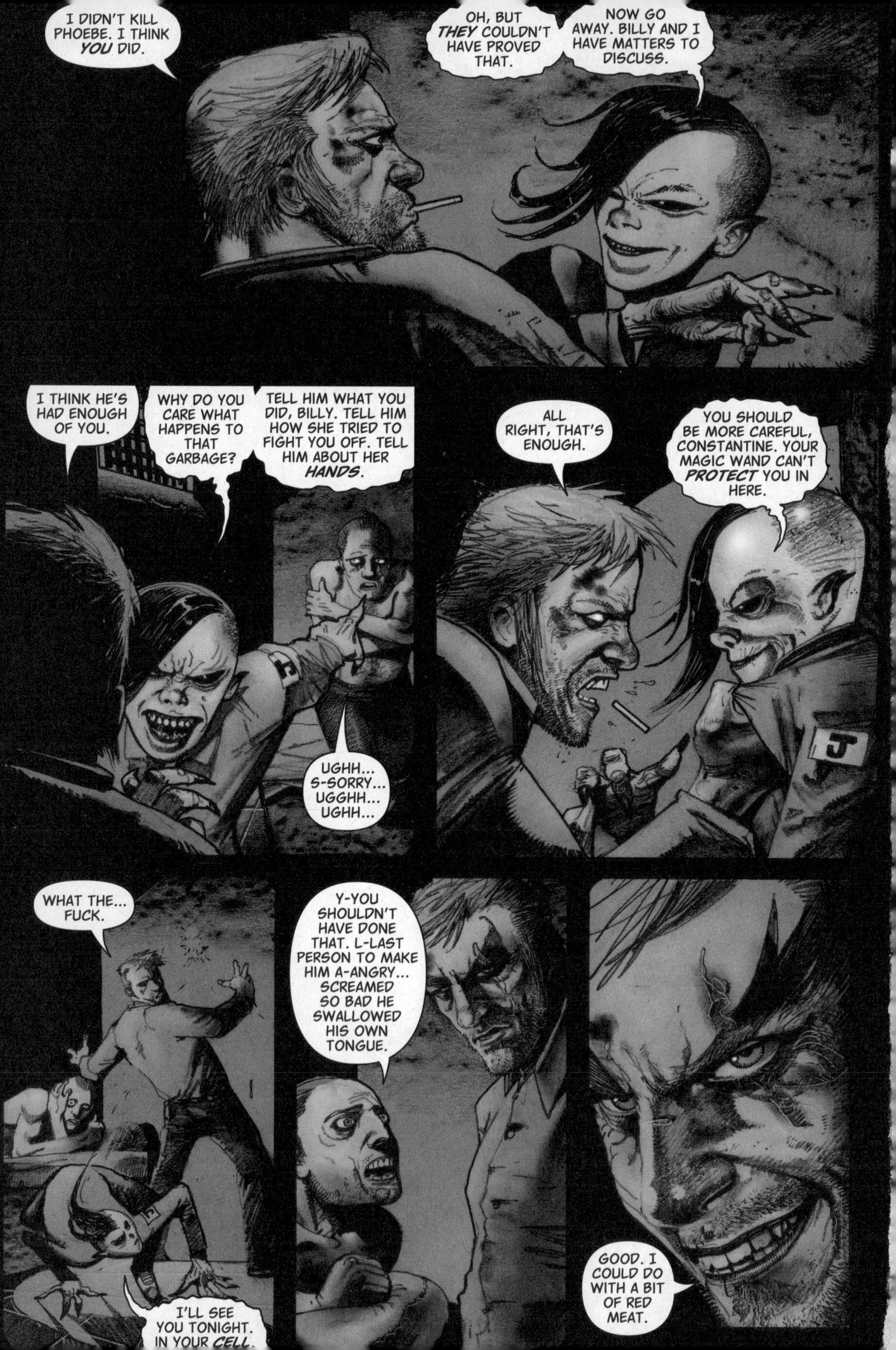
I DIDN'T KILL PHOEBE. I THINK *YOU* DID.
OH, BUT *THEY* COULDN'T HAVE PROVED THAT.
NOW GO AWAY. BILLY AND I HAVE MATTERS TO DISCUSS.
I THINK HE'S HAD ENOUGH OF YOU.
WHY DO YOU CARE WHAT HAPPENS TO THAT GARBAGE?
TELL HIM WHAT YOU DID, BILLY. TELL HIM HOW SHE TRIED TO FIGHT YOU OFF. TELL HIM ABOUT HER *HANDS*.
UGHH... S-SORRY... UGGHH... UGHH...
ALL RIGHT, THAT'S ENOUGH.
YOU SHOULD BE MORE CAREFUL, CONSTANTINE. YOUR MAGIC WAND CAN'T *PROTECT* YOU IN HERE.
WHAT THE... FUCK.
I'LL SEE YOU TONIGHT. IN YOUR *CELL*.
Y-YOU SHOULDN'T HAVE DONE THAT. L-LAST PERSON TO MAKE HIM A-ANGRY... SCREAMED SO BAD HE SWALLOWED HIS OWN TONGUE.
GOOD. I COULD DO WITH A BIT OF RED MEAT.

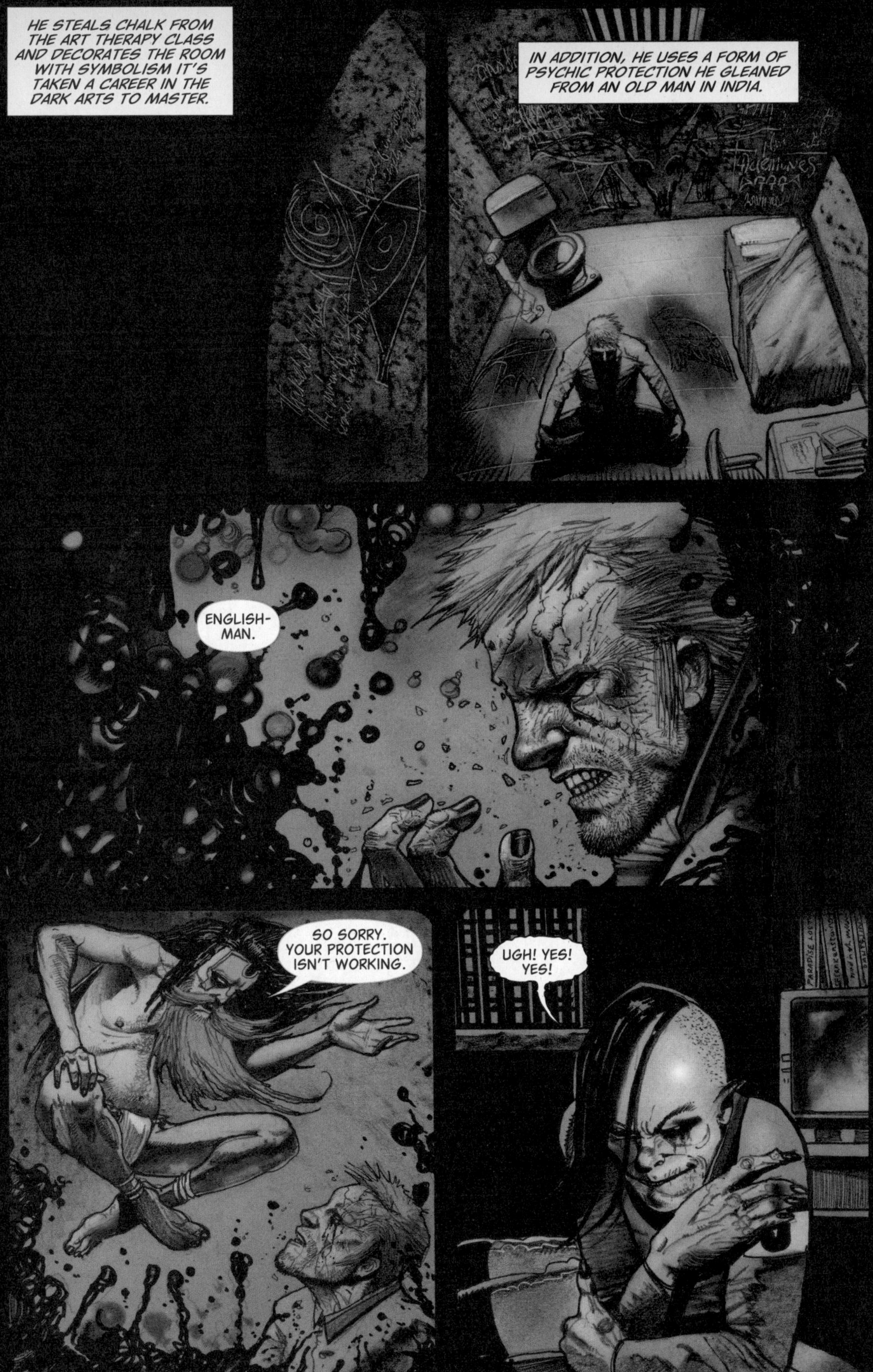
HE STEALS CHALK FROM THE ART THERAPY CLASS AND DECORATES THE ROOM WITH SYMBOLISM IT'S TAKEN A CAREER IN THE DARK ARTS TO MASTER.
IN ADDITION, HE USES A FORM OF PSYCHIC PROTECTION HE GLEANED FROM AN OLD MAN IN INDIA.
ENGLISH-MAN.
SO SORRY. YOUR PROTECTION ISN'T WORKING.
UGH! YES! YES!

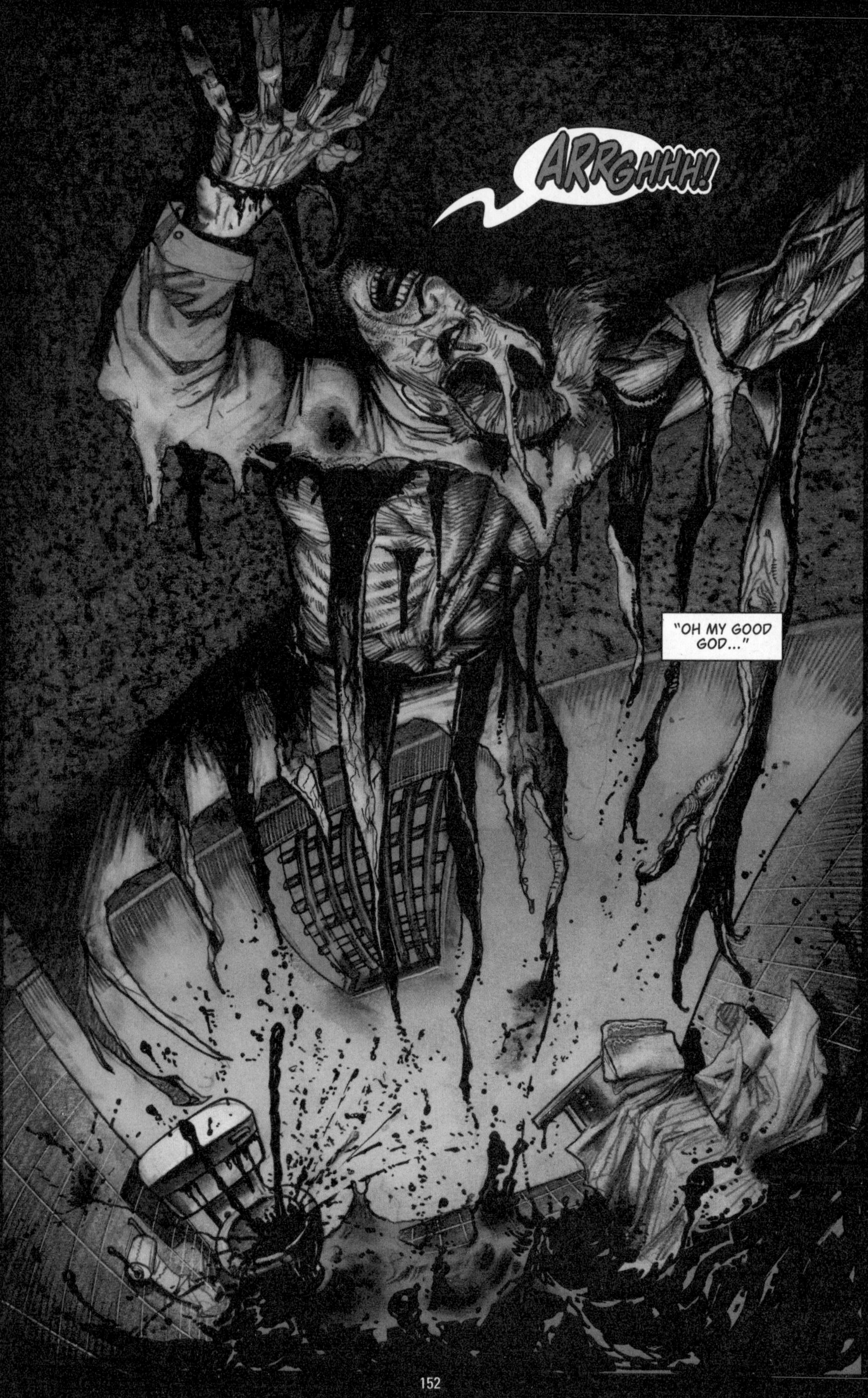
ARRGHHH!
"OH MY GOOD GOD..."

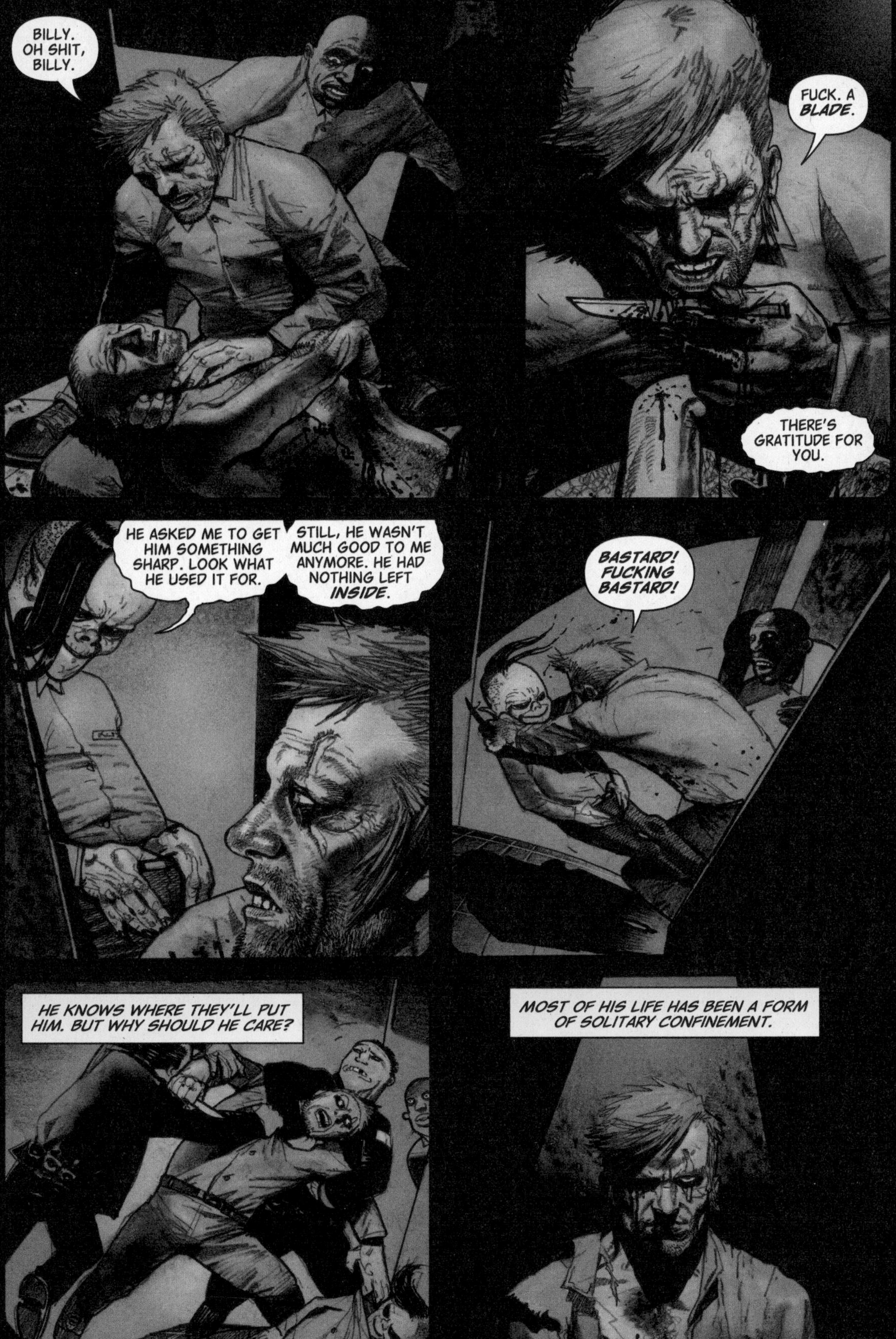
BILLY. OH SHIT, BILLY.
FUCK. A *BLADE*.
THERE'S GRATITUDE FOR YOU.
HE ASKED ME TO GET HIM SOMETHING SHARP. LOOK WHAT HE USED IT FOR.
STILL, HE WASN'T MUCH GOOD TO ME ANYMORE. HE HAD NOTHING LEFT *INSIDE*.
BASTARD! FUCKING BASTARD!
HE KNOWS WHERE THEY'LL PUT HIM. BUT WHY SHOULD HE CARE?
MOST OF HIS LIFE HAS BEEN A FORM OF SOLITARY CONFINEMENT.
"I KNOW, I KNOW..."

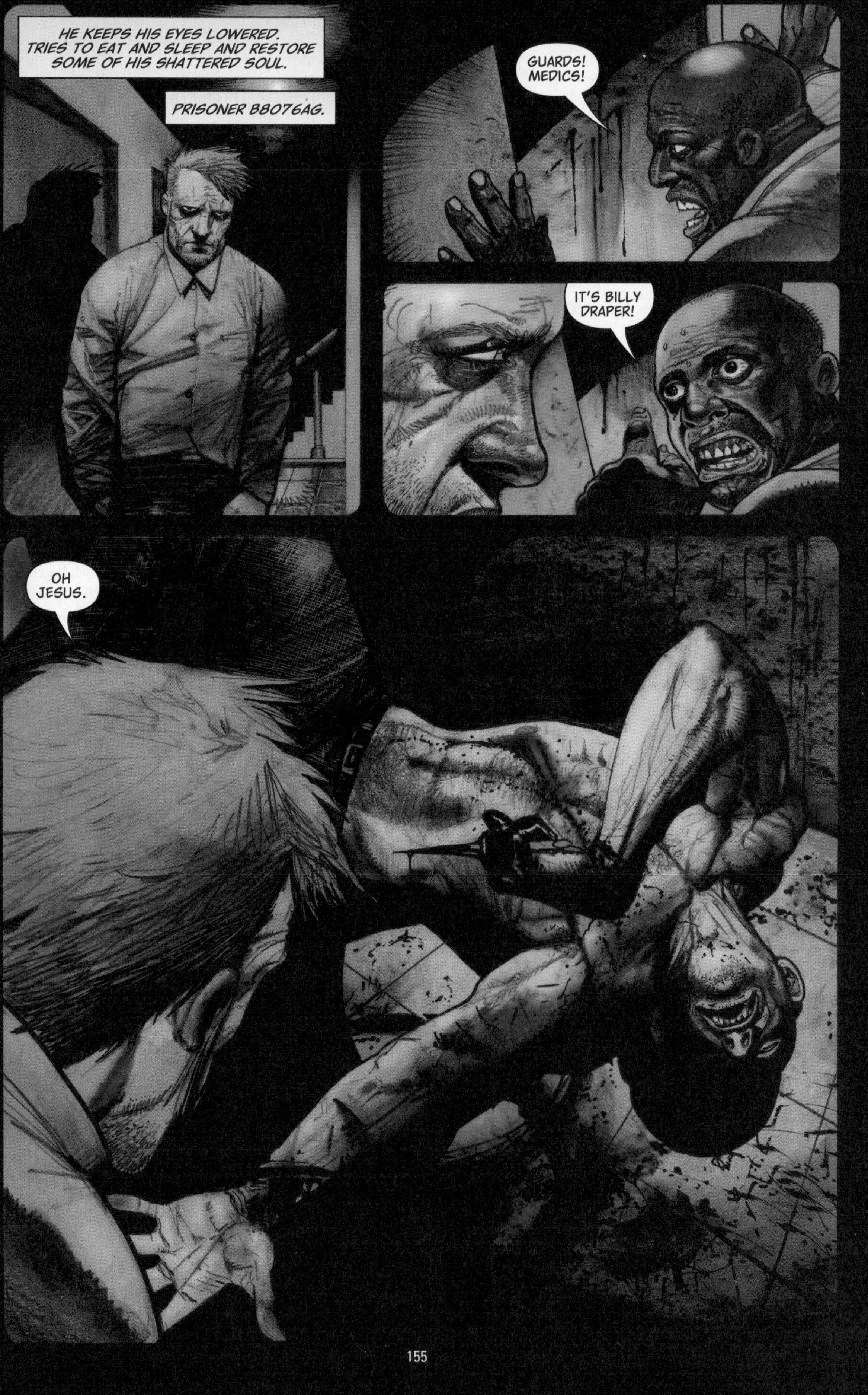
HE KEEPS HIS EYES LOWERED. TRIES TO EAT AND SLEEP AND RESTORE SOME OF HIS SHATTERED SOUL.
PRISONER B8076AG.
GUARDS! MEDICS!
IT'S BILLY DRAPER!
OH JESUS.

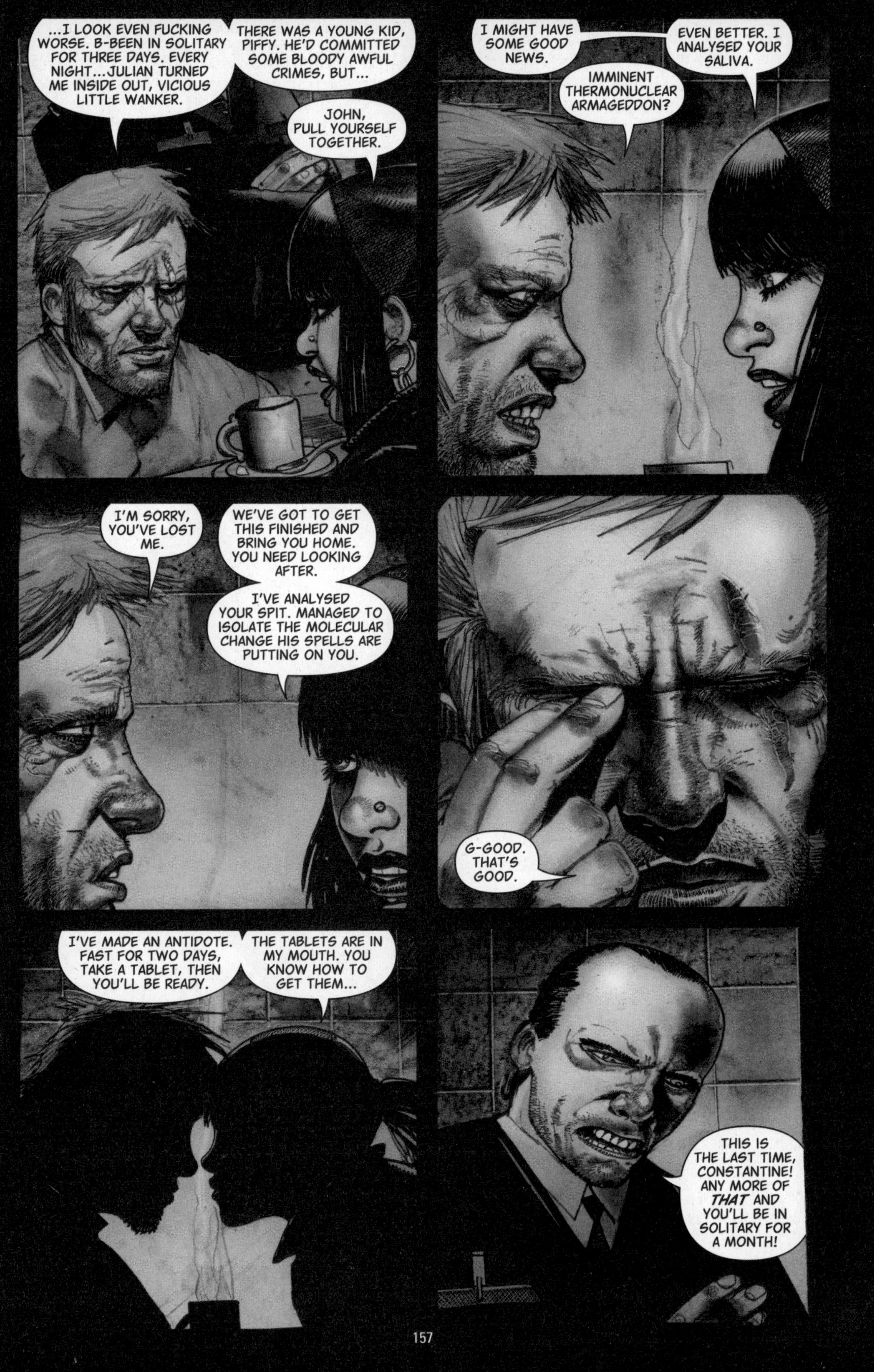
...I LOOK EVEN FUCKING WORSE. B-BEEN IN SOLITARY FOR THREE DAYS. EVERY NIGHT...JULIAN TURNED ME INSIDE OUT, VICIOUS LITTLE WANKER.
THERE WAS A YOUNG KID, PIFFY. HE'D COMMITTED SOME BLOODY AWFUL CRIMES, BUT...
JOHN, PULL YOURSELF TOGETHER.
I MIGHT HAVE SOME GOOD NEWS.
IMMINENT THERMONUCLEAR ARMAGEDDON?
EVEN BETTER. I ANALYSED YOUR SALIVA.
I'M SORRY, YOU'VE LOST ME.
WE'VE GOT TO GET THIS FINISHED AND BRING YOU HOME. YOU NEED LOOKING AFTER.
I'VE ANALYSED YOUR SPIT. MANAGED TO ISOLATE THE MOLECULAR CHANGE HIS SPELLS ARE PUTTING ON YOU.
G-GOOD. THAT'S GOOD.
I'VE MADE AN ANTIDOTE. FAST FOR TWO DAYS, TAKE A TABLET, THEN YOU'LL BE READY.
THE TABLETS ARE IN MY MOUTH. YOU KNOW HOW TO GET THEM...
THIS IS THE LAST TIME, CONSTANTINE! ANY MORE OF THAT AND YOU'LL BE IN SOLITARY FOR A MONTH!

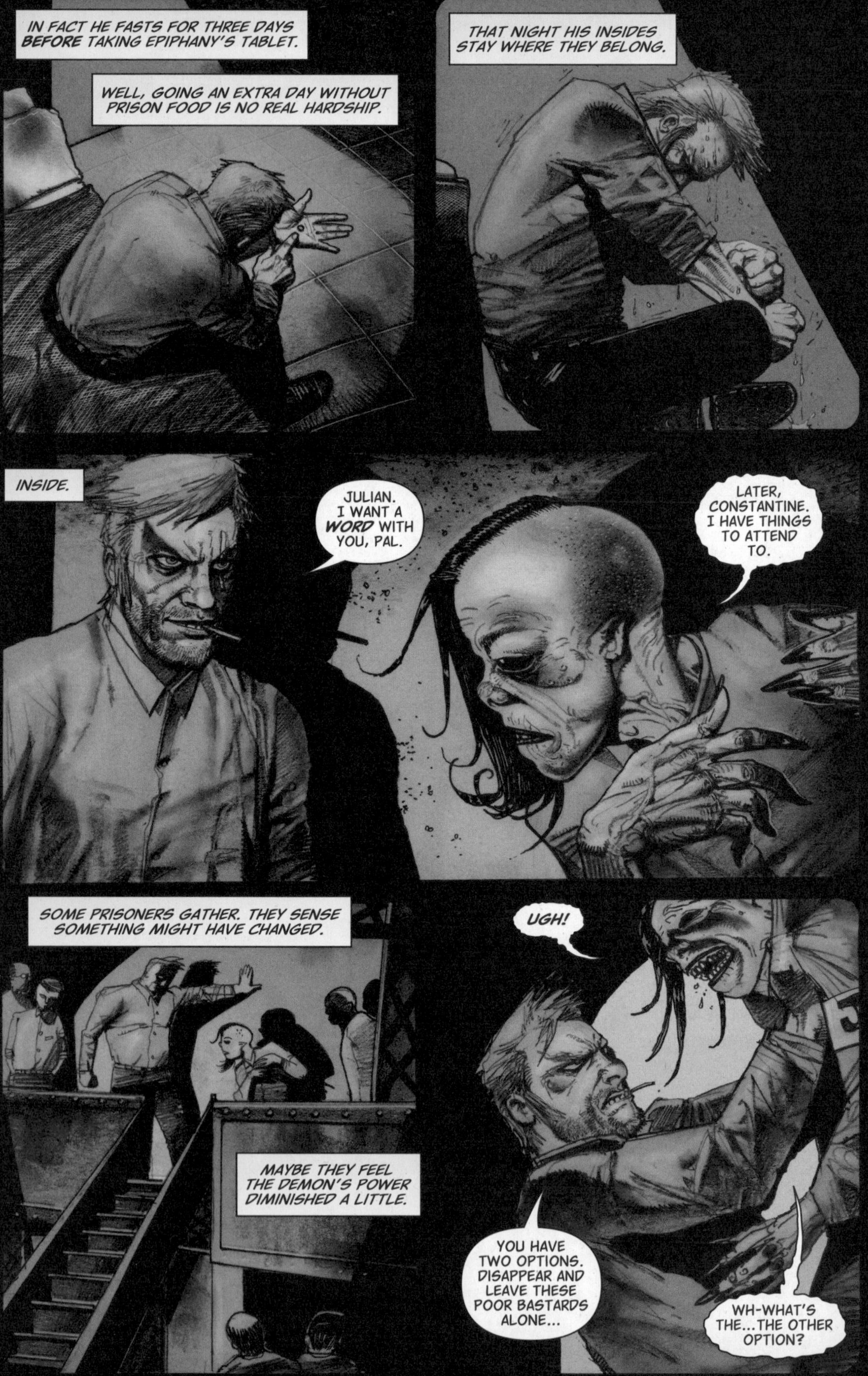
IN FACT HE FASTS FOR THREE DAYS BEFORE TAKING EPIPHANY'S TABLET.
WELL, GOING AN EXTRA DAY WITHOUT PRISON FOOD IS NO REAL HARDSHIP.
THAT NIGHT HIS INSIDES STAY WHERE THEY BELONG.
INSIDE.
JULIAN. I WANT A WORD WITH YOU, PAL.
LATER, CONSTANTINE. I HAVE THINGS TO ATTEND TO.
SOME PRISONERS GATHER. THEY SENSE SOMETHING MIGHT HAVE CHANGED.
MAYBE THEY FEEL THE DEMON'S POWER DIMINISHED A LITTLE.
UGH!
YOU HAVE TWO OPTIONS. DISAPPEAR AND LEAVE THESE POOR BASTARDS ALONE...
WH-WHAT'S THE...THE OTHER OPTION?

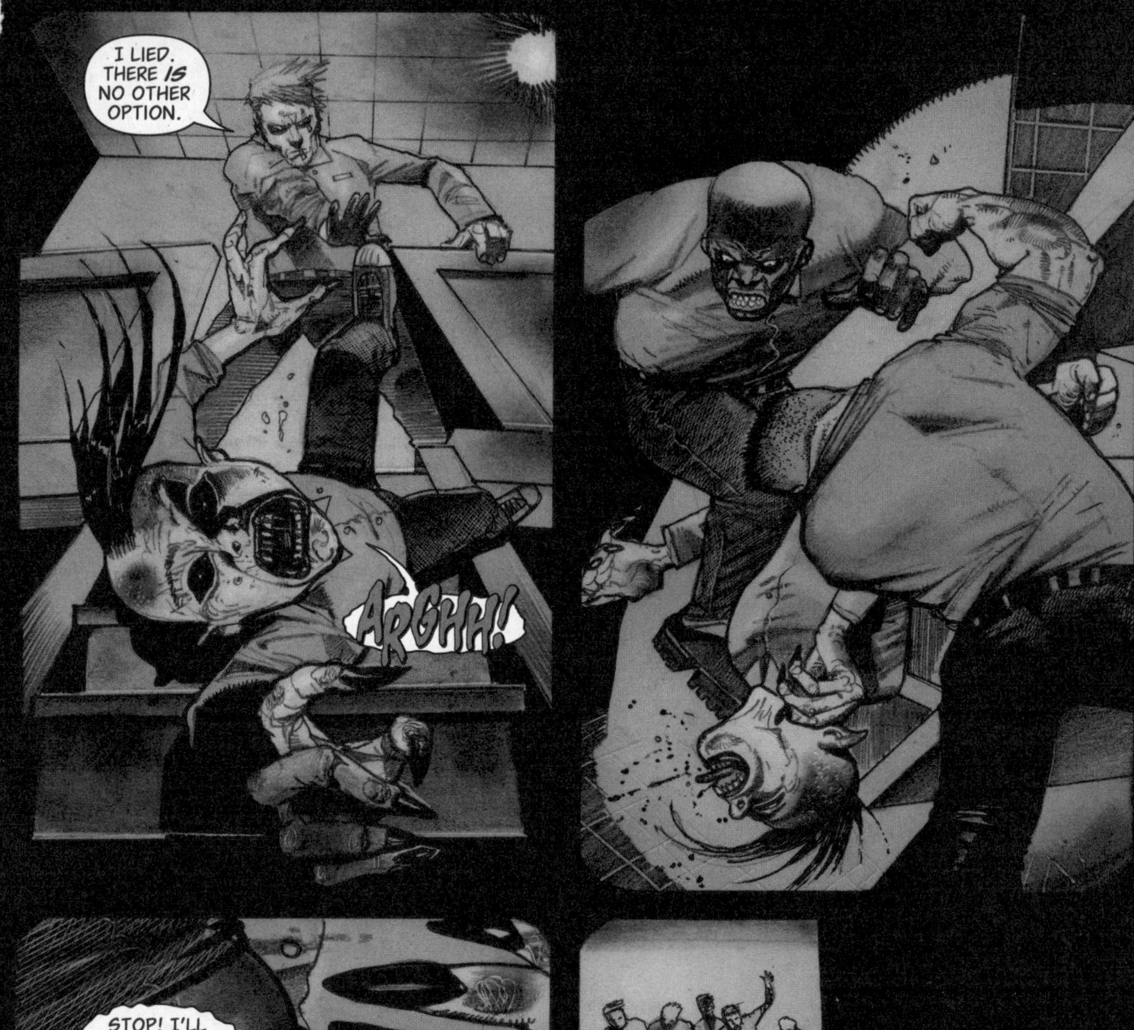
I LIED. THERE *IS* NO OTHER OPTION.
ARGHH!
STOP! I'LL VISIT YOU IN YOUR CELLS! I'LL TURN YOU... INSIDE OUT!
BUT SOMETHING HAS CHANGED.
A SPELL HAS BEEN LIFTED.

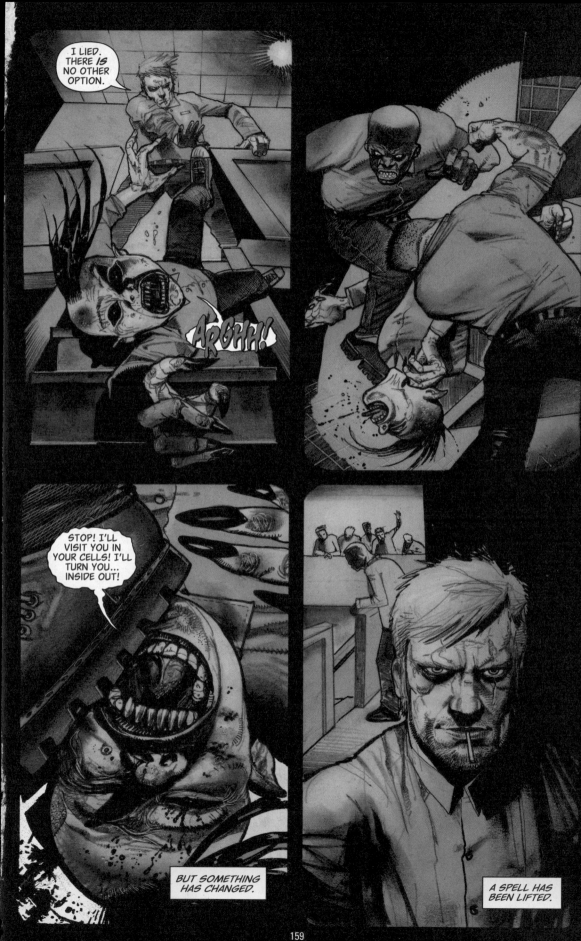

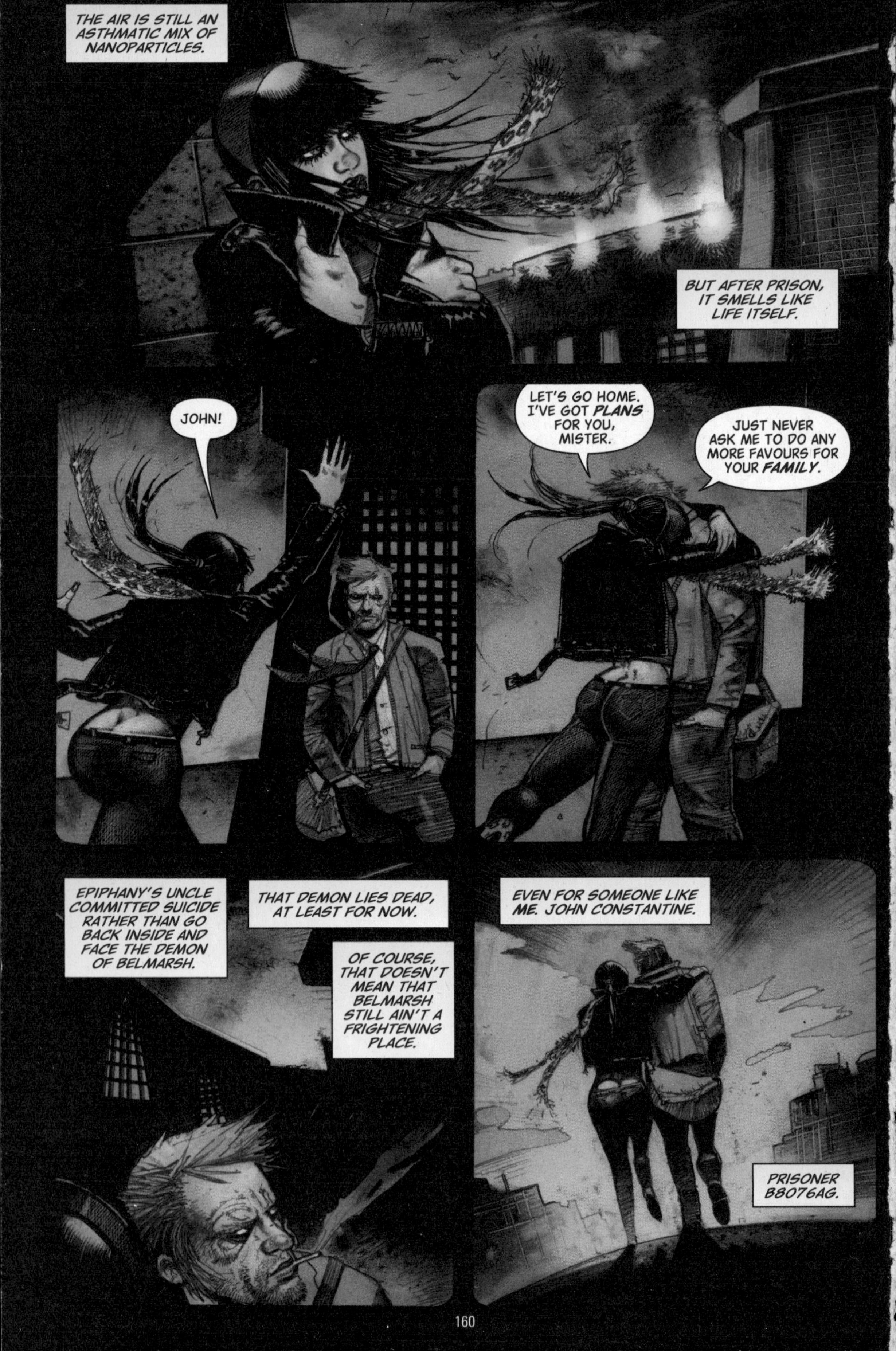
THE AIR IS STILL AN ASTHMATIC MIX OF NANOPARTICLES.
BUT AFTER PRISON, IT SMELLS LIKE LIFE ITSELF.
JOHN!
LET'S GO HOME. I'VE GOT PLANS FOR YOU, MISTER.
JUST NEVER ASK ME TO DO ANY MORE FAVOURS FOR YOUR FAMILY.
EPIPHANY'S UNCLE COMMITTED SUICIDE RATHER THAN GO BACK INSIDE AND FACE THE DEMON OF BELMARSH.
THAT DEMON LIES DEAD, AT LEAST FOR NOW.
OF COURSE, THAT DOESN'T MEAN THAT BELMARSH STILL AIN'T A FRIGHTENING PLACE.
EVEN FOR SOMEONE LIKE ME. JOHN CONSTANTINE.
PRISONER B8076AG.